Religious Feminism in an Age of Empire

CMS Women Missionaries in Iran, 1869-1934

GULNAR ELEANOR FRANCIS-DEHQANI

CCSRG Monograph Series 4

Centre for Comparative Studies in Religion and Gender
Department of Theology and Religious Studies
University of Bristol

2000

Published by the Centre for Comparative Studies in Religion and Gender,
3 Woodland Road, Bristol BS8 1TB

Copyright © 2000 Centre for Comparative Studies in Religion and Gender,
Department of Theology and Religious Studies,
University of Bristol, Bristol BS8 1TB, England

ISBN 0-86292-489-8

Printed by the University of Bristol Printing Unit, Old Park Hill,
Bristol BS2 8BB

Preface to CCSRG Monograph Series

This monograph is part of a new series of publications on religion and gender which are based on research undertaken at the Centre for Comparative Studies in Religion and Gender (CCSRG) in the Department of Theology and Religious Studies at the University of Bristol. The Centre encourages innovative interdisciplinary and comparative research on inclusive gender issues in different religions, relating to women as well as men. It is the intention of this series to make the Centre's research on different religion and gender topics more widely available to others.

Research undertaken at the Centre can be grounded in different methodological paradigms; it can be primarily empirical or theoretical; it can be interdisciplinary and comparative, or focused on a single religious tradition. Or it can be applied and action- or policy-oriented with the aim to contribute to the transformation of existing gender injustices in religious and social institutions.

Besides the publication of the Research Monograph Series the Centre organises regular research seminars and encourages networking among scholars working on religion and gender issues. The Centre welcomes applications for associate membership or for postgraduate research leading to a higher degree.

This is the fourth monograph since the series was started in 1999. Whether historical, contemporary or comparative in its approach, whether dealing with doctrines, rites, symbols or people, each of these research monographs makes its own distinctive contribution to current debates about religion and gender.

Ursula King
Series Editor
University of Bristol

This work is dedicated to my grandmother

Meg Thompson

and my mother

Margaret Dehqani-Tafti

women of strength - never "just a little 'm' "

*with gratitude for fostering in me a love for Iran
and planting the seed of faith*

Acknowledgements

For much of the time that I was researching this book, I travelled along parallel paths with my time divided between this work and training towards ordination. As my journey progressed I became conscious that the research and my personal formation in preparing for ordination were joining forces, urging me ever deeper into a search for my roots and identity. The research illuminated old memories from Iran and strengthened my awareness of being Persian. In addition, the spiritual pilgrimage drew me back in time and space to the Anglican Church in Iran which nurtured my early faith and has enriched its later development. It is twenty years since my enforced absence from Iran and the physical distance now feels greater than ever, just as the emotional ties have grown stronger.

The inevitable frustrations in producing this work have been significantly minimised through the help and support of several people to whom I would like to express my appreciation. To Professor Ursula King I am immensely grateful for her wise and gentle advice. Her honest and insightful approach was consistently balanced by sensitivity and understanding towards my personal circumstances. This project would have neither started in the first instance, nor been completed without her enthusiasm for the subject and her confidence in my abilities.

I am indebted to the many libraries and their staff who aided my research, in particular, Colin Rowe and Elizabeth Williams from the Mission Studies Library at Partnership House, for their patience and expertise. For financial support my thanks go to Bristol University, the St. Boniface Trust, the Jerusalem and the East Mission Trust, the Reformed Mission League in the Netherlands, and the American Presbyterian Church's Global Education and International Leadership and Development scheme. To the parish of Mortlake with East Sheen, especially the Revd Peggy Jackson, I am grateful for the regular periods of study leave they permitted me in the early months after my ordination. My parents have patiently anticipated the completion of this project and I hope they will think it worth the wait. I thank them for their support and also for my father's generosity in lending me books and providing me with advice and information.

Finally, I want to express my love and appreciation to those who have survived the past few years living with me. To our pet labrador Comfort - often my only companion - who helped keep life in perspective; and above all to my husband Lee, for his positive outlook and extraordinary reserves. His encouragement, sense of humour and enduring love were my greatest companions along the journey.

CONTENTS

INTRODUCTION   1

Part I

1. IMPERIALISM AND FEMINISM:
   IN SEARCH OF AN INTEGRATED METHODOLOGY   10
   - The interdisciplinary nature of missionary women's historiography
   - Approaches to the study of history
   - Women, history and the faith/feminism dialectic
   - The genderization of missionary imperialism
   - Sources and methods

2. A MEETING OF WEST AND EAST:
   THE VICTORIAN/QAJAR PERIOD CONTEXTUALIZED   26
   - Iran: Land of Diversity
   - Social and Political Upheaval
   - Women in late-Qajar & early-Pahlavi Iran
   - Britain: An era of change and development
   - British women and the dawn of opportunity
   - Victorian and Qajar women: Closer than either realised

3. THE CMS PERSIA MISSION AND ITS WOMEN MISSIONARIES   44
   - The History of Christianity in Iran
   - The Church Missionary Society in Iran
   - The Role of Women in the CMS Persia Mission

4. ATTITUDES TOWARDS ISLAM AND THEOLOGICAL SELF-PERCEPTIONS   59
   - The theological dimension to missionary motivation
   - Views from the 1910 World Missionary Conference
   - CMS women, Islam and the Muslims of Iran
   - An assessment of missionary attitudes towards Islam and Iran
   - The use of theological language in expressions of missionary motives

Part II

5. MARY BIRD: A PASSION FOR EVANGELISM AND A HEART
   FOR THE WOMEN OF IRAN   84
   - The role of evangelism in the work of missionary women
   - The beginnings of a missionary career
   - Establishing work amongst Muslim women and
     laying the foundation for future efforts
   - Professionalisation of the mission: Phase two of Bird's work, 1897-1904
   - A life spent in the service of God: Phase three of Bird's work, 1911-14
   - Interpreting and evaluating Bird's life and career

6. ISABELLA READ: MISSION AS AN OPEN WINDOW ON EDUCATION 114
   - The feminisation of missionary education
   - Read's unconventional place within the CMS Persia mission
   - Retrieving the past and weaving a forgotten history
   - Isabella's attitude towards life in Persia and work as a missionary teacher
   - Intuitive empathy underlying empire's dominant ideologies

7. EMMELINE STUART: MEDICAL MISSIONS
   AND THE HISTORY OF FEMINISM 142
   - Women's medical work in mission history
   - The career of Dr Emmeline Stuart and her impact on the CMS Persia Mission
   - Growing confidence and feminist defiance
   - Social critique and missionary feminism

CONCLUSION 172

Notes 179

Appendices 222

Bibliography 235

List of Photographs

Unless otherwise stated, all photographs are hitherto unpublished and have been taken from the family albums of Agnes and Donald Carr, and Margaret and William Thompson, who all worked as missionaries in Iran during the period 1869-1934. Where possible exact or approximate dates have been provided. The photographs vary in size and quality according to the original. For a greater variety of photographs related to the topic of this book see Gulnar E. Francis-Dehqani (1999), *Religious Feminism in an Age of Empire: CMS Women Missionaries in Iran, 1869-1934.* Bristol University: PhD Thesis.

Mary Bird as a girl in 1875, and a young missionary in 1891	89
Accommodation at the Murchehkhor caravanserai, 1901	90
Patients arriving at the Julfa general Mission Hospital	99
Patients at the Jubareh mission dispensary in Isfahan, c 1905	102
Children suffering from curvature of legs due to long hours of carpet weaving	105
Daughter of an English missionary with two twenty year old carpet weavers	106
Group photograph including Isabella Read, her husband and children	122
Isabella Read's children: Nevarth, Armenouhie and Apgar, 1902	123
Miss Parry, CMS missionary, on mule back, c 1910	132
A Persian couple travelling in palakis	132
Missionaries travelling in kajavehs, c 1907	133
Missionaries travelling "old style" and "new style" in Persia	134
Patients outside the Julfa general Mission Hospital prior to Stuart's arrival, 1895	149
The Julfa Women's Hospital, 1904	150
Dr Stuart operating in the Julfa Women's Hospital, c 1899	151
Dr Stuart operating on a small girl, c 1907	151
Dr Stuart in Bakhtiari tribal clothes, smoking a hubble-bubble, 1902	158
A group of missionary women in the CMS Persia mission, 1904	160
St. Luke's Church, Isfahan	166

Glossary of Persian Terms

andaroon	women's quarters in the home, literally, inner part
bast	sanctuary
birooni	men's quarters in the home, literally, outer part
chador	Full length veil worn outdoors by women for modesty
dhimmi	religions granted minority status by Islam
farangi	foreigner
fatwa	a formal, written religious decree
hakim	doctor
kajaveh	mode of transport in Qajar Iran
khanum	lady
madresseh	theological college/Seminary
majles	parliament/Assembly
maktab	traditional elementary school
mujtahed	high-ranking Muslim clergy
mullah	low-ranking Muslim clergy
shah	king
shari'a	religious law
ulama	clergy (plural)
zaifeh	term used to refer to women, literally, weaker sex

Abbreviations

BCMS	-	Bible Church Missionary Society
CEZMS	-	Church of England Zenana Missionary Society
CMJ	-	Churches Mission to the Jews
CMS	-	Church Missionary Society (now Church Mission Society)
FES	-	Female Education Society (short for Society for Promoting Female Education in the East)
FMI	-	Female Missionary Intelligencer
IETD	-	Indo-European Telegraph Department
LGB	-	Local Governing Body (of the Persia mission)
LMS	-	London Missionary Society
PC	-	Parent Committee
PCC	-	Parochial Church Council
SC	-	Standing Committee
SMS	-	Scottish Missionary Society
SVMU	-	Student Volunteer Missionary Union
WMC	-	World Missionary Conference (Edinburgh 1910)
YWCA	-	Young Women's Christian Association

INTRODUCTION

The gradual progress of Britain as a world power, coupled with the impact of various religious revivals, resulted in Christian missionary activity burgeoning in England towards the end of the eighteenth century.[1] The geographical conquests of colonialism opened the way for those spiritually inclined to take the gospel to the furthest corners of the earth. In many cases churches were unwilling to give official recognition to such projects and efforts were left to individual initiative, reliant upon voluntary financial support. As a result, many societies were founded by groups of like-minded and committed people, eager to encourage the missionary task.

One such organisation was the Church Missionary Society (CMS), set up in 1799 by several Anglican evangelical clergy.[2] During the early years, progress was slow and missionary numbers remained few. Gradually, however, public interest developed and the stature of the society heightened. Concurrently, initial emphasis upon the ordained pattern of ministry gave way and CMS - like many other missionary organisations - became a prominent vehicle for the religious expression of lay people. As the nineteenth century progressed, CMS came to rely more, not only on the membership of male lay workers, but that of women also. Discovering the advantages of influencing indigenous women through female missionaries, the society began encouraging women's participation and was soon dependent upon their involvement. By the end of the century women provided a large amount of support for CMS, both as missionaries on the field and as fund-raisers or patrons at home.[3]

During the course of the nineteenth century CMS firmly established itself within British society and began working in many diverse parts of the world. Not until 1869, however, did work begin in Iran, or Persia.[4] Though missionary wives were present from that date, it was from 1882 and more particularly from the 1890s that single women's involvement became a major part of the missionary endeavour which led to the founding of the Anglican Church in Iran.

There are countless books written on the history of Iran, and literature analysing the work of western missionaries, including that of women, has also expanded considerably in recent years.[5] However, there has not yet been an occasion when the two subjects have converged in any critical study.[6] In this book Persian studies and the field of missionary scholarship are introduced to one another, reflecting the encounter between English Christianity and Iranian Islam during the late nineteenth and early twentieth centuries. The sixty-five year period (1869-1934), referred to as the Victorian/Qajar era, represents an age which witnessed the meeting of West and East, with particular consequences for the position of British women and the history of the western feminist movement.

Soon after the 1979 revolution catapulted Iran from a despotic, militaristic monarchy into an Islamic Republic, and almost exactly one hundred years after CMS began work there, all foreign missionaries left the region. To date, none have returned or been replaced and there seems little likelihood of the situation changing in the near future. However, the tiny Episcopal Church which began as a result of the work of CMS, has survived against all odds. Despite much persecution, confiscation of institutions under its care, drastic reduction in numbers, and the loss of life, the community still maintains a Persian Christian presence in Iran. Made up of Muslim, Jewish and Zoroastrian converts, and gradually including second and third generation Christians also, this group has continued under dedicated leadership throughout the turbulent years since 1979 and remains a member of the world-wide Anglican Communion. The women missionaries who participated in the early years of the Persian church's evolution are vital to its continuing story, for they played an integral role in establishing early working methods as the foundation for later development.

When I first began researching the CMS women in Iran I was haunted by anxieties about the topic. I felt certain that the missionary methods they utilised would be judged unacceptable by contemporary socio-religious values to which I am committed. At the same time, I was uneasy about approaching the subject if my evaluations were to prove entirely negative and the end result was to be a severely critical appraisal of a group of women silenced by the passage of time and with no chance to defend themselves.

Accordingly, all three approaches with which I considered tackling the subject appeared to present deadend options. First, placing the CMS women within the overall history of feminism and its related structures seemed somewhat hazardous. Feminist scholarship has increasingly realised that women are not always part of the underclass but that many have participated in the oppression of other women through the abuse of racial and class-based superiority.[7] It seemed likely that the CMS women in Iran would fall within this category through their maternalistic and often condescending attitude towards the indigenous population. Secondly, a post-imperialist analysis seemed inappropriate, for critics from this school of thought are usually extremely captious of any past contact (especially during the British colonial era) between the western world and its politically and economically weaker eastern counterpart.[8] Finally, the realities of an increasingly pluralist western society, together with insights from studies in the theology of religions, offered a doubtful path for a beneficial study of CMS women in Iran. The influence of this strain within theology has caused many Christians to question the wisdom of previous encounters with other religions especially through Victorian missionary methods.[9] On all three fronts, therefore (feminism, post-imperialism and the theology of religions), it seemed I would have no choice but to judge my protagonists harshly and find them wanting.

As my studies progressed, I began to realise my concerns were misdirected. Further reading and familiarisation with the CMS women led me to consider the project from a different angle. The question I had been so obsessed by - "were the CMS women right or wrong, good or bad?" - began to fade in significance as I grew to understand that it was, in fact, unanswerable and therefore somewhat irrelevant. For how can we today sit in judgement over people whose context presented them with very different values and priorities? My emphasis began to shift from a desire to judge them by late twentieth century standards towards a longing to understand them within their own context. To move from a simplistic question, inevitably loaded with contemporary ideological baggage, towards a more complex interpretation of their motives and actions against the backdrop of the period in which they lived.

Less troubled by the irreconcilable nature of their methods in today's world, I have tried instead to discover what motivated them and how they achieved their goals in an age when women's place in society was complex and ambiguous. This approach has liberated the entire topic. Merely highlighting their mistakes and shortcomings would ultimately mean discarding them as quaintly irrelevant historical relics. A more positive or open approach, however, presents the potential for dialogue with the past from which we can better understand the present and hope to learn for the future. As my research continued, therefore, I became more interested in conversing with the women in order to learn from them. Clearly, this necessitates consideration of their limitations but it also requires an openness to positive elements they may be able to offer.

As recently as one decade ago the more open approach I am proposing would have been difficult to justify within the academic climate. Feminist scholars were little interested in gaining insights from religion, marginalizing the influence of late nineteenth and early twentieth century religious impact on women as ineffective at best and harmful to the women's movement at worst. Writers influenced by post-imperialist insights ensured that any favourable interpretation of Victorian missionary activity was sidelined as self-interested apologetics.[10] To gain credibility within the academic world, it was easier to maintain an anti-mission stance which included harsh criticism of the role of missionary women. Commonly, the modern missionary movement was dismissed as an extension of British colonialism and the western imperialist agenda. This view usually interpreted Christianity simply as another unwelcome or even destructive aspect of western culture imposed upon the East.

From the 1930s onwards, scholarly respect for the missionary movement had gradually given way to disdainful reproach. Concurrently, writers began reifying indigenous societies within an environment of popular cultural absolutism. In the post-colonial world, western societies experienced an outpouring of collective guilt for which they punished themselves through "cultural masochism".[11] A kind of hyper-moralism seized western scholarship in which "absolute cultural relativism and cultural absolutism became the order of the day".[12] Traditional indigenous societies were regarded as wholly good and any attempt to influence them, especially religiously, was deemed cultural genocide. Accordingly, the church and the missionary movement experienced especially severe criticism.

Such views underestimated traditional indigenous societies in three significant ways. First, they disregarded the reality of cultural malleability and interdependence, promoting the false notion of a glorified past in which non-western cultures existed in perfect form, untouched and unchanged by external influences. Secondly, in an attempt to cleanse themselves from a paternalistic and patronising past, western scholars merely constructed a form of neo-paternalism by once more assuming that they knew what was best for the non-western world. Thirdly, by presupposing that the arrival of Christianity through missionary activity had been entirely negative, this anti-mission stance condescendingly portrayed local Christian converts as helpless victims of western intrusion. According to Hiebert:

> The irony of all this breast beating on the part of the West is that in one sense it functioned as a kind of residual paternalism to keep the West as judge of what is good or bad for the non-Western world ... A theological romanticism that regards

all other cultures as good in reaction to the past when they were seen as barbarian still is demonstrating an epistemological arrogance. It still takes the prerogative of having the last word when judging other cultures, even if it is a positive word.[13]

Today, increasing numbers of indigenous Christian scholars are heard defending their right to choose Christianity as a universal religion, transcending cultural barriers.[14] It is demeaning to continue insisting that indigenous churches were formed merely as a result of western coercion or that Christianity was somehow forced upon them by missionaries. Moreover, it is vital to understand that conversion to Christianity is not synonymous, in the eyes of most converts, with the acceptance of all that is western. It represents, rather, encounter with a faith which becomes central to people's lives and, engaging with its new context, is re-worked and frees them to become more fully themselves.

Acknowledging this process of inculturation means the spread of Christianity can no longer be explained simply in terms of the history of western imperialism. Rather, as Sanneh has pointed out, the only effective way to analyse the historical transmission of Christianity under western initiative is to subordinate it to its "local assimilation and adaptation under [indigenous] agency".[15] Regardless of what one may think of the modern missionary movement and despite much valid criticism, indigenous churches have grown up as a result of mission work. Christians throughout the world are now eager to trace their roots and create their own histories. It is their dignified and insistent voices that allow for a more open and positive approach to the study of missions.

Indeed, what we are now concerned with is more than *mission* history. For the modern missionary movement played an integral part in the creation of the Anglican Communion and is in part responsible for what is understood by the term Anglicanism.[16] It is through the efforts of organisations such as CMS that the word "Anglican" has ceased to mean simply English or European but has become instead, "a term for the particular embodiment of the historic faith, order and worship of the Catholic Church that is the heritage of the Communion".[17] Indigenous churches, therefore, have their own place within the Anglican story. The small Christian community now present in Iran, despite its virtual invisibility in western scholarly and ecclesiastical circles, is no exception. Missionary labourers sowed the seed that developed roots and, adjusting to its new context, grew into the existing indigenous church - a member of the world-wide Anglican Communion.

None of this can be used as an excuse for producing uncritical descriptions of missionary activity. The past is not something sacred, standing beyond the judgement of new insights. It is important to temper historical accounts through contemporary critical questions, thereby encouraging dialogue between past and present. For this to happen successfully, the context must be firmly established. British Victorianism and Iran under the Qajar dynasty need to be understood with particular regard for the position of women in both societies. Having ascertained the context, it is then possible to probe it analytically by means of contemporary concerns arising from reflections on the politics of imperialism and the influence of feminism. The important point is that the CMS women should not be judged merely by late twentieth century priorities but according to those which are relevant to their own time. Throughout this book, therefore, there is an underlying tension between past and present. If approached imaginatively this can become a positive force, allowing the women to speak with an authoritative voice of their own whilst also challenging them with modern concerns.

In effect, my work is a didactic historical study, aiming to illuminate the past, better appreciate the present and more fully prepare for the future. It seeks both to understand and learn from a specific group of women who, whilst deeply influenced by the contours of Victorian society, were trying to expand their opportunities. Their contribution is analysed as part of western culture during the late nineteenth and early twentieth centuries. As Christian women in the British empire, they were involved in the negotiation of racial, religious and gender ideologies, each affected by orientalist, evangelical and sexual conventions of the day. Striving to improve the position of their sex, the women continued to live on the margins of society's organisational structures. Therefore, their efforts towards progress proceeded through a careful mixture of subversion and compliance with expected norms.

Each of the three ideological frameworks - orientalism, evangelicalism and gender assumptions - will be discussed throughout the book and provide the underlying themes for the remainder of the material. My research inquires into ways the missionaries, conditioned to accept particular interpretations of these principles undergirding Victorian society, accommodated them within Islamic Iran between 1869-1934. I argue that the most complete understanding relies on appreciating the paradoxical ways in which they both conformed to and subverted the restrictions imposed upon them by societal conventions.

For example, the CMS women betray typical features of the orientalist outlook prevalent at the turn of the century. Typically, their language is littered with exotic descriptions of the East as essentially different and "other". Western civilisation is commonly contrasted in a superior manner with the weaknesses and deficiencies perceived in an alien eastern society. However, these women were also amongst the earliest westerners to experience sustained contact with the peoples of the East. As the years progressed they developed friendships which grew into deep and valued relationships. Thus, their written accounts were incipient in providing British people with more authentic descriptions of a hitherto unknown and exotic Orient. In this way, despite stubborn adherence to the linguistic and ideological restrictions of orientalism, they played a significant role in the growing western move towards greater understanding and deeper appreciation of the East.

Evangelicalism was perhaps the single most influential factor restricting the public role of Victorian women and preventing their progress. The tenacity shown by the CMS women in their loyalty to evangelical convictions is evidence of its extended influence both in church and society more generally. However, within ecclesiastical structures and late Victorian theology, adherence to evangelical standards was slowly becoming an act of resistance compared with the more positive poise it had represented in the late eighteenth and early nineteenth centuries. Whilst evangelicals were still in a relative position of strength, they were increasingly defending themselves in an environment where other theological views were also gaining ground. Those willing to defend it risked becoming entrenched in a defensiveness that ultimately restricted their vision. Not withstanding these changes in the religious climate, evangelicalism still shaped many of the social ideologies at the heart of Victorian society and legitimised the acceptable customs and conventions of the day. For example, it provided religious justification for many gender assumptions and effectively controlled the progress of women. Also, its emphasis upon personal salvation through Christ alone sanctioned the anti-Islamic stance of empire, further fuelling racist sentiments already prevalent within orientalism.

Despite such negative factors, the modern missionary movement was instrumental in demythologising western attitudes towards Islam. Written accounts of contact with Muslim people and descriptions of their lives helped provide a human face for Christianity's great rival. As it became more familiar, the religion that had hitherto been denounced under a shroud of mystique and exotic imagination, began shedding some of its more fictitious associations. The missionary movement generally, and writers such as F.D. Maurice specifically, made British awareness of Islam a positive determinant in the founding of a theology of religions and the future of Christian-Muslim relations.[18] The CMS women in Iran were part of the process in which Islam became known in a more real sense. Their written accounts contributed to the widely disseminated missionary literature, providing descriptions of individual Muslims as ordinary human beings with similar needs and desires. Despite continued limitations, the effect was to humanise Islam for westerners and provide a foundation for a future based on greater, more appropriate understanding.

The restraints of evangelicalism were also apparent upon the lives of Victorian women, whom it confined and limited in many respects through spiritual justification of accepted social norms. However, the strictures themselves were adopted by women as a positive tool for improving their position in church and society. This paradox is a peculiar feature of religious feminism during the late nineteenth and early twentieth centuries. For whilst religion largely restricted women to the private world, it also provided the way to an expansion of that role into the public realm. Women motivated towards greater public participation found acceptability through the extension of home-based ideologies and an understanding of religious vocation as a calling from God.

The Victorian gender ideologies and their appropriation by religious women signifies perhaps the most pertinent ingredient in a study of female missionaries during the age of empire. For negotiating the complexities of gender expectations held unique consequences for women, whereas the other cogent constituents (orientalism and evangelicalism) were equally influential upon the lives of men. Through a mixture of co-operation and subversion many women created space for themselves, gradually expanding their possibilities. Carefully manoeuvring the subtleties and working with inherent contradictions, they forged change without the need for rebellion and the risk of losing the little they had gained.

Essentially, the CMS single women (the primary subjects of this study) were more explicitly part of a movement successfully challenging gender presuppositions, whilst leaving intact many of the assumptions at the heart of orientalist and evangelical attitudes. They were adventurous pioneers, participating in a level of public involvement never before achieved by women. Where they did not succeed for themselves they prepared the ground for future generations. It is their relative success in expanding the scope of gender boundaries, whilst failing to dispute orientalist and religious ideologies, that provides a basic theme within this book.

My contention is based on a fundamental dualism at the heart of the CMS women's involvement in late nineteenth and early twentieth century feminism. In short, whilst playing a significant role in expanding the position of British women, they conformed to certain undesirable tenets of orientalism and evangelicalism. Indeed, by acquiescing with unegalitarian convictions operating at the core of empire through orientalist and evangelical influences, their part in the feminist movement became possible. For in embracing certain conventions they found space to develop in other ways, and by conforming in some areas they expanded the boundaries elsewhere.

These women undoubtedly forwarded the public position of British women and can, therefore, take their place in the historical feminist movement. However, their success was based upon an undermining of the egalitarianism that is the essence of feminism in its search towards equality for *all* women. For as they expanded the possibilities for western women, they defined themselves in relation to Persian women whom they considered subordinate and dependent in many respects. Therefore, the evolution of the western feminist movement advanced, whilst at the same time its progress relied upon an unequal relationship between the CMS women and the women of Iran. It is my aim throughout the book to delineate the paradoxes inherent in this situation, and to understand and assess the missionary contribution within this overarching contradiction.

The information outlined in the following chapters has been structured around the triple impact of imperialism, gender ideologies and the theology of religions. For in short, it is concerned with the study of religious women in an age of empire. The book is divided broadly into two parts. The first (chps 1-4), outlines the theories and methods of research and provides the religious, social and political background for the work of the CMS women. The second (chps 5-7), consists of three case studies in which close investigation of individual women provides the means by which the more general material is contextualized. Throughout Part II, biographical detail is nuanced by careful attention to material from Part I. Each chapter highlights matters pertinent to one of the three underlying issues, namely the theology of religions, imperialist and orientalist concerns, and gender imperatives.

In chapter 1 the fundamental methodological principles of the research are presented in terms of an interdisciplinary approach, straddling aspects of women's history and its encounter with imperialism. (Although the impact of evangelicalism upon the lives of Victorian women is detailed, the theological dimension concerning Christian attitudes to other religions has been excluded so that it may be dealt with more fully later.) The tensions inherent in historical research are outlined, and the women's movement is depicted according to its late nineteenth and early twentieth century manifestations. An attempt is made to define imperialism in a post-colonial context, to understand the effect of feminism and imperialism on one another and to delineate the status of British women in the empire. The chapter closes with a discussion of sources and methods used in the effort to establish epistemological coherence and integrity.

In chapter 2 the methodological theories are given a foot-hold as the Victorian/Qajar period is contextualized with specific reference to the position of women and the impact of imperialism. The religious, socio-economic and political ingredients in British and Iranian society act as a backdrop for the unfolding events. In understanding them, the meeting of these two cultures can be better appreciated.[19] The missionary women were rarely aware of the extent to which social conventions affected them. It is vital, however, that the impact be analysed from a historical perspective. The result is that despite immense divergence between East and West, the position of women in both societies was closer than either realised. Essentially, Persian and English women lived under similar restrictions (albeit to different degrees), arising from the widespread influence of basic cross-cultural gender ideologies.

Having established the methodological and contextual ground, it is possible to look towards more concrete details. Chapter 3 presents a history of Persian Christianity and an outline of CMS's early years in Iran. Against the background of the previous two chapters, the foreground begins to take shape, as CMS organisational structures and key personalities are introduced. Attention is then turned to the participation of missionary women. Information is provided concerning selection and training, the role of married women and the three-fold categorisation of "women's work" as evangelism, education and medicine. The chapter closes with a discussion concerning the paradoxical ways in which the CMS women utilised dominant Victorian ideologies through a careful balance of subversion and compliance.

Part I concludes with chapter 4 - a general theological reflection on the missionary women in Iran. Although religion has been an underlying factor thus far, here its implications are subject to more explicit analysis. The chapter incorporates aspects of personal religious motivation whilst also including broader elements pertinent to the study of Christian missions in Muslim lands. In a continuing effort to stress the importance of contextualization, the women are placed firmly within the late nineteenth and early twentieth century missionary milieu generally and that of CMS in Iran specifically. Their attitudes towards Islam are assessed and their part in the development of a more positive theology of religions considered. The chapter ends with an examination of the theological language employed by the missionaries as a means of sustaining motivation and expressing religious sentiments.

Part I incorporates a gradual move from the general to the particular. It begins with the comprehensive brush-strokes of methodological theories and travels via historical scene-setting to the work of CMS in Persia and the role of women missionaries. In chapter 4, the women generally are subject to a specific theological investigation as a means of completing the tripartite approach of imperialist, feminist and religious enquiry. In Part II, the particular takes centre stage and biographical detail becomes the means by which the general can be better understood.

Chapters 5-7 consider the contribution of three individuals, offering insights into their distinct situation whilst also illuminating broader aspects of women's work in the Persia mission. Isabella Read, Mary Bird and Emmeline Stuart between them cover fifty-two years (1882-1934) of CMS's early years in Iran. They represent the three aspects of "women's work" through particular involvement in areas of education, evangelism and medicine respectively.

Characteristic of their female colleagues in many respects, each was also unique and exceptional in her own way. The details provided in these final three chapters highlight aspects of the underlying contradictions within the collective effort of CMS women's desire for female progress.

Ultimately, this book narrates the struggles of a group of women through the vicissitudes of late nineteenth and early twentieth century Victorianism. It is concerned with how they negotiated expectations and mediated change. Combining reform with a respect for tradition, they participated in an important and transitional stage from past restrictions to a future paved with hope and opportunity. Concurrently, they were influential in establishing working patterns in the early days of CMS in Persia, thus co-operating in the inception of Iranian Anglicanism. Whatever we think of them, they are our religious foremothers. Unless we try to understand them, we fail to fully comprehend the present, for they are part of the past which has led us to where we are today.

Part I

CHAPTER ONE

Imperialism and Feminism:
In Search of an Integrated Methodology

The interdisciplinary nature of missionary women's historiography

In order to ensure that this research does not simply fall between disciplines but weaves them together in a practical and profitable manner, this chapter is dedicated to a delineation of my methodological approaches.[1] To begin with, however, I must outline two important points which underlie the entire discussion, acting as a kind of *motto perpetuo*. First, retrieving the past is always a project fraught with difficulty which cannot, or should not, be approached by any single method or methodology. While the *idea* of a universally applicable and ideal methodology may be attractive, the full realisation of this goal "remains elusive".[2] Indeed for some, the very notion of such an absolute reeks of the "tyranny of methodolatry" and should be avoided at all cost.[3] The solution lies in applying to historical research what Knott claims for the feminist approach to the empirical study of religion:

> We would do well to stop worrying about whether we are shifting paradigms or establishing a single method ... This is to use benchmarks provided in the competitive world of academic life which may be of dubious contemporary value. Instead, we might continue to examine and share our processes, recognizing and learning from what we as women do and have done in our research and writing.[4]

Secondly, it is important that terminologies are clarified so they can be used with unambiguous specificity throughout the book. All too commonly academic research is littered with words like "method", "methodology" and "epistemology" without any clear identification of what they mean. Sandra Harding, amongst others, highlights the differentiation between these terms, arguing that though there are important connections between them, their individual features distinguish them from one another.[5] According to Harding, a research method is a technique or way of gathering evidence by means, for example, of interviews, observations or analysis of historical data. Such methods need not be mutually exclusive but can be used concurrently and as the context requires. Closely connected, methodology refers to the way in which methods are carried out. A theoretical understanding of how research should proceed, it is methodological discussions which will undergird much of the interdisciplinary deliberations of this chapter. Finally, epistemology is concerned with theories of knowledge and how resources are used to generate hypotheses and provide evidence. It is not a question of "what" we know but "how" we know that is of interest to epistemologists. Increasingly, researchers are enquiring into how parameters are set for the questions and answers deemed valid, against those considered "nondata".[6] Who makes the rules and why? Both post-colonialism and feminism, in particular, have challenged the epistemological *terra firma* by disputing old assumptions and refusing to be confined by traditional standpoints. This represents a significant transformation in the appropriation of knowledge and the manner in which the researcher approaches her/his data, for, "changes in *what* we know are normal; changes in *how* we know are revolutionary".[7]

Approaches to the study of history

There is growing historiographical interest in new research methodologies that place ideas within a wider social and intellectual context. Concern over the relationship between "now" and "then" raises questions about the "meaning" of history and even the feasibility of accurately defining the word history itself. Bradley and Muller, for example, refer to "the problem of the past" in terms of an inherent difficulty in distinguishing between past events and their written contemporary accounts.[8] The past, they argue, is never simply the past but always remains intimately, though equivocally, connected with the present. According to Said, past and present "inform each other", coexisting in a complex and ambiguous relationship in which the past shapes our understanding and views of the present.[9]

In former years, and perhaps even today, many assumed that "because there is *one* reality, there can be only one correct understanding of it".[10] Such a philosophy neglects the basic fact that documents surviving from the past describe only the viewpoint of the person or people who wrote them. Indeed, history usually represents "the world view and value system of those who have 'won', [and] it is to that extent a distortion of the totality of reality systems which could be extant at any period of time".[11] Moreover, acknowledging historical evidence as an accurate portrayal of just one reality among many can prove equally problematic in undermining the strength of the multifarious forces impacting on the author. Any combination of cultural, religious, social and political influences can have a distorting effect, "intentionally or unintentionally stand[ing] in the way of a clear understanding of [the] author's mind".[12]

The dilemmas involved in historical research lie not just in the past, however, but in us and our connection with the past. For we ourselves are a product of the past and cannot simply disassociate it as an entity to be studied objectively. Constantly torn between "seeing the 'like-unlike', the 'self but not self' which lies in the past", we project our own perspectives, moulded by contemporary contexts and expectations, into the history which has formed us and brought us where we are.[13] All reality, ours and that of those whom we study, is subjective, for no story can be told until a selection is made from available events, and that selection represents a judgement passed upon their relative importance.

The challenge is to function within the paradoxes involved in any historical study, aiming to pursue balance and objectivity without abdicating personality or involvement. True objectivity arises from a willingness to let past voices speak in their own terms, whilst also exercising critical judgement based upon candid recognition that empathy and bias will always be a part of the project. This is a double-edged sword, constantly at risk of manipulation. It is likely, for example, that research will at some stage create negative emotions for the investigator who may feel uncomfortable with her/his findings and its repercussions for present day realities. Pursued in an insufficiently contextualized manner, such a reading of history risks falling prey to zealous "present-mindedness",[14] ultimately resulting in a misunderstanding both of past events and their relevance for today. This desire to assess the past entirely on the basis of its direct contribution to contemporary values and ideologies - what Gill calls "a teleological reading of history"[15] - can only provide a distorted image of an already fragile reality, of little worth to the student of history.

The methodological solution adopted within this book is to operate within a wider spectrum outlined by Eleanor McLaughlin. She seeks to present a history that is both "responsible" by being "grounded in the historicist rubric of dealing with the past on its own terms", and "usable" through examination of the past "with a new set of questions that arise out of commitments to wholeness ... for all humanity".[16] Accordingly, I propose allowing the CMS women to speak from their own experiences and from within their own particular context, thus granting them epistemological dignity by acknowledging them as a valuable source for the creation of knowledge.[17] Concurrently, the methodological resources of various disciplines will challenge them with exacting questions concerning the dynamics that shaped their lives. Exploring the tension within McLaughlin's framework allows for a listening approach without regarding the past as an authoritative voice for present reality or future inspiration.

Women, history and the faith/feminism dialectic

Women's history or feminist history?

In recent years there has been growing concern to distinguish between what is meant by women's history as distinct from feminist history.[18] Women's history tends to be defined more by its subject matter, demonstrating a concern for the retrieval and exploration of the lives of past women. This task of restoring visibility dates back to the nineteenth century which saw the publication of many hagiographies celebrating the lives of exceptional women. Whilst modern biographies show greater interest in ordinary women and are generally more analytical, the emphasis remains on description and retrieval.[19] By contrast, feminist history has been defined as "a pursuit committed to the present"[20] which, while imbued by concern about the past, is fuelled primarily by a desire to contribute to contemporary social change by challenging the continued oppression of women.

Criticisms have been voiced of both these approaches as unsatisfactory and unhelpful. Compensatory history is accused of merely "filling-in-the-gap" and falling short of the full potential of feminist analysis. Critics argue that the method risks focusing on exceptional women involved in activities traditionally regarded as important. This not only undermines the majority of women but judges the minority on the basis of how successful they were in a "man's world". Moreover, a methodology limited to simplistic replication of historical documents by and about women, fails to appreciate the constraining effect which pressure to conform has upon such evidence.[21]

Feminist historiography arose from "a need for a past with which the feminist movement and women individually could identify".[22] Nevertheless, it has caused concern regarding its tendency to judge women of different eras according to present day ideological and practical priorities. Bock warns of the danger inherent in such "professional vice" which sees the past merely as "a function of, and as an instrument for, the present".[23] Ignoring historical diversity, this methodology refuses to allow women to emerge as individuals in their own right with concerns that may conflict with ours but are no less significant. Women in all ages speak with a variety of voices and whilst some undermined the confines of nineteenth century patriarchy, others found collusion to be their only method of survival. They may seem unenlightened and insignificant now, however, today's priorities are only possible because of those early context-specific attempts to improve the condition of women. The intrusion of late twentieth century assumptions as an absolute by which previous generations are to be judged neither does credit to the past nor truthfully helps make sense of the present. Unless we try to understand Victorian women within the context of their own concerns and realities, we present a one-sided and over-simplified reading of history. Forced to falsify their part in our present, we deny ourselves true dialogue with them and fail to appreciate the historical complexities of the choices facing them.[24]

My assertion is that elements from both women's history and feminist history are needed for a balanced approach to emerge. Furthermore, the boundaries between them need not be as sharp as some commentators suggest. There is no such thing as one feminist- or woman-orientated methodology. Indeed, feminism itself confronts the notion that one person or group has the right to impose definitions of reality on others. The same, then, is true of feminist scholars (and scholarship) who should "avoid doing the same thing in research situations".[25] Instead of searching for a single methodology, far better to work under the standard of a feminist epistemology which presents an alternative way of seeing reality, without imposing specific investigative conditions. This style sees research not in terms of particular techniques, but offers "a feminist perspective on the research process",[26] permitting greater flexibility in the application of various methodologies. Retrieval of women's past remains vital in the restoration of a more accurate historical narrative and it would be foolhardy to give up too soon what we have barely had at all. Meanwhile, maintaining a critical edge on historical events through concerns and priorities of feminism today, need not result in methodological or political determinism that only succeeds in smothering the diversity of past voices.

The impact of faith and feminism on women

A more holistic approach to a feminist epistemology that oversees the implementation of methods and methodologies is particularly appropriate when considering the role of religion in the lives of Victorian women. Whilst traditional accounts of Victorian church history have included little by way of gender analysis, contemporary feminist historiography has largely ignored or treated with suspicion the religious element in women's history. Despite the efforts of a few commentators to bring the disciplines closer, they still remain markedly disparate, with secular scholars wary of including religion as an analytical category in gender studies.[27] Those willing to admit the significance of Christianity and the church, mostly regard the impact as negative. Religious women, evangelicals and those involved in purity campaigns and the defence of Christian morality in particular, are often seen as betrayers of the women's movement, acting as a kind of brake on its forward motion. Meanwhile, scholars happy to accord religion a more positive status in the progress of women, do so primarily on the basis of a broader understanding and more comprehensive definition of nineteenth century feminism.[28]

The 1960s witnessed the advent of what is often described as the "second wave" of the women's movement. During this period feminism was frequently defined, somewhat narrowly, in terms of a doctrine of equal rights for women, based on a theory of sexual equality. Nineteenth century religious women, concerned less with political, legal or economic equal rights with men, and more with basic welfare rights for women, were easily excluded from this definition and placed outside the historical women's movement. Historians, however, soon found such straightforward classifications crude and unsatisfactory. There was growing realisation that a comparative historical approach necessitated a broadening perspective if the wide-ranging activities of earlier women were not simply to be condemned.

A two-fold understanding developed which lead to deepening appreciation of the past. First, it was increasingly acknowledged that "feminist theory is not monochrome",[29] but holds within itself a plurality of reflective analysis and practical strategy. Secondly, feminism came to be regarded as context related. For women's opportunities and priorities differ according to time and place, resulting in changing manifestations of feminism which is always deeply embedded in its surrounding culture:

> There have been significant shifts in the range of ideas, attitudes, and concerns of feminists ... but these were changes within feminism rather than involving a change from something which was pre-feminist or non-feminist to feminism.[30]

Such a broadening notion helped historians re-define feminism along very different lines. Banks, eager to re-appraise the relationship between nineteenth century evangelicalism and gender, uses the term in referring to those "that have tried to change the position of women, or ideas about women", whilst Offen regards it as "the impetus to critique and improve the disadvantaged status of women relative to men within a particular cultural situation."[31]

In a strictly historical sense, use of the term feminism, however it is defined, is problematic in relation to British Victorian women. Coined in France during the nineteenth century, the word did not find common usage in England until after 1910.[32] Moreover, it was never used by the CMS women in Iran to describe themselves or their work. Whilst recognising an inherent anachronism in this situation, it still remains possible to continue using the expression. Quite simply, in the absence of a suitable alternative, "feminism" is a useful shorthand too convenient to lose. More positively, no other term adequately conveys the extent or intensity of concern regarding the position of women or the sense of injustice at the oppression many experienced. Above all, "feminism" - utilised in its inclusive form - encourages appropriate analysis of the complex and multi-layered nineteenth century "woman question" as more than just the radical suffragette movement, which developed as a branch of contemporary liberalism during the early twentieth century. Accordingly, the entire nineteenth century women's movement - in all its diversity - can be acknowledged as predecessor to today's feminist concerns. The religious element can thereby claim its place as one strand in the historical evolution of feminism. For whilst placing more emphasis on women's Christian duty and less on their equal rights, religious feminism strengthened the women's movement by bringing into it many who would not have been motivated by a desire for equality.[33]

Of course, Victorian religious feminism, far from representing a hegemonic entity, was itself "a cause with many sides".[34] It included radicals who joined the fight for suffrage and raised controversial issues such as women's ordination, and moderates eager to persuade church authorities through committed philanthropic service that the female force was strong and valid. Many in the latter category, including most missionaries, would never have explicitly aligned themselves with a radical feminist cause. Nevertheless, they were part of the broader movement in terms described by Levine as distinct, due to its "conscious woman-centredness".[35] In contrast to active engagement in organised politics or ecclesiastical controversies, this form of feminism represented a change in outlook. It involved the adoption of alternative values which, common to much nineteenth century feminism, was interested in improving the rights of women without showing undue concern for achieving equality with men.[36]

This brand of feminism, rooted in the dominant ethical value of its day, was based on the philosophy of separate spheres and steeped in Victorian evangelical culture. Negotiating and manipulating acceptable parameters, churchwomen were walking an ideological tightrope. Had they proved too radical they might have fallen off without achieving anything. Therefore, many played according to conventional social rules, all the time carving out for themselves ever growing niches in which their potential blossomed. We should be wary of determining the success of Victorian feminism only in terms of public achievements by assuming these women were passive objects compared with their more radical sisters. To be sure, domestic ideology and evangelicalism provided the language for their cause which, based on sexual difference, stressed the Christian duty of women and the "centrality of potential or actual maternity".[37] This notion that the women's movement apparently included distinctly anti-feminist values, serving only to restrict women, could be regarded as an unacceptable contradiction. Alternately, it could represent the extraordinary achievement of countless women who successfully used their subordinate position as an ideological vehicle for expanding their possibilities.

The primary aim of this section has been to argue for diversity as the essential feature of Victorian feminism. Indeed, the sheer breadth of the movement was a factor in its refusal to submit to one formal organisational principle. There is no single women's movement or phenomenon describing the position of all feminists. Moreover, Caine rightly warns against a simplistic division of moderate feminists (those stressing women's "difference" from men), and radicals (emphasising "equality").[38] For when paired dichotomously, these constitute an impossible choice, belying the reality whereby most women worked with the advantages of both.

The modern missionary movement and women's participation within it remains unpopular and much maligned by critics regarding it as an exploitative arm of British imperialism. Women's role is often seen only in terms of a futile power struggle between superiority lauded over indigenous women and ultimate submission to the male authority of mission hierarchy. Such ideas fuel the notion that the Victorian church was an anti-feminist institution and that the closing years of the nineteenth century represent a blank period in the history of Britain's religious feminism.[39]

In fact, female participation in the missionary movement should be regarded as one strand in an increasingly diverse movement.[40] Struggling with very different concerns, many of them controversial today, missionary women were no less involved in conscious woman-centred work. This resolute concern for the welfare of their sex is a common theme amongst female missionaries, evidenced from one worker in India who expressed her calling in terms of "a passion for woman".[41] To be sure, their involvement was based upon a re-interpretation of the separate spheres philosophy and the essential difference between men and women. However, even the harshest critics of missionary activity admit that female missionaries helped stimulate the movement towards women's emancipation in the East.[42] Though they did not call themselves feminists and were far from aligning themselves with radical groups demanding sexual equality, missionary women's participation in the development of feminism should not be undermined. Nor should it be forgotten that conditions abroad were often more favourable than those at home in allowing the possibility for change.

> It was ... in the mission field, far away from the institutional and social confines of Victorian England, that the greatest opportunities for women to exercise responsibility and initiative ... occur[red].[43]

A comprehensive historical understanding of Victorian feminism acknowledges that the multi-faceted movement, steeped in the dominant values of its day, was expressed through prevailing linguistic tools. This approach denies feminism a false hegemony, and acknowledges a place for religious and missionary women within the developing movement. Underlying it is the paradox of the faith/feminism dialectic in which religion both empowered and shackled women. Christianity was central in the lives of all Victorians and for women it frequently provided strength and self-belief in taking up their cause. Concurrently, the church imposed the full weight of the separate spheres ideology upon women, drastically limiting their opportunities. In response, religious women ingeniously used the domestic ideology to their advantage, thus becoming active agents in the making of their history. The very essence of what impeded them became the source of their liberation. Despite their limitations and shortcomings, these resourceful women should not be denied their rightful place in the making of modern feminism.

The genderization of missionary imperialism

Whilst it is possible to place the CMS women within the context of feminism's development in Britain, there are also significant factors differentiating their situation from that of women in England. The missionaries were venturing into new racial and religious terrains as well as grappling with gender and class issues. In this section I examine the connection between the missionary movement and imperialism, exploring in particular gender questions pertinent to the position of women. The link between missionary work and imperial expansion has long been established although the manner in which commentators interpret the relationship varies.[44] By comparison, the more specific field of gender and empire is relatively new and one that both secular and religious scholars are only just beginning to tackle.[45]

Defining imperialism in a post-colonial context

Any study of imperialism is fraught with difficulties. A complex etymology means its contemporary usage is controversial, polemical and loaded with ideological premises. Entering the English language during the 1840s, the term originated in France with unpleasant connotations from its earliest days.[46] Attempts were made to improve its reputation during the 1860s and by the end of the century two diverse interpretations had emerged. To the majority, it was "a larger patriotism"[47], growing from pride in an expanding empire. Accordingly, the imperial mission - a topic of unembarrassed attention in Britain at the time - was based on an obligation to spread the benefits of western civilisation to less fortunate peoples. This philosophy was founded on an unconsciously held view of "natural" English superiority operating across society, providing "cultural hegemony" and a "unified discourse".[48] Though the vocabulary of the time is littered with value-laden terms such as "inferior", "subject races" and "subordinate peoples", the underlying premise of this understanding of imperialism was an eagerness to act responsibly for the benefit of those being ruled. Conversely, a different strand associated imperialism with wars, bloodshed, exploitation and the search for profit. Later the term was absorbed into Marxist ideology, and since the advent of post-colonialism in particular, has been a convenient multi-purpose, anti-western slogan.

Despite the efforts of a number of commentators to elucidate it, imperialism remains difficult to define and, carrying strong emotional overtones, is often confusing rather than clarifying. It is, therefore, a word to be used with extreme caution. According to Said, imperialism is "the practice, the theory, and the attitudes of a dominating metropolitan centre ruling a distant territory", in contrast to colonialism which, "almost always a consequence of imperialism, is the implanting of settlements on distant territory".[49] Similarly, Eldridge refers to it as an "'umbrella-word'" encompassing not only events which led to the establishment of colonies, but also the motives behind those events and the theories underlying them.[50] In other words, imperialism includes aspects of a theoretical ideology as well as practical implications. Though the political idea failed, faith in the idea remained alive in the thought and action of governing classes in Britain until the end of the Second World War. Iran is not commonly included among the acquisitions of the British empire. However, taken as a principle or idea, the impact of imperialism was as strong in Iran, which was never colonised, as it was anywhere. For empire was more than physical invasion; it was

> a relationship, formal or informal, in which one state controls the effective political sovereignty of another political society. It can be achieved by force, by political collaboration, by economic, social, or cultural dependence.[51]

It is in this context that Said uses the term imperialism in his book *Culture and Imperialism*. Arguing that cultural links are more potent than direct domination through physical force, he considers imperialism to be

> an ideological vision implemented and sustained ... much more effectively over a long time by *persuasive means* ... [through] ... the daily imposition of power in the dynamics of everyday life, the back-and-forth of interaction among natives, the white man, and the institutions of authority.[52]

The cultural imperialism implied here was at the root of the informal imperialism operating in Iran during the Victorian/Qajar era. Throughout the empire, western culture "constructed privileged norms and unprivileged deviations",[53] against which it judged indigenous societies. Missionaries are frequently accused of having been "a quintessential feature of British expansion" as primary agents in the transmission of cultural imperialism.[54] Perhaps surprisingly, in *Culture and Imperialism*, Said makes no explicit mention of missionary activity. However, in his seminal work, *Orientalism*, he identifies religion as a primary area of interest over which Britain felt it had legitimate claim and, quoting Tibawi, accuses the missionary societies, including CMS, of "openly join[ing] the expansion of Europe".[55]

Feminist Imperialism

Empire was essentially a patriarchal structure founded upon masculine ideologies. Firm views on traditional gender roles helped maintain the male balance of power.[56] Nevertheless, women, often accused of "complicity with patriarchy and imperialism",[57] are not immune from the charge of imposing an imperial agenda, and feminists still struggle with how best to include them in the process of historical analysis. British women throughout the empire had no authoritative part in formal organisational and administrative structures. However, they did influence official policy in important ways. The majority were infused by the widespread values and beliefs of an imperial worldview and, at some level, strongly identified with its masculine ideologies. Others, however, attempted to develop a feminine version of "benevolent imperial social reform".[58] Often displaying condescending elements, this adaptation involved a dualistic approach towards indigenous women. It regarded them as sisters whose stereotypical role in society should be challenged, but at the same time, as "passive and silent victims in need of the protection of white women".[59] Burton interprets this as a kind of feminist imperialism, prevalent among the middle-classes, which regarded white women as prime agents of western civilisation, motivated in their work by a sense of duty to help their eastern sisters.[60]

Whatever it is called - maternalistic, benevolent or feminist imperialism - its roots were in the dominant evangelical culture of the time. This promoted the notion that spreading the gospel was a duty resulting from God's munificence showered upon Christendom. It provided moral justification for imperialism in a doctrine of trusteeship over so called "backward" races. The feminisation of this theology in the missionary movement resulted in women colluding with its basic ideology, whilst at the same time challenging it through their very presence. The continuation of Christian civilisation was still considered dependent upon women conforming to the traditional role of wife and mother. However, single women missionaries stepped outside the traditional bounds of the domestic sphere both in their own social context, by rejecting marriage and working outside its confines, and by questioning the position of indigenous women in relation to Persian cultural norms. Due to their self-perception as better equipped (through their western and Christian heritage) than Iranian women to ensure the latter's liberation, and in common with much contemporary evangelical and imperialist thought, "their charity seems often to have been accompanied by a patronizing attitude".[61]

The status of women in the mission hierarchies

The mixture of "complicity and resistance",[62] common among women of the empire, indicates their ambivalent position within the hierarchical structures. According to Foucault's concept of power as omnipresent and decentralised,[63] the CMS women were active participants in the politics of the mission field. However, they played different roles according to whether they were reacting to the dominant male mission culture, or the perceived inferior indigenous culture of Persian women. In the former case, the CMS women were involved in "reverse discourses", subverting and resisting institutional power where they could and following the "path of convention" where it best suited.[64] By contrast, in the inverted non-egalitarian relationship between them and Persian women, the missionary women became the dominant activators to which their eastern sisters reacted with their own reverse discourses. In short, like many other western women in the empire, the CMS missionaries "played ambiguous roles as members of a sex considered to be inferior within a race that considered itself superior".[65] The result was equivocal, enabling identification with the oppression of Persian women, whilst at the same time, nurturing a sense of superiority.

The nature of the unstable power relationships with which the CMS women continually juggled is evident in their racially orientated approaches to the separate spheres philosophy. Recognising the strictures created by the Iranian version of the domestic ideology, the missionaries aimed to help Persian women towards liberation. What they actually did was to impose their own (often subconscious) western version of the ideology on a new context. In other words, they wanted to *improve* the private world of women rather than eradicate it in favour of equality with men. Whilst the CMS women themselves had rejected traditional roles as wives and mothers, they endeavoured to teach Persian women about the inherent virtues of this model, hoping they would adhere to it in the new Christian society imagined for Iran.

The CMS missionaries were not simply attempting the regeneration of a new Persian womanhood, but were also in the process of clarifying their own role and identity. In *Orientalism*, Said argues that all societies or groups acquire their identities by developing a notion of "self" based upon some "other" in binary opposition. Thus, the Orient, whilst representing one of the Occident's "deepest and most recurring images of the Other", more importantly helps the westerner "define Europe (or the West) as its contrasting image, idea, personality, experience".[66] Thus the "orientals" Said writes about are little more than western innovations (equivalent to Foucault's insane, perverts and criminals) who, deviating from imposed European norms, are falsely constructed and at the same time help construct the westerner.[67]

This concept of "otherness" may be applied methodologically to other disciplines, geographical entities or historical settings, and proves particularly fruitful in areas of feminism and racism. Its application in the context of this book underlines how, during their time in Iran, the CMS missionaries developed their own self-identity, not just through new and groundbreaking work, but in direct opposition to their construction of indigenous women as "other". Comparable to their role in the convoluted power relationships (mentioned above), the women were part of a structural hierarchy which also regulated their sense of "self" and "other". In relation to their male colleagues they were the "other" fabricated in opposition to the male notion of "self". Concurrently, however, they formed the dominant group, defining "self" according to their perceived version of the Persian women as "other". Haggis writes about London Missionary Society (LMS) missionaries in India involved in "a process of 'othering' which construct[ed] Indian women as the converse of their English 'sisters'".[68] The CMS women in Persia were doing likewise, but all the time they were also being categorised as the "other" invented by male colleagues.

Exposing the myths of imperialism

There are dangers in portraying the West-East relationship in crude terms, as a straightforward superior/inferior power domination. A number of qualifications are necessary to avoid simplistic conclusions akin to a battle between the virtuous, idyllic East versus the evil, destructive West. Notwithstanding the strength of western technology, economics and ideological self-confidence, the success of both imperialism and the missionary movement necessitated co-operation on both sides. Just as women colluded, to a degree, with the ongoing dominance of patriarchy, so the East chose to accept elements of imperialism, and the missionary movement endured because of its perceived benefits.[69] The entire imperialist enterprise provided a mixture of humiliation and benefits for indigenous recipients. This was equally true of the missionary movement, perhaps especially with respect to women's contribution.[70]

It is, moreover, demeaning and patronising to assume that when faced with the Christian message brought by missionaries, Persians simply surrendered to the might of western power. First, this presupposes far greater contact and assimilation of ideas than was actually the case. The extent of social interaction between missionaries and Persians was modest at best, and the number of converts, infinitesimally small. Secondly, it is based on the model of Persians as gullible, hopeless victims with scant capacity to think for themselves and filter the missionary message. Indeed, many enjoyed the benefits of missionary education and medical care without any inclination towards conversion. Finally, it undermines the decision of those who did convert, often in the face of hostility and opposition. Several writers have shown how the missionary message was embraced as an attractive alternative, addressing important aspects of everyday life inadequately dealt with by indigenous religions. For women in particular it offered hope in the face of social evils such as poverty and disease, helping them face death in very different ways.[71] It is not surprising, therefore, that - as was the case in Iran - missionaries found the majority of their early converts among poorer women.

A further important point should be noted regarding the nature of western cultural hegemony and/or the Christian civilising message and its supposed impact upon eastern societies. Porter is extremely suspicious of the notion that missionaries were involved in the process of cultural imperialism.[72] He believes it is based on a mistaken assumption that there was an identifiable entity, called imperial culture, which missionaries were trying to transmit. Rather, he argues, the inherent difficulties with the term "imperialism" are further compounded by the addition of a qualifying adjective such as "cultural", itself open to contrasting interpretations. It is wrong, therefore, to present western culture as highly integrated, persistent, monolithic and immune to change, imposing itself on some idyllic version of indigenous civilisation which, fragile and weak in comparison, crumbles in the face of its superior counterpart. Said agrees, maintaining that such a view envisions the "outlying regions of the world [as having] no life, history or culture to speak of, no independence or integrity", leaving westerners "at liberty to visit their fantasies and philanthropies upon a mind-deadened Third World".[73]

In reality, cultures do not survive in isolation but are interconnected and interdependent. This presupposes that any social contact between two groups impacts upon both sides, rather than influencing one and leaving the other in its original state. Therefore, the missionaries and their Christianity must have been affected through contact with Persian society. Indeed, for their universal message to enjoy any form of efficacy it required negotiating and adapting to fit its new localised context. Compromise and malleability were essential elements in the meeting of these two worlds and missionaries unable to comprehend this, soon found "the penalty for inflexibility was commonly rejection".[74]

The question remains whether the CMS women were *aware* of this need for the fusion of ideas and cultures, and whether they were open to change for themselves as well as the Persians they tried to influence. "Was the glass two-way? Did [they] learn from the culture... they sought to transform? How far were their own values modified by their experiences?"[75] Stanley believes most nineteenth century missionaries did allow
> their personal experience of other cultures to re-define their norms of civilization to the limited extent that their moral and theological convictions allowed.[76]

This, however, raises serious methodological difficulties due to the nature of the original sources available. Limited by their language and the audience for whom they wrote, missionary letters and articles must be read with care. Literal interpretation is often inadequate, for it does not necessarily serve as an accurate indicator of the authors' real views.

If their language was restricted by prevalent orientalist ideologies,[77] then we too must be wary of the boundaries that fence us into all too narrow conclusions of our own time. Historiography that is overly concerned to maintain "political correctness" (racial or gender based), is in danger of limiting its insights. Hyam, for example, writes about the "poverty of feminism", with its "self-imposed parameters" and "humourless rules" which operate only according to the militant agenda, consistently hostile to any study of women as victims who, through their resilience, could turn their exploitation into advantage.[78] Similarly, Rodinson warns against a kind of distorted orientalism that simply classifies the "other" in a diametrical manner. Rather than rendering it diabolic, it goes to the other extreme and through an extraordinary "ideological about-face ... practically sanctif[ies] Islam" and the East. This European version of "Muslim apologetics", through its refusal to be critical of Islam in any way, loses its analytical advantage and becomes little more than indulgent description.[79] There must be no discrimination, vilification or scorn, but there is no obligation to applaud all Muslim ideas and deeds. If past voices are to speak on their own terms, scholars must be wary of imposing such a heavily biased twentieth century agenda that their sources are silenced. An anti-imperialist sentiment, when combined with Christian ecumenism (eager to make amends for past enmity), can result in distorted historiography based on fear that any racial or religious criticism will exacerbate old imperial attitudes.

The CMS women lived, worked and were influenced by dominating contours of their era: high imperialism, missionary confidence and feminism. Caught between the "interplay of imperial mission and gender imperatives",[80] they sometimes challenged the predominance of restrictive ideologies and at other times did not. Negotiating the converging and conflicting fields of gender, race, class, nationality and religion, they were forced to improvise and innovate whilst operating within a paradoxical feminised empire. For offering women benefits of a life-style and responsibilities they could never have achieved at home, it still contained them within overall Victorian gender norms. Able to identify with Persian women on some level, the missionaries recognised various social problems and sought to alleviate them. However, they were too easily persuaded that these resulted from the evils of indigenous culture and religion, failing to see them as a product of gender oppression from which they too suffered in different ways. Believing that they possessed the key to Iran's problems, they regarded Christianity as the source of western greatness and the solution for Persian society. East was compared unfavourably with West, and Islam denounced as the cause of Iranian (especially women's) degradation.

Away from home for long periods at a time, it was easy for the missionaries to remember a glorified version of Britain, far from the real country they had left behind. Forgetting the tensions at almost every level of social, political and religious life, each struggling with new ideas of modernism and feminism, they presented a distorted image of Victorian Christian Britain as a shining example of civilisation, particularly in respect to women and the exalted position it accorded them. "Victorian class and gender stereotypes were transferred into racist ideology"[81] as their convictions moulded by the tenets of empire proved stronger than their will to question the conventions of imposed sexual norms. The former placed distance between the British and Iranian women, whilst the latter, a cross-cultural issue, brought them closer than either side recognised.

Sources and Methods

In applying various methods to the research process, the important point is to remain self-conscious, always submitting oneself to critical scrutiny. Sensitivity towards sources is also essential if the power relation between researcher and researched is not to be abused.[82] However, the limitations and restrictions of sources must be recognised if they are not to be mistakenly idolised as presenting "the truth".

Main sources used

British women's religious history is plagued by practical difficulties regarding scarcity of information and limitations of available material.[83] The principal sources used in this study, likewise, presented disadvantages, affecting research methodology.

The most important primary source material has been the private missionary letters, available in CMS archives. All missionaries were expected to write an "annual letter" describing the events of their past year. Many wrote more often, and for the period between 1869-1934, their correspondence was filed chronologically.[84] The collection is not complete and frequent gaps and censorship of sensitive information make it difficult (sometimes impossible), to follow the outcome of an entire incident.[85] CMS publications, including journals and newsletters, also included missionary contributions. Articles were sometimes written for a specific occasion or to match the theme of an educational or medical journal. More commonly, suitable sections from missionary letters, especially annual letters, were extracted and inserted into relevant volumes or compilations.[86]

Both these sources present similar limitations. First, there is comparatively little information provided by women. Official decisions were always taken by senior men, responsible for informing CMS of their actions. Most of the correspondence, therefore, is by men, though it frequently includes information *about* female colleagues. Articles, and sometimes entire periodicals, were often demarcated by gender. This produced a hierarchical distinction between general missionary work, carried out by men, and "women's work" as a separate adjunct. Letters and publications by women rarely include anything other than straightforward descriptions of their specific areas of work.[87]

Secondly, these written sources were not private letters but written in a highly self-conscious manner and for a specific audience. As public material, therefore, they were restricted in tone and subject matter by readers' expectations. Printed information was produced primarily to encourage financial giving and was not the occasion for expressing pessimism or articulating doubt. It necessitated a positive portrayal of missionary work so that readers would be persuaded that their generosity was proving successful and worthwhile.

Finally, these primary sources are limited due to the prescriptive power of the dominant religious and racial discourses of the time. Victorian evangelicalism created a highly charged language which missionaries were not only expected to reproduce, but were firmly and subconsciously bound by. Whilst their narrow perceptions and prejudices were frequently modified as a result of experience, missionaries usually remained unable to appropriate the new theological language necessary to express these changes. Therefore, how they "interpreted their experiences is interesting and telling, but it is not necessarily the final word".[88] The distinction engendered by the orientalist discourse between western superiority and eastern inferiority was also extremely powerful, limiting even some of the most imaginative and broad-minded people of the age.[89] This theoretical orientalism, referred to by Said as a "wholly bookish Orientalism", was built upon a long literary tradition of intellectual scholarship and represented a formidable force during the age of empire.[90] Those who found their personal experience differed from prescribed views were seldom able to express this and eventually converted the experiential into recognised codes of orientalist language. Within most texts, a "metamorphosis from personal to official statement"[91] occurred, strengthening the existing persistence of orientalist discourse.

Like the missionary archives, most late nineteenth and early twentieth century literature betrays the influence of imperialist thought patterns and unprecedented British self-confidence, and should be used with care. More recent secondary missiological sources must also be utilised sensitively for they seldom relate directly to Iran.[92] Whilst providing general methodological and epistemological guidelines, analogy and analysis must be applied to the particulars of this book scrupulously.

As a means of enriching the textual material, I have also included photographs within the book. They appear only within the more biographical context of Part II, and seek to endorse other source material. Photographs help contextualize written evidence and, providing an ethnographic dimension, aid in conveying the Persian milieu that the missionaries encountered.[93] In addition, further supporting material may be found in the appendices.

Integrating the general and particular

My aim throughout this project is to combine the general and particular as "two perspectives on the same material".[94] Used independently, each is in danger of distortion and inaccuracy, however, when integrated, the general helps illuminate the particular and vice versa.

Feminist historians have recently tended to stress the "collective" over the "exceptional".[95] This is based on a desire to understand more about the lives of the ordinary majority instead of focusing on the extraordinary minority. However, emphasising the general need not necessarily ignore the exceptional, for an integrated biographical method enables recognition of individuality whilst reconciling it within the wider context.

Accordingly, the three women discussed in Part II are not presented as exceptional characters but as representatives of the more general. Each was, in her own way, unique and extraordinary; however, they are more significant as figures delineating aspects of the overall position of their female colleagues in Iran. Restricted by their class and religious affiliation, each was both victim and agent in a male environment that sought to confine women within certain limits.[96] Their individual successes and failures are, in one sense, particular but at the same time help to elucidate the wider issues faced and negotiated by their contemporaries.

The personal dimension as an epistemological source

Traditional research methodologies are increasingly criticised for "professional obsessiveness with 'scientific objectivity'".[97] Feminist and post-imperialist awareness of the positive implications of racial diversity attempt to redress the balance by stressing the need for honest clarification of personal involvement and subjectivity. Post-modern scepticism about attempts to tell "true stories" allows historians to avoid the pretence of objectivity and enjoy the benefits of carefully practised subjectivity. Researchers now understand that, "it is the *unexamined* exercise of cognitive authority ... which is most to be feared",[98] not the considered path of personal experience laid open to critical scrutiny.

My own involvement in this research is deep and intimate. The topic is part of my personal history and has played a significant part in my growth and development. For I am, in part, a product of missionary efforts in Iran. My mother, the daughter and grand-daughter of CMS missionaries, was born in Iran and spent most of her life there. She married my father, a Persian Muslim who converted to Christianity as a result of his encounter with the mission. Together they have dedicated their lives to the service of the church in Iran. I was born in Isfahan and spent my formative years amidst a Muslim environment at school and a Christian one at home. My family has been in England since shortly after the Islamic Revolution and, to date, we have been unable to return due to politico-religious reasons.[99]

This brief personal narrative is offered not by way of descriptive light relief but serves as a useful bench-mark, locating me and my research "vis-à-vis the Orient".[100] My story signifies involvement in both Persian and British cultures, presenting me as a product of both. Never entirely at home in one or the other, I live with the sometimes painful and yet enriching reality that each has influenced me profoundly. The Islamic culture of Iran and the CMS missionaries with their particular brand of Christianity are equally part of my heritage and my research is an attempt to explore this history rather than repress or deny it. Patricia Hill Collins has written about black women as "outsiders within" whose marginality offers them a unique position from which they can contribute to feminist thought.[101] As an "outsider within" who frequently feels on the margins of both western and eastern societies, involved in and yet distant from both, I hope to make use of the creative potential in my personal biography as a significant epistemological source.

Clearly, as an Anglican clergywoman, I write as one who has chosen Christianity. Yet I still feel deeply Persian and preserve the connection with my roots through family and friends, contact with the church in Iran, knowledge of the language and a sense of belonging within Iranian culture. Far from trying to ignore the emotional dimension, I attempt to capitalise on the creative tension it creates as a positive "source of insight" in "the production of knowledge".[102] Recognising the importance of the personal is fundamental to feminist philosophy and scholars recognise it as a crucial variable present in any attempt to do research, for "idiosyncrasies of person and circumstance are at the heart not the periphery of the scientific enterprise".[103] A range of technical difficulties may arise as a result of being "in" the situation one seeks to analyse, and awareness of this is vital. However, if achieved successfully, "personal experience has an immediacy that honestly reflects its role in the formation of intellectual judgement".[104] Passion and emotion, whether they arise from intellectual curiosity, personal experience or a combination of both, are necessary for a satisfactory outcome. Yet ultimately, "history as one knows it in one's own person is always more compelling than history as it may be written in the cold analysis of documentary research".[105]

I aim through my work to combine personal history with the documentary research necessary for creating an intellectually credible analysis of the subject under study. According to feminist methodology, I seek "to bring together subjective and objective ways of knowing the world"[106] by using both methods abundantly. Like many women, I need to relate to my foremothers as a means of appreciating my past,[107] and more importantly, better understanding my present. In this book I try to combine the particular with the general in a variety of ways. One of these is to fulfil my personal quest for historical rootedness whilst also contributing to the wider history of women and religion. The specific situation of CMS women in Iran represents a narrow and particular story. Yet it also helps illustrate something of the strength of evangelical culture which combined with imperialism to create an ambivalent environment at once liberating and confining women.

CHAPTER TWO

A Meeting of West and East:
The Victorian/Qajar Period Contextualized

Iran: Land of diversity

The historically sensitive stance with which I am eager to approach the subject of my book requires that the context in which the CMS women lived and worked be delineated. Building upon the methodological principles outlined in the previous chapter, this section focuses on the religious, political and social environment of British and especially Iranian society during the Victorian/Qajar period, with particular reference to the position of women.

The term Qajar is applied to the Persian dynasty whose first shah, or king, originated from the Qajar tribe during the eighteenth century. Technically, the years 1869-1934 are not confined to the Victorian and Qajar eras. Queen Victoria died in 1901 and the Qajar dynasty, which began in 1787, was overthrown in 1925.[1] However, in its formative years, the Persia mission was shaped and influenced by the nuances of what may be called Victorian/Qajar factors. Much of the essence of Victorianism continued to influence British life long after the death of Queen Victoria herself, giving credence to my premise symbolically, if not literally. Likewise, the early years of the Pahlavi regime (1925-1979) represented a time of tremendous change and upheaval so that its true nature and method of government did not become apparent until the 1930s.[2]

Geography, climate and population

Geographically, the Iranian plateau covers a vast area of the Middle East. Its 636,000 square miles includes an extensive central desert region and several formidable mountain ranges (see Appendix I for a map of Iran). The climate provides veritable variety with pleasant springs and autumns separating the greater extremes of summer and winter. In 1932 Sir Arnold Wilson warned would-be travellers that, "according to the season [they] will be grilled by the sun, or buffeted and frozen by the wind".[3] The severe climate, rugged terrain and long distances were compounded, during the nineteenth century, by bad roads and poor communications, resulting in a fragmented population living in secluded villages, isolated towns and nomadic tribes. It is commonly accepted that in 1850 the population was approximately ten million, of whom twenty percent were urban dwellers. By 1900 Iran's populace had grown to twelve million while the 1956 census records just under nineteen million. Today there are in excess of sixty-five million people living in Iran.[4]

Persia is a land of "racial diversity which over the centuries has been welded into the Iranian nation".[5] An amalgam of different peoples and cultures, it is further complicated by its mixture of religious and linguistic minorities.[6] Difficult travelling conditions, poor communication and a weak central government meant disparity was a feature of Persian life during much of the Victorian/Qajar period.[7] Many communities existed as virtually self-sufficient groups, economically autonomous and predominantly self-governing. Various strata of communal life were organised according to networks operating as small pyramids, analogous yet independent. Nomadic tribes were an important element in Iran throughout the century, preserving their distinctive identity despite continued government efforts to bring them under control. Each had its own dialect, genealogy and system of authority. Though officially appointed by central government, leaders were more like hereditary nobles, selected in the tribes before being confirmed in office as a formality. Villages functioned on a similar basis, whilst a more complex social framework operated in cities and urban centres.[8]

This multiplicity of town, village and nomadic structures commonly operated within one larger region. In central Iran, for example, Isfahan contained a number of villages, tribal populations and other districts including two for non-Muslims: Jubareh for Jews and Julfa for Armenians. However, this somewhat idyllic "mosaic of social units" should not deflect from the reality which often transformed diversity into conflict.[9] The struggle for scarce resources, a belief that one group could only prosper at the expense of another, and the competition to fill local government offices ensured that "factional strife, in one form or another ... remained a feature of Persian life down to modern times".[10]

The fundamental problem was a weak and ineffective Qajar government, lacking in solid central administration. Officially, the shah granted Governor-generals and Prince-governors sanction to control different regions.[11] However, until the late 1930s when Reza Shah established a one-nation state under the Pahlavi dynasty, large parts of Iran were ruled by warlords, tribal chiefs and bandits. "In theory, the [Qajar] shahs were omnipotent; in practice, they were politically impotent".[12] Ruling Iran through retreat in the face of dangerous opposition and manipulation of internal conflicts and rivalries, the Qajar dynasty was a failed imitation of the absolutist oriental despotism many in the West considered it to be. Iran survived on "minimal government",[13] with the power balance shifting between tribal leaders, *ulama* (religious leaders), and foreign nations, whose subtle but effective authority held sway in Iran throughout the Victorian/Qajar era and beyond.

The *ulama* and foreign powers, in particular, were extremely significant components in the development of late-Qajar Iran and its relationship with CMS missionaries. The tolerance of the Persian government and people towards the mission was co-dependant upon the relative popularity of the British and strength of the Muslim clergy at any given point. Indeed, throughout nineteenth and twentieth century Iran the position of all religious minority groups, including missionaries and converts, continually changed as they were "exposed to the vicissitudes of prosperity and persecution, according to changes in the political climate".[14] The authority of Iran's own particular brand of Islam, together with the effectiveness of foreign domination (through Russia and especially Britain), are integral factors in understanding the situation of nineteenth century Persia.

"Moslems with a difference"

Despite Iran's multi-racial and factional nature, and notwithstanding its many internal strifes, the country remained an integrated whole throughout the Qajar period. This was largely due to the unifying influence of Islam operating across sub-sections of society. Though non-Muslim minorities existed, they were never very influential and in the hundred years from 1850 onwards, only accounted for three percent of the population.[15] For the remainder, the various linguistic and ethnic communities maintained a religious synthesis in the shape of Islam. Since its political and geographical conquests from the seventh century, Islam had been more than just a faith. Acting as the ultimate basis of identity, it provided a primary focus of loyalty and supreme source of control. Kings and sovereigns attempting to limit the authority of Islam or the *ulama* did so, and continue to do so, at their peril. Muhammad Reza Shah proved this when his endeavours to westernise Iran and undermine religious supremacy culminated in the Islamic Revolution.

In the West, Islam has generally been understood as it is manifested in Arab countries or perhaps the Indian subcontinent. Iran's Islam, solid and deep-rooted as anywhere, is different however, in two essential and interconnected elements. First, the majority of Iranian Muslims are Shi'ites, not Sunnis.[16] Secondly, unlike most other Muslim nations, the people of Iran "retained an awareness of their pre-Islamic past",[17] never losing their Persian identity by total submersion into Arabic culture. By contrast with other Middle Eastern regions, Iran is Muslim but most definitely *not* Arab.

Some consider the distinctiveness of Shi'ism in terms of a victory of Persians over Arabs - the creation of a "Persianized Islam" or an expression of "Iranian National Consciousness".[18] In fact, Shi'ism is Arab in origin and the hypothesis that it was a specifically Iranian invention or phenomenon is entirely incorrect. From the earliest days, though, Persians found this brand of Islam adaptable to local circumstances and tolerant enough to allow the absorption of pre-existent customs.

Shi'ism, the minority faith, and the Iranians, the most civilized and individualistic converts to Islam, exercised a strong mutual attraction for each other ... an attraction which was finally consummated in the establishment of Shi'ism as the official religion of the state under the Safavids.[19]

Richard refers to the "Iranization of Shi'ism" as "twofold".[20] Politically, the sixteenth century Safavid dynasty put in place a Shi'ite system in which spiritual leaders (*mujtaheds*) were above kings in religious matters. A structure of mutually supportive recognition developed whereby the state accepted advice and guidance from the religious establishment who, in turn, authorised the legitimacy of sovereigns and governments. Thus, foundations were laid for a Muslim institution in which religious figures gained increasing influence on secular matters. For the masses, the *mujtahed* became a kind of "ruling elite"[21] and, since the nineteenth century in particular, Iranian clerics have consistently and effectively intervened in political affairs.

Culturally, "Iranized Shi'ism" is manifested in emotive religious rites surrounding the lives and especially martyrdoms of the *imams*. These ostentatious displays of mourning are peculiar to the people of Iran. They have little to do with obeying the commands of clergy or other ruling bodies but indicate national outbursts of "spontaneous ritual" that most Sunnis regard as an "orgy of Imamolatry".[22]

Iranian Shi'ism is unique in the way it maintained a non-Arab nature through deep roots in a pre-Islamic Persian history. Many Arab attributes were imported into Iran during the Muslim invasion. Shi'ite prayers and theological texts, for example, are in Arabic and many Arabic words filtered into every-day Persian language. Furthermore, with Mecca as their religious focus, Iranians are acutely aware of belonging to a spiritual community dominated by Arabs. Undoubtedly, the Arab conquest permeated deeper into the structure of Iran's civilisation than any other external influence before or since. Yet it did not wholly destroy or absorb indigenous Iranian traits. The Persian language survived with its essential characteristics and roots intact. Several pre-Islamic customs also resisted extinction such as those connected with New Year - *Noruz* - still celebrated each spring. These are outward and visible expressions of a reality which Mottahedeh refers to as "that world of ambiguity between Iranianness and Islam".[23] It is not simply that Persians have guarded their language and traditions but that they do so with deep pride and a sense of achievement. To be sure, memories are often more mythic than historic but no less vivid or significant because of that. Legendary characters and events, such as those depicted by the great eleventh century poet Ferdowsi in his epic work *Shahnameh* (The Book of Kings), retain a vital place in the Persian psyche.

No account of the dynasties of Iranian history would be complete without some reference to the Iranian legend, the national myth with its kings and heroes and lovers who loom larger perhaps in the mind of many Iranians ... than most historical figures.[24]

The arts and literature provided the field in which tensions between Persian and Muslim elements were enacted. Poetry, in particular, became "the emotional home in which the ambiguity that was at the heart of Iranian culture lived most freely and openly".[25] There is little doubt concerning the sincerity with which most Iranians embraced Islam. However, a spontaneous pleasure remained in the distinctive re-telling of a pagan past in uniquely Persian terms.

In short, a perplexing tension exists in the Iranian subconscious between its Islamic and pre-Islamic roots. People know they are Muslims but also consider themselves cultural heirs of a pre-Islamic Iran depicted by the ancient fables of Ferdowsi and others. It is this paradox in the Persian nature that makes Iran a nation of Muslims but "Moslems with a difference".[26]

The English/Persian love-hate relationship

One of the most interesting factors about Iran, and perhaps the reason why it has not been subjected to serious missiological study, is that the country was never formally colonised under western rule. Generally, British missionary societies were active in regions where the British government had political autonomy and mission studies has concentrated most of its research into such areas.[27]

Though Iran was never under direct imperial rule, I have already argued that during the Victorian/Qajar era it was virtually a colony in all but name. Geographically, the country formed a buffer zone between Russia and Europe and as a gateway between India and the West, it was strategically critical to several interested parties.[28] For the world powers concerned, Britain in particular, the major issue was not trade and commerce (though these became increasingly significant), but that Iran should "maintain its independence and integrity as a vital element in the defence of their Indian empire".[29] Lord Curzon stated categorically:

I am profoundly convinced that England neither wants to possess, nor ought to possess, nor ever will possess, those territories herself ... I can see no reason for suppressing [Persia's] independent existence.[30]

Britain and Russia both believed they could best maintain their interests in the Middle East by a rivalry that ensured Iran retained a degree of stability and was never occupied by either one of them. Thus, western involvement in Iran

> lay not in her own civilization or splendour or mystery, but in her possibilities as a field of expansion among rival great powers - or rather, to be more precise, as a field in which expansion of one great power should be limited by a rival power; and it was precisely this rivalry... which enabled Iran to preserve her independence.[31]

During the Qajar dynasty, Iran experienced increasing contact with the West and foreign ideas, products and values were imported at considerable speed. Moreover, feeble governments ensured that Iran remained powerless in the face of foreign pressure, effectively being carved up into various spheres of influence. In short, Britain successfully wielded tremendous political authority without ever colonising Iran, and Persians experienced a type of "informal imperial control".[32] It has been argued that this is the most harmful form of foreign influence a nation can undergo, resulting in an encounter with all that is negative about colonial subjugation and little, or nothing, that is positive. Constituting a form of complete commercial control without acceptance of any moral responsibility, it is far from the "benevolent colonialism" which became British policy from 1813, and consciously took responsibility for the welfare of its inhabitants.[33]

The effect of this form of foreign influence left a legacy upon the Persian mentality in its attitude towards Britain and the West generally. Wright highlights the unusual association between Britons and Persians, "in psychological terms as one of love-hate", and the contradiction is well expressed by Farman Farmaian who writes, "we Iranians didn't exactly hate the British - or rather, we hated and admired them at the same time".[34] The British, then, enjoy a special position in the Persian psyche, often "without any logical reason, given either credit or (more usually) blame for developments beyond [their] ken".[35] Ambiguity in the Persian disposition towards Britain continues and it would be unjust to suppose there were no explanations for this. A survey of British involvement in Qajar Iran makes the reasons for such confusion all too clear.

Iranians grew increasingly divided and uncertain about the advantages of association with the West. There developed a kind of dependency, but an unhealthy and confused dependency which, ultimately, had monumental consequences for the country's future. Many fervently believed in the superiority of western science, technology and outward forms of life-style. Yet insufficient thought was given to deeper sociological issues which provide a society with its values. This subject has been expressed by one of Iran's best known twentieth century writers, Jalal Al-e Ahmad. Mottahedeh explains how Al-e Ahmad developed a critique of Persian society, its selfishness and lack of emotional and moral authenticity.[36] He considered this a disease which had infected Iran and, in describing it, coined a new term, *Gharbzadegi*, as the title of his seminal 1962 book. The literal meaning of the word is "West-stricken-ness" though this does not adequately convey the intensity of the Persian original.

[*Gharbzadegi*] is like cholera [or] frostbite. But no. It's at least as bad as sawflies in the wheat fields. Have you ever seen how they infest the wheat? From within. There's a healthy skin in places, but it's only a skin, just like the shell of a cicada on a tree.[37]

This obsession with superficial things of western life, or modernisation as it was thought of by some, became the *raison d'être* of the Pahlavi regime from the 1960s, eventually resulting in the collapse of the ancient Persian monarchial system in 1979. Abrahamian believes the cause of the Shah's downfall lay not in the unacceptability of political developments or the improving socio-economic programmes, but in the relationship between the two which he describes as the "politics of uneven development".[38] This included "socioeconomic development" in efforts towards modernisation, and "political underdevelopment" through intense centralisation and desire for absolute control over every aspect of peoples' lives.[39] Both could not co-exist forever and, though the situation remained hidden until the 1970s, pressure mounted as resentments grew over increasing social inequalities. Internationally, Iran was soon considered "one of the most inegalitarian societies in the world" and "once cracks appeared in the Pahlavi regime, they rushed forth in a torrent to engulf the whole society".[40]

The complex attitude of Iranians towards the West and its socio-political influence has played a significant part in Iran's modern history. The purpose of this chapter is not to analyse these issues but draw attention to them. For these factors were consistently, though not directly, relevant to the way in which missionaries were viewed and treated. The work of CMS, from its earliest days to its final exit, was either hampered or aided by Anglo-Persian relations. "A turn in the political wheel [could] at any time change the situation for better or for worse".[41] Moreover, the mission was affected not only by changes in official relations between governments, but more importantly, in the perceptions of ordinary Persians towards the British and their interests in Iran.

Social and political upheaval

The periods of increased tension between Iranians and CMS often resulted from the interplay between several factors, most significantly, those already mentioned: the position of Muslim clerics *vis-à-vis* foreign influence (direct or indirect), at any given time. The socio-political strain often manifested itself in public eruptions of emotion or more gradual, but equally significant, movements for change. These frequent episodes of social upheaval and political unrest were a mark of the Victorian/Qajar period during which CMS was active in Iran. Some of the more significant events are outlined in this section as they inevitably impacted on the mission. Iranian perceptions of CMS, regarded by many as an arm of the British government's interest in Persia, easily shifted with negative public opinion disrupting work and the ease with which missionaries could function.[42]

During the nineteenth century growing economic and ideological contact with the West provided the driving force for Iran's transformation. However, due to frequent opposition from *mullahs* or the masses generally, change did not manifest itself suddenly but as a slow and gradual process. The making and breaking of political and commercial treaties was a common feature of Persian politics from 1800 onwards. Britain's involvement depended largely on its relationship with Russia at any given time. Consequently, it never seemed to tire of signing treaties with Iran and later retracting them because of new alliances formed with Russia. Iran's motivation in granting concessions was not merely pecuniary, for the Qajars hoped the agreements would ensure British protection against constant threat of Russian invasion. Though Persian optimism was soon shattered, ineffectual Qajar governments continued with their policies, leaving the country little alternative other than to accept its fate.

By mid nineteenth century Britain and Russia had obtained a series of commercial capitulations enabling them to open consular and commercial offices anywhere in the country.[43] Even more significant were the remarkable concessions given to the naturalised British businessman Baron Julius de Reuter in 1872.[44] Announcement of the terms even shocked the British government which was particularly fearful of Russian reaction. According to Curzon the settlement contained within it

> the most complete and extraordinary surrender of the entire industrial resources of a kingdom into foreign hands that has probably ever been dreamed of, much less accomplished, in history.[45]

Ultimately, it was not only the Russians but Persian people themselves whose feelings against the surrender of their nation's birthright was further stirred up by the *mullahs*. The Shah eventually bowed to mounting opposition, cancelling the concessions one year later in November 1873.

A similar occasion arose in 1890 when the Tobacco Concession granted a fifty year monopoly of the production, sale and export of Persia's entire tobacco crop to the British citizen Major Gerald Talbot. Once again, popular feelings against the British surfaced and disturbances were reported in Mashad, Isfahan, Shiraz and Yezd.[46] A remarkable response followed when a leading *mujtahed*, Mirza Hassan Shirazi, pronounced a *fatwa* forbidding the sale or use of tobacco until the concession had been repealed. The boycott was so effective that the humiliated Naser-e-din Shah was obliged, at great cost, to re-purchase the concession in December 1891. The episode represented a landmark in modern Persian history and was, "in a sense, the beginning of a national awakening", demonstrating that

> there was a limit to what [Persians] would endure, that they were not the spiritless creatures which they had been supposed to be, and that henceforth they would have to be reckoned with.[47]

The 1907 Anglo-Russian convention was the final nail in the coffin of English-Persian relations and perhaps epitomises the feelings of frustration felt by Iranians. The British, concerned about German infiltration, allied with the Russians to sign a treaty, effectively carving Persia into two spheres of influence - the northern section under Russian domination and the southern under British. "Justifiably or not, most Persians would, from then on, be prepared to believe only the worst of England".[48] The cumulative result of all these affairs, especially the latter, was the development of complex ambivalence, already mentioned, in the attitude of Iranians towards the British.

Feeling utterly betrayed by the British, many Iranians remained captivated by western notions of modernisation. Political and economic liberalism was regarded as the basis of the West's power, wealth and influence. Tentative early nineteenth century experiments in modernisation developed into more radical ideas, forming the basis of a nationalism which progressed towards the Constitutional Revolution of 1906. The struggle was a movement of the people in which the *ulama* and British played central parts, though not always on opposite sides. One famous incident took place in the Summer of 1906 when, demanding their rights for a Constituent National Assembly, fifty merchants and *mullahs* appealed to an ancient custom for protection and took up residence in the British Legation in Tehran. Numbers gradually increased until there were fourteen-thousand Persians taking *bast* in the Legation grounds. The situation lasted for three weeks until Muzaffar-e-din Shah gave in to the people's demands. This period, during which the virtually bloodless revolution was followed by civil war in 1908-9, and the First World War in 1914, was a time of tremendous disturbance in Iran's history. The constitutional movement was, in a very real sense, "both religious and nationalist", and ultimately succeeded in incorporating "the traditional gospel of Shi'ism ... into a modern structure of government".[49] The disruptions continued alongside a rising sense of nationalism, until the overthrow of the Qajars in 1921 and the establishment of the Pahlavi dynasty four years later in 1925.

After the outbreak of war, Iran was quick to declare neutrality in November 1914. However, sympathies clearly lay with Russia's enemies and the summer of 1915 witnessed increased German influence throughout Persia.[50] In response, the British government ordered the evacuation of all its citizens, including the CMS missionaries. During the war, Iran - strangled as never before between the military interests of various world powers - experienced invasion from all sides. This, together with the presence of large numbers of foreigners in the country led to strong nationalist feelings. The October 1917 Russian Revolution saw Iran's northern enemy withdraw (for the time being) from the struggle for power in Persia. This encouraged the British into a concerted effort to secure their predominance by means of the 1919 Agreement that was to provide them with a protectorate in all but name. The treaty was signed in August and hailed as a great triumph by the British government. Rumours of corruption were soon widespread, however, on the discovery that Britain had paid bribes to Persian ministers in order to obtain necessary signatures. Though they accepted the money, the Iranian ministers had no intention of betraying their country and the British plan was foiled. The Agreement was not placed before the Persian Assembly and was consequently never ratified.[51]

In 1921 a group of moderate nationalists, headed by Sayyid Ziya and the military force of Reza Khan with his Cossack Brigade, marched into Tehran and seized power in a virtually bloodless coup. Four years later, Reza crowned himself Shah and so began his drastic plans for Iran. Driven by vehement nationalism and a desire for modernisation, yet reinforced by ardent anti-religious and anti-foreign elements, he soon turned Iran into a one-nation despotic state which was finally brought to its knees in the dramatic events of 1979.[52]

Women in late-Qajar and early-Pahlavi Iran

The Iranian movement for women's emancipation should not be seen in isolation from similar developments in western Europe. Chronologically the events were not in tandem, nor the details identical, yet all attempts sprung essentially from the same root: a desire to improve the status and condition of women. In a society, such as Qajar Iran, where virtually the whole population was exposed to exploitation or oppression of some kind, women were undoubtedly amongst the most vulnerable of all.

> Women were peculiarly exposed to ill-treatment and violence in a society where the normative manner of exercising authority was capricious and brutal. Women were frequently the principal victims when misfortune struck a family or a community.[53]

Little is known for sure concerning accurate details of Persian women's lives during this period. Nineteenth century literature, Persian and foreign, is conspicuously silent on the subject, though western commentators, who often had no direct contact with Iranian women, were not shy of sweeping generalisations on the basis of "supposition, gossip, and stereotypical commentary".[54] This often resulted in the propagation of extreme views as universally true of all Persian women. Sykes, for example, described them as unhappy "victims of Islam", whereas Shuster regarded them as "the most progressive, not to say radical, in the world".[55]

Several significant distinctions should be noted when considering the situation of Iranian women. The respective position of urban and rural women resulted in diverse life-styles. Peasant and especially tribal women, were usually unveiled and often involved in physical work more strenuous than that of men.[56] By contrast, the socio-political system in towns ensured that urban women's lives were more limited to the home. Seclusion was the norm and home boundaries acted as an "almost completely self-contained world".[57] Wherever men and women were present together, at weddings or other social gatherings, rigid segregation laws kept them apart. These regulations were stricter for middle- and upper-class women whose veiling and seclusion were carefully guarded as a means of ensuring the protection of their sexual morality. It was unusual to see these women out of their homes and on such rare exceptions, they were anonymously hidden behind long shapeless *chadors* and, sometimes, a thin face veil in addition. Lower-class women and their rural counterparts, while working harder, often enjoyed greater freedom than upper-class metropolitan women who spent their days in idleness.[58]

Lack of statistics and historical data means the kind of questions now often asked about past women cannot be answered with accuracy for Qajar Iran.[59] However, it can safely be affirmed that

> every woman, without exception, was subordinate to the authority of and under the restraint of a particular man (i.e., father, brother, husband, son), and that her material well-being and personal happiness were entirely dependent upon the benevolence, sense of justice, worldly success and good fortune of whatever male happened to be exercising that authority over her at any given time.[60]

Other generalisations, such as the importance of marriage in women's lives, cannot be evaded. A matter in which the female population had no say, marriage was considered God's law and woman's destiny. At the behest of their fathers, girls from the age of eleven were wedded to much older husbands and, once married, enjoyed few legal rights. Divorce, virtually impossible for women to secure, could be obtained by a man without any legitimate reason. Family law ensured that daughters above the age of puberty and sons over seven stayed with the father. Meanwhile, desertion, polygamy and temporary marriages made life for women painful and complicated.[61]

Little value was placed on the lives of women and the birth of daughters was commonly not an event to be celebrated.[62] A wife's status was immediately improved if she produced a son and heir for her husband. Taught from an early age that the "proper condition of females [was] one of near-invisibility", daughters were expected to be meek and self-effacing.[63]

The latter part of the period covered by this book was, in particular, an era of great change for Iranian women. Many reforms, however, retained a hollow superficiality, affecting only the middle and upper strata of urban society. A collective women's consciousness began to develop during the constitutional struggles from 1905 onwards. Prior to this, women had participated in occasional riots though there is little evidence of their active involvement in social and political affairs.[64] As popular pressure mounted against the Shah's policies, women became increasingly involved in the fight for a constitutional Assembly. They participated in the spreading movement for nationalism, often risking their lives by demonstrating in the streets, standing in the way of the Shah's troops, or hiding active revolutionaries.[65] Women's protests were organised during the sit-in at the British Legation and, after the granting of a constitution, they joined in street parties and public feasts for the first time.

Arguably the most famous incident confirming women's political involvement occurred in 1911. The Russians had objected to Iran employing an American as financial adviser and convinced the British that it was against the spirit of the 1907 Anglo-Russian convention. Demonstrations followed in which three-hundred women marched into *majles* (parliament) with rifles under their *chadors*, threatening any delegates willing to submit to Russian intimidation. In response, *majles* refused the ultimatum and Russian troops advanced towards Tehran. Concerned about the possible outcome, however, Cabinet dissolved parliament, leaving the Russians triumphant.[66]

Despite failure, the event was symbolic of Iranian women's national awakening and marked their entry into the political arena. They had shown that "if they wished, they could assert their presence in a male-dominated society".[67] The years following the revolution saw a great surge in political fervour, with women playing a significant part in the new parties and groups that mushroomed across Iran.[68]

Women's education and other partial improvements

There were no government schools for girls in Iran until 1917 and, when Reza Shah came to power, almost the entire female population was illiterate.[69] *Mullahs* provided most of the organised education for boys through the *maktab* and *madresseh* systems. The former provided primary education in basic literacy skills and knowledge of the Qur'an. Some boys went on to *madressehs* which increasingly included a variety of secular subjects. The emphasis, however, was on theology and the law. These seminaries were bastions of male supremacy concerned with training future clergy and religious leaders. Formed in the Islamic world around the eleventh century, a handful of *madressehs* provided religious tutelage for women but most were exclusively male territories.[70]

Girls were commonly educated alongside boys until around the age of eight. After that the only skills usually learnt were those considered necessary to make them pious wives and good mothers. Often referred to as *zaifeh* - weak one - a woman was believed to have limited abilities which made it futile and dangerous to teach her more than was needed for becoming a housewife. After the American Presbyterians opened their first school for girls in Urumiyah during 1835, a scattering of missionary and other private schools followed suit.[71] Despite the example set by these establishments and calls for improved female education during the Constitutional Revolution, the situation had barely changed by 1925. When Reza Shah began his modernisation programmes, especially during the 1930s and 40s, he targeted education as a primary concern. With the enforced closure of private schools, government establishments mushroomed and girls' education was encouraged alongside dramatic changes in the secularisation of boys' schooling. Whilst Reza's efforts were praised by many, the long-term result of such drastic centralisation was the creation of an "intellectual elite" made up of the middle- and upper-classes, but by-passing the majority of Iran's rural and working-class population.[72]

Other areas of the Shah's westernisation programme suffered from the same inherent weaknesses. Many of the changes were shallow and superficial, affecting only the higher echelons of Persian society. His reign should be remembered for considerable advances in women's public life, but perhaps "the *partial* emancipation of women" (my emphasis) better describes the reality, for many of the innovations were "little more than cosmetic".[73] Urged to emulate their western sisters in education, dress and social activities, women's status improved a little and many conventional restrictions were removed from the 1920s onwards. However, Reza Shah's civil code still reflected traditional Islamic assumptions regarding the relationship between the sexes and their roles in society. Muslim family law was retained and little effort made to alleviate the age-old juridicial subjugation of women who remained disadvantaged partners in marriage, exploited employees in the job market, and politically paralysed without the vote until 1963.[74]

Having encouraged Iranians to wear western clothes from early in his reign, in 1936 Reza Shah passed a law making it illegal for women to be veiled in public. In his desperate drive for modernisation, the edict was enforced brutally and lead to intolerable suffering for many women who imprisoned themselves at home rather than face the shame of exposure. Welcomed by a minority of the educated, unveiling was regarded by the majority as "a blasphemous act and vehemently opposed by the clergy".[75] The law was eventually revoked in 1941 and, while western fashions remained popular among middle- and upper-class women, the majority reverted to wearing the *chador* in public.

The ideological significance of the *chador*

The *chador*, together with the architecture of Persian houses, which enabled women's seclusion, were both visual symbols of an ideology separating the lives of men and women in Qajar Iran. Most Persian houses were subdivided into sections, functioning as physical boundaries between the sexes, whilst also representing deep-rooted psychological divisions. The *andaroon* (literally, "inner") part of the house was reserved for womenfolk, and ensured they remained isolated from all men except close family. However, this physical enclosure expanded into an ideological symbol of women's entire lives as a domestic existence in which they concerned themselves only with household and private matters. The *birooni* (literally, "outer") section, surrounded the *andaroon* and provided a space sanctioned as the realm of men. The term *birooni* itself, and its actual vicinity, closer to the outside world, represented men's place in that great sphere beyond the home.

The *chador* acted as an augmentation of this dualistic ideology from the home environment into the public domain. By providing visual separation between the sexes, it protected women's security and symbolically extended their private sphere even while they were in the public realm of men. It acted as a kind of mobile *andaroon*, enabling women to venture into the *birooni*, physically if not ideologically.

It is my contention that this duality was of great importance in the encounter between missionary and Iranian women. Presenting an invisible and subconscious bond between them, it was no less significant because of that. The single missionaries, in particular, were regarded by many Persian women as liberated and capable of success without the need for a man.[76] To be sure, they were also considered unusual and somewhat strange, nevertheless, their independence was often recognised. Likewise, the women missionaries believed they were far ahead of their eastern sisters whom they regarded as less fortunate, restricted by Muslim customs and subservient to male authority. What neither group acknowledged was the analogous strength of Victorian conventions, confining English women. The public/private division of labour in British society was equivalent to that in Iran, associating women with the domestic realm and men with the public sphere of work. Whilst there were differences in the type and extent of strictures imposed, hidden similarities existed which remained silent and unacknowledged by both sides.

Britain: An era of change and development

Late nineteenth and early twentieth century Britain was a society in flux, experiencing myriad changes in social and religious life. England was still a religious nation and the church enjoyed considerable status in national life.[77] However, by the turn of the century the mood was changing and old securities were crumbling. Traditional standards of decency and morality were being challenged, religion was increasingly considered "old-fashioned" and church attendance was in decline.

Several socio-religious factors underlay the changing nature of faith and society.[78] A period of western optimism and confidence was shattered by the Great War and twenty years of "uneasy peace"[79] that followed it. During this time of tremendous national soul-searching, the church's influence dwindled in areas such as education. Though Sunday schools continued flourishing, financial restraints, together with the growth of state education, ensured that the church lost much of its control in educating the young. Oxford and Cambridge remained devout centres of religious learning but the new universities marginalised religion in an effort to minimise controversy. The uneasy relationship between religion and science, a feature for much of the nineteenth century, accelerated with the publication of Darwin's *On the Origin of Species* in 1859. The evolution debate, however, was just one component in an atmosphere of growing religious doubt, further fuelled by the advent of biblical criticism.[80] Liberalism was a feature of society generally and was firmly established ecclesiastically in 1917 when the liberal churchman Hensley Henson was consecrated Bishop of Hereford.[81]

The rise of the Oxford Movement and tractarianism during the late nineteenth century threatened the strong foothold of evangelicalism. Intensifying battles between ritualists and anti-ritualists led to ecclesiastical sagas such as the trial of Edward King, Bishop of Lincoln (1889-90), and the Prayer Book fiasco (1927-8).[82] Furthermore, growing interest in the Christian socialism of F.D. Maurice and the *Lux Mundi* (1899) school of theology highlighted the divergence between the evangelical and high church traditions. The history of evangelical social action was embodied in figures such as Josephine Butler (1828-1906) and Lord Shaftesbury (1801-85). Remaining true to the spirituality that fuelled it, evangelical benevolence was closely linked to the notion of personal conversion as the panacea for the evils of society. Belief in individual salvation as the beginning of social reform often left unchallenged the political systems which created the problems in the first instance. The incarnational theology of Charles Gore and other like-minded thinkers was critical of evangelicalism's "excessive individualism",[83] its stress on sin, the fall and a transcendent God atoning through the cross of Christ. Emphasising the immanence of God, Gore's incarnational theology in particular, was influential in developing late-Victorian Christology with ideas of Christ's kenosis, or self-emptying, as the essence of divine strength through weakness and self-sacrifice.

Evangelicalism and Victorian Culture

Despite its shrinking authority, evangelicalism - which had its roots in eighteenth century revivalism - remained a significant and influential element throughout the period 1869-1934.[84] By 1900 it had been largely hijacked by the upper middle-classes, even becoming an avenue for upward social mobility. In the process of being "'taken up' by polite society",[85] however, it lost a certain amount of its incisiveness. According to Bebbington, late-Victorian evangelicalism experienced a decrease in the spontaneity of its revivals, moving towards more arranged forms of spiritual regeneration. Thus, the second evangelical awakening of 1860, considered by many to have begun in the States before arriving in England via Ulster, marked a new phase of "organised evangelism" far removed from the unprompted nature of early revivals. "This distinction is the key to understanding what happened to British Evangelicalism in 1859-60".[86] Certainly, it would never again dominate British society as it had during mid-Victorianism especially once the divisions of the 1920s destroyed its unity.[87]

Notwithstanding major changes, evangelicalism's primary characteristics (conversionism, activism, biblicism, crucicentrism) remained intact, providing a milieu in which the missionary societies continued flourishing, and significant developments began taking place in the lives of middle-class women.[88] As "the defining characteristic of Victorian culture",[89] or more precisely urban middle-class Victorian culture, the influence of evangelicalism remained alive throughout the Victorian/Qajar years and is of special significance for understanding the context of this book.

British women and the dawn of opportunity

Renegotiating traditional gender boundaries

As female evangelical missionaries, the CMS women in Iran were clearly influenced by the interrelationship between British society, evangelicalism, and the position of women. Christianity in general, and evangelicalism in particular, were highly relevant factors in the changing situation of British women during this eventful period which witnessed the rise of the women's movement from the 1860s onwards.

The "feminisation" of the Victorian church is a term commonly used to indicate the extent of women's involvement in religious activities.[90] While church leadership remained overwhelmingly male, nineteenth century pews were filled by a "mainly female rank and file".[91] More importantly, it was a time during which women's public role, through better education and work outside the home, increased considerably. The "woman question" emerged as a major theme in all levels of society with "the walls of exclusion from public life" crumbling all around; and the church was no exception.[92] This re-forming of gender boundaries involved considerable tensions and ambiguities, operating as it did in the midst of complex socio-economic, religious and class confines.

During the nineteenth century the church came to a gradual realisation of the grinding poverty and poor social conditions which plagued much of British society.[93] Numerous religious groups became involved in working for change and evangelical activism, in particular, carried over into social concern, transforming the Victorian era into one of philanthropic frenzy. Many middle-class women became major participants in voluntary programmes across the nation. Barred from most employment opportunities, they relished the prospect of this new and acceptable (within limits) form of self-expression. Philanthropy, the most prominent feature of Victorian religion, was thus "womanized",[94] providing the most obvious outlet for the energies of countless women.

Consideration has already been given to the extent which religious, and missionary women in particular, may be regarded as feminists or active participants in the women's movement. For the purpose of this contextualizing chapter, two important points should be noted. First, although a developing understanding of genderization was in progress and some women were becoming active in affairs outside the home, "few criticisms of the social structures, to which most were firmly wedded, entered their minds".[95] In other words, the phenomenon was almost entirely an upper middle-class one in which women remained unable (or unwilling) to include a class-based critique. Secondly, and with relevance to the comparable private versus public world of Qajar Iran, the changing role of British women (especially religious women) was firmly confined within the parameters of the dominant Victorian separate spheres ideology.

The doctrine of separate spheres and expanding notions of motherhood

Complex and convoluted, the separate spheres doctrine developed out of the eighteenth century "principle of subordination" and was cultivated alongside the peculiar moral superiority with which evangelicalism burdened women.[96] Georgian society was based on an hierarchical ordering in which economic, class and gender differentiations were regarded as God-given and beneficial. Thus, woman's subordination to man was considered neither unjust nor undesirable, but part of a reciprocal and interdependent arrangement. Evolving largely as a result of socio-economic factors, this principle of subordination continued into the nineteenth century, ensuring that women's roles were still defined in relation to men and their needs.[97]

Nineteenth century economic changes meant fewer women needed to work, therefore, a sharpening distinction appeared in some strata of society between the worlds of men and women. Concurrently, powerful religious factors were at play as an authoritative and self-confident middle-class church defined female respectability in terms of that separation between the spheres of home and work. Such socially-orientated theologising relied on the ability to sustain a life-style in which women were above the need for paid employment. Whilst presenting wealthy women with a secure path to the approved devout life, this gendered ideology guaranteed the class marginalization of their poorer working-class sisters.

The ground, however, would soon shift under the separate spheres doctrine with middle-class women seizing upon a contradiction in the dominant theology of womanhood and turning it to their own advantage. Central to evangelical piety was a belief in women's moral and religious superiority, acting from within the home, as a regenerative source for the well-being of society in general. This conservative and limiting definition of spiritual femininity provided the justification for women extending their "natural" aptitude into the public realm of social reform. Manipulating the separate spheres ideology constructed the paradox at the heart of the changing situation of middle-class women. Believing in the power of their own special virtues became a means to emancipation yet, at the same time, greater social involvement remained intimately linked to women's subordinate position and operated strictly within the rules imposed by the separate spheres ideology. For at the heart of the philosophy separating the worlds of men and women was the notion of a "natural" basis for sexual difference. Therefore, only jobs considered appropriate to women's home-orientated, feminine instincts were acceptable for their public role which was always carried out under the ultimate authority of male superiors.

Distinctive female traits of compassion, modesty and self-sacrifice sat uneasily alongside belief in woman's original sin and disobedience.[98] This conflicting image of women as potentially more sinful *and* more pure than men, was resolved in a class distinction which further justified some women's growing involvement in social reform. A differentiation was idealised between "chaste, innocent, and passionless middle-class Christian woman, and the sexually depraved and voracious fallen woman of the streets",[99] or indeed, the so-called "heathen" woman of the East.

This feminine classification developed into a capacious notion of motherhood far beyond the confines of biology and domesticity. Nineteenth century eugenics, nationalism and social Darwinism combined to positively emphasise the physical function of mothers as a means of increasing the population and improving racial stock. Good motherhood, regarded as essential in preserving national health, reached cultic proportions as the most exalted symbol of femaleness. Women were encouraged to pursue their duty as mothers and better education was promoted as a means of ensuring these obligations were carried out.[100]

The notion of motherhood was then expanded, creating a means by which single women could transcend the parameters of their private sphere. By arguing for an extension into "social motherhood", infinite new possibilities opened up for "surplus" women.[101] The motherly instincts of womankind - "the only truly unselfish feeling that exists on this earth",[102] became the prototype for good pastoral care, enabling the motherhood motif to break through the old private/public barriers of the separate spheres ideology. In 1912 one writer explained the potential usefulness of single women in this way:

> Everyone knows maiden aunts who are better, more valuable, completer mothers in every non-physical way than the actual mothers of their nephews and nieces. This is woman's wonderful prerogative, that, in virtue of her *psyche*, she can realize herself, and serve others, on feminine lines, and without a pang of regret or a hint anywhere of failure, even though she forego physical motherhood. This ... therefore, is a plea not only for Motherhood but for Foster-Motherhood - that is Motherhood all but physical. In time to come the great professions of nursing and teaching will more and more engage and satisfy the lives and the powers of Virgin Mothers without number.[103]

Missionary maternalism

Heeney has shown how the Victorian church, by emphasising the maternal duties of all women, helped develop a vocation for single women based on self-giving service.[104] Its consequences were a kind of "benevolent maternalism",[105] extending the influence of middle-class women in wider society *vis-à-vis* other women less fortunate than themselves. This theory has also been delineated to include women on the mission field. Ramusack argues that independent female missionaries working with Indian women between 1865-1945 displayed similar traits as "maternal imperialists". Often functioning as allies eager to improve women's rights, many were able to form bonds of friendship and affection with their eastern sisters. Nevertheless, the "mother-daughter" relationship remained prominent and its unequal, authoritarian style meant Indian women were more often treated like children being prepared for adulthood, than equal partners in friendship based on mutual trust and respect.[106]

In practical terms on the mission field, the motherhood ideal was frequently transformed into a form of cultural or racial superiority. This is, perhaps, an aspect of what Jay considers the paradox of evangelicalism's "wholescale commitment" which as its strength can also "result in the repressive sanctimoniousness, entirely at odds with the service of a God of Love".[107] Nevertheless, the spiritual source of social maternalism was one of humble, self-giving sacrifice. Active motherly instincts were promoted as a prototype for good pastoral care predicated upon a theology of female suffering internalised by many women. For some, the Virgin Mary provided the most salient model of ethereal motherliness. However, amongst many Anglicans - and certainly for most CMS women - Mary was a controversial figure they were wary of emulating for fear of risking Mariolatry. Thus, the redemptive power of female suffering developed more within the contemporary Christological debates. Ellice Hopkins, for example, drew on the incarnational theology of Gore and the *Lux Mundi* school, advancing the notion of kenosis as necessary for women to partake in the transformation and redemption of humanity. Similarly, Florence Nightingale wrote positively about the concept of women embracing suffering and deduced the need for a female Christ figure before their position in society could be improved. Few, if any, evangelical missionaries thought in quite these terms, though they showed a predilection for understanding their vocation in terms of an imitative relationship with Christ. Belief in a call to total sacrificial surrender and Christ-like service had a certain fascination for women in an age when feminine submission was a vital element in the shaping of female piety.[108]

Victorian and Qajar women: closer than either realised

During this chapter I have attempted to show that the separate spheres ideology, reinforced by the doctrine of submission, operated at the heart of British Victorian society. Nevertheless, many women were able to justify a more public role for themselves through manipulation of this dominant philosophy. That does not mean the public/private spheres that separated the sexes were disintegrating. Indeed, the parameters were still jealously guarded by most of society and, where women did manage to cross the physical boundaries, invisible rules of submission to male authority and adherence to appropriate womanly behaviour still limited their activities.

In addition to negotiating gender and class boundaries, the CMS women were actively involved in the mediation of racial factors which affected their self-understanding and relationships with Persian women. In Britain, as in Iran, the separate spheres were much more strictly adhered to among the middle- and upper-classes. The gap between the ideology - which underlay respectability - and reality, was dependant upon women's financial and social capability in maintaining the appropriate life-style. In neither country did prescriptive theories correspond to reality in a straightforward manner and there were enormous differences between "what was and what ought to have been".[109]

In England the ambiguities and contradictions inherent in notions of contemporary womanhood lead many middle-class women to engage in philanthropy among the working classes, in an effort to convince them of "respectable" standards of living. By contrast, the missionaries in Iran, involved in additional considerations of racial components, preferred to direct their work more towards Persian women of equivalent class status to themselves. This shift in emphasis is significant for two reasons. First, it represents a transferral of benevolent maternalism from a class-based superiority to a racial superiority. Secondly, it indicates the missionaries' conviction that the upper strata of any society was the real agent for change. For their desire to influence the gentlewomen of Iran was based upon the conviction that only these women could introduce cogent change. Maintaining that their own social group was affecting change for all women in Britain, they conveyed this philosophy of women's multifarious place in society to the Persian context, presenting it, *inter alia*, as the solution for the problems of Iran.

It has already been argued that the missionary women were prone to presenting a glorified version of British culture far from the restrictive reality. For most of the period between 1869-1934 women were virtually powerless in the Church of England's decision-making bodies and invisible in liturgical leadership.[110] Moreover, a deep-rooted class system ensured that where gendered ideologies were challenged, social structures were seldom disputed, leaving the deplorable position of the female population of Britain's under-class largely unchanged.

The degree of restrictions varied considerably between the women of Iran and Britain. Yet the favourable comparison of Christianity against Islam made by the CMS missionaries was not entirely justifiable. This subconscious internalisation of what can only be described as a kind of hypocrisy played an enormous part in the relationship of missionary women towards their Persian sisters. The separate spheres ideology of both cultures - in terms of physical boundaries and invisible conventions - was deeply imbued in Iranian *and* British women. Yet the constraints it caused were recognised explicitly only in relation to Persians. The private/public parameters were clearly different for the missionary women, but the essential ideology inevitably influenced their work, theology and self-understanding.

Primary methodological principles, together with the context in which the CMS women lived and worked, have now been delineated. In the next chapter more specific details are presented concerning the work of CMS and its women missionaries in Iran.

CHAPTER THREE

The CMS Persia Mission and its Women Missionaries

The history of Christianity in Iran

Christianity has existed in Iran since its earliest days. Traditionally, the three magi are from "Persian lands afar" and on the day of Pentecost, Parthians, Medes and Elamites (inhabitants of Persia) were present among the disciples (Acts 2: 9). Later legends suggest St. Thomas visited Persia on his way to India whilst others claim Simon the Zealot brought Christianity to Iran.[1] One way or another, by the end of the fifth century, there was an organised form of Christianity in the region, though Zoroastrianism remained the official religion of Iran. A bishop from Iran was present at the Council of Niceae in 325 and later, in 635, the Persian bishop known as Alopen arrived in China on a missionary expedition.[2]

Christianity continued in Iran following the seventh century Muslim invasion. Thereafter, however, the fate of Christians became more closely linked with socio-political changes in the country, resulting in periods of relative freedom separated by spells of hardship and persecution.[3] From the earliest days of its territorial expansion, Islam granted *dhimmis* (religious minorities), or "tolerated unbelievers",[4] certain rights and protection. Their situation varied according to the relationship of Muslim rulers with Rome and the West at any given time. Nevertheless, they were always regarded as inferior and separate from Muslim nationals. Accordingly, Christian, Jewish and Zoroastrian groups have continued until today, living in cultural pockets, maintaining their own customs, languages and religions.

Despite many restrictions, religious liberty has, perhaps ironically, been greater for *dhimmis* than Muslims in Iran. Able to make active choices in their spiritual quest, members of religious minorities are free to convert to Islam, whereas for Muslims apostasy is both a crime and a sin. The violation amounts to treason, desertion and betrayal of a community to which one owes loyalty and is punishable by death. The country's legal system has not always practised this religious tenet, nevertheless, churches in Iran have had to be extremely cautious evangelistically, and the work of foreign missions has likewise been restricted.

The ancient churches

The oldest churches in Iran - those existing prior to the nineteenth century - may be described according to three broad categories, of which two experienced internal fragmentation, causing rifts and splinter groups. First, the most ancient Christian presence in Iran was the Assyrian Church of the East, whose adherents are commonly known as Nestorians.[5] A disagreement in 1552, led to an eventual rupture with a significant number changing allegiance to Rome, thus forming the Catholic Chaldean, or Uniate, Church.

Secondly, the Armenian Apostolic Church has had long-standing influence in Iran due to historical and geographical connections as one of Persia's northern neighbours. This association was further consolidated during the sixteenth century Safavid dynasty. Shah Abbas, the most famous and ruthless Safavid King, began a programme of compulsory mass movements, transferring populations within the Persian empire to strengthen and sustain it. He moved in the region of seventy-thousand Armenians to southern Iran, approximately half of whom settled in Isfahan, creating the district of Julfa.[6] During the seventeenth century, roughly nineteen-thousand Armenians, including a number from Julfa, converted to Roman Catholicism. Though there are not many left in Iran today, the rift came as a bitter blow to the Apostolic Church.

Thirdly, apart from the Chaldeans and Armenian Catholics, a long tradition of missionary commitment, including seventeenth and eighteenth century Carmelite involvement, has ensured the influence of other Roman Catholic groups in Iran. Today, the majority are foreigners though their church membership includes some Persians especially those influenced through the educational work of missions.[7]

Modern missionary endeavours other than CMS

During the nineteenth and especially the twentieth century many new churches and Christian groups mushroomed across Iran.[8] The period witnessed the arrival of several foreign individuals and missionary organisations eager to embark on evangelistic activity especially through medical and educational establishments. In this section, a number of the more significant people and societies will be highlighted.

One of the earliest and most notable missionaries to visit Iran was Henry Martyn. In India from 1805, Martyn translated the New Testament into Persian and in 1811, shortly before his untimely death, passed through Iran to spend time in Shiraz revising his work. At the time, missionary work in Islamic lands was considered a dangerous enterprise and foreigners were frequently refused permission to stay in Muslim districts. Assurances were sent from India to British government officials in Iran that Martyn would not cause disruption and that he had "no thought of preaching to the Persians or to entering into theological controversies".[9] Soon after his arrival, however, he was drawn into the age old tradition of Islamic debates which, far from angering the Persians, appears to have fascinated them. It seems "everything about Martyn was intriguing to the Shirazis", and that he won their affection by nature of his apparent humility and patience.[10]

Several other individuals also travelled through Iran, working as freelance missionaries interested mainly in educational and medical work.[11] In 1843 the Archbishop of Canterbury sent Reverend G. P. Badger on an exploratory visit among the Assyrians of eastern Turkey and North-western Persia. Later, a mission station was established in Urumiyah where a number of schools were opened between 1885 and 1914. Work never re-started after the First World War led to the departure of all missionaries.[12] Among other nineteenth century missionaries were the French Roman Catholics from 1875, and the Churches Mission to the Jews (CMJ) from 1876.[13] The Scottish Missionary Society (SMS) began functioning in Iran from 1803 and was replaced in 1827 by the German speaking Swiss Basel Mission. This organisation was concerned primarily with Bible translation.

The most significant pre-CMS missionaries to work in Iran were the American Presbyterians who, stationed in Urumiyah, concentrated their efforts in the North-western territories. The American Board of Commissioners for Foreign Missions began work in 1835 with the specific aim of revitalising the Assyrian church community. However, several members from the Church of the East defected, forming the Presbyterian Evangelical Church of Iran. In 1870 work was transferred to the Presbyterian Board of Foreign Missions, USA, and concurrently aims broadened to include projects among Muslims. Their educational work was of particular importance, especially amongst the female population. Missionaries began closing their institutions during the 1950s and gradually withdrew from the country. Today the Presbyterians include independent groups (worshipping in Assyrian, Armenian and Persian) with a central Church Council.

As a result of the 1895 Baghdad Missionary Conference, CMS and the Presbyterians reached an agreement that neither would encroach on the other's territory. CMS would restrict its activity to the South (which incidentally, the 1907 Anglo-Russian agreement marked as the area of British "influence"), while the Presbyterians would concentrate on northern Persia. The two organisations, together with the Persian churches resulting from their efforts, worked closely over the years, though discussions for unification were never ratified.[14]

The Church Missionary Society in Iran

From a tentative start to the laying of foundations

Earlier in the history of missions there was considerable optimism regarding the impact of Christianity upon its Islamic rival. In 1597 Philipp Nicolai developed a "geography of missions", as proof that the gospel had been preached throughout the world in the Apostolic age. Concerning Persia, he wrote:

> The Christian faith grows amidst the Persians, gains in importance and leads those peoples dependent upon Islam to largely abandon the superstition of their barbaric religion ... Islam could easily be done away with, so that, while the *Qu'ran* is slowly fading away, Christendom alone will be victorious.[15]

This was, of course, the wishful thinking of an imaginative mind. Yet early in the nineteenth century, Henry Martyn fostered high hopes that, in the face of the Bible, "the Qur'an would pale into insignificance".[16] It is no surprise, therefore, that in its initial two annual reports, the newly founded CMS committee (meeting for the first time in 1799), expressed interest in mission work amongst the Muslims of Persia. The necessary moves were not made, however, and it was some years before CMS was established in Iran.

When work did start, it was more by accident than design. In 1869, a CMS missionary by the name of Robert Bruce interrupted his journey to India by stopping in Iran to learn Persian.[17] As foreigners they were prohibited from residing in Muslim areas, so Bruce and his wife Emily settled in Julfa for the two years they were expecting to remain. During that period the country experienced a severe famine in which the Bruces tried to help the people of Isfahan. Amongst other things, they set up an orphanage with money sent from Germany. Preparing to leave in April 1871, several Muslims requested baptism and Bruce took this as a sign from God that he should stay in Iran. CMS initially opposed him and it took Bruce considerable time and effort to persuade the society that Persia was fertile ground for missionary work. A station was finally given official recognition by CMS on 14 June 1875 and the educational, medical and evangelistic work gradually began.[18]

Robert and Emily worked alone for several more years, in particular co-operating with the Armenians of Julfa in educational work among the young. In 1879 Rev Dr E.F. Hoernle arrived to undertake medical work and by the early 1880s a small band of missionaries was well established, though efforts were still largely restricted to Julfa. Church services were held in Persian, medical and educational work developed and Bruce continued working on his revision of Martyn's Persian Bible. In 1883 Bishop French of Lahore travelled through Persia and, with a commission from the Bishop of London, performed sixty-seven confirmations and one ordination.[19] The diocese of Iran was created in 1912, led consecutively, by four missionary bishops until 1961 when for the first, and to date, only time, a Persian Muslim convert - Hassan Dehqani-Tafti - was consecrated Bishop in Iran.[20]

When Persia was formally recognised as a CMS mission field, it was coupled with the station in Baghdad under the heading, Turkish-Arabia mission. For several years, the two co-existed as one administrative unit. Indeed, the first CMS women to work in the region arrived in Baghdad in 1890, one year before their counterparts reached Julfa. It soon became apparent, however, that though both were Muslim countries, the distinction between an Arabic and Persian environment was too great to sustain an identical strategy. Furthermore, geographical distances were too large for maintaining reasonable contact and communication between the two regions.[21] In 1897 the stations were separated and the Persia mission began operating independently.

Around the turn of the century, the earlier optimism of Henry Martyn and others was giving way to a realisation that Islam represented "the stoniest ground"[22] for missionary endeavours. The 1910 World Missionary Conference reported widespread dissatisfaction with Islam but could not hope for greater openness to the Christian message. Fourteen years later, at the 1924 conference in Jerusalem, few considered the task any easier. One missionary explained: "our task is to induce the proudest man [sic] on earth to accept the message he detests from a people he despises".[23]

Meanwhile, Iran was considered one of the most promising Islamic fields, with many believing it had great potential in yielding to Christian evangelism. Indeed, in the early part of the twentieth century, although converts were few, "the number of baptisms was significantly larger than those of any other CMS mission in Muslim lands".[24] With the benefit of historical hindsight, it is obvious these signs were not leading towards a burgeoning Iranian church. However, even more extraordinary than the apparently fanciful hopes of overly-sanguine missionaries, is that their efforts did lead to the creation of an indigenous church, albeit an extremely small one.

Missionaries were active in other Muslim countries throughout the Middle East but nowhere was a convert church formed in the same way as in Iran. From the earliest days services were conducted in the Iranian national language and efforts were made to translate Christianity into a relevant cultural concept for Iranians. Once an Episcopal Church was established, the majority of worshippers were Persians rather than Armenian or Assyrian converts and the aim

was always to "Christianise" not "westernise". Dehqani-Tafti strongly affirms this, arguing that the missionaries
> wanted the church to maintain its Iranian essence ... The belief that missionaries tried to break the culture of the country they worked in was utter nonsense. In fact, in Iran it was completely the opposite. I remember as a child ... we were all encouraged to keep our Persian culture.[25]

Numbers remained small and the church always retained an irrevocably foreign (or British) taint in the eyes of most Iranians. Its membership, and increasingly its leadership, was Persian, yet despite efforts to the contrary, it failed to shake off its image as an arm of British interest in Iran. This is partly because early missionaries were reluctant to relinquish power to Persian Christians and, however willing in theory, were too slow in trusting the indigenous faith community to construct its own future. Moreover, CMS in Iran, like many missionary organisations elsewhere, submerged itself under a "conviction that the progress of Christianity is intimately related to bricks, mortar and educational qualifications."[26] The church in Iran, "small and comparatively weak ... seeking to show the love of Jesus in action ... built up a network of institutions rather out of proportion to its size".[27] Many of the workers necessary for maintaining hospitals and schools were foreigners and the church, closely connected with these institutions, was considered by most Iranians to be essentially alien.

This has been a great disadvantage for the tiny Anglican community especially since the Islamic Revolution. For Muslims who become Christians are considered by their compatriots to have betrayed their identity and allied themselves with the West. The complex of establishments run primarily by missionaries heightened the sense of "otherness" with which most Persians viewed the church. These two elements created a false perception of Persian Anglicanism as entirely foreign, when it was in its early days and remains today, truly indigenous in many respects.[28]

There are several reasons why the efforts of CMS lead to the formation of an indigenous church in Iran when it failed in other Muslim countries. The socio-political climate of Qajar Iran meant the mission's philanthropic work was appreciated by many. Moreover, British influence was sufficiently strong to give missionaries some status, thus allowing them considerable freedom in carrying out their activities. More significant, however, is the complex issue of Persian identity as Muslim but not Arab. The paradox at the heart of being Persian is a tension between accepting a well established Muslim heritage, whilst striving for a connectedness with pre-Islamic culture and civilisation.

Dehqani-Tafti believes it is this component in the collective consciousness of Iranians that helped lay the foundations of a Persian church and sustained its development throughout the turbulent years of the later twentieth century. A Persian, he maintains, is "psychologically a divided personality" - this includes a strong pre-Islamic element
> that goes right back to Cyrus and Darius [and feels] a terrible revulsion against the Arabs who invaded our country - almost an unconscious anti-Islamic feeling. And yet the other side is a thousand years of Islam: Arabic, Qur'anic verses etc.. These things are part of our nature too.[29]

Although both these constituents co-exist, they clash in the Persian psyche, allowing for a greater possibility of one defeating the other. If pre-Islamic Persian-ness gains the upper hand, Islam becomes easier to relinquish. This makes embracing Christianity a more viable option for Iranians than many other Muslims whose entire Arab culture is steeped in the Islamic tradition. Iranians can reject Islam and retain dignity through Persian roots, whereas for Arabs their entire notion of self is enveloped in an Islamic culture where religion forms the largest part. Thus the struggle for identity, difficult enough for the Persian Christian, is intensified for an Arab Muslim convert.[30]

Defining the period under study

The period covered by this book has been restricted to the years 1869-1934 due to a combination of circumstantial reasons and deliberate choice. As the history of CMS women in Iran has not previously been studied, the early era provides an appropriate starting point. These women were amongst the first to work officially as CMS missionaries and their lives and careers deserve careful consideration. Although single women are the primary focus of my research, and 1882 was when the first began work in Persia, missionary wives remain of interest.[31] Emily Bruce, wife of Robert Bruce who founded the Persia mission, was present from its inception in 1869 and, together with missionary wives who followed, played a vital part in early developments. 1934 represents the sixty-fifth anniversary of CMS's venture in Iran.

1869-1934 was a period in Victorian/Qajar history when both Britain and Persia faced new challenges. The socio-political climate in Iran fluctuated and the missionaries were constantly negotiating shifting fortunes according to local circumstances. In Britain, economic factors and changes in religious outlook were further heightened by the rising women's movement. The CMS missionaries in Persia characterise one way in which British women responded to their new position in society. Moreover, the Victorian-Qajar encounter, within the imperialist context, created a particular dynamic that may be depicted by the relationship between missionaries and Persian people.

Primary sources, in the shape of CMS archives, also helped define the period covered by this book. The society's filing system changed in 1934, providing a convenient cut-off point. Furthermore, from that time, professionalisation resulted in committee minutes and official reports becoming more common than letters from individual missionaries. Therefore, the sense of personal contact with women, who remained excluded from most senior posts, was minimised. Finally, Emmeline Stuart, chronologically the last woman I have included in the book as a case study, retired in 1934. With her departure, following a career spanning nearly forty years, came the end of an entire era in the CMS Persia mission.

Organisational structures and key personalities

As a result of its unconventional start, the various administrative layers of the CMS mission in Iran developed slowly. Nevertheless, a pattern soon emerged and as missionary numbers increased, the station formalised its decision-making processes. Some familiarity with the structures is essential so that necessary references may be made to committees and conferences.

Although missionary conferences of some form operated during the 1880s,[32] it seems the process was formalised some years later when the first Persia-Baghdad Missionary Conference was held on 26 July 1894. Conference provided a forum, usually once or twice per annum, where the largest number of missionaries gathered for discussion and voting on certain subjects. Although Mary Bird was an active participant in the first meeting of Conference, the constitution of the Persia mission was soon ratified, denying women the right to vote.

Conference elected two or three senior male missionaries onto the Standing Committee (SC) which included the bishop and mission secretary as ex officio members. SC, known as the Local Governing Body (LGB), formed the most powerful decision-making group. As the missionary enterprise expanded, sub-committees were formed for matters concerning specific branches of work such as education and medicine. During the early years, women had no real power in terms of changing policy. Yet they were vital in the day to day running of the mission and were usually present during Conference where they exercised influence by participating in discussions.

Conference and all committees were ultimately answerable to CMS head-quarters in London. Major decisions could not be taken without being sanctioned by the Parent Committee (PC) responsible for missionaries in Iran. The mission secretary in Persia - always a senior man - maintained regular contact with PC which preserved final veto on significant issues, effectively controlling the style and scope of missionary output. The mission secretary and bishop were the two most powerful missionaries, assigned the task of maintaining order and efficiency. Despite occasional and inevitable friction between missionaries, efforts were usually made to keep matters under control without the need for informing PC unless absolutely necessary. Between 1869-1934 several senior men became key personalities with significant influence on the life of the mission. The following is a list of major characters whose names will appear throughout the book.[33]

Name and most significant position held	Presence in Iran
Robert Bruce -founder of the Persia mission	(1869-1894)
Charles Stileman - mission secretary, bishop from 1912	(1892-1916)
William St. Clair Tisdall - mission secretary	(1893-1907)
Edward Stuart - bishop	(1894-1910)
Donald Carr - medical doctor	(1894-1930)
Walter Rice - mission secretary	(1901-1921)
James Linton - educationalist, bishop from 1919	(1908-1935)
William Thompson - educationalist, bishop from 1935	(1914-1961)

The seniority of individual missionaries depended upon length of service. Without the vote, however, women were clearly subservient to men (many of them clergy) in a carefully constructed gendered hierarchy. A further imperial layer operated according to a spatial differentiation, elevating authorities in England over working missionaries in Persia. A complex system of hierarchies co-existed, therefore, with unwritten sexual, imperialist, and theological codes.

Missionary relations with British diplomats and government officials in Iran

The CMS mission's inescapable reputation as an extension of British political and economic interest in Iran has already been mentioned. Today, missionaries generally, are frequently condemned for maintaining unsuitably close ties with colonialists or influential British officials.[34] Certainly, in common with most Victorian missionaries, the majority of CMS workers in Iran regarded themselves as members of that superior western civilisation to which all Britons, including diplomats, belonged. However, interpreting the relationship between missionaries and British officials in terms of straightforward mutual benefit would be to misunderstand the inherent complexities.

Close and regular contact existed between diplomats and missionaries in Iran. As British subjects, the CMS workers usually felt bound to obey their government's orders, however unwillingly, and on occasions they requested support and protection. Yet the missionaries experienced far greater contact with ordinary Iranians, developing a keen sense of loyalty towards the locals. This, together with their evangelistic zeal and commitment to carry out the work they had been commissioned for, often resulted in clashes with British diplomats. Government employees were, on the whole, uncomfortable with missionary presence in Iran and embarrassed by their work amongst the Persian people.

The relationship between these British residents in Iran, each motivated by different concerns, is best described as somewhat uneasy and equivocal. Diplomatic representatives found the missionaries disconcerting and regarded them as an unnecessary complication within Anglo-Persian relations. Even after a Persian church had been established and British diplomats were required to communicate with its Iranian leaders, there remained a tangible sense of embarrassment at the presence of an establishment which seemed neither fully British nor entirely Persian. Dehqani-Tafti confirms the continuation of an ambiguity inherent in the relationship between British embassy and Persian church. During his episcopacy from 1961 onwards, he believes, the diplomats were uncomfortable with the notion of a Persian bishop:

> With me, I felt that the embassy had a difficulty. They couldn't deny that I was the Anglican Bishop, on the other hand, they didn't want to identify with the mission of the church ... [they] kept a friendship but did not want to be identified with us ... They wanted to keep their distance from me ... This was the tension and I was aware of it.[35]

During the Victorian/Qajar era British missionaries and diplomats were united by their western heritage and many of its imperialist assumptions. Yet their reasons for being in Iran, and the type of contact they enjoyed with Iranians, was incomparable. Their disparate hopes and aspirations for the country kept them apart. Missionaries, eager to retain independence, did not always ratify government suggestions whilst diplomats, in turn, were unwilling to actively support many aspects of the mission's work.

The role of women in the CMS Persia mission

CMS single women and missionary wives in Iran were not officially involved in any policy matters or decision-making processes. Without them, however, it is unlikely that the mission could have established itself as a viable organisation in Persia. The presence of women was vital to the enterprise and, though denied formal power within the administrative structures, they formed a large and potent part of the workforce. Much of the day-to-day running of the mission fell upon their shoulders and in practical terms they enjoyed a significant share of responsibility in the life of the small community and its growing institutions. Dehqani-Tafti was a young boy during the latter part of the period and lived with the missionaries during school terms, for his family was too far away. Whilst acknowledging that in some ways "it was very unsatisfactory for a young person to grow up like that", he recalls with fondness the enormous effect some of the women had upon his life.[36]

A cursory glance at the statistical information displays an extraordinary array of data concerning the CMS women in Persia.[37] From 1891 (when CMS first sent single women to Iran), not only until 1934, but through to 1980 when all missionaries left the country, there were more women than men working in the Persia mission. Moreover, from 1903, even after wives are excluded from calculations, there was still a significantly larger number of single women than all male missionaries added together (for a complete breakdown of annual figures see Appendix IV).

The average number of years served by the seventy-eight single women recorded as CMS missionaries in Iran between 1891-1934 was 15.8 (for a chronological list see Appendix V). Of these:

    48 (61.5%) stayed for ten years or more
    26 (33.3%) stayed for twenty years or more
    16 (20.5%) stayed for thirty years or more
    10 (12.8%) married missionary husbands and, though taken off the CMS records, continued working in Persia
    10 (12.8%) died in Persia or on the way home to Britain

These figures bear witness to a remarkably high level of commitment, shown by relatively few women, towards their work amongst Persian people. It is more than mere hypothesis to declare that the current church in Iran owes much in its past to the presence of these women. The actual significance of their involvement was far greater than their formal visibility suggests. The large number of female missionaries and the average length of dedicated service belied the modest amount of official power they were granted as they became deeply influential in the life of the mission. Undoubtedly, mistakes were made and methods utilised which today seem incomprehensible. Yet by participating in new activities for women they became active agents for change, whilst playing a major part in the establishment of a mission and the formation of a Persian church.

Preparation for missionary work

Little bibliographical information is available about the women before their arrival in Iran, as application forms and candidates' papers did not survive the bombing of London during the Second World War. However, in common with most Victorian single women missionaries, who were expected to be "ladies of some education, culture and refinement", the majority were from middle-class families.[38] The missionary women in Iran were mostly well educated though few, other than the doctors, had university degrees. Financially, many were comfortably secure, often partly or even fully supporting themselves. Several worked as honorary missionaries, receiving no stipend from CMS, whilst others paid for the training and expenses of colleagues. The majority were English although an increasing number were attracted through local CMS associations, from countries such as Ireland, Canada and Australia.[39]

Throughout the period up to 1934 little attention was paid by CMS to the training of women missionaries. Prior to 1891 approximately one-third of the society's female candidates received some instruction at The Willows, a private foundation established in 1888. From the 1890s onwards several other institutions were also developed.[40] As the years progressed, there was growing realisation of the need to improve missionary women's training.[41] Nevertheless, CMS continued relying on women's experience of philanthropic activities, Sunday school teaching and professional training through nursing or teaching. These were regarded as a useful prelude for the missionary vocation of women which was justified as a further extension of the private sphere into the public realm. Arguments promoting benevolent maternalism, allowing women in Britain to expand their activities beyond the home, inevitably relied upon a class-based ideology which perceived middle-class women as ameliorating the situation of their working-class sisters. By relying to such an extent on their experience of welfare work in England, instead of providing more relevant missionary training, organisations such as CMS colluded with the transferral of this classed-based superiority into a racial one on the mission field. The women, used to regarding themselves as quasi-social workers, required only a subtle change of emphasis to interpret their missionary role as "saviour" to the less fortunate "heathen" women of the East.

Most CMS women arrived in Iran with very basic missionary training, in no way geared towards the specific needs of Persian people. Informed of their destination towards the end of their training, they were commissioned, or "dismissed", by CMS officials before leaving Britain. Once in Iran they immediately began studying the language in which they would later be examined for proficiency. Other necessary skills were learnt through trial and error and with advice from senior colleagues. Those who remained long enough were permitted furlough (home leave), lasting up to two years, at approximately five-yearly intervals. For the remainder of the time, life changed dramatically as they began mediating an entirely different religious and cultural environment.

Classifying "women's work" and introducing three case studies

CMS in Persia was no different to mission stations in other, especially Islamic, regions in realising the advantages of employing female workers. The view that a nation could only be

changed through its women, who carried the greater burden of rearing and influencing the next generation, was prevalent in the late nineteenth century. Writing from a different missionary context but expressing the general mood, the Bishop of Grahamstown, South Africa noted:
> We know that home is the centre and foundation of social life; and woman is the centre of home. Such as the women are, such are the homes, and such the civilization and the Christianity of society.[42]

Keen to promote Christianity in Persian society, Robert Bruce soon recognised the need for women missionaries to partake in the Christianising programme. Female workers were necessary in order to gain easier access to Iranian women who lived, largely, in seclusion.

As women missionaries increased numerically, their tasks were divided into three distinct categories: evangelism, education and medicine - known collectively as "women's work". In Part II of this book, the life and work of three individuals is explored as a means of outlining their particular contribution in each area. The commitment of Mary Bird, Isabella Read and Emmeline Stuart to the particular fields of evangelism, education and medicine respectively also indicates the more general approach of CMS within each sphere of "women's work".

Protestant and Reformed missionaries had long stressed the importance of education as part of mission strategy. Literacy was essential, for it provided converts with the capacity to read the Bible. Moreover, educating indigenous women was regarded as the key to elevating their position, thereby improving the entire nation.[43] In Iran there was an additional understanding that the country could ultimately only be evangelised through the work of Persian Christians. Great stress was placed on the need to educate converts and prepare future leaders for the local church community. Accordingly, many CMS women were educationalists who worked in the developing network of schools and other learning establishments.

The lack of existing female education in Iran made CMS's work amongst Muslim girls and women especially significant. Apart from a handful of schools set up by religious minorities for educating their own girls, and the efforts of the American Presbyterians in the North of Iran, the CMS missionaries were embarking on a new and ground-breaking movement towards improving the condition of Persia's women. In the early years, when work in Isfahan was not yet possible, efforts were concentrated in Julfa. Isabella Read was the first single female missionary to work as a teacher in the Armenian Girls' School set up by Bruce soon after his arrival in 1871.

Whilst education was important, CMS soon discovered that medical efforts were a much more efficient means of gaining contact with Iranian women. Moreover, on witnessing the suffering of many Persians, they were keen to provide physical aid wherever possible. For thirty-seven years, between 1897-1934, the women's side of CMS's medical work was supervised by Dr Emmeline Stuart. During that time she witnessed the arrival and departure of many other female nurses and doctors (see Appendix VII for a chronological list of the CMS women doctors), oversaw the building and maintenance of several hospitals and established a pattern of medical work which continued developing long after her departure.

Education and medicine were regarded as important and valuable tasks for alleviating suffering and hardship endured by many Iranian women. However, they were worthless unless carried out within the context of evangelism which undergirded the entire missionary enterprise, marking it as religious rather than secular welfare work. In theory medical and educational missionaries were also expected to operate as evangelists. In practice, busy schedules left little time for this basic form of outreach. Instead, additional women were set aside as evangelists whose time was spent visiting, teaching Bible classes and preaching the gospel whenever opportunities arose. Mary Bird was undoubtedly the most prominent of the early women evangelists and was remembered fondly by many long after her untimely death in Iran. Though she was well known for her basic medical skills, it was above all as an evangelist that she thought of herself. Bird's style and approach set the pattern for much of the women's work in the Persia mission and her influence was deep and long-lasting.

The CMS women participating in these three areas of missionary work were part of the ongoing evangelical tradition of social action rooted in an individualistic understanding of spirituality dependent upon personal salvation. A religious change of heart was regarded as the ultimate solution for the problems in society. However, it was necessary for the love of God to be shown through benevolent action in order for people to experience and understand the need for change. For many this now represents a patronising assumption at best and an insuperable deadlock at worst. For contemporary efforts to improve social conditions are usually considered entirely separate from evangelistic work leading to religious conversion. Within the Victorian context, however, the connection was taken for granted and seldom questioned. Both elements - spiritual and physical - were believed to be necessary parts of the missionary equation, and welfare work was carried out within this overarching framework. The source of missionary motivation was undoubtedly spiritual and expressed through a desire for personal religious conversion. However, this did not represent a disingenuous attitude towards welfare work but, rather, a context-specific holistic approach to the missionary task. For the majority of CMS women in Iran would not have conceived of working for one, without a desire for change in the other.

Married women

Mission researchers often raise the problem of the "invisibility" of missionary wives in archives and other historical sources.[44] The records of CMS's activity in Iran, likewise, present a paucity of information on married women. Yet their tacit participation provides a great deal of material for interpretation. Whilst that task falls beyond the scope of this book, the project would be incomplete were no acknowledgement made of the role played by wives during the early years of the Persia mission.

In countries where missionary societies were active for many years before the advent of single women, pioneering wives usually established a large and significant field of work. Haggis argues that in southern India, "women's work" was initially demarcated by married women defining and providing the appropriate parameters.[45] Though these did not change with the arrival of single women, the importance attached to them shifted significantly as the enterprise was professionalised under the efforts of single women's specialisation.

Haggis' analysis of missionary wives creating spheres of work that soon demanded the efforts of single women is not directly relevant to the situation in Iran. For numbers were too small and time too short for progress of any consequence to take place prior to the arrival of single women.[46] However, if her data about *change*s in the understanding of "women's work" carried out by wives to that undertaken by single women is not directly applicable to the circumstances in Iran, many of her insights about the *difference* in perception between the two are highly pertinent and have been assimilated into my arguments throughout this section.[47]

During most of CMS's early period in Persia, married women laboured alongside single missionaries as silent partners in work that was, for the most part, indistinguishable. Whilst many were extremely influential, they were not accorded the official status of a missionary by CMS. Margaret Thompson (née Carr) was born in Iran to missionary parents and worked tirelessly for the mission, first as the daughter of Dr Carr and later the wife of Bishop Thompson. Never, however, was she recognised by the society as an active participant in her own right. Referring to herself as "just a little *'m'* ", she would explain that the only proof of her existence in several CMS documents was a letter *'m'* printed next to her husband's name, indicating he was married.[48] Women who arrived as single missionaries and later married colleagues were compelled to resign their post. Though the majority continued working, their stipend was withdrawn and their name wiped out of the record books.[49]

The problem was that if wives had been recognised officially, the justification for permitting women to work as missionaries would be seriously undermined. For,
> the *raison d'être* behind the women's missionary movement of the late nineteenth century was that single women, without the encumbrances of husband and children, would be able to devote their entire lives to missionary work.[50]

Generally, married and single women co-operated in similar work and were identical in status on committees and decision-making bodies. There was, however, a different emphasis in how they were perceived, based entirely on an ideological distinction, expressed through the relative invisibility of wives, their title as "missionary wife" (compared with "lady missionary" used for single women) and their lack of financial remuneration.

The latter was particularly significant in affecting the position of wives. By virtue of their salary (albeit smaller than that of male colleagues), single women were regarded as professionals, qualified for their job and accorded worth through financial reward. Married women, embarked upon very similar work, experienced a qualitative reduction in the value placed upon them by receiving no financial benefits. CMS could effectively ignore their presence and strip them of any identity other than "wife of Mr X". Agnes Carr was in Iran for thirty-six years together with her husband Donald. On their retirement, CMS recorded their gratefulness to Dr Carr for his services to the Persia mission. In a long account, Agnes is mentioned only once, as "the wife" who shared his career.[51]

In short, the position of wives was exploited by CMS who took married missionary women for granted. Had they not been there, or simply refused to participate in the work, their absence would have been keenly felt. Their involvement, however, at minimum cost to the society,[52] was an unspoken expectation, implicit within the missionary code. If a wife was thought to be opting out of her duties, this was a matter for comment by others. Charles Stileman wrote to

CMS in 1899, concerned that Mrs Blackett was failing to carry out her responsibilities in Kerman:

> Complaints here [have been] made to me ... that Mrs Blackett refused to see the Persian ladies when they sent to ask if they might visit her ... I mention this because the usual idea in this mission is that when a married couple occupy a station, the wife does some pioneer work amongst the women, thus preparing the way for single ladies, this pioneer work is not being done and the sooner the single ladies go there the better it will be for the work.[53]

The presence of wives accorded missionary societies with ideological and theological justification for the work of single women. The Victorian apology for women's involvement in the workforce was based on a particular interpretation of the separate spheres philosophy in which public work was regarded as an extension of the domestic realm. If this logic was to continue corroborating women's cause, the domestic world needed to remain discernible. For expansion of the private realm depended upon its continued existence as a coherent reality. Missionary wives, therefore, completed the total image of womanhood by ensuring the domestic world remained intact. Fulfilling the role of home-maker and providing familial stability, they represented the essence of Christian morality based on monogamous marriage, Christian motherhood and womanly self-sacrifice. Meanwhile, single women were liberated to reinterpret the private world, expanding it beyond the safe domain of domesticity into the public world of work. The result for married women was paradoxical. Their role provided them with a kind of status as upholders of the basic Christian virtue at the heart of stable society. Yet it also restricted them professionally and limited them financially.

Within the mission there were inevitable disagreements and controversies, arising from the relationship between wives, single women and male missionaries. The ambiguous role played by married women meant the stronger personalities wielded greater power. Equally, they were easier targets of personal attacks by other missionaries, especially men, who felt justified in commenting on them, for they were not officially regarded as colleagues. Soon after arrival in Persia, Tisdall wrote to CMS with general opinions on the state of the mission. Amongst other things, he remarked on Mrs Bruce, considering her "a most unpleasant woman, miserly in the extreme among her other bad qualities". She had, he believed, "much influence on her husband and biase[d] his mind against people ... I can understand how troubles have arisen in the past. A great many of them have been due to Mrs B. doubtless".[54] For the most part, the distinct constituencies within the mission circle worked alongside each other peaceably. Single and married women provided ideological justification for one another's presence and between them depicted the ideal of Christian womanhood, fulfilling responsibilities at home and in the public domain.

Interpreting the paradoxical nature of CMS women in Persia

My contention that historical subjects are best understood within the broad spectrum of "usability" and "responsibility" creates a tension within the research process. For it requires that past women are both understood contextually and challenged by contemporary assumptions. This tension is best resolved by efforts towards a paradoxical interpretation of data rather than a search for straightforward simplicity. Accordingly, if the CMS women are to be credited with a distinct, but no less significant, part in the development of feminism, it is necessary to highlight several contradictory elements within their gender, theological and imperialist perceptions.

First, their work and self-understanding was limited by Victorian gender boundaries. They viewed the world in terms of separate male and female spheres and did not, on the whole, conceive of destroying or removing these boundaries. Instead they operated within the defined parameters, using the restrictions to their advantage and ingeniously finding ways to expand the customs deemed acceptable for women. The legitimacy of their part in the women's movement is based on an astute interpretation of a conservative and potentially limiting ideology, rather than an attempt to demolish that ideology. They avoided the risk of full-scale male [and some female] opposition, by ensuring the ideology remained in place. It is, therefore, important to judge them more by their actions than their words. Uninterested in shifting philosophical ground under prevalent gender assumptions, they seldom argued for equality with men. Yet they participated in significant moves towards change, through work which took them beyond the physical confines of home.

Secondly, the CMS women embodied the paradoxical nature of religion in the lives of Victorian women. Dominant evangelicalism restricted their vision to a traditional theology of womanhood. Concurrently, it promoted the spiritual and domestic superiority of women, providing the impetus needed to work for change. Like many religious women at the time, the missionaries discovered the capacity to face the struggles from an entirely spiritual source. They found their motivation for new and ground-breaking ventures in a personal faith and a belief that God was calling them.

Finally, one of the most common paradoxes within the imperialist agenda influences the task of interpreting the CMS women. A basic contradiction meant they maintained an overall attitude of superiority towards Iran whilst also developing close friendships, based on warmth and mutuality, with individual Iranians. Said has written extensively about the orientalist tendency to incorporate generally accepted views about Islam, with a more personal experience of it.[55] He evinces a distinction between the "particular" and the "general" in a western approach to the East, arguing that people learn "to separate a general apprehension of the Orient from a specific experience of it", whilst allowing both to coexist.[56] Accordingly, the CMS women were usually willing to criticise the entire nation or pronounce judgement upon Islam generally. Yet their encounters with individuals brought them close to a real understanding of Persians on their own basis, not as potential converts. By operating according to this paradox, the CMS women remained within the linguistic and ideological boundaries expected by supporters in England whilst in reality their attitudes were often changing, even if subconsciously, through personal experiences of the people amongst whom they lived and worked.

This dichotomy will be further explored in the next chapter which analyses the CMS women's theological framework. Their theoretical understanding of Islam is set against their personal encounter with it, providing a basis on which to understand their position in Iran.

CHAPTER FOUR

Attitudes Towards Islam and Theological Self-Perceptions

The theological dimension to missionary motivation

Thus far the CMS women in Iran have been discussed in relation to the broad influences of their day. They have been considered within the light of dominant orientalist and feminist ideologies, each given religious justification by the authoritative voice of evangelical Christianity. They have also been placed within the Iranian setting and that of the CMS Persia mission where they worked. The present chapter draws these themes together through an exploration of theological issues with specific reference to interfaith concerns and the Christian encounter with Islam. My intention is to analyse the theology that motivated the women both professionally, in their work amongst Muslims, and personally, through a consideration of the motifs and models which helped them maintain an inner faith and relationship with God.

The chapter is divided broadly into three sections. The first contextualizes the CMS women's views towards Islam and Muslims through a consideration of ideas expressed at the 1910 World Missionary Conference (WMC) in Edinburgh. This was undoubtedly the most significant international missionary gathering during the sixty-five year period covered by this book. For present purposes, the most relevant WMC contribution was the report of Commission IV, "The Missionary Message in Relation to Non-Christian Religions". It is an important source from the Victorian/Qajar era concerning missionary approaches towards other faiths and their adherents. A delineation of the material available from the Commission IV report will serve as a useful backdrop for the remainder of this chapter.

The second and most substantial section is an examination of theological attitudes shown by the CMS women in Iran towards Islam, which also drove them to labour amongst Muslim women. Assessed in detail, their views and perspectives will be compared with prevalent themes expressed at the Edinburgh conference. The final section provides an analysis of the theological language employed by the women as they articulated their religious self-understanding and motivated themselves to work more effectively.

Views from the 1910 World Missionary Conference

Recent studies such as Kenneth Cracknell's *Justice, Courtesy and Love* have shown that despite mistakes and the lack of a consensus, the dialogical approach to other religions, usually thought of as an invention of the 1970s onwards, did exist in embryonic form as early as 1910.[1] Commentators frequently justify this assertion through examination of the views expressed in the responses to the missionary questionnaire sent out by Commission IV prior to the WMC which, they believe, present a remarkably positive attitude to the world faiths. Detailed forms were sent to 149 active missionaries, representing different denominations and geographical regions, to assess their opinions and approaches towards other religions and their adherents. The report of Commission IV, compiled in time for the Edinburgh conference, was based largely on the results of these questionnaires and reflected the prevalent mood amongst missionaries at the time concerning the world faiths.

Throughout this section, considerable use will be made of Cracknell's analysis of the questionnaires and the Commission IV report. I intend to describe his findings, before providing my own critique, with particular reference to the work of missions in Muslim lands. Cracknell maintains the mood of the Commission, and the structuring of the questionnaire itself, reflected an open and generous approach to other faiths.[2] The complexities of interreligious encounter were addressed, with a greater concentration on the "why" of the missionary movement rather than the "how" of the missionary approach. Edinburgh was promoted as a working conference for active missionaries to confer and debate, not as an opportunity for triumphalism or raising home support. In short, the Commission IV report marked the earliest positive attempt this century to outline a generous Christian perspective towards other religious traditions.

Whilst his conclusions are based primarily on an analysis of the questionnaires, Cracknell includes two other significant sections. His book ends with details of the report's positive reception by two theologians, Temple Gairdner and James Hope Moulton.[3] More significantly, since the ideas expressed at Edinburgh did not appear in a vacuum, Cracknell begins by providing contextual background through outlining the views of thirteen pre-1909 theologians and missionaries whose ideas were seminal in the formation of a theology of religions.[4] To assess these correctly, several negative elements which shaped the missionary framework are defined in terms of fixed attitudes towards theological views prevalent at the time, namely, millenialism, millenarianism, radical intellectual anti-idolatry, uncompromising hyper-Calvinism, radical anti-intellectualist revivalism, and intense Biblicism.[5] Inevitably, elements from these "were part of the mental furniture of each of the missionaries and theologians",[6] but their achievements should be measured by reflecting upon their individual points of departure.

In analysing the responses to the questionnaire, Cracknell celebrates the overwhelmingly positive attitude shown by many missionaries towards other faiths. He subdivides the majority views (many of them implicit but present nevertheless), under a variety of headings, including sympathy and appreciation, identification and solidarity, genuine fellow pilgrims, theology of religions, evolution, logos, fulfilment.[7] Negative approaches by missionaries regarding other religions as distortions or imperfect responses to the Christian revelation were present but in a clear minority.[8] Overall Cracknell is convinced that today's more open approach advocated towards interfaith ecumenism by many Christians is not a peculiarly late twentieth century phenomenon. Rather, contemporary attempts at serious interreligious dialogue and encounter are a fulfilment of the earnest beliefs and desires of our forebears in faith, which somehow got buried in the intervening years.

The negative significance of Islam

Though convincingly argued, Cracknell's case is based largely on a significant error of judgement, for he undermines the importance of the Islamic factor. A closer inspection of his theory, by anyone with a keen interest in Islam, reveals a weakness in his argument. First, the conspicuous virtual silence, for the first two-hundred pages of the book, on attitudes towards

Islam, damages Cracknell's thesis considerably. None of the thirteen theologians and missionaries whose contributions he outlines are concerned with Islam. Secondly, the positive trend formulated through examination of the questionnaires was, in fact, virtually irrelevant with regard to Islam and missionaries working in Islamic contexts. Practically none of the positive categories used in Cracknell's analysis were employed by missionaries working primarily with Muslims. One is compelled to ask whether these points are not too significant to be ignored?

There are a few exceptions, notably William Shedd, an American Presbyterian in Persia, and Anna Smith of the Church of England Zenana Missionary Society (CEZMS) in Bangalore.[9] However, Cracknell himself admits that Smith, in particular, was unusual in acknowledging the existence of truths in Islam which Christians could learn from, even discerning the presence of the Holy Spirit in the Muslim community and faith tradition.[10] It is in the minority *negative* views that missionaries from Muslim lands are most prominently represented.[11] Moreover, their minority status does not underestimate the significance of their negative views. For of those responding to the questionnaire, only a small proportion were from Muslim lands; therefore, it is obvious that their views would represent a minority attitude. Of the 149 respondents, twenty were from Muslim countries. A further fifty operated in regions where Islam existed, but worked chiefly among adherents of other religions, especially Hinduism, Confucianism and Buddhism. Had more responses represented work in Islamic contexts, the negative views would probably have increased. Moreover, these numerical facts are not presented by Cracknell whose readers may not realise the minority view is directly proportional to the small number of responses from Muslim lands.[12]

Just as the reader may assume that Cracknell has ignored the significance of Islam almost entirely, he presents a section entitled "The special case of Islam".[13] In it he outlines the reasons why the positive trends in evolving missionary thought did not impact upon those in Muslim lands. Islam could not be treated like other religions, for unlike them, it had not appeared *before* Christianity. As a later revelation, it knowingly rejected Christian truths and could not, therefore, be interpreted as a nascent tradition, open to fulfilment or completion through Christian transformation. Notably few respondents denounced Islam as satanic and, on the whole, courtesy was advocated in relationships with Muslims. However, most believed the only hope for Muslim salvation was in whole-hearted acceptance of Christianity and complete discontinuity with an Islamic past.

Missionary opinion representing CMS in Iran

Two senior men, Walter Rice and William St. Clair Tisdall, represented CMS in Persia as respondents to the Commission IV questionnaire. Not only are their replies typical of missionaries in Muslim lands, but Cracknell considers them amongst the most emphatic concerning the need for displacement in a move from Islam to Christianity.[14] Indeed, Tisdall was well known as a fierce critic and author of some repute on Islamic matters.[15] Yet despite his impassioned response to the questionnaire and acclaim as a writer, he remained noticeably under-used by the WMC Commission. This is probably because the report included a surprisingly positive section on Islam for which Tisdall's insights were unhelpful.[16] Even allowing for orientalist and evangelical linguistic restrictions, his views are uncompromising and dogmatic. Maintaining an entirely negative understanding of the essence of Islam, Tisdall believed "the missionary gladly recognises the truths that he [sic] finds hidden and buried under masses of error ... [but] endeavours to cleanse the jewel from the mire into which it has fallen".[17]

Notwithstanding the relatively generous section on Islam in the Commission's report, Tisdall's views were, in fact, largely in line with many CMS colleagues both in Persia and other Muslim contexts. According to Cracknell, the reasons for this (apart from the later revelation of Islam mentioned above), may be two-fold.[18] First, the similarities evident in these two monotheistic religions of Islam and Christianity were a source of tension between them. Amongst other things, both include a strong missionary incentive and share a long history of antagonism, hatred and misunderstanding. Such factors heighten the sense of rivalry and increase the potential threat of danger each feels from the other.

Secondly, the prevalent anti-Islamic missionary stance may have resulted from the "influence of some powerful (domineering is a better word) personalities within the CMS (Robert Stirling in Jerusalem, William Miller in Nigeria and Tisdall in Iran to name but three) who had fixed negative views on Islam".[19] Therefore, not only Tisdall, Rice and a handful of others, but large numbers within CMS maintained a hard line in their disposition towards Islam. By contrast with several other missionary societies, CMS was one of the least forward-looking with "the general attitude of the ... General Secretary Eugene Stock set[ting] the tone at this period".[20]

The overall missionary responses in 1910 remained surprisingly positive, acknowledging the need to find new and more appropriate ways of contact with other religions. Many wrote warmly about personal encounters and friendships, revealing the desire for better relations and more understanding. Such appreciative expressions and the acknowledgement that truths could be found in other faiths, make it possible to argue that the WMC findings provide the early stages of a positive theology of religions.

However, both the Commission IV report and Cracknell's analysis fail to grasp, seriously enough, the conservative views proffered by the majority of missionaries working in Muslim environments. Whilst it is possible, therefore, to regard Edinburgh as a watershed in the history of Christian mission, this cannot be interpreted as a true reflection of the missionary situation in Muslim regions, especially those within CMS jurisdiction. And it is within this more specific context that the women in Iran should be studied. Their contribution must be judged according to points of departure from their contextual norm, created by CMS structures operating within a Muslim environment.[21]

CMS women, Islam and the Muslims of Iran

In *Justice, Courtesy and Love*, Cracknell suggests various approaches which may have aided missionaries offering positive responses towards other religions in their Commission IV questionnaires.[22] Two of these prove especially useful as a means of structuring the data about the women in Iran. First, there was a sense of the replies being couched in terms of people rather than whole religious systems.[23] Many showed an instinct for the personal - the individuals they knew - rather than the abstract. Anna Smith of Bangalore for example, demonstrating remarkable forward thinking, clearly had her eyes on the people, rather than their religious doctrines, and was able to recognise in them the presence of God.[24] This meant regarding the faith in its present form, here and now, not according to its past history. Secondly, most positive respondents were unwilling to judge other faiths on the basis of unacceptable social manifestations, though these were acknowledged and frequently criticised.

Muslims and Islam, or the particular versus the general

The paradox of relating to the particular in a positive way whilst judging the general negatively (based on Said's theory that both can co-exist within the orientalist mindset), has provided a *leitmotif* throughout this book. For westerners during the age of empire frequently related warmly towards individual Muslims whilst condemning Islam by means of unqualified generalisations. It was the ability to emphasise individual friendships over and above entire religious systems that allowed many respondents of the WMC questionnaire a more generous spirit towards other faiths. An inspection of the CMS papers, however, reveals the women in Persia wrote more in terms of "Islam" as an institution than "Muslims" as people with whom they formed relationships. Accordingly, it was relatively easy for them to denounce the whole nation without personally involving individuals whom they encountered.

Two themes emerge in this context, namely, "the land" *en masse*, which they considered was in darkness, and "the people" as a unit, whom they believed to be lost. In 1892 Mary Bird expressed hopes of building up house visiting so she could be used for God's service "in this dark land".[25] Out of this developed a call for "the evangelization of the land"[26] as the means by which God's spirit would become active in Iran. This rather abstract idea of "the land" found its reflection in the notion of a "thirsty perishing *people*"[27] (my emphasis), for which missionaries laboured to "gather many souls out of the darkness into His marvellous light".[28] Occasionally, "the land" and "the people" were ambiguously combined, in references such as the "evangelization of *Persia*"[29] or "the salvation of this erring *nation*"[30] (both my emphases). In either case, both land and people were regarded as residing in darkness, and the missionary hope and belief was that the Lord would "answer the many prayers for these lands speedily".[31]

Though "land" and "people" formed the most comprehensive units, the CMS women's efforts directed their attention more towards the female population of Persia. It is perhaps not surprising that they too were usually mentioned in terms of a distinct, definable category, often referred to simply as "Muhammedan women". Three themes in particular run through missionary attitudes towards this unified group. First, personal contact was essential, for Persian women had to be *reached* if the missionary endeavour was to be successful. Secondly, they were on the whole regarded as uninformed and ignorant. Finally, the missionaries expressed pity towards Persian women, convinced they could only be helped by means of the gospel message.

The common belief that to change a nation, its women needed to be reached was central to missionary ethos by the late nineteenth century. Certainly, from the earliest days of CMS's presence in Persia, contact with women was regarded as essential. Soon after her arrival in 1891, Mary Bird wrote that her time was occupied in learning Persian so she could take best advantage of any opening among the Muslim women.[32] The following year she affirmed the importance of visiting women "where ever I can gain admittance, so as to win their confidence, and get opportunities of hearing and speaking, and thus paving the way for future work".[33] For prior to the growth in educational and medical work, home visiting was regarded as the most effective means of encountering women whose lives revolved around the private world of domesticity.

Having made contact with Muslim women, missionaries were quick to express generalised opinions about them as a group, regarding them, on the whole, as ignorant and uninformed. However, during the early period when Persia was part of the Turkish-Arabia mission, a distinction appeared between views postulated by CMS women in Iran compared with those in Iraq.[34] For the former, any ignorance they perceived as a trait of Persian women was usually considered an environmental fault within a society where female education was not encouraged, whereas for the latter, Arabian women of Baghdad were reproached due to their apparently inherent limitations from a very young age.

Isabella Read, for example, showed great concern for Iranian women's lack of education and refused to believe them incapable. Similarly, Emmeline Stuart, commenting on high levels of female illiteracy and lack of educational opportunities, concluded that these were due to mistaken assumptions within Iranian thinking that women lacked the capacity for learning.[35] By contrast, Arrabella Wilson writing from Baghdad in 1890 was much more critical of Arabian women and girls:

> I have begun an infants class on Sunday afternoon just to teach them to repeat and, as far as I can, to understand verses of the Bible. It is work I dearly love, but they need an immense amount of patience for thinking is not in them and you may tell them a thing again and again without their taking it in, even the simplest thing...[36]

The missionaries in Iran were equally fond of generalisations, many of which were far from flattering. However, their comments about Persian women's ignorance were based more on sociological observations concerning society's treatment of women, whereas in Baghdad unqualified remarks were presented as innate truths.

By far the most common feeling expressed by CMS women towards Iranians was one of pity. This is distinguishable from sympathy or compassion, also a typical missionary response, but one that usually developed over a longer period of time and grew from personal contact. By contrast, pity was a sentiment many expressed in broad terms and with little knowledge of particular circumstances. Its corollary was unequivocal assurance that missionaries themselves, as channels for the Christian message, could help relieve the misery of Persian life. Thus, pathetic, pitiable lifestyles were often assumed for "the people" of Iran even by the most recent missionary recruits. Laura Stubbs, soon after reaching Julfa, recalled her journey across Persia:

> As we passed through the villages one felt so sorry for the people. We longed to be able to speak to them and to tell them the 'Old, old Story'. They looked so like 'sheep having no Shepherd'.[37]

These observations were based not on knowledge of Iran, but on theological suppositions and confident evangelical theories, buried deep in the subconscious and stubbornly immutable. Ten years later Stubbs' sentiments persisted as she sadly recalled passing through villages near Yezd, knowing they were in utter darkness without a single missionary: "Oh that God may make us [Mary Bird and herself] channels of life to these dying souls".[38] Not surprisingly, such generalised comments were frequently directed towards Iranian *women* specifically. Philippa Braine-Hartnell first went to Persia in 1892 as helper to the Tisdalls whilst also doing missionary work in an unofficial capacity. Three years later she was eager to be taken on as a full CMS missionary. In her letter of application she expressed a desire to work "among the poor downtrodden women of Persia".[39]

This emphasis on missionary help as a necessity for compensating the supposedly lamentable circumstances of Persian lives was essentially an expression of theological significance. The tiny band of missionaries was in no position to solve the problems arising from socio-political and economic structures within Qajar Iran. Whilst they recognised their human limitations, however, most believed the religious conversion of Iranian individuals and the nation as a whole could alleviate much of the suffering. This hypothesis was based on the commonly held evangelical belief in personal salvation as the antidote for all societal problems. Ultimately, it provided the CMS women with a resolute motivation to work for the achievement of their goals.

Inevitably, the desire to palliate the ills of society by redemption through personal conversion was accompanied by a condescending demeanour, at its worst, intimating arrogance. The patronising attitude to which so many missionaries adhered was a typical feature of contemporary evangelicalism's overly enthusiastic approach. It originated from a deeply held belief in Christian superiority placing a burden of responsibility upon all who accepted it. In militaristic terms common at the time, the gospel was used as a weapon in the battle to win souls. For many believed conversion, followed by personal salvation, would lay the foundations for a new spiritual and physical community. As deliverers of the Christian message, missionaries were convinced they possessed the necessary solution to ensure a positive future for Iranians. Their motivation was genuine, as was the desire to alleviate suffering. However, the figurative generalisations to which they clung in order to express their ideas, together with deeply embedded assumptions of superiority, meant a patronising tone remained inescapable.

It should be noted that the type of contact missionaries had with ordinary people in Iran was a rare experience for Europeans at the turn of the century. They are, therefore, amongst the most reliable social commentators from that period and it is incumbent upon us to take their comments seriously.[40] They witnessed hardship and suffering in the lives of many and elucidated this by means of the familiar linguistic framework of Victorian evangelicalism. The oppressive structures of their language should not, however, diminish from the underlying reality of their words. To acknowledge the poor condition of Iranian society, especially with regard to the position of women, is not to discriminate against Islam or condemn all that is Persian. Rather, it is a rejection of that particular brand of distorted orientalism which loses impetus in the search for truth and fails to understand the nineteenth century within its true context.

There are two exceptions to the CMS women's widespread classification of Persian Muslim women as a single homogenous group. The first is more general, regarding the distinction often made between rich and poor. The second concerns those occasions when missionaries did move beyond generalisations and related to *individual* Persian women.

From the earliest days CMS was aware of profound implications for its work in the social chasm between Iran's rich and poor. Access to wealthy women was generally more difficult, allowing the mission fewer opportunities to influence this group. The conventions of the Islamic separate spheres philosophy were adhered to more strictly for wealthy urban women compared with their poorer and/or rural counterparts. Furthermore, rich townswomen were not required to work but had regular staff to carry out all household duties. This, according Bird, created a superficiality which made wealthy women "so frivolous, so taken up with their gorgeous dresses and ornaments, their endless cups of tea and pipes, and so self-satisfied".[41]

The difference between rich and poor was frequently expressed in terms of a typically English fascination with class distinction. For eagerness to influence the upper echelons of Iranian society was based upon a transferral of the British class-based ideology, in which middle- and upper-class women were regarded as affecting change for their supposedly helpless working-class sisters. The theory extended to the Persian context, developing into a belief that only gentlewomen could forge real change within the country.

This did not mean the social and religious requirements of poorer women were neglected but simply that they were considered entirely different. Jessie Biggs, for example, was concerned about educating various classes of women separately so that each could be taught according to their needs. English, French and science were of little use to poorer girls who needed to be "taught to earn their own living ... according to the customs of the country".[42] Whilst this was an articulation of characteristically class-based superiority, it also arose from practical requirements. Poorer women with no other means of income were given appropriate skills for earning money at a time when Persian society had little use for developing intellectuals amongst such women.

In contrast to general remarks about the women of Iran and the distinction recognised between rich and poor, there are countless examples of detailed narratives concerning the lives of individuals.[43] What these accounts have in common is that the majority refer to people who, under the influence of the mission, were either showing keen interest in Christianity or had already been baptised. There are, for example, detailed descriptions of the faithfulness and courage displayed by a number of female converts. Likewise, enquirers not yet ready to commit themselves to the Christian way of life are entrusted to the prayers of readers at home in the hope that conversion may soon follow.[44]

The CMS women's capacity for referring to individual Persians who were of professional interest, whilst continuing their tendency to generalise about the people as a whole, may be interpreted in a variety of ways. It is possible to argue that they were only willing to develop relationships with those from whom they had something to gain. Accordingly, their association with Persian women was based on a power balance in which they had something to offer, but nothing to receive in return. Alternatively, the women they met through work were obviously also those with whom they formed relationships and it was natural, therefore, that these should be the people about whom they wrote as individuals. The pertinent point is that developing personal friendships did not eliminate the generalisations but co-existed alongside them. Whilst an attitude of superiority seeps through the missionary letters, it is balanced by genuine warmth and friendship. This is one more element within the paradoxical nature of missionary presence in Iran.

To be sure, CMS letters were aimed at a specific audience eager to hear positive results about missionary efforts in Iran. The language and tone of much of the material is designed to satisfy these requirements and adumbrates a pattern within which the CMS women felt secure. However, the archives also include authentic expressions of humility and admiration for the strength and courage shown by converts experiencing persecution. While the language conforms to expected norms, there remains a real sense in which the missionaries regarded Persian Christians as fellow pilgrims along the journey of faith. For many years they continued insisting that the growing indigenous church needed nurturing and developing through seasoned missionary expertise. However, they also acknowledged their own need to learn from the Persian experience, particularly with regard to accepting the burden of suffering.

The CMS women are typical of Said's orientalists whose individual and general approach to the East and its people co-existed, each apparently unencumbered by the other.[45] Inevitably, this resulted in a complex relationship between missionary and Persian women. An inability to recognise inappropriate universalised assumptions resulted in an air of superiority running as a major theme throughout the mission's first sixty-five years. Furthermore, the appropriation of the early stages of a positive theology of religions, in the way expressed by many missionaries at the 1910 WMC, is not possible. The generalised approach employed by CMS women persistently suggested the mission had something to offer the people of Iran for which nothing could be given in return.

Nevertheless, analysing missionary attitudes towards individuals introduces a variant approach indicating the composite nature of their relationship with Iranians. Friendships undoubtedly developed and many missionaries were profoundly influenced through the Persians whom they knew. They remained unwilling or unable to supersede the theological framework in which they operated, never displaying radical change from the traditional CMS approach. However, this should not lead to the assumption that their relationships were all one way. Many were aware of gaining more than they had given and learning more than they had taught. The majority developed a deep love for the people of Iran which grew primarily from experiences of personal friendship. Their shortcoming was the inability to recognise the paralysing effect of generalised assumptions with regard to the people of Iran and the indigenous church community.

Despite this, their writings act as a kind of counterbalance to much contemporary post-imperialist literature which, with its fiercely anti-mission stance, refuses to concede the right of non-western individuals to choose Christianity for themselves.[46] There is a tendency to assume that all who converted as a consequence of missionary efforts did so merely in the face of coercion and intimidation, and that subsequent generations have followed suit because of the overwhelming power of western cultural imperialism. This neo-paternalistic hypothesis inverts the arrogance of nineteenth century orientalism, but still maintains an attitude of superiority by defining what is best for peoples of the East.

By contrast, genuine admiration for the courage of converts enabled the CMS women in Iran to reveal their faith in a Christianity that transcends cultural and national boundaries and adapts to its new environment. For despite the contours of their orientalist mindset and the limitations of its accompanying vocabulary, essentially they were eager not to westernise Persian society, but Christianise it. Today we may be unable to detect the difference, yet for the missionaries the distinction was self-evident. For some, the benefits of Christianity were inexplicably linked with the influence of western civilisation. Generally however, the Persia mission made an early and conscious effort to separate these two dimensions, believing it was both possible and desirable. Annie Gauntlett, for example, argued that "the need for the Gospel and *the Gospel only* in Persia, has grown with the facilities for preaching it" (my emphasis).[47] Yet, as explained by Dr Winifred Westlake, this was not synonymous with a case for westernisation:

> We don't want to Anglicise the Persian women, do we? No, if we may be used to set them free from the trammels of Mohammedanism, placing them in the light of the Gospel of Christ, they will develop as God wills, and who can tell what they may do in His honour and glory.[48]

Whilst we may reject many of their sentiments and the manner in which they were expressed, amidst the rhetoric it is possible to hear missionary voices carrying across the generations, challenging us to respect personal conscience in the quest for religious wholeness. Since western global ascendancy and the age of empire in particular, choosing Christianity can all too easily be regarded as alignment with the superiority of strength and power. For, at the very least, being a Christian is a symbolic association with the force of western domination. The CMS women's insights, however, challenge this often subconscious assumption, presenting the possibility of a faith that does not restrict new cultural expression but encompasses the richness of human experience.

Islam and its unacceptable social manifestations

Cracknell's second proposition concerning the positive respondents to the WMC questionnaire is that they showed an unwillingness to judge other faiths on the basis of unacceptable social manifestations, though these were both acknowledged and criticised.[49]

The CMS archives include much material linking missionary assessments about Islam to perceptions of its Iranian social reality. A deep rooted and widespread interpretation was one based on a straightforward cause and effect relationship between religion and social degradation. Accordingly, the very existence of Islam was posited as the direct source of Iran's social problems, engendering belief that if the former were destroyed the latter would automatically improve. This negative appraisal of Islam based on a particular interpretation of its cultural manifestation appears to have been imbued in the CMS women before they arrived in Persia.[50] However, contrary to many respondents of the WMC questionnaire,[51] experience of living amongst a different faith community seems to have intensified rather than changed their views.

> In England one realizes to a certain degree the great need of these people who do not know Christ as their Saviour; but I think this realization becomes far deeper

and stronger to those who come out amongst them. I can truly say my missionary zeal and prayer have become intensified since I came to Persia.[52]

The reasons for an intensification of such preconceptions were essentially social. Missionaries who remained in Iran for long periods persisted in constructing Islam as the theological foundation for the ills of society, interpreting many events in Persia as indicative of the "horrors of a religion of man's making".[53] After ten years experience, Stubbs still found that, "Daily the wrongs and sins and sorrows of this land of Islam dawn upon me".[54]

The harmful impact of Islam was delineated not only in vague terms on the basis of its overriding presence as an institution or religion. The missionaries also proffered more specific examples. Dr Stuart, for example, in writing about one of her trips to a village near Julfa, used the episode as an opportunity to explicate the dubious effect of Islam upon the behavioural patterns of Persian women.[55] She describes the arrival of a woman paid by the *mullahs* to agitate a gathering of villagers through reciting the death narrative of the martyr Hassan. The wild gesticulations, loud hoarse tones, wailing and beating of chests that followed were, for Stuart, indicative of how ignorant people could be stirred up by fanatics to participate in deeds of violence.

The appalling state of Iran's medical care was further regarded as an implicit consequence of Islam. According to Stuart, almost every patient seen by the mission was "a sufferer from the ignorant treatment of Persian doctors".[56] Whilst missionaries recognised this was partly due to lack of education and technology, they also considered it the result of a corrupt system. Mary Bird, for example, wrote about a baby, first misdiagnosed by a Persian doctor and then refused treatment due to the family's shortage of funds. In the brief article, emotively titled "A Baby Murdered", Bird explains that by the time the child was brought to the mission there was nothing they could do to save his life.[57]

Not surprisingly, the forms of social degradation that most concerned the female missionaries were those which impacted upon Iranian women. Indeed, it was woman's status that represented the most unacceptable face of Islam's social reality, proving it was a false religion. This common theme was adhered to by many missionary organisations at the time. Writing in 1910 from an American perspective, Helen Barrett Montgomery expressed the then uncontroversial sentiment that "the darkest blot upon the prophet Muhammad is the low appreciation of womanhood".[58] Amongst the missionaries in Iran, Dr Stuart was one of the most passionate on the subject, believing the scandal of Islam's treatment of women was manifested most strongly through polygamy, divorce and child marriages. She was not alone, however, and the archives are littered with similar references by many of her colleagues.

Missionary analysis of the Iranian situation was based upon an understanding of the natural link between a false religion and its resulting social degradation. By extension, Christianity was regarded as the solution to this problem and the means of breaking the destructive cycle. In an uncomplicated way the CMS women passionately believed the national embracing of Christianity would establish necessary theological structures from which alleviation of Iran's social problems would flow. Accordingly, they perceived themselves as requisite catalysts for bringing about the necessary transformation. For by proclaiming the gospel message they could lead the nation and its people out of darkness, into the light of Christ. Writing about potential converts, Dr Stuart explained: "they are seekers after truth and *we* intend to give them the opportunity of finding it" (my emphasis).[59] Similarly, on her transfer from Isfahan to Yezd, Biggs was encouraged to be "the messenger of glad tidings to very many, who humanly speaking would otherwise have no one to lead them to the Truth".[60]

Two pertinent issues are raised by the missionary women's interpretation of Iran's socio-religious degradation and their perceived role in its redemption. The first concerns the inevitable ambiguities resulting from their participation within the feminist movement during the age of empire. Through attempts to define their own identity and justify a woman-centred public role, the CMS missionaries undoubtedly participated in developing the women's cause. However, they also continued succumbing to basic tenets of the imperialist agenda, defining the Orient and Occident as diametrically opposed and behaving with a kind of benevolent maternalism towards Iranian women. The second relates to their somewhat schizophrenic approach in understanding the social reality of their day. These two topics will be subject to discussion for the remainder of this section.

The construction of a direct causal relationship between Iran's religion and its social problems, together with faith in the catalytic nature of CMS's efforts, means the encounter between missionary women and Persian women could be interpreted as a straightforward power relationship. For implicit in this meeting between West and East was a belief that missionaries were in possession of what *they* believed the women of Iran needed. However, for the purpose of this book, concerned primarily with the role of CMS women within the context of Victorian Britain, a more complex critique is essential.

By proclaiming their vocation and delineating its objective, the British women were, in fact, defining themselves and discovering their identity as Christian missionaries and western women freer to participate in the church's mission abroad than at home. Through this process, however, they concurrently defined Iranian women according to their own perception of reality. Persian women - regarded as those who needed what the missionaries offered - became the "other", thereby giving credence to the CMS women's developing notion of "self" as autonomous human beings with a valid and justifiable religious calling. In thus defining Iranian women, the CMS missionaries created and defended their own identity whilst denying their Persian sisters the freedom to do likewise.

The equivocal position of women in mission hierarchies was discussed earlier according to Foucault's theory of power discourses and reverse discourses, and Said's notion of "self" based upon some "other" in binary opposition. For the CMS women in Iran the resulting reality was a dualism in which they co-operated in the imperialist agenda whilst at the same time participating in the progress of the feminist movement. As they legitimised their role in working alongside male colleagues, they united with growing numbers of their western sisters in proclaiming the right of all women to define themselves and participate in the public arena of work. Meanwhile, their self definition was achieved at the expense of Persian women, cast in the role of "other" and used as justification for the female missionary purpose. In short, the perceived need of Persian women for the emancipatory Christian gospel became the apology for CMS women's public vocation. Thus, the prevailing imperialist agenda, together with its underlying evangelical tenets persisted, whilst the widespread western gender assumptions, separating the private and public world of men and women began to crumble.

Through willingness to attribute the problems of Persian society wholly to the Islamic way of life, the CMS women exposed a significant rupture in their comprehension of Victorian Britain's social reality. For extremely critical of the unacceptable social manifestations of Iranian Islam, they continually displayed stubborn resistance in the face of problems emanating from their home society with its hypocrisy and oppression of women. Rationalising the Persian situation was straightforward, for adherence to a false religion produced poor social conditions (especially for women), ultimately resulting in a corrupt and immoral society. However, a comprehensive understanding of the British scene necessitated a certain amount of ideological gymnastics based on ambiguous, even paradoxical interpretations of social reality.

Theoretically, the CMS women distinguished and, therefore, separated Christianity from its wider cultural and social environment. However, on a deeper more subconscious level, they accorded the benefits of western civilisation - especially its affluence and the high position they claimed it offered women - to the influence of Christianity. Therefore, just as they interpreted the religion of Islam as directly associated with their perceptions of Iranian social reality, so too they coupled their judgements of British society with prevalent views about Christianity. Whereas a wholly negative relationship was transposed onto the socio-religious connection in Iran, an unrealistically positive gloss was employed in describing the western/Christian correlation in Britain. Several factors combined to enable this generous portrayal of the home environment that had restricted them so definitively until they had chosen to leave.

First, by physically removing themselves from Britain the CMS women effectively freed themselves from the shackles of impeding home conventions and strict gender confines. Their purpose was described in terms of responding to the call of vocation and the Christian duty to follow God's will. However, many were probably aware of the greater opportunities available to them through participation in missionary work. Certainly, once abroad they were released to be more fully themselves in a way that British society, and the church in particular, would not allow at home. Finding scope to develop their talents and utilise their skills in new and stimulating ways, they mistakenly came to regard this freedom as reflecting the situation of all British women. These feelings were compounded by long periods away from home, obscuring memories and concealing the multifarious socio-economic problems facing Britain at the time. Such an apotheosis of British society presented a distorted image of Victorian England and a false representation of the position of women within it.

Secondly, based on the writings of Adrienne Rich, Nancy Paxton has referred to the problem of loyalty facing late nineteenth and early twentieth century British women abroad.[61] The pressures of imperialism and pride in the homeland led to many inconsistencies within the feminist movement, often compelling women to choose between the extreme poles of allegiance or infidelity towards the country they had left behind. The matter was considered entirely straightforward and, ultimately, women were forced to regard themselves either "loyal or disloyal to [British] civilization".[62] While many, in Iran and elsewhere, would have preferred to maintain a critical stance, under severe pressure to conform they ultimately gave in to total allegiance, impeding any possibility for captious or objective analysis. The imperialist agenda was internalised so effectively that rebellion was seldom achieved, for resisting complicity threatened the fragile position which women were beginning to create for themselves.

Overall, the CMS women in Iran reveal mixed responses in their negotiation of the new gender, imperialist and religious questions facing them. Essentially conditioned to accept the basic gender assumptions of their day, they began challenging these by claiming the autonomy to define themselves, travel abroad and take up more public responsibilities within the mission structures. Encumbered by fewer restrictions they tentatively experimented with their new-found liberty. By stretching the ideological boundaries, they participated in improving the future for British women, yet all their efforts remained contained within the non-controversial confines of standard evangelical and orientalist frameworks. Islam was vilified with both religious and social justification, whilst the position of women provided the main motif in undermining the theological and societal structures of Iran. Therefore, the language used to describe their work presents an entirely negative evaluation of Islam, providing no indication that the CMS women participated in the formative advancement of a theology of religions.

Contextualizing and reinterpreting missionary opinions

The information thus far appears to offer little that is positive in terms of openness and sympathy shown by the CMS women towards Islam. The archives suggest their views were in conflict with many of those expressed by the WMC respondents and the report of Commission IV, whilst broadly in line with the general CMS ethos. However, in order not to judge them too hastily or discard them as irrelevant, several qualifications should be noted. These help contextualize the women both within their period and according to their particular circumstances in Iran.

The pressure of conforming to expected linguistic models, writing for an evangelical audience, and working in what was considered a more hostile Islamic environment, all compounded to restrict significantly the expression of views presented by CMS women in Iran. To appreciate them more fully it is vital to look beyond the obvious and superficial, and to search for more subtle means of understanding deeper perceptions and emotions. For the most part the missionaries remained bound by theological and orientalist conventions undergirding Victorian language. However, it is possible to look beneath their words, scrutinising the experiences and events that altered their lives. Indeed, it is through the very act of stripping back the descriptive material which survives, that glimpses of their deepest feelings - which supersede language and touch the very core of humanity - become apparent.

The superficial elements undoubtedly conformed to expected norms, for these women knew nothing of post-imperialist insights and were unaware of the subtleties of gendered language or the intricacies of religious pluralism. Nevertheless, they had embarked on a journey that took them beyond the familiar and kept them there for many years. To survive without becoming despondent, and continue despite constant failure (in missionary terms) implies that the substance of what they experienced was deeper than hitherto suggested. It indicates that their life's work was not so much a concern about ideas but a passion for people. That despite their writings, their deepest motives were nourished through relationships developed with individual friends and the love affair enjoyed by many with the country as a whole. The women remained unable to express these experiences and were perhaps even unaware of them. Yet without the forming of mutual relationships, the palpable depth of love and concern shown towards Iran and its people would have been impossible to sustain.

A broad interpretation of the archival material generally helps delineate the notion of developing mutuality in the relationship between missionary women, Iran and its people. Two issues arise in particular. First, though the women often wrote about Persia and its populace in abstract and detached tones, this should not undermine the genuine warmth and love felt towards the country. Secondly, as the years progressed they remained in Iran because they believed the people wanted them. The missionaries clearly acted on the conviction that they were responding to a need expressed by those amongst whom they lived and worked. A survey of their writings helps depict these themes.

Due to take furlough in 1907, Biggs was clearly not looking forward to her departure and wrote, "This land and people have won my heart and I am very reluctant to leave".[63] In Kerman, Mary Bird was delighted to witness Muslim children read and write during a prize-giving ceremony at a Parsee (Zoroastrian) school. Despite feeling an opportunity for Christian instruction had been lost, her pleasure in seeing the young students fulfil their potential is unmistakable:

> It really was wonderful to hear the girls reading the Koran, and Persian history and ... answering questions in geography, doing arithmetic and writing, and reciting a long Moslem catechism.[64]

During 1900, Henrietta Conner wrote from Ballyneen in Ireland hoping to return to Persia now her health had improved. To endorse the application she enclosed a letter from Bishop Stuart in which he wrote to her, "I know you are a persona grata to the Persian women: for you have sympathy and love for them...".[65]

Yezd seems to have had particular impact on the missionaries, with many revealing immense fondness for the place and its people. Reflecting on her first trip to the city, Biggs remarked, "the people, I think, no one could help liking".[66] Similarly, Dr Elsie Taylor expressed great sadness at the prospect of leaving Yezd after her marriage: "I love it, and the people - and I shall leave a great many friends behind".[67] A number of references show the missionaries regarded Yezd, in some way, as being "home". During the period of British evacuations in the First World War, Stirling wrote from Tehran, thankful to be safe but constantly "wishing and praying for the day to come when we may return to our Yezd homes and our Yezd work".[68] Likewise, on return from furlough in 1923, Ellen Brighty wrote: "Here I am at last safely back in Persia - though I am not to go back to my 'home' in Yezd just yet"; and although busy training hospital assistants in Isfahan, she admitted, "my heart goes out to my own dear people in Yezd".[69]

The sadness often expressed by those approaching retirement or leaving the country for other reasons was usually a result of their depth of feeling for Iran. After thirty-one years as a missionary, Braine-Hartnell wrote: "Such as I love Persia, I suppose it must be retirement now"; and Stirling, approaching her fortieth year in Iran, admitted deliberate delay in sending her letter of retirement: "I suppose having been allowed to be in dear Yezd for so many years makes it all the harder to settle down at home".[70] In 1929 Frances McKitterick was asked to leave the mission as Bishop Linton was not satisfied with her work. Expressing unhappiness at the manner in which she was notified of the decision, her greatest sadness was having to leave Iran: "I am very sorry to give up my work amongst a people I have learnt to love, and am very glad that I have had an opportunity of helping them, even if it has only been in a very small way".[71]

Notably, the affection expressed by missionaries was not exclusively one-sided. Records provide evidence of the love extended by many Persians towards the British women and indicate the high esteem in which they were held. Mary Bird is perhaps the most outstanding example, though letters of gratitude were sent about several individuals, and others were implored to stay in Persia after retirement, though this was against missionary regulations. For example, His Britannic Majesty's Consulate (HBM Consul) wrote to CMS expressing the appreciation of Parsees in Kerman for the work of Dr Ironside who later died in Iran:

> The Parsees said that never before have they received such skilled and sympathetic treatment and especially appreciate the work done by Dr Ironside among their women.[72]

Writing in 1930, Lucy Molony was anxious that PC should not think she herself was asking to remain in Persia after retirement and explained that the suggestion had come entirely from the Bishop and the Persian Church.[73]

Episodes such as these intensified the feeling amongst missionaries that their work and presence, far from being an unwanted intrusion, was welcomed by many Persians. Countless examples show they continued work on the basis of a genuine belief that they were responding to the will of indigenous people. As early as 1897 Bishop Stuart commented on being accompanied by his daughter Annie on one of his journeys in Iran: "My daughter was very cordially welcomed by the ladies of the anderoon at all [the] central resorts, and pressed to come again".[74] Delighted by any warm reception, the missionaries were eager to stress that they did not force themselves upon the people. Mabel Ward, writing about two girls adopted by missionaries, informed CMS of their recent baptism, carefully emphasising that the decision was entirely their own.[75] The overriding sense that the CMS women were responding to an expressed need is perhaps best encapsulated by Biggs:

> It is not us thrusting ourselves upon people but that they go home disappointed for we have not enough workers to do all the visits people would like us to do ... It would be easier if they did not want us but when they ask for us to visit them it makes it double hard to refuse.[76]

It is possible, of course, that Persians were merely captivated by the novelty and unfamiliarity of foreign ways and beliefs. For, notwithstanding the benefits of CMS's medical and educational establishments, missionaries were also a source of diversion - a kind of amusement in the otherwise ordinary lives of many Iranians. Indeed, the missionaries themselves were not unaware of this, though their analysis was usually more optimistic. Soon after beginning work in Yezd, Mary Bird commented that homes were opening up, not just for medical work or out of curiosity to see a foreigner but for teaching and prayer also.[77]

An appropriate contextualization of CMS women in Iran between 1869-1934 should include recognition that complete mutuality between those representing British and Persian cultures was extremely unlikely, if not impossible. At the time, East and West were almost total strangers to one another. Contact between the two worlds was relatively recent and the way towards common understanding and sympathy had barely begun. Indeed, if we are critical of orientalist attitudes common amongst westerners, we should not forget the scorn with which foreigners were often treated by peoples of the East. With specific reference to Qajar Iran, Wright correctly points out that whilst the CMS missionaries represented a motley group, "some broad-minded and tolerant, others ... bigoted and narrow-minded", so also, "arrogance and contempt for the foreigner were not an exclusive British monopoly", for linguistic, religious and cultural differences created misunderstanding and resentment on both sides.[78]

An assessment of missionary attitudes towards Islam and Iran

My eagerness to emphasise context and search beneath the superficiality of historical records underlies the notion that researchers should neither expect nor seek out neatly packaged resolution or straightforward analysis. Human nature, adapting to a new environment or set of circumstances, seldom responds in simple patterns which remain conveniently identifiable after the passage of time. Victorian missionary methods and motives, particularly concerning women, involved a complex reaction to an array of theological, socio-political and economic factors. Moreover, any contemporary evaluation is itself reacting to similar ingredients whose emphasis and priorities, however, have changed considerably.

It would be unsatisfactory, therefore, to judge the CMS women in a simplistic or uncomplicated manner. For the truth is they represent an amalgam of mixed motives and diverse results. Understanding themselves as participants in God's mission for the world, they believed in what they did as worthy and good. Within the context of Victorian evangelicalism, where salvation was only considered possible through Christ, their longing to convert the Iranian people was based essentially on admirable motives. And their desire to alleviate poor social conditions in Persia was a human response to the suffering encountered. Nevertheless, compared with other missionaries of their day, as represented by the WMC questionnaire, their theological views were conservative and exclusive. The generosity shown by many of their colleagues and the positive mood reflected in the Commission IV report does not reverberate in the writings of CMS women active in Persia.

Problems in relating to individual Muslims and linguistic constraints restricting expressions of friendship, were probably less detrimental to their overall views than the criticisms of Iranian society directly attributed to Islam. It is notable that the tendency towards generalisations *vis-à-vis* the country and people of Iran is more typical of the earlier years. There are few such references beyond 1903, and by 1913 they have virtually disappeared. This is most likely a result of developing friendships and deepening love for the nation leading to an unwillingness for universalised condemnation. The same is not true, however, of writings concerning the social ills of Iranian society based on the theological imperfections of Islam. Here, early feelings, expressed through strong language, recur time and again, persisting into the late 1920s.

It seems that as the years progressed, increased contact with Iranian people and developing relationships did impact on preconceived missionary opinions. Subconsciously, a depth of understanding was cultivated and natural affection for the country surfaced. Meanwhile, however, the women remained unable, or unwilling, to express this change in the essence of their writings. They were either incapable of discovering the necessary framework for expressing the shift, or remained cautious about causing controversy amongst their readership. Concurrently, the reality of Iran's social problems constantly troubled them, reinforcing negative views about Islam and the need to work for its destruction. Equally important was the religious assurance of evangelical Christianity with its bold confidence in providing the theological structures for social change. The missionary women's use of religious language and imagery remains consistent throughout the period, reflecting the uncompromising certainty with which they viewed their faith.

They were, on the whole, concerned not to force themselves or their views onto people, believing that in most instances they were responding to a call from the indigenous population. Moreover, where their letters indicate anti-Islamic views, it should be remembered they were designed for a specific audience. In conversation with Iranians efforts were made to avoid offensive or insulting remarks in favour of polite and courteous discussion. This, however, did not diminish personal theological convictions. Today, in an environment of liberalism, this trait makes many Christians uneasy. For uniformity, or at least unanimity, are frequently hailed as the best approach to mutuality and co-operation. Regardless of how inappropriate their theological and sociological agenda may now seem, the missionary women's love for those amongst whom they lived and worked remains authentic. To be sure, it often began as a love they were duty-bound to feel as Christians responding to their Lord's command. But for many, this blossomed into genuine and deep affection, upon which were built relationships of mutual friendship.

There is little in the archives to suggest widespread and rational appreciation of Islam or sympathy towards its theological integrity. However, whilst CMS women remained convinced that religious change and discontinuity were vital for Iran, their overall contribution to the growth of understanding between East and West should not be diminished. Amongst the earliest western women to live for long periods in an eastern environment, the CMS missionaries experienced unprecedented contact with the indigenous population. They operated within the dominant theological and orientalist restrictions of their day, often conforming to, rather than challenging, basic negative assumptions. Nevertheless, through early efforts such as theirs barriers began to break down and eventually the Christian world started to wake up to the need for a more open understanding of its Muslim counterpart.[79] Historically the CMS women were part of a movement promoting greater contact between the peoples of the world, bringing closer together those who had once been total strangers.

Contemporary ideas in interfaith dialogue and global ecumenism are possible largely because of the nineteenth century missionary movement which participated in a move towards globalisation. As a result, the world has become a smaller place and its inhabitants are more aware of their intrinsic relationality. The CMS women in Iran played a less explicit role in the development of religious tolerance than some of their colleagues elsewhere. This should not, however, undermine their implicit participation - through presence amongst, and contact with, the indigenous population - in laying foundations for a more open and sympathetic future.

The use of theological language in expressions of missionary motives

The nature of the archival material available on the CMS women makes it impossible to formulate systematically their use of doctrinal language with specific reference to their attitudes towards Islam and Muslims. It is possible, however, to examine the material, thereby ascertaining the kind of theological images they used to express themselves in relation to their life and work.

The Muslim environment of Iran means trinitarian language is, unsurprisingly, absent from the missionary archives. Images pertaining to the Trinity would have been entirely unhelpful in an Islamic context where the notion of a triune God is utterly abhorrent. For Muslims, the concept of the divine relies wholly on a unitarian depiction.

Allah is first and before everything else One, and it is the Oneness of God that lies at the center of both the Quranic doctrine of God and Islamic spirituality.[80]

More notably, trinitarian expressions are also absent from extracts conveying the CMS women's own understanding of mission. I have already demonstrated how their writings tended more towards missionary work in the abstract rather than emphasising personal relationships. The image of God in a community of three persons - a divine dependency of social affiliation - was, therefore, somewhat redundant. Nevertheless, the three persons of the Trinity appear in the records independently, each employed to express fairly specific aspects of missionary work.

The term "Father" was especially useful as a means of indicating the women's own personal sense of being loved and cared for by God, in work, through safety in travel, accepting disappointment or other similar circumstances. For example, soon after her marriage to a missionary from another society, Mrs Zwemer (neé Wilkes) of Baghdad explained, "I am thankful to our Heavenly Father that although leaving your Society I still have opportunities of engaging in similar work of witness for Him...".[81] Whilst Ethel Procter, on arrival in Persia wrote about her "pleasant journey - just full of causes for thankfulness to our Heavenly Father under whose protection we felt so perfectly safe".[82] And, writing of Florence Wilmott's untimely departure from the mission due to bad health, Bird conveyed her colleague's "bitter disappointment of having to give up the active service in the front of battle", whilst also recognising "her Father's will and hand in withdrawing, as well as sending her out for His service".[83]

Whereas the concept Father was usually used to express a more personal dimension of the missionary women's faith, the Son - in the person of Jesus or Christ - was a salvific figure, leading others to Christianity. Guiding people to a knowledge and experience of Christ was the missionary *raison d'être*, as explained by Miss Guy during her interview for work in the Persia Mission:

> I should try to teach a Moslem (woman) that Christ through His Great Love came to take our sins upon Him (although Sinless) and to suffer and die for us, that we through accepting Him, repenting and coming to Him for forgiveness, may receive pardon for our sins, and Life Everlasting.[84]

Christ encompassed the perfect and integral Christian message. The comforts available to suffering humanity through personal experience of him provided the fundamental difference between Christianity and Islam. The missionary task, as explained by Ruth Salisbury in 1912, was to make him known amongst the people: "I do pray that I may be used very fully in making Christ known and loved in that land".[85]

A personal encounter with Jesus was regarded as sufficient for drawing people towards Christianity without the missionary even realising she had been involved in the process. In 1900 Dr Stuart wrote of a fourteen year old bride brought into hospital after her husband had attempted to set her alight. Describing the girl's poor condition, she explained how attempts were made to ease the pain, for her life could not be saved.

> Then to our surprise she [the girl] began asking for 'the Book' to be read to her and begged us to tell her more about Jesus. In her village she had once before heard of Jesus from a missionary and been touched by the gentle Jesus described and longed to know more of Him ... Ignorant of nearly everything else in the Bible, she yet had grasped in the most wonderfully clear manner the leading truths. She had received so little love in her short life - it was the love of Jesus that attracted her first and remained with her to the end.[86]

These excerpts are an indication of how the second person of the Trinity was interpreted in contrasting ways. First, there was a clear notion of the need for salvation through Christ who has authority to forgive sins and grant everlasting life. This was a more detached conception based on the supreme powers of a transcendent saviour. By contrast, the figure of Jesus expressed the intimacy of human relationships with a loving and imminent companion. Both these representations were necessary for a complete depiction of the Son to emerge in the missionary context.

Finally, the Holy Spirit appears to amalgamate the roles fulfilled by the Father and the Son, through both aiding the missionaries in their personal strength and motivation, and helping create change in Persia and its people. There are frequent prayer requests similar to that of Margaret McClure's in 1900: "May I ask for your prayers that I may be fitted and filled with His Spirit for the work which He has prepared for me".[87] The missionaries whose work was always carried out "in dependence on the help of the Holy Spirit",[88] remained confident that he would provide the appropriate gifts needed at any given time. Describing the urgent need to learn Arabic so she could communicate with the Iraqi people, Wilkes explained in trusting anticipation, "It will be glorious when the Holy Spirit has given the new tongue - His gift".[89] If the Spirit provided linguistic and other relevant skills, the missionaries also maintained he was working amongst Persians to transform the nation. Thus, positive results were often accredited to the third person of the Trinity, such that Wilmott could acknowledge in 1902 that, though the three mission stations - Julfa, Yezd and Kerman - were each at different stages, all showed signs that the Holy Spirit had been at work.[90] Moreover, as explained by Brighty, it was through the missionaries that the Spirit would become active and achieve success: "... all are united in longing for the Holy Spirit to work through us in our mission work".[91]

By far the most common theological motif employed by the CMS women was, simply, God - a broad term, covering the multitude of experiences and emotions encountered. The concept of God was useful in two particular ways. First, the notion of a *loving* God was stressed as the central Christian doctrine within a Muslim environment where absolute divine sovereignty was a far more potent idea. Secondly, the use of God-language reflects, to an extent, the "first stirrings of the importance for missiology of 'theocentricity' rather than 'christocentricity'".[92] This was especially true of Christian missions in Islamic lands where the concept of God was shared by both religions, providing a sure and safe foundation for contact between the faiths.

Both the CMS women's sense of vocation and the specific location to which they were sent, were invariably regarded as explicitly directed by God. On hearing of the decision to send her to Persia, for example, Dr Taylor wrote, "I like to feel that it is the place that God has chosen for me".[93] Similarly, Adamson spoke of "the privilege of being chosen to serve in Persia" as

> still further proof of God's loving guidance, for all along He has so lovingly and patiently led me step by step towards the work He so clearly called me to ... I know God's hand was in it all and I thank Him for the many lessons He has taught me through it.[94]

This notion of being chosen was often referred to in terms of a calling from God. Dr Evelyn Constable, for example, having already left Persia before hearing news of her former colleague's death, wrote to CMS confident in her sense of vocation:

> Whilst realizing my own utter unworthiness I am convinced beyond any possible shadow of doubt that God is calling me at once to fill the vacancy in Isfahan left by the Home Call of my beloved friend Dr Catherine Ironside. I go in direct opposition to my mother's will but Matt X.35 and X.37 justify my action.[95]

The women were equally inclined to see the hand of God calling them away from a particular place, even if he had recently led them to it. One year after she arrived in Persia, Kate Mothersole was ordered home due to medical reasons. She wrote at length about the strangeness of having been called to Persia only to leave it again so soon, but was sure that everything was part of God's plan, both for her and the school in Yezd where she was working.[96] Similarly, Lily Buncher expressed great disappointment when, on furlough, she was declared unfit to return to Iran. However, "I feel sure it is God's will for me, and therefore accept it as straight from Him, knowing He must have some wise purpose in it all!"[97]

This simple faith enabled the CMS women to see God in everything, continually detailing all aspects of their life. In happiness at her impending marriage, Martha Adamson wrote, "It is an unexpected joy that has filled my life; and we both trace the hand of God in the way we have been brought together...".[98] Equally, reflecting on the recent death of Mothersole, Brighty commented,

> How strange God's ways are sometimes to our poor human sight, and yet I am confident that He makes no mistakes and that 'all is right that seems most wrong' in this as in all His dealings with us - for He loves and knows.[99]

And reflecting on the cancer from which his wife suffered, Bishop Linton noted, "[she] feels so sure that God is going to bring blessing to others through her pain".[100]

The convenient use of theological shorthand means there are virtually no references to the missionaries' *own* views or personal feelings about unfolding events. One unusual exception appears in a letter by Annie Stuart, asked to stay in Kerman longer than she had expected: "I feel very strongly that I <u>ought not</u> to be away from my work longer than a year: it is a larger and much more important work than what I am doing here".[101] For the most part, that which the women longed or hoped for was seldom expressed openly but camouflaged by religious language that made it seem acceptable. In 1914 Gauntlett, keen to give up nursing and become a full time evangelist, wrote,

> It is with a strong sense of my unworthiness for such work but at the same time with an acute sense of the hand of God upon me that I offer to resign my present post as nurse (when I can be relieved by another taking my place) and suggest myself as a candidate for the position of assistant evangelist to the Women's Hospital.[102]

Outlining a number of considerations that led her to this decision, she identifies the first as "the manifest call of God".[103]

The evangelical culture and gendered hierarchy of the mission structures combined to create an atmosphere in which the explicit expression of personal opinions was virtually impossible. It has already been argued that modification rather than destruction of the separate spheres ideology was a path followed by certain strands within the Victorian women's movement. Moreover, the extension of women's roles, especially within religious feminism, relied upon a development of female vocation based upon self-giving service. This emphasis on the sacrificial aspect of women's vocation produced a paralysing effect, muting the expression of the CMS women's personal views. For their duty as evangelical missionaries was further compounded by their conditioning as women to submit their lives to obedience of God and service of others.

The tendency towards Calvinistic predestination allowed for elements of fatalism in the missionary women's approach towards life and work. This, in a sense, united them with Iranian women who, through their own culture's gender limitations, were also disempowered from affecting change. Ironically, the Persian predilection towards fatalism was severely criticised by missionary women as a further reminder of the evils of Islam.[104] Yet at the same time, they cultivated the notion themselves by accepting the decisions of CMS and interpreting them as the actual word of God to be quiescently obeyed.

Paradoxically, however, the women were not entirely passive victims within the mission structures. For just as they worked within acceptable gender boundaries, developing notions of social maternalism and other means of improving their position, so too they utilised the benefits of conservative theological convictions to their own advantage. Religious rhetoric provided camouflage for resistance, by disguising personal views in terms of God-language and divine will. This presented the women with a further means of subtle subversion, aiding the advance of feminism without the need for open rebellion.

Whilst believing that the three persons of the Trinity, or more generally God, would work through them to bring about change in Iran, the women's evangelical convictions meant they laid great emphasis both on the Bible, as an essential tool of evangelism, and the gospel, as a powerful instrument of conversion. Simply hearing the gospel - the good news of Christ - through teaching or proclaiming God's word in the Bible, could lead to a change of heart. Accordingly, many prayed that they would not hinder the power of the good news but allow it to "have free course and be glorified".[105] From the earliest days, the CMS missionaries were unequivocal in their belief that the only necessity was for the word of God to be preached as widely as possible, and all their efforts were directed towards making that possible. Mary Bird unashamedly explained this to those who came to her dispensary:

> There are several other villages within easy riding distance from which patients have come, and now are asking to be visited, though I have told them, if Christians come we must bring the Gospel with us.[106]

The early educational work also reflected this missionary incentive as explained by Isabella Read: "Persian is taught in the school in the hope that when doors open, some of these girls may be able to carry the gospel to their Mohammedan fellow-country women".[107]

The CMS women were passionate about their duty to proclaim the gospel in Iran. Their presence and the example of their lives was never considered sufficient as a means of evangelism. In 1894 representatives of the British government in Persia, concerned about demonstrations against the mission, pleaded with CMS to abate explicit evangelisation whilst continuing with their humanitarian activities. The missionaries reacted with a formal statement:

> ... While ready as loyal subjects of Her Majesty to render all due honour and obedience to Her Majesty's representatives in all matters in which we can conscientiously do so, yet we cannot deem ourselves justified in ... desisting for one moment from endeavouring to evangelise the Muslims of Persia. Our reason for this resolution is that our Divine Lord's last command was to preach the Gospel to every creature and to carry it to the uttermost parts of the earth...[108]

Whilst declaring loyalty as British citizens, their religious convictions demanded greater allegiance and without the gospel, their work was of little value. For all medical, educational and other philanthropic efforts were nothing if not employed within the gospel context which ultimately held the solution for all Persia's problems. As Stirling wrote in 1896: "The women in this land do so much need the Gospel message to help them in all the difficulties of their life".[109] This missionary insistence on both spiritual *and* physical well-being - most apparent in the example of Mary Bird - is in stark contrast to later more secular ideas about mission as social justice. Yet within the context of Victorian evangelicalism the missionary ideal of combined efforts for the benefit of body and soul "embodied a significance that only the unimaginative could deny".[110] Today's priorities, which often lead to embarrassment in the face of explicit religion or unease at spiritual potency, should not be used as a yardstick by which to determine the rights and wrongs of a previous generation's missionary methods.

The longing of the CMS women in Iran was to lead individuals to personal faith in order to extend the kingdom of God. However, it is not always clear whether the kingdom was seen in terms of the afterlife or the faithful community here and now. God - transcendent and other - was sovereign of his kingdom but he could rule on earth as well as in heaven. So, news of a death in the mission was often presented in metaphorical language which was, nevertheless, quite clear: "On Advent Sunday morning [Miss Valpy] went in to see the King in His beauty".[111] By contrast, references to the king's *realm* were usually less specific. For example, Stubbs' precise meaning is unclear when she prays "that God may fill us with His Spirit, so that we may glorify Him, in thought, word, and action, and so win others for His Kingdom".[112] Similarly, Adamson's reference is ambiguous: "It is so comforting to know that He understands all one's longings and sees every effort which is made to extend His Kingdom ...".[113] Such equivocal allusions to the kingdom of God were probably intended to encompass the significance of Christ's body on earth *and* the salvation of souls in eternal life. For both aspects were equally important within the religious understanding of the women, thus becoming almost indistinguishable in their references.

Accordingly, they represent the paradox of the "now" and the "not yet" which is of great significance, socially as well as theologically, to the contribution of the missionary women in Iran. For diverse interpretations of the eschaton are helpful in understanding the hopes and aspirations of their feminist motivation as well as their religious *raison d'être*. Each generation that has contributed to the ongoing women's movement has hoped for more than immediate success in the improvement of their own conditions. Rather, they have participated in a wider operation which spans generations, always longing and working for a better future for those who have not yet been born. In other words, the historical feminist movement encapsulates the "now" and the "not yet" in a comparable way to the Christian doctrine of God's kingdom, and both these elements may be seen in the thoughts and actions of the CMS women in Iran.

This reflection upon the theological language utilised by the women has highlighted the extent of religious motivation in their missionary work. They were resolute and single-minded in carrying out their duty to spread the good news across the world, for they believed it was the only way in which "truth" could be encountered. In many respects they conformed to the standard patterns of Victorian evangelicalism, whilst at the same time ingeniously adapting some of its tenets. Their good intentions were often patronising in tone and yet the spiritual source of their life's work was a deep and genuine humility which took them close to the people whom they served and helped them develop sincere relationships. Always aware of their human frailty, they considered themselves to be "God's messengers"[114] who could do nothing alone, but were willing to be used as servants in a higher plan.

Looking beyond the superficial and searching for the reality that motivated these women, one can see genuine love and deep religious motivation. Undoubtedly, the linguistic and ideological contours of Victorianism continually limited their outlook and the tenor of their writings. Nevertheless, they achieved much whilst also remaining aware of their own need to receive anew the message they were seeking to pass on. Lily Buncher speaks for them all when she asks, "please pray that I may first be taught of God myself, before I attempt to teach others".[115]

The themes explored in Part I provide the theoretical and ideological background for the work of CMS women in Iran between 1869-1934. Victorian British society, and its manifestation within the empire, has been examined according to several dominant discourses in areas of orientalism, feminism and evangelicalism. In this chapter, the CMS women themselves have taken centre stage and been introduced within the theological context of their age, with specific reference to the newly developing theology of religions.

In Part II each of these areas will receive closer inspection through the biographical details of three individual women. Mary Bird whose work in the area of evangelism represents the essence of the missionary aim will be discussed first. Her life and work highlight, in particular, further considerations arising from this chapter regarding the attitude of CMS women towards Islam and Muslim women. Having set the broadest missionary context through the work of evangelism, Isabella Read - chronologically the first of the three women - is presented as an educationalist and one whose ideas cast light on the pertinent influence of orientalism. Emmeline Stuart, a later medical practitioner, is the subject of chapter 7. As an influential figure she had a profound impact upon the Persia mission and the role of women within it. Her contribution is of particular interest with regard to the development of western feminism.

Part II

CHAPTER FIVE

Mary Bird:
A Passion for Evangelism and a Heart for the Women of Iran

The role of evangelism in the work of missionary women

Women's work within the CMS Persia mission has been described in terms of three primary categories: evangelism, education and medicine. Each of these should be regarded as playing a significant part in the progress of the British women's movement within the missionary context generally. For opportunities to evangelise, teach and practise medicine allowed Victorian women to develop their skills and improve their own condition whilst also striving to ameliorate the position of indigenous women.

Though the three areas of women's work seem distinct and self-contained, in fact there was a significant degree of overlap between them. Ultimately, the primary aim of each missionary was evangelism and all strove to spread the gospel message of salvation as the basis of social improvement. Theoretically, therefore, the practical work of teachers, doctors and nurses was set within the context of the missionary task to evangelise and remained subordinate to it. However, the paucity of workers and the physical needs of people they encountered meant in practice, time was often unevenly divided between explicit evangelism on one hand and the exercise of professional skills on the other. Those set aside as evangelists frequently found themselves drawn into the realm of more practical activities. Meanwhile, educationalists and medical workers struggled to maintain the required balance between welfare work and spiritual responsibility. This inherent tension will become increasingly evident during the course of the next three chapters.

The phrase "evangelisation of the world" had gained common usage by the end of the nineteenth century.[1] A deep longing to see this task fulfilled, and the faith that made it seem possible, provided the motivation for many potential female missionary candidates.[2] The intentions embodied within the term "evangelism" or "evangelisation" were understood in fairly specific ways. The word was used in reference to the process of spreading the gospel through proclamation of salvation in Christ and the call to repentance, faith and new life in the Holy Spirit. This method relied upon belief in the power of God to act through missionaries as passive vessels or messengers of the gospel.

On the mission field, however, this idealistic concept required tempering if it was to become a realistic vision. Missionaries soon found meeting the physical needs of the people amongst whom they worked was an essential component of their task. The CMS women in Iran were not exceptional in their early realisation that efforts to Christianise were more likely to succeed if they had something more tangible - such as medical treatment or educational opportunities - to offer Persian people. In addition, the CMS women were moved by the suffering they witnessed to progress beyond preaching into activities for advancing the physical condition of Iranian women and elevating their position in society.

It was, therefore, through a combination of desire for professional success and more altruistic motives that the missionaries recognised the need for a more practical gospel. The theory of pure evangelism remained at the heart of mission ideology and continued infusing the evangelical language it relied upon. However, its application expanded to incorporate practical elements in an effort to improve social conditions.

This tension between the words and actions of missionaries, or their "sayings" and "doings", is an underlying element within the work of the CMS women, and nowhere is it more obvious than in the person of Mary Bird. Her language consistently conforms to the standards of nineteenth century evangelicalism at its starkest. Yet her conduct presents a notion of mission far greater than the narrow confines of pure evangelism. Eager to win individuals for Christ in an effort to procure their salvation after death, she also represents an ardent desire to work for the redemption of whole *people*, not merely souls, in terms of all their relationships. Her concern was for salvation here and now, as well as in the life to come, thus reflecting the tension between the "now" and "not yet" inherent also in the doctrine of the kingdom of God.

Throughout her career in Iran (1891-1904, 1911-1914), Mary Bird remained committed to the notion of evangelism as the essence of missionary activity. Despite her practical skills and the extraordinary manner in which she employed them, she always considered herself, first and foremost, an evangelist. For her enthusiasm and commitment were based wholly upon a desire to lead people to Christ. However, whilst her writings may suggest adherence to narrow evangelism in the worst sense, her life was an example of a more rounded approach. Bird, fully persuaded of the need to carry out Christ's commission to preach the gospel throughout the world, never lost sight of his teachings on issues of human dignity and justice. In achieving this balance, she set a pattern for women's work in the CMS Persia mission and laid the foundations for future work amongst Muslims.

Bird's significance within the Persia mission and her challenge to contemporary feminism

Mary Bird is undoubtedly the most famous CMS woman to have served in Iran. Her name lived on for many years in Persia where she worked for a total of sixteen years, died unexpectedly and was buried. Also, unlike most of her colleagues, she is occasionally mentioned in more general missiological studies.[3] More importantly, Bird is one of very few women from the Persia mission who wrote a book about her time in Iran.[4] As a result of these and other archival sources, more is known about her early life and time in Iran than any other female missionary. Despite this, the resources remain frustratingly limited, for there is not yet any analytical study reflecting on the impact of her work from a late twentieth century perspective. Publications are restricted to uncritical reminiscences of her life or to passing references in which she is only briefly quoted.

Nevertheless, Mary Bird enjoys the privilege of being the best remembered of all her female co-workers. This is partly because she was one of the earliest single women to work for CMS in Iran at a time when little was known about Persia. At the end of the nineteenth century, the very idea of a young unmarried woman travelling such distances to work in a land shrouded in the myths of an exotic and unfamiliar East was still unusual. The dangers involved fed the imagination of missionary supporters and fuelled stories about untold bravery and romantic possibilities. Consequently, Mary Bird (and Laura Stubbs with whom she travelled) are often affectionately remembered as "the first unmarried lady missionaries to visit Persia".[5] This is in fact incorrect, for Isabella Read of the Society for Promoting Female Education in the East (FES) had already been in Julfa for nine years before Bird's arrival. However, Read's work was amongst the Armenians and it was alongside her that Laura Stubbs would operate. Bird, meanwhile, was the first CMS woman especially assigned to work amongst Muslim women in Iran and in that sense she was clearly a pioneer.

Bird was, in short, a colourful and potent personality, deeply committed to her vocation and much loved by a wide range of Persians and Britons alike. In the archival sources alone, though her writings are not as prolific as some, she stands out as an extraordinary woman, determined and strong, yet with a gentle disposition. Compared to many, her time in Persia was short but her impact was keenly felt and her influence long lasting. She paved the way for later work amongst Muslim women, unconsciously leaving a trail in which others found it difficult to follow. One missionary preparing to work alongside her was warned, "You are going to have a fellow-worker who does the work of six men and lives on biscuits and eggs. Don't copy her".[6] Bird's love for the women of Iran, combined with intense commitment to evangelism, render her a fascinating and important figure in the overall evaluation of the CMS Persia mission and its female missionaries.

Clearly, she played an important role in the early history of CMS in Iran. More than that, however, Bird's life issues a challenge to late twentieth century feminism. For it would be easy to dismiss her as a woman of restricted vision, enslaved by linguistic, religious and ideological expectations of her day. The challenge, however, is to look beyond the superficial in a willingness to learn lessons from Bird without expecting to endorse all her ideas and the manner in which she expressed them. She herself would probably be appalled and confused at the possibility of being termed a feminist, and many today would regard her as having no place within the women's movement. In her achievements, however, and the way in which she won the love and respect of those whom she met, Bird defies an entirely negative appraisal and demands an unconventional place in the history of the women's movement.

Her methods would be unacceptable today, but considered within the context of her time, she is impossible to dismiss. Bird combined genuine humility with utter confidence, and an unfailing spirit of adventure led her into new possibilities that extended the boundaries of acceptable behaviour for British women. Moreover, her life was spent in an effort to improve the condition of other women, and for that alone she takes her place within the historical women's movement. Mary Bird represents a religious strand within nineteenth century feminism whose expression was somewhat contorted due to the language and influence of evangelical and orientalist ideologies. This strand did not motivate women towards active involvement in organised politics or the fight for equality. Nevertheless, it emanated from a similar source, for it grew from a concern for the well-being of womankind and found its expression in a woman-centred approach to life and work. The aim of this chapter is to reflect upon Bird's career and assess her contribution critically, whilst remaining open to the possibility of learning from her in unexpected and surprising ways.

Chapter Five

The beginnings of a missionary career

Early life and development

Mary Rebecca Stewart Bird was born, the fifth of six children, on 23 June 1859 in County Durham. Her father, the Reverend Charles Bird, was Rector of Castle Eden and her mother, Harriet Oliver, was the daughter of a doctor from whom she learned elementary medical skills. The Bird family was well connected, including such names as Isabella Bishop (neé Bird) - the travel writer - who was a cousin of Mary's father, and the famous religious figures, Archbishop Sumner and William Wilberforce. Mary's credentials for missionary work, therefore, were in place from an early stage.

From childhood, her nature was "a large unselfish one",[7] whilst her physique was small and delicate. "Tiny" - the name given her by siblings - was the first of many nicknames used by others and herself. From a young age, she had a great love for animals and showed a keen desire to be helpful whenever possible. Accounts portray her as a happy and playful, yet somewhat unusual child, with single-minded determination to become a missionary. Descriptions from her early life reflect the romantic Victorian fascination with exotic foreign lands which ensured that missionaries on furlough were showered with high esteem and lavish adulation.[8] According to Clara Rice, a missionary from Africa visited the rectory when Mary was five and aroused her interest with vivid stories about his work, asking if some day she too would like to be a missionary: "'Yes,' she replied, and always after considered herself pledged to this work".[9]

Powell believes that, unknown to anyone, Mary began preparing herself for work abroad as one by one her siblings left home.[10] Learning much from her mother's dealings with parishioners, she was also a companion and "right-hand man"[11] to her father, for much of her girlhood was spent visiting and teaching the poor and needy. At a time when female missionary candidates were assessed according to their experience of philanthropic work, Mary's home life provided valuable training for her future.

Imagining Mary Bird growing up, one sees a playful and carefree character cultivating a solemn intent from an unusually young age. This is just one small example of the many contradictions that made Mary the perplexing person she was. On one level, she was the most straightforward of women, clear in her intentions and fearless of expressing them. Yet the dichotomy between her words and actions, flowing at times in tandem and then drifting apart, make her difficult to comprehend, for she seems to defy definition. Ultimately, to grasp her intent and appreciate her life, Bird must be seen within the context of her time.

Exceptional in many respects, Bird was not an innovator ahead of her age but rooted deeply within the nineteenth century and its dominant ideologies. Essentially a product of the social and religious environment of her day, Bird regarded the influence of "the false prophet Mohammed" as responsible for turning Persia into "this seething mass of moral and social corruption".[12] However, to dismiss her on the basis of words like these would be to profoundly misunderstand her nature. For Bird also had a vision of a better future in which women, free from suffering, would be fulfilled and whole. Her life was spent in an effort to bring about this future in the only way she knew how.

Perhaps more than any other CMS missionary her strong and earnest desire was for Christianity to be established in Persia. Christ alone, she believed, was the solution to the country's problems and it was her duty, therefore, to evangelise: "We are 'put in trust with the Gospel'; dare we hold it back from those who are perishing for lack of it?"[13] She gave what she could, in order to secure a better life for the women of Iran, intending to improve their immediate conditions as well as their spiritual life after death. In short, her career was an expression of deep love and commitment towards the people amongst whom she worked, and her achievement was in the love and affection returned to her by them.

Arrival in Persia and the first phase of Bird's work, 1891-97

In 1886 Mary's father died and she announced her desire to become a missionary, though it was not until 1890 that she began the limited preparation CMS offered her. The few months spent at The Willows training centre for women proved a difficult time. Used to working on her own initiative, Mary found the restraints of community life with its inevitable rules and regulations trying. She also struggled with the nature of an entirely female environment. Echoes of this are evident in a letter she wrote to her mother some years later:

> It seems to me women living alone, or even together, get into ruts and narrow little ways much sooner than men, and generally find it harder to give and take, though, of course, there are grand exceptions to the rule.[14]

The constraints she expressed concerning an all-female institution reflect something of the frustration Mary felt within the bridle of Victorian society generally. For the restraints on women - contained within the dominant separate spheres ideology - were simply more pronounced within an environment where men were absent. The Willows was an establishment where *all* inhabitants, by nature of being female, were expected to conform to certain norms of acceptability, and in which there was no expression of the male experience needed to make reality seem complete. The result was an intense encounter with the crippling limitations of the women-only realm of Victorian Britain. That which made up the sum of women's admissible experience was exposed starkly, and its inherent frailty was felt palpably by those with an adventurous and sensitive nature such as Mary's. However, unable to express this from within her nineteenth century context, Bird regarded it as a problem emanating from woman's nature as narrow and shortsighted. For her, reality was wider than those experiences in which women were legitimately permitted to partake and during her time in training she began to feel this keenly.

On 7 April 1891 Bird was formally approved as a CMS missionary. Africa was the land that sparked Mary's initial interest in a missionary vocation, and it was there she had hoped to work. However, Persia became her destination in an appointment considered by CMS to be a dangerous and risky experiment. It was with a sense of uncertainty about the future that on 18 April 1891, Bird and Stubbs set out on their voyage which lead eventually to Julfa in Persia (see photograph 5a).

The journey took the women via Berlin to Odessa, where they crossed the Black Sea to Batoum. They travelled through Russia to Baku and boarded a steamer across the Caspian Sea to Enzelli, where another boat took them along the lagoon to Resht on the northern edge of Persia.

Chapter Five

Having already journeyed two-thousand miles, they still had a five-hundred mile trek across Persia, taking a further twenty-one days on horse back. According to Chappell, "the journey was a tedious one, though they experienced several modes of transit".[15] Mary herself does not speak of tedium, though she writes graphically about the experience of travelling in Persia, mentioning in particular the over-night accommodation, very far from standards to which she had been accustomed in England (see photograph 5b). The rooms were

> ... built of mud, festooned with cobwebs and soot, a hole in the roof to let out the smoke of the fire, a lattice, sometimes no opening but the doorway to admit light and air, which is the more easily done when the door is missing![16]

5a. Mary Bird as a young girl in 1875, and as she was in 1891 when she set out for Persia[17]

Few Victorian missionaries wrote in detail about their outward journeys or the problems that they encountered. For many, despite inevitable discomfort and difficulties, the experience remained novel and exciting. However, according to Byrne, they seldom offered particulars because they "were not travelling for travel's sake",[18] but aimed to arrive at their destination and begin the work they were sent to do. Certainly, Bird's letters relate more to her understanding of *why* she was on the journey. Her enthusiasm is evident, both in her generous nature and in these early attempts to make spiritual connections for readers at home. For example, struck by the lack of water as they crossed the desert, she persuaded their muleteer to share their supply with a group of Persian travellers. She wrote, "We had yet to learn no water meant no life - God grant that Persians may soon learn that no living water means perishing souls".[19]

5b. The accommodation at the Murchehkhor caravanserai, 1901.

Changing strategies and conflicting ideologies in the CMS Persia mission

It was a small group that Mary joined in Julfa early in June 1891, yet those first few years were an important and formative time in the mission's development. After fifteen years official presence in the country, since 1875, CMS was now becoming more established. Hitherto, most of the work had been carried out amongst Armenians as Isfahan remained largely closed to foreigners and access to Muslims was extremely difficult. Mission strategy to influence Muslims through the Armenian people had inadvertently resulted in a number breaking away from the Orthodox Church to set up a separate congregation. The educational work in the CMS schools in Julfa, meanwhile, continued its objective to train Armenian youngsters for work amongst their Muslim countryfolk.

Bird's arrival represented a shift in the emphasis of missionary work, for the CMS team was now resolved to "devote our efforts in the main to direct work amongst Persians, rather than to seek to influence them indirectly through the Armenian congregation".[20] Within this broad agenda, Mary was assigned to pioneer work amongst the women of Iran and accordingly played an important and influential role in setting patterns and establishing future methods.

Her priority on arrival was to learn the language, so most of Bird's time was spent studying. However, always anxious to be active, Mary taught English classes in the Armenian Girls' School and gave Bible lessons on Sunday afternoons. As soon as possible she began visiting Persian women wherever she found a welcome. The inevitable culture shock is underplayed in her writings, though it was clearly deeply felt.

> Miss Bruce has taken me to visit some Persians who live near. It all seemed so strange. At the door you take off your shoes; there are no chairs or tables in the rooms, you sit cross-legged on the floor. Soon cups of very, very sweet tea without milk, and fruits, are brought in on trays and set before the principal guest; taking the cup in both hands they hand it, saying, 'You are welcome in the name of God'; you must answer, 'May your hands never be tired'; they reply, 'May your

head never be tired.' Then the questions begin. 'Why do you not paint your face?' 'Why are your nails and hair not dyed red?' - this is supposed to show holiness ...[21]

These early days, as she struggled to express herself in a new language and begin the work she had come to do, were a real test of Bird's patience. Accepting that "this waiting time is very good for my impatient spirit",[22] she longed to be effective in the mission, to talk about Christ and to share her faith with the people she met. However, she dared not "speak on religion just yet, as they would begin to argue, and many words with totally different meanings are so alike in sound, that I might assent when I ought not to".[23]

Mary was convinced of the need to influence the female component within Iran's population if change was to be effected in the country as a whole. However, the transformation she envisaged and which motivated her efforts, was never straightforward or clear-cut. Her theology shaped her belief in the women as "a matter of the greatest importance in the evangelization of Persia",[24] suggesting she regarded them as the most likely means of ensuring the success of her religious ambitions. However, Mary was also driven by an acute awareness of the physical anguish she perceived, regarding the women as "the greatest sufferers"[25] in Iran. She noted that from birth, the lives of girls counted for little next to those of their brothers. Not considered worthy of education, they often married as young as ten and were later frequently required to endure the humiliation of polygamy or divorce.

The misfortunes she witnessed, combined with the Victorian ideologies and religious sentiments that had shaped her, encouraged Bird in her efforts to ameliorate Persian women's condition in this world *and* the next. Evangelical assumptions meant she associated the suffering she encountered with the religion of Islam whilst confidently presenting Christianity as the solution to all social problems. Meanwhile, appropriation of the imperialist agenda meant she regarded herself in a superior position, able to provide the necessary help. However, it was the woman-centred approach to her work, emanating from the same concern for female progress in Britain, that convinced Mary of the need to improve the condition of women in Iran. All these factors combined to ensure Bird willingly provided for the physical needs of Persian women, whilst never relinquishing the longing to accommodate their spiritual needs through the hope of salvation now and after death.

One sees in Mary Bird's life the conflicts arising for missionary women from prevalent ideologies in Victorian Britain. This tension runs through her career, reflecting both negative and positive impacts. A blind passion for religious conversion as the solution to Persia's problems and an inherent superiority in western capability is balanced by a genuine desire for the progress of womankind. Though these contradictions were not unusual in theory, Bird maintained their balance in such a way that her contribution stands out over that of many others.

Undeniably, the source of her motivation was always religious and, ultimately, she regarded inner peace as more important than physical comfort. Concerned that "... in the hour of anxiety, sorrow or death, the Moslem faith gives its followers no sure and certain hope nor divine consolation", Mary continually told the women that the gospel contained within it, "the secret of life, peace and joy".[26] Yet the depth and sincerity of her religious convictions meant the outpouring of her faith in the shape of benevolent works was more than a belief in her own superiority and a very genuine desire to lessen suffering and pain where she could.

Realistically, however, this was seldom possible. For the physical problems of Persia were too immense even for the best and most motivated philanthropic will in the world. This left only the spiritual dimension, both as a reservoir to encourage the missionaries themselves and as a source of hope to offer the women they encountered. The hopelessness of the social reality made it difficult for the missionaries to maintain ceaselessly the impetus for continuing work. But assurance in eternal life, together with the peace which faith could provide for mortals, provided an underlying framework for the CMS women's motivation. Mary believed that if she could guide Persian women towards personal faith, then she had helped them find something greater than the possibility of temporal alleviation in this life. For inner joy and comfort were realities that no-one could take away and, if sustained from within, would ultimately lead to the possibility of social change for women. Regarded in this way, Bird's life can be interpreted in a more rounded manner. The dualistic separation of spirit and body, apparent in much of her writings, becomes less difficult from a late twentieth century perspective when considered within the context of her entire contribution. For ultimately, Mary was concerned for the well being of *whole* women, perceiving no need to prioritise between spiritual and physical needs.

Never wavering in her assurance that Christianity offered the perfect solution, Mary was acutely aware of the magnitude of the task ahead of her, feeling great inadequacy in the face of it. "The more I see of the work which ... lies before me", she wrote in her first annual letter, "the more I feel how unfit and unworthy I am for it".[27] Such sentiments reflect genuine humility as a substantive part of Bird's personality. Always maintaining a realistic sense of her own abilities, she longed to be made more suitable for God's service. Her letters frequently include prayers that God would "cleanse and sanctify me that I may be fitted for His service, and enabled to testify for Him by a consistent life as well as by word".[28] Humble and modest though she was, Mary was also boastful and jealous of the God in whom she had complete confidence. All her abilities, she believed, were divinely given and only found fulfilment in God's service. Success, likewise, was always credited to God, for "issues of life and death" were all with "the Great Physician".[29] Though she enjoyed her work and found it satisfying, its purpose was to glorify God, not achieve a personal agenda. "I am sure", she wrote, "if God should see fit to use me to help any of these poor people, they will see at once the power is His, not mine".[30]

It is difficult to imagine how daunting the future must have appeared to Mary in those early days with no role models or proven working techniques. She was neither medically trained nor a teacher qualified to pioneer educational work for Muslim children. Yet her delicate physique hid a strong and stubborn personality, fearless in facing the unknown and optimistic enough to bypass early disappointments. Thriving on sheer faith, Mary had the assurance to know she was doing God's will, and that confidence gave her courage to face the uncertainty and danger she encountered.

Certainly, her task was exciting as well as challenging, but it would be wrong to think of her career as romantic. The life of a single foreign woman in Qajar Persia was far from idyllic and Mary Bird should not be remembered in the fanciful terms perpetuated by Victorian orientalist ideology concerning the exotic East. She was, rather, setting out on a lonely path which would lead her into unknown dangers and an early death. Yet it was this woman who became the foremother of much that followed in the Persia mission. For Birdie, as she came to be known, was fully involved, alongside the early men, in establishing the whole ethos of the mission as it changed its focus from Julfa towards Isfahan and developed greater work amongst Muslims.

Establishing work amongst Muslim women and laying the foundation for future efforts

Transformation of a class system within missionary women's imperialism

To ascertain a pattern for work among Muslim women, Bird began by familiarising herself with scenes and customs of Persian life.

> The women were the principal subjects of her study, as she sought to acquire a sympathetic understanding of both their outer and inner life.[31]

She was keen to make contact with as many Persian women as possible in order to gain their trust. Her efforts to form friendships with the rich were occasionally successful, however, generally she found the poor more accessible. Bird's eagerness for contact with wealthier women reflects a more general attitude within the mission as a whole. For Mary and her colleagues believed that lasting social change for Persian women could most successfully be realised through the efforts of their own counterparts, in other words, the middle- and upper-class women of Iran. This faith in the higher echelons of Persian society was based upon an appropriation of a similar class-based ideology underlying the western women's movement at the time. For in Britain, the upper-classes were regarded as responsible, and better able, to ensure lasting social change for their working-class sisters.

However, the transferral of this philosophy into an Iranian context relied on a subtle shift in emphasis. In British feminism, upper-class women were contrasted in a straightforward and diametrical manner against the lower- and working-classes. In Iran, whilst there was eagerness to reach wealthy women, ultimately *all* women were grouped together, and set up in antithesis to the missionaries themselves. A class-based ideology still existed, and is apparent from the missionary desire to influence wealthier women in Iran. However, an added imperialistic dimension based on a religious definition of Muslim versus Christian, and/or a racial definition of eastern versus western, also entered the equation. This justified the female missionary vocation to convince *all* Persian women of the need for conversion and change. Accordingly, whilst eager to reach the upper-class women of Iran, Bird was equally critical of them, finding them too interested in material things and little inclined to show interest in religious matters. Indeed, she considered them in many respects "more shameless than the poor".[32]

Whilst the missionary aim was to aid women, in the process an invisible yet impenetrable barrier, constructed from the values of empire, was set up differentiating between eastern and western women. The intrinsic ingredient of orientalism, regarding East as essentially "other" and by implication inferior, entered the woman-centred agenda of the missionaries, distorting - though not negating - their role within the history of feminism.

Victorian evangelicalism and the liberation of British women

Realising that contact with all types of Persian women was more difficult than she had expected, Mary soon found they received her more readily if she had something to offer. In this, she represents the realism of missionaries in the face of theoretical evangelical theology with its emphasis on pure evangelism as the sole required ingredient for conversion. Mary began her early tentative steps by teaching a number of girls and women to read and knit in the few homes where she found a welcome. Returning from one such visit, she noticed a woman crying in the street and on enquiry discovered her boy was ill and she could not afford the doctor's fees. Uncertain about Mary's proposal that they should pray, the woman eventually acquiesced before willingly accepting quinine which Mary hoped would cure the boy of what she believed was malaria.

Occurring within several months of Bird's arrival in Iran, this incident marked the initiation of her future work and, on reflection, represented to Mary herself, the opening of a door by God.[33] The boy's health was restored and "no sooner was he better, than the mother told all her neighbours [Mary] was a doctor".[34] No amount of protestation availed and Bird soon found women and children visiting her daily in the hope she could cure their physical ailments. Despite her own concerns, Robert Bruce encouraged Mary, assuring her that the women were safer in her hands than many of their own superstitious Persian doctors.[35] According to Powell, Bruce convinced Mary that though she was not a doctor, she could offer the women of Iran "a little English common-sense, a good deal of English cleanliness and hygiene, and - the maximum amount of Christian faith and charity".[36]

Very quickly Bird's work, and with it her reputation, began to grow. A room was rented in Julfa, acting as a dispensary for two or three days each week. Mary studied any medical books available and, before the arrival of new reserves, made use of stores left over from Dr Hoernle's time.[37] Women soon began to trust her, coming to the dispensary in increasing numbers and begging her for home visits. She became affectionately known as *Khanum Maryam* (lady Mary) or *hakim Maryam* (Dr Mary) and the mission soon understood the significance of her accomplishments. In July 1893 Tisdall paid her the highest tribute by recognising her work as a "medical mission", informing CMS that within the last twelve months she had received 9401 patients.[38]

Despite the apparent success, Mary maintained a clear sense of her limitations. She never attempted treatment beyond her capabilities, nor claimed any form of medical expertise. Jokingly referring to herself as a "quack", she was anxious to avoid misunderstanding and stressed, "I am *not* a 'qualified' person ... nor do I wish to advocate 'quackery'".[39] Perhaps mindful of a medically trained sister at home, initially appalled on hearing of Mary's activities, she remained cautious and was respected by later medical missionaries for this.[40] Nevertheless, Bird firmly believed that God had called her to this work and would not, therefore, send away those who came for help but was glad to "do a little for these dear women".[41]

Despite the success of such unconventional medical work, evangelism remained at the centre of Bird's missionary agenda. Her practical skills provided the opportunity of reaching people and, whilst she willingly helped them physically, it was the desire to share her faith and preach the gospel which motivated her actions. Her efforts to alleviate corporal suffering were underpinned by a deeper longing to bring the people to a place of inner healing and spiritual health:

> From the first my greatest desire was to tell the sick ones of the Great Physician who still, though now invisible, goes about doing good to *soul* and body.[42]

Religious preconceptions convinced Mary that Muslims knew nothing of a loving God they could turn to for comfort. It was her duty, therefore, to help them towards understanding the divine Father who loved all his children equally. The prioritising of evangelism in Bird's life and work was perhaps exacerbated by the fact that she was trained for no other profession. Instead, she found meaning in her strivings when embarked upon the one area in which she felt assured. For Mary was sent to Persia to evangelise and it was through participation in that aspect of missionary work that she found confidence and security.

Accordingly, the medical care she provided was never isolated from an opportunity to evangelise. Unlike Persian doctors, Bird accepted no money from patients but they soon understood that the Christian message was a component in the package she offered. Prayers and readings were an established part of the dispensary pattern and patients knew exactly what to expect. Initially many objected to prayers in Persian rather than Arabic, as was the Muslim custom. However, soon their complaints subsided and some, who had first come only for treatment, grew willing to listen to the gospel, frequently asking for it themselves.

From a late twentieth century perspective it is easy to see limitations in Bird's attitude to life and work. The naivety of her faith in a quasi-medical approach and the priority of evangelism in her missionary method may now seem unsophisticated at best and crude or even dangerous at worst. Within their historical context, however, these elements are marks of the way in which British religious women participated in one strand of the developing women's movement. Despite the restrictions of evangelical ideology on the role of women within the acceptable private sphere, many - like Bird - used faith as a resource for expanding their opportunities. It was Mary's uncomplicated evangelical beliefs that convinced her of her vocation to help the sick and suffering women of Persia. Her ardent religious faith enabled her to take risks in the hope that new possibilities would arise for herself and the women of Britain, as well as those she met in Iran. Without this assurance, Bird was unlikely to pursue such an unorthodox and potentially reckless career, for the safety of convention and precedent had a strong hold over Victorian women.

Faith also gave to Mary Bird the confidence to express her calling and vocation in definite terms and act accordingly. Her perceptions were hampered by linguistic and ideological restrictions. Yet her vision for a better future for women drove her to work for change and improvement in their social and spiritual condition. Like many in her day, she remained uncritical of methods based on mistaken assumptions and limited understanding of eastern people. However, her efforts to ameliorate the position of Persian women, whilst expanding the possibilities for British women, characterise her enterprise as woman-centred, giving her a place in the history of feminism.

Christian imperialism or a mission of wholeness?

Having sought to justify Bird's significance within the wider context of the historical women's movement, it remains necessary to consider more closely the methods that she utilised. For it would be easy to regard her as excessively spiritual, caring little for the ills of the body as an end in themselves but using them merely as a means to conversion and religious change. Indeed, her writings did tend towards a more potent expression of this side of her personality. However, it should be noted that Mary was naturally attracted to a more practical approach to life and the spiritual dimension was the one she strove to improve. "Energetic and ready for any secular task", in her youthful enthusiasm in particular, she often displayed an "evident disinclination for definitely spiritual work".[43] Her struggle to redress this instinctive imbalance was life-long and perhaps intensified the religious aspect of her writings. Colleagues recognised that her self-conscious efforts towards spirituality caused a tension in which "the *intense* side of her character was the religious one", whilst in her actions she remained ready for "whatever came of spiritual or secular work".[44] For Mary herself, the conflict was never resolved and after years of missionary work she still strove to withstand the temptation of preaching less and doing more:

> Sometimes lately it has been such a temptation to cut short the teaching, the sick ones need so much attention, and it is a difficult question to know what to give up. The Devil always whispers, 'Teach less to-day, to-morrow you will be less hurried,' and as I listen I know it is a lie - he will do his utmost to make it still more difficult to-morrow.[45]

This desire for emphasis upon the explicitly spiritual was typical of many Victorian missionaries. There appears, at times, to have been an almost intolerable tension between the philosophy of their methods, based upon the evangelical ideal of pure evangelism, and the reality of need for social action. Nevertheless, both elements continued in a surprisingly comfortable coalition. Theoretically, social action submitted easily and was subsumed in the jargon of missionary philosophy. In practice, it retained a vital part within the missionary method, though it was seldom given equal expression.

This co-existence of spirit and body is an apparent feature in Mary Bird's life and is best expressed in terms of a dichotomy between words and actions. For she remained entirely within bounds of the language expected of her, yet her efforts to improve the social condition of Persian women are no less significant because of this. Considered in its entirety, it is clear that Bird's contribution was not based upon a dualistic advocation of soul over body. However, she expressed these elements in different ways. Whilst her concern for the spiritual is most fully asserted in writings that adhere to expected norms, her actions speak volumes about the regard she had for the temporal needs of people. Even amongst her contemporaries Birdie was known as one whose "doings [were] much greater than her sayings",[46] and this should be remembered as a significant factor in interpreting her life.

Bird represents a missionary approach of holistic care *expressed within the context of late nineteenth century Victorianism*. Close examination reveals a woman for whom body and soul were intimately linked, but whose theology ensured the emphasis of salvation through Christ over and above the need for participation in humanitarian acts. Her medical skills were used in an effort to reach people's souls, however, that need not imply that the corollary was an unloved or uncared for body. Rather, it suggests that her *raison d'etre* was found in the combined healing of body *and* soul. Both elements were equally necessary for, as explained by Mary in answer to critics of the missionary movement, the extraction of one distorted the fullness of the vision:

> Some people in England seem to think 'it is a hardship and unfair to *force* religion upon those who do not wish for it,' but where is this done? As I often told any women who wanted to have medicine given them before prayers, 'You know our rule is to have prayer and Bible teaching, yet you have come of your own accord; if you do not approve, you are free to leave us and go to your own Moslem doctors.' Ought we not to apply the same reasoning to spiritual matters as to temporal? Which of us would applaud the surgeon who, rather than cause his patient an hour's suffering, refused to use the knife, but thought nothing of sacrificing his life? Would it be less culpable for missionaries to shrink from offering those who come to them a perfect cure, which has never been known to fail, because it might entail suffering for a time?[47]

Bird never considered turning away any who came for help, for she resolutely believed in the importance of medical work in providing "for the care of suffering bodies as well as souls".[48] She displayed no partiality in treating those with an inclination towards conversion, compared to the majority without. Her single rule was that patients should *listen*, in the hope that their hearts may be touched. For she was ultimately a missionary, not a social worker - motivated by the spiritual, not so much the physical. Her methods were explicit and rooted within the same source that gave rise to her sense of vocation. Nevertheless, her life in its fullness was an example of the complete care to which Cragg refers as the essence of religious calling. For, he argues, "Christians are not called to organize philanthropy dissociated from the love of God in Christ. Nor are they called to a rescue of the soul that ignores society and sickness".[49] Mary Bird was an example of one whose life and work were a self-conscious effort to achieve the right balance between these two aspects of the missionary vocation.

Growing opposition and the threat of female initiative

Bird's methods were apparently proving successful. Her medical efforts expanded so considerably that by mid 1893 the mission was urging CMS for more staff to help with the growing amount of work.[50] CMS eventually responded and, as additional women were sent to aid Birdie, a pattern began to establish itself with routine dispensary arrangements in Julfa. Prayers were said twice daily as work began, and again two hours later for the benefit of subsequent arrivals. A number of Persian women enjoyed the religious content, often returning once their treatment was complete or staying for the second session having already received their medicine.

Growing confidence from achievements in Julfa soon convinced Mary to venture into Isfahan. This city, well known for religious fanaticism, had hitherto remained closed to missionary activity and foreign presence generally.[51] In a respectful attempt to show solidarity with Muslim women, Bird's first visit was made in native outdoor costume. However, on hearing that people thought she was ashamed or afraid to be known as a Christian and was attempting to gain admittance into their houses in disguise, she gladly changed the *chador* for an English cloak and veil.

Both Bird's initial decision to wear a *chador* and the Persian reaction to that choice are notable. I have previously discussed the CMS women's developing notion of "self" in opposition to their construction of Persian women as "other", suggesting that the perception of differences between the women aided the missionaries in their search for identity in an otherwise male context. The contrast between the attire represented by the two cultures was undoubtedly a powerful and potent symbol of that difference, and one noticed by both English and Iranian women. Yet on this occasion, Bird made a deliberate choice to minimise the visual distinction in an extraordinary act of mutuality. Given the relief with which she discarded the *chador* and the dangers she later faced, it is unlikely the gesture was undertaken merely as a means of self-protection. Rather, it was a sign of her commitment to the work she was called to do. Mary's affection for the women of Persia gave her a sense of affinity with them which superseded, in most respects, the differences she perceived. The result was a desire for closeness, in order to better understand and know them. Perhaps more than any of her colleagues, Mary was able and willing to blur the boundaries of difference between her notion of "self", and Persian women as "other". However, her faith and ardent belief in the superiority of Christianity ensured that the differences remained, leaving an inevitable chasm between English missionary and Persian women.

It is significant that the Persian reaction to Mary's efforts for commonality proved it to be misguided. The ideological importance of the *chador* in representing the public/male and private/female division of roles in Iranian society was extremely powerful. In this instance, Mary's choice to wear the veil was perceived as a threat to the normality and security of social convention. An unknown foreigner did not fit into the recognised sphere of Iranian womanhood merely by virtue of her sex. In fact, her deliberate choices to part from the commonly accepted female role placed her more within the public realm of men. In other words, Persian women also recognised an "otherness" between themselves and the CMS missionaries. Whilst they sometimes respected and even envied the possibilities represented by these British women, they were, certainly in the early days, threatened and uncertain. For Mary Bird, as a single autonomous woman with a mission, presented them with a public dimension to the familiar private world of women.

Despite initial problems, Mary's open personality and persistent character, together with the medical advantages she offered, gradually broke down barriers. As the women began to trust her, relationships were formed and friendships created. During this period Mary became increasingly active in the mission hospital, helping with the treatment of patients wherever possible. The fame of the mission's small medical team had already spread far and wide and patients travelled great distances in the hope of receiving a cure (see photograph 5c).

Chapter Five 99

5c. Patients arriving at the hospital lying on a donkey, and in baskets or panniers across the back of a mule

Concurrently, however, as she won the confidence of women, Bird also attracted growing hostility from the Muslim leadership in Isfahan. The real breakthrough came when, on 4 January 1894, a women's dispensary was opened in the Bidabad district of town. Popular with many ordinary people, those in authority grew increasingly concerned that Bird's work was leading to the conversion of their womenfolk. She herself only wished "that the statement were true!"[52] In reality, conversions were virtually non-existent, yet Mary had touched a nerve by influencing the women to act independently in visiting her dispensary and continuing contact with her. The threat they perceived was not Mary herself but the effect of her work upon their women. For the authorities were fearful that if women's position in Iranian society were to change there would be a shift in the social equilibrium.

By February Mary was regularly attracting hostility instigated by local leadership. Assaulted with verbal abuse, she was pelted with stones and mud whilst cycling or riding to work. Soon the *mullahs* were preaching openly against her and forbidding women from attending the dispensary. Many persevered, however, coming either at daybreak or in secrecy across the flat rooftops of neighbouring houses.

Years later, after Bird's death, a fellow missionary commented that Mary had "alarmed the opponents of the Gospel ... far more than the rest of us put together".[53] Certainly, she became the magnet for most of the opposition faced by the mission in those early years. The events are recorded in detail throughout the archives though, notably, never by Mary herself. There are countless letters by male colleagues and British officials in Persia about Bird's influence between 1893-5. But history has recorded her, primarily, as an object of other people's responsibilities, concerns and solutions rather than the subject or active agent within unfolding events. Though she refers to these episodes in passing, modesty and a service mentality appropriate for Victorian women prevented her from dwelling upon them in detail.

The growing threat of serious violence eventually led the mission to request help from the British Consul in bringing the situation under control. Bird herself seemed uneasy about this, feeling keenly the privilege of having "so much protection as British subjects".[54] In the event, the British Minister did little other than oppose Christian missionary work in Iran and request that it be abated. Initially the mission refused compliance and soon the situation was further inflamed when a local *mullah*, Agha Najafi, called for Bird's execution. However, on this occasion, the Shah himself intervened, ordering the Prince Governor to ensure Bird's safe-keeping.

Subsequently conditions eased as the missionaries agreed that Bird would not visit Isfahan during the holy month of Ramazan. However, no sooner did she recommence her duties than the problems were inflamed once more. Eventually, after the owner of the dispensary was beaten for letting property to Christians, the clinic was moved to Dardasht, a Jewish and less volatile quarter of Isfahan. Work resumed intermittently, whilst opposition persisted and the *mullahs* continually tried to prevent women from visiting Bird. She believed, however, that their actions were merely harming their own cause whilst benefiting that of the mission.[55] For though threats were constantly issued against her and women banned from visiting, large numbers still appeared, with as many as 168 registered during one day.[56]

The above events depict the ambiguous feelings of Persians towards Mary Bird in particular, and the mission and Britain in general. On one hand, she was loved, or at least respected, by those who continued to visit the dispensary despite warnings and threats. On the other hand, opposition grew both towards the mission and herself.[57] For *Khanum Maryam*, as well as being a friend to many, came to be perceived as a threat to Islam and the Persian way of life.

By the end of 1896, CMS had nineteen missionaries stationed in Iran. Eleven were women, of whom five were single and, therefore, registered officially. As the first phase of Bird's life in Persia ended, four female converts represented the fact that her efforts and those of her colleagues had not been in vain. The story of Sakineh in particular, the "first-fruit" of missionary labours among Persian women, became famous in mission circles and led to a great deal of suffering and persecution on behalf of the woman herself.[58] Yet, together with the other three converts, she was a sign of hope for the future and the cause of much rejoicing.

Professionalisation of the mission: Phase two of Bird's work, 1897-1904

Having worked tirelessly to pioneer "medical work by and for *women*"[59] in Persia, Mary Bird approached her first furlough in 1897. Arrangements were in place for the arrival of the first woman doctor, Emmeline Stuart, later that year. The mission, however, grew increasingly convinced of the need for an overlap period between Bird's departure and Stuart's arrival.

> It is very important that Miss Bird's most valuable work should, as far as possible, be carried on without any break - Her dispensary must be closed if she goes away before Dr Stuart arrives, no other lady here being qualified to carry on that part of Miss Bird's work.[60]

PC was eventually convinced, agreeing that Bird would delay her departure to allow for an overlap between the two women.[61]

Soon after Bird's departure, however, it became apparent that the nature of work would change considerably under the leadership of Dr Stuart. The emphasis would shift from the somewhat ad hoc dispensary and house visiting towards a more formalised approach in establishing a women's hospital in Julfa (see photograph 5d). Whilst some missionaries expressed reluctance, perhaps feeling protective of Bird, change was inevitable and, as rationalised by Bishop Stuart, there was no reason why "Miss Bird's work, however much we have had reason to be thankful for it, could not be improved upon".[62]

There is little reason to suppose Bird was worried by these developments. Indeed, the arrival of a female doctor and the opening of a hospital were the fulfilment of what she had been working towards. There are no indications that she found it difficult to work with new or better qualified colleagues. By contrast with several other strong personalities or influential characters in the mission, Bird was never knowingly the cause of any controversy. Expressing genuine delight at the arrival of doctors, she extended a generous welcome to both Donald Carr and Emmeline Stuart. Looking back, she wrote, "We thank God He had put it into their hearts to devote their talents and life to the sick and suffering ones in Persia".[63]

5d. Although the emphasis of the women's medical work shifted more towards the hospital after Dr Stuart's arrival in 1897, the dispensary continued as a vital part of the mission's outreach. This photograph shows a group of patients waiting to be treated at the Jubareh dispensary in Isfahan, c 1905.

Despite Birdie's generous spirit, sensitivity prevailed and the mission agreed that, "To keep her in Julfa, working side by side with Dr Stuart, would be a most undesirable loss of power".[64] It was decided that on her return, she would initiate work at the new missionary station in Kerman.[65] Unexpectedly, however, and not long before departure from England, an objection was raised about her new appointment. A male missionary in Kerman by the name of Blackett, "urg[ed] that Miss Bird should not be allowed to proceed to Kirman ... as he considered that her presence would be an embarrassment rather than a help to the work".[66]

Blackett disapproved of Bird not being a qualified doctor, and also expressed concern that she was female. Believing the Kermanis would only accept the presence of a woman if she were a doctor, Blackett insisted that "the advent of a lady missionary will at present be fraught with serious consequences".[67] The integrity of his reasoning is doubtful, however, for just two months later he was equally vehement against the appointment of Dr Urania Latham.[68] Whilst the precise nature of his displeasure remains unclear, it seems likely that Blackett was uneasy about working with female colleagues, especially those who were skilled and successful. Such competition from male missionaries was probably not unusual at a time when women's increased involvement issued a threat to male supremacy. Nevertheless, Blackett's attempt at such explicit control remains an exception within the life of the Persia mission between 1869-1934.

The remainder of the mission resolutely opposed Blackett, urging PC to inform him that his views were "entirely at variance with those of all his fellow missionaries".[69] Blackett, however, refused to withdraw his objections, forcing SC to pass resolutions against him, in

Chapter Five

support of Bird.[70] Disregarding this, he further angered missionaries by appealing to the British Consulate to convince CMS in England that the presence of women in Kerman was unacceptable. Conference urged PC to ignore the threat, deeply regretting Blackett's actions in undermining CMS's authority.[71]

Amidst the controversy she had unwittingly caused, Bird arrived back in Persia and was ordered to Yezd whilst attempts were made to resolve the impasse. There for nearly two years, she once more maintained the silence considered appropriate for a woman's calling to Christian service and became the object of other people's concerns and opinions. Never expressing partiality, she simply stated her position as "ready to go or remain here, just as it seems God's will, if He will only allow me to bring back one lost sheep, it matters not where it may be".[72]

In May 1901 the final decision was taken and Bird prepared to leave for Kerman. At the last moment she was detained due to Dr Malcolm's (neé Latham) sudden nervous breakdown. Clearly affected by the previous years' events and having made a home for herself in Yezd, Bird finally ventures her own thoughts on the entire episode. Characteristically, however, her views are disguised in theological terms, and never expressed as personal preference. Sending a letter to CMS, she enclosed a copy to Bishop Stuart to whom she wrote, "I do not know if your Lordship will agree with [the enclosed] or not, but it does seem to me that God's restraining hand has been so plainly stretched out that it would be wrong for me not to let the P.C. know".[73]

To CMS she explained that this was the third time the door had been closed, preventing her arrival in Kerman. She was now forced to consider whether her appointment might be blocking the way for work to begin there. Far from interpreting Blackett's stance as a personal slight she regarded the events as being entirely under God's control. By effectively removing Blackett from the process in this way, Bird subtly undermined his authority by reducing it to subservience under the divine will. At the same time, her letter is an example of genuine humility and a desire for the best advancement of the Persia mission:

> The more I pray and think about it the more the conviction is laid upon my heart that God sees He cannot use me for His honour and glory in Kirman, and that is why He has shut the door each time. When I was in London I was told the C.M.S. committee wished me to do pioneer work, and could I do so I would oh so gladly, but indeed I do not think I have any very special qualifications for it more than some of my fellow workers. The only special reason I can see for it is in the medical line, as being unqualified and quite unable to undertake surgical work, I am only fitted to do a little weeding and digging in preparation for a proper medical mission, and as soon as fully qualified workers are sent to move on; but this is not a sufficient reason for my practically standing in the way of other workers being sent to Kerman.[74]

PC, however, disagreed with Bird and, as a clear indication of its authority, instructed her immediate transfer to Kerman where she stayed for the remainder of her time in Iran.

Contrary to Blackett's fears concerning the effect of a woman upon the missionary endeavour, Mary was delighted that "God has granted us a wonderfully open door in Kirman".[75] Not so fanatical as other Persian cities, she experienced less Muslim opposition from the people and found herself free to ride or walk in the streets and bazaar without the threat of hostility. Comparatively little information is available detailing this new phase in Bird's life and the initiation of women's work in the southern region of Kerman that it represents.[76] Much of her time was spent alleviating the suffering caused from widespread opium addiction, and long hours of enforced carpet weaving amongst children in particular. Many of the cases touched her deeply and the experience had a profound influence upon her.

Mary's passion for evangelism undoubtedly remained central to her missionary motivation. Yet the acute anguish she daily confronted, together with the gospel of love in which she believed, continually moved her beyond preaching into actions of all kinds. The Kerman years consolidated the pattern her missionary career had taken thus far. The following is one example of the many incidents she encountered.

> On Friday I saw a poor wretched woman leaning against the doorway ... As soon as I went near I knew by her contracted pupils that she had had a large quantity of opium ... Throwing back her chadar [sic] I found such a fine boy of about a year old dying in her arms ... we tried all we could, but in vain; the little pet died in my arms ... the baby, [the woman] remembered, was playing with pellets of opium; more she did not know. She died the next day, leaving three tiny children, all opium inhalers from birth.[77]

Equally traumatic were encounters with children physically mutilated through hours of carpet weaving (see photographs 5e-g). Girls in particular, some as young as five, were forced to sit in one position for long periods. Scantily fed and unsuitably clad, many suffered from starvation and extreme curvature of the legs. They were expected to walk to work in all weathers until,

> when through extreme weakness and deformity the little ones cannot walk, they are carried to and fro daily ... Then perhaps, one morning they are deposited at the hospital doors for treatment as in-patients.[78]

Bird's time in Kerman was brief, for in 1903 she returned to England to care for her ageing mother. Despite its brevity, however, her influence was deeply felt. A male colleague, Dr Summerhayes, summing up the impact she had made wrote, "There is a wave of feeling in favour of the mission due to Miss Bird's wonderful Christlike work".[79] Upon her departure a testimonial of gratitude was written by the leading inhabitants of Kerman (including the chief *mullah*), which spoke of "Her Highness the English Mariam Khanum",[80] and her care for the sick of Kerman. In a typically Persian association, Mary's religious virtues were linked with her country's political institution as gratitude was extended to the "English Government and nation ... because of such favour and kindness".[81]

Leaving Persia was not easy for Mary whose vocation to the missionary life had neither wavered nor diminished. However, love and loyalty for her mother, together with Victorian social expectations concerning an unmarried daughter's responsibilities, took her back to England for nearly ten years. The tension evident in Mary's experience represents the plight of many single women in England at that time. Regarded as primary carers for ageing parents, pursuing personal goals or responding to a vocational call was firmly relegated to second place.

Mary conformed to this pattern, not complaining, but regarding it as another important phase in her life, ordained by the hand of God. In a letter to her mother, she wrote,

> I know you gave me up fully, gladly, for God's service in Persia, but if you would like to have the poor old spinster daughter with you, I am sure it will be truly God's service to minister to my dearest mother, as well as my delight.[82]

Meanwhile in Persia, her loss was keenly felt both by those within and without the mission circle.

5e. Four little girls brought to the mission suffering from curvature of the legs due to long hours of carpet weaving

5f. The same children after being operated on at the mission hospital

5g. The twelve year old daughter of an English missionary photographed with two twenty year old Persian carpet weavers - showing the extreme effect of long term weaving.

A life spent in the service of God: Phase three of Bird's work, 1911-14

On 17 February 1911 a telegram was sent from the Persia mission to CMS head-quarters, recommending that Miss Bird, whose mother had now died, be invited to fill a vacancy.[83] PC cautiously approved the decision, providing Bird agreed to abide by certain conditions and limitations. The mission's medical work had advanced a great deal since Bird was last in Persia and there was some concern that she would not adjust to the new structures. Bird herself, fully aware that her role would be substantially different, was unworried by the strictures imposed.[84]

At the age of fifty-two, twenty years after she first arrived, Birdie was welcomed back to Persia in September 1911. Work had expanded considerably with the mission boasting forty-five missionaries in total. Of the thirty-two women, nineteen were single. The medical work included several nurses as well as four male and four female doctors. Though Mary had a lower profile now than when she had departed, both colleagues and Persians were glad to have her back. For the first two years she was posted to Yezd where her time was spent visiting in the town and surrounding villages. Still remembered by many as *hakim*, she continued caring for the sick when she could, though the emphasis of her work had shifted more towards teaching and evangelism.

By contrast to the previous occasion, Kerman missionaries were now vying for Bird's presence amongst them. Whilst those in Yezd requested that she stay with them, the Kerman sub-conference passed a resolution saying, "We urgently need Miss Bird here for evangelistic work which no one else can do".[85] In the event, the southern most city was triumphant and at the end of 1913 Bird transferred her educational and evangelistic work to the surrounding villages and city of Kerman, where she also set up a dispensary.

Contact with ordinary folk remained Mary's first love, for it gave her the opportunity of preaching the gospel and "telling the 'Old, Old Story'".[86] Her final article describes a visit to Khebis, a village on the outskirts of Kerman, and indicates that she had retained the ability to communicate with the people of Iran.

> No notice of my coming had been given but the next day by 8.00 am women were beginning to gather to enquire if I knew Persian and whether I had brought medicines for them. Only 35 came and were willing to listen to the Gospel. During the two weeks I was there numbers steadily grew, the highest being 157 in one day. On Sunday I had told them there would be no dispensary but many came to hear the Gospel.[87]

And it was not only women whom she impressed. Persian men, who seldom had contact with European women, often treated *Khanum Maryam* in a very different way. Rice explains how many took her seriously, willing to listen, and argue with her.[88] On this particular occasion in Khebis, some of the village women had assembled while Mary spoke of her faith. "Suddenly", Bird wrote, "I heard a man's voice behind me and saw that the village men had gathered behind a mulberry tree and said they were glad to listen."[89]

Her death, when it came, was sudden and unexpected. Just two weeks after succumbing to ill health, Mary Bird died on 16 August 1914. One of her male co-workers wrote of the shock and "little preparation for so great a loss that we, individually, and as a Mission, have sustained in the 'Call Home' of our veteran Missionary, Miss Bird".[90]

It was customary for the missionaries to have a break from the city during the heat of the summer. In 1914, a number were escaping to the relative cool of a small village, Sirj, in the mountainous region, about forty miles east of Kerman. By mid July all had left except Bird who intended joining them at the end of the month. In the wake of a typhoid epidemic, she was determined to remain until the end of July, keeping open the dispensary and nursing two convalescing patients. Eventually she left Kerman on 3 August, arriving at the Dodson's holiday home at Deh Saheb, fifteen miles outside the city, at midnight, after a long and tiring journey. The following day Bird had a fever and it soon became apparent she had contracted typhoid during her last few days in Kerman.

Emma Petley and Dr Winifred Westlake arrived from Sirj to help the Dodsons care for Mary during her last days. For much of the time she was semi-conscious, passing in and out of delirium before she "quietly passed away on Sunday morning".[91] Her colleagues were devastated by the loss:

> Thus it has pleased our God and Father to call to His perfect rest one [who] has always been to us all a beautiful example of perfect loving devotion to her Master and to those for whom she had been chosen as a witness; and although, humanly speaking, we cannot do without her life and testimony, yet we do know that her life will always be an inspiration to us in Persia.[92]

As in life, so in her dying hours, Mary proved an example to those who were with her:

> Through her illness till unconsciousness set in, she was ever as sweet and considerate as she was in health, and we could not but be struck, how her mind was constantly running on her work here, as she frequently talked in Persian, at one time to patients, giving them detailed instructions about food and medicine, and at others pleading with them to accept our Lord Jesus Christ.[93]

That same evening her body was carried to town on a make-shift stretcher by eight villagers. The weather being hot, her funeral was arranged in haste and she was buried early the following morning at the small European cemetery on the eastern side of Kerman. Conducted by the Rev. A. Boyland, the service was attended by most of the Europeans in town, together with a sprinkling of Persians. This did not seem a fitting end but "under the circumstances things had thus to fall out, and the very many Persian friends who would have been present had they had the news were therefore unavoidably absent".[94] There was, great sorrow far and wide once news of her death became known and the missionaries, despite their own sadness, felt "that the loss really falls heavier on the mass of folk here, rich and poor, for whom Miss Bird would still have spent her untiring energy and intense sympathy, had she been spared for more service".[95]

Bird's life was cut short as she laboured among those whom she loved. In her final letter to a friend she expressed what, for many, summed up her career, yet she still strove towards: "Do pray for me that I may grow in grace, tactfulness, courage, and love. I so much need them for the service God has entrusted to me".[96] Tragic and premature though her death was, Bird would have been happy to die in the service of others. She had frequently answered the question, "'Is it worth while to spend so much time and trouble on such people, to say nothing of the expense?'" with an unequivocal "yes", for she earnestly and passionately believed it was the "highest honour to spend and be spent in His service for 'such people'".[97]

On Sunday 16 August 1914 an era in the CMS Persia mission ended. The memory of Mary Bird and her influence, however, did not die with her. A grave on the outskirts of Kerman, in the southern deserts of Persia, still stands witness to her life and work. As a forerunner of work amongst women, she remained an inspiration to those who followed. For Persians there may have been "but one Khanum Maryam",[98] however, other missionaries continued to receive a warm welcome in many remote villages in her name and for her sake. Soon after she died, Dr Winifred Westlake, who had nursed Mary in the final days, wrote about the impact of her final months.

> The great help Miss Bird rendered to woman's work in Kerman for nine months before her death can never be fully estimated ... In visiting and teaching indefatigable, in medical treatment most successful, Miss Bird reached an enormous number of people of all classes. Her command of Persian conversation, manners, habits, and customs, was truly splendid, and all her gifts were grandly used to the one end of bringing her Persian sisters to Christ.[99]

Interpreting and evaluating Bird's life and career

The ideal of (social) motherhood and a missionary spirituality of self-denial

As a single British woman at the turn of the last century, Mary Bird was not unusual in advocating the importance of motherhood. Contemporary ideas in the field of eugenics had increasingly placed positive value upon the physical function of mothers, adding new dignity and significance to the role. Bird conformed to such ideas through her understanding of motherhood - or rather, Christian motherhood - as essential to any nation's greatness. Indeed, she considered herself lacking in appreciation of the divine because of her status as a single woman without children.

> I think one realizes more fully than ever the preciousness of a mother, a Christian mother, living in [Persia]. The very backbone of English greatness is its Christian home-life. Look what this land is without that! I always feel parents must gain a clearer insight into God's fatherhood than we can, who have not experienced either the greater joys or sorrows of a parent's heart.[100]

Christian motherhood was the foundation of a healthy society and a means of better understanding God. The motif was central to Bird's missionary aim, for "judging from the vast influence of Christian mothers in England, it must surely be a matter of the greatest importance in the evangelization of Persia, that the women and girls should be reached as soon as possible".[101]

Nevertheless, Mary apparently saw no contradiction in her own rejection of this ideal in favour of a spinster's missionary life. She even turned down a marriage proposal from a man she loved, convinced that her future lay in mission work abroad.[102] Her misfortune, like so many women at that time, was being forced to make a choice. For marriage and the potential of motherhood on one hand, and a sense of vocation on the other, represented opposing and inherently incompatible options.

If that was women's tragedy, the response of those who remained childless was not to reject the potency of motherhood imagery, but apply it to their own advantage. Like many others, Bird employed themes from the motherhood motif, using them to legitimatise a move from the private sphere to the more public realm of men. Accordingly, it was possible for single women to retain the central importance of mothers as the basis of society, whilst choosing an alternative lifestyle for themselves. The genius of this was that the social *status quo* was not disturbed. Men were unthreatened, for the ideology which brought women into the public arena was essentially that which legitimised their role in the private world. And single women with a vocation could justify their ventures beyond the conventionally acceptable. Moreover, Christian motherhood was retained as the mainstay of British greatness, thus upholding the traditional values of Victorian society.

At the heart of the motherhood motif lay feminine attributes of compassion, self-denial and service. It was this suffering through sacrificial surrender of self, most acute in a woman's love for her child, that formed a vital element in the shaping of Victorian female piety. A mother's self-giving love was the model to which all women aspired in their service of God and others.[103] For women such as Mary Bird, the example of feminine submission and self-sacrifice was heightened within the missionary context. For suffering through sacrificial surrender was not only the basis of *women's* spirituality but also formed the foundation of *missionary* spirituality. According to Andrew Walls, the modern missionary movement at the height of its success cultivated its own brand of spirituality, expressed essentially through a "self-denying life", with individuals sacrificing country, comforts, prospects and health for the sake of the gospel.[104]

Given the Victorian context of female and missionary spirituality, it is hardly surprising that self-denial and suffering were at the heart of many missionary women's motivation. The theme of purging through suffering, common to many Victorian women, also appears in the writings of Bird. Strangely comforted by the opposition she encountered at the hands of Muslim authorities in Isfahan, she wrote:

> Personally, nothing has helped me so much in my work as this little persecution. The women always said, 'It is all very well; you are a *farangi* [foreigner]; you are safe; but we should be killed if we became Christians.' Now I feel we are much on the same level, and it makes it easier to talk to them.[105]

Indeed, it was the suffering endured by women converts that gained them great respect in the eyes of Mary Bird and her colleagues.

As a Victorian woman, Bird's attitudes were coloured by contemporary ideologies. Imperialistic and evangelical traits meant her missionary approach at times betrayed the patronising tone of racial, cultural and religious superiority. Yet she was more successful than many co-workers in coming close to the people and especially the women of Iran. To be sure, she became a "mother" figure to some but others also called her "sister".[106] For Mary respected the people of Iran and did not look upon them merely as objects of mission but regarded them and their experiences seriously. Above all, she was eager for people to see Christ *in* her before she talked *about* him, understanding that "kindness and courtesy go a long way towards breaking down prejudices, and forming friendships".[107] Any maternalism evident in her approach was a product of the age in which she lived, for she undeniably operated within familiar models. However, Bird's real achievement was her capacity to employ the common motifs of motherhood, service and suffering both towards her own and British women's progress, and as an aid to bring her closer to the people whom she served.

Achieving much within the confines of Victorianism

In his study of women's role in the modern missionary movement Sean Gill makes a passing reference to Mary Bird as just another example of how Islam was viewed in "stock Victorian terms as a religion of the sword whose precepts had little practical effect".[108] On one level this cannot be denied, for Bird was extremely critical of Islam and its social manifestations.[109] Even when acknowledging minimum value, she accorded this to Judeo-Christian influences.

> The symbol of the Muslim faith is the crescent moon, and like the crescent, the religion has but a little light, and much shadow, and its lights, like that of its symbol, is a reflected one borrowed from the Jewish and Christian religions.[110]

In light of later developments in the theology of religions, Bird and her attitude towards Islam and Muslims can hardly be regarded as innovative or forward-looking.

However, as I have tried to stress throughout this chapter, Bird's life must be evaluated contextually and she should not be judged merely on the strength of her written words. In a sense, Mary Bird represents her age *fully*, for her life is an example of the best *and* the worst of late-Victorianism. Certainly, she had little positive to say about Islam, yet as a deeply religious woman she fearlessly followed her calling and paved the way for others to follow. Moreover, Mary was not a negative person. Everything she did emanated from a strong and earnest belief in the positive power of Christianity. She sincerely believed that Christ was the only solution for the problems of Persia and it was that belief which gave meaning to her life, inspiring her to help others find meaning for theirs.

Recognising the constraints which limited her, three things in particular may be said of Mary Bird. First, in her day, "she was not looked upon as a woman with a narrow outlook, or a prejudiced mind".[111] Notwithstanding her evident zeal for spreading the Christian faith, she was in fact, considered open-minded and tolerant, always willing to acknowledge nobility and truth wherever she saw it. Indeed, she was recommended by the Principal of The Willows as the most entirely trustworthy of the students then in training to become the first woman from CMS to be sent to Persia.[112]

Secondly, it must be noted that her writings, which often adhered to the strongly anti-Islamic tone typical of the time, were aimed at a *Christian* audience. For she wrote not even for the general British public but for a specific group of CMS supporters, expecting to be regaled by details of missionary success. Evidence suggests that in conversation with Muslims her use of theological expressions was much more abstract and inclusive.[113]

Thirdly, despite what now seems unpalatable in much of her writings, Bird's life in action does not bear witness to the negativity portrayed in the evangelical and orientalist language she utilised. Unable to express herself in terms of any other framework, it was for her deeds she came to be known, and for those, Mary was motivated by much more positive factors. Letters and articles may suggest a missionary motivation based on anti-Islamic fervour. In fact, it was deep faith in the Christian message which provided the stimulus for her work. Bird's life, considered in its entirety, reveals actions that sprung, not in negative response to Islam, but from an earnest and positive desire to share the most valuable gift she believed could be offered. Clara Rice describes her thus:

> She reproved sin and its consequences, and deplored the darkness of the hearts of men [sic], but more by holding forth the true Light than by seeking to make darkness visible. There was more in her teaching that was positive than negative. It was for building up, not casting down.[114]

Bird was certainly unafraid of criticising social norms where she believed it necessary. But for that she should not be condemned. All cultures have elements worthy of rebuke and Persia at the turn of the century was no exception. Mary's medical work, in particular, meant she witnessed aspects of a society which treated women with little respect, placing scant value on their worth. Married whilst still children, polygamy and divorce often made their lives unbearable. Whilst speaking against social ills where possible, Bird soon discovered the mission was powerless to bring about change. Yet energised by her Christian faith she tried to ease suffering whenever possible, as evidenced by her efforts amongst carpet weavers and opium addicts in Kerman. She apparently enjoyed some success, for the common saying, "'opium has no cure' ... changed to: 'if any one wants to give it up he [sic] can; the Christians have a medicine for it'".[115]

The difficulty from a late twentieth century perspective is that whilst Bird was alive to the wrongs of Islamic Persia, she remained blind to the evils of her own British culture. Unable to identify her experience of relative freedom as the result of living abroad, she rendered invisible the problems of women in England. Discovering her own potential *away from Britain* she reached out in a kind of irrational loyalty to a homeland recreated through distant memories and wishful beliefs. Certainly, the freedom she enjoyed to work, travel and pursue a life outside the home, could be compared favourably with much that she witnessed in Iran. However, it hardly justified such a glorified portrayal of "England and how marvellously God has prospered us since we became a Christian nation".[116]

Exceptional in many respects, Mary was unable to dispute the nationalist agenda within the ethos of the British empire. Willing to challenge sexual stereotypes in Persia, she seemed unaware (or uncritical) of those operating at the heart of English society. Her achievements were in spite of such restricting ideologies and should not be denied because of them. Nevertheless, Mary and many of her colleagues fell prey to the temptation of wholesale comparison, by associating the social ills of Persia with Islam, whilst losing sight of the evils in Victorian Britain, in particular regarding its attitude towards women.

Today many will not understand Mary Bird, just as countless Persians could not fathom her then. Some, of course, will believe she was misguided and wrong, and with the benefit of

Chapter Five

historical hindsight, there is indeed much to criticise. Nevertheless, amongst her contemporaries Mary Bird was an outstanding example of courage, determination, commitment and love. Entirely a product of Victorian attitudes, she overcame many restrictions without disturbing the accepted boundaries of female behaviour. In a secular book on women travellers Jane Robinson writes of Bird and how Persian women's "curiosity soon turned to trust, and trust to love", for,

> Mary was not one of the betrousering and civilizing brand of missionary: at home in her Jolfa dispensary and on her extensive travels with Whitey the donkey into the outlying areas, she grew to respect (if not condone) the Muslim traditions of the Persians, and was able to explain the Christian faith with a potent mixture of deference and authority.[117]

She grew to understand Persians perhaps better than any of her colleagues. Experiencing the extremes of their temperament, from great warmth to violent opposition, she was always eager to make friends and was genuinely moved by expressions of friendship shown towards her.

Above all, Bird passionately believed that Christ could offer the women of Persia comfort in the suffering that no-one else could alleviate. In a mysterious way this touches on something significant. Countless came and went without ever becoming Christians, yet clearly Mary made a strong impact on the lives of many such Persians. Her success is ultimately incalculable for no-one will ever know how many found solace through her vision of a loving saviour, caring for them as friend and brother in their often unhappy and lonely lives.[118] But "results ... are more than those that are measurable",[119] and once more Mary evades being judged by definable criteria.

Eager to speak of her faith whenever possible and rejoicing at individual baptisms, Bird remained aware of the complexities in converting an entire country. She understood that "foreigners can never evangelize a nation", but trusted they had a part to play in "train[ing] the first generation of workers".[120] She may have disapproved of prolonged missionary presence in Persia, for perhaps she had greater faith in the power of God and the wisdom of local Christians. Such notions are mere conjecture, but Mary's part in laying the foundations for the growth of an indigenous church community remains indisputable. Whilst weeping for the plight of Iranian Christians today, Mary would also rejoice at their perseverance and commitment. She would not doubt for one moment that her life's work had been worthwhile, even in the face of such small and apparently insignificant results. For Mary Bird believed in the value of each individual, body and soul, and her passion was undiminished by the numerically small number of respondents.

CHAPTER SIX

Isabella Read:
Mission as an Open Window on Education

The feminisation of missionary education

In the previous chapter I showed how the work of late nineteenth and early twentieth century Protestant missionaries was carried out within the overall context and aim of evangelism. The CMS women in Persia complied with this model which formed the theological bed-rock of the modern missionary movement. As exemplified in the life and work of Mary Bird, all educational and medical work was subordinate, ideologically if not in reality, to the task of pure evangelism. I also sought to indicate the tension this situation created for many individuals. In the first place, a growing realisation developed that as missionaries they would be more welcome if they offered local people a more tangible commodity than merely an alternative faith. Moreover, the physical needs perceived through encounters with the indigenous population led many towards a more practical expression of their missionary task.

Significant growth in educational work was part of this expansion towards a more holistic concept of Christian mission. Increased emphasis on female education in particular created more possibilities for women's participation in the late-Victorian missionary movement. The contribution of Isabella Read as described in this chapter can be regarded as part of this broader development within the overall missionary endeavour.

Protestant and Reformed missions had from the earliest days been pioneers in the field of education. Locals frequently sought after Western education and missionaries were always keen for an opportunity to deliver it. For the centrality of the Bible in these particular Christian traditions meant literacy was essential for would-be converts. As a result, church and school often stood alongside each other on the mission compound as a visible symbol of the missionary aim.

In addition to the emphasis on literacy, missionaries recognised education as a means of social improvement. Whilst religious input was designed to nurture people in the ways of Christian living and ethics, the secular curriculum enhanced employment opportunities and helped develop local industries. Educating indigenous women, regarded as essential vehicles for change, was doubly important, for it was a means of elevating individuals and enhancing society generally. Accordingly, women and girls' education became a vital element within the missionary programme, concurrently giving rise to the growth in numbers of female missionary workers.

The purpose of this feminised education in Persia (as elsewhere) was first and foremost to reproduce the Christian home environment as an indispensable base for a sound and healthy society. Concerned with enhancing the domestic attributes of Iranian women, girls' education was inevitably sexist in emphasis. This included a bias towards homecraft and practical skills such as weaving, sewing and cooking. Nevertheless, girls were also taught to read and write and encouraged to become proficient in less traditional subjects. The early missionary schools for girls represented a dramatic contrast from attitudes towards female education in Qajar Iran.

Increasingly, tension did develop between the desire to cultivate good wives and mothers whilst at the same time producing a vanguard of women as Christian messengers for their families and Persian compatriots. Realisation grew that women could and should work outside the home. Later, especially towards the middle of the twentieth century, training schemes were designed by missionaries and the Iranian church, providing professional qualifications particularly in the traditionally feminine fields of nursing and midwifery.[1] In short, much of CMS's feminised education in Iran developed along stereotypical models, generally remaining within bounds of acceptability. Nevertheless, even the earliest efforts represented a new venture for Iranian women at a time when Persian society provided virtually no place for them in the public domain.

Read's unconventional place within the CMS Persia mission

Strictly speaking, Isabella Read does not fit the subject of this book, as she did not go to Persia under the auspices of CMS. However, the apparent diversion is necessary and important within the overall context of the history of the Persia Mission. For Read was the first single Anglican woman to work as a missionary in Iran, and the first from any denomination to work in the southern part of the country.[2] Sent by the Society for Promoting Female Education in the East (FES),[3] she spent most of her life working alongside CMS colleagues, was answerable to the head of the Persia mission as much as to her own society and was, for a time, paid by CMS. Her deserved distinction for being "first", however, has been overshadowed by Mary Bird to whom history has been much kinder. This chapter offers an opportunity to redress the balance and restore Read's name to its rightful place.

Isabella arrived in Persia long before CMS permitted the employment of independent single women, and she laboured for almost ten years before Bird and Stubbs joined the team in Julfa. Work amongst Persian Muslims being, for the main part, impossible, Read's efforts were directed towards the Armenian population. The influence of Mary Bird in establishing future working patterns cannot be claimed for Isabella Read. Yet her contribution as the authentic forerunner of female missionary presence in southern Persia deserves recording as part of Iranian church history.

The Society for Promoting Female Education in the East: Its ideology and practical significance

To understand Read's life and work, it is important to contextualize it with information concerning the history and aims of her own missionary society. FES was founded as an interdenominational organisation on 25 July 1834 under the full title, Society for Promoting Female Education in China, India and the East. Four years later this cumbersome designation was abbreviated by dropping the references to China and India. The original stimulus for its creation was an appeal by an American missionary, Rev. David Abel.[4] Having worked in China for many years, Abel had grown increasingly concerned that indigenous women, largely inaccessible to the work of missionary men, could not be reached through ordinary efforts. As a result of his powerful and emotional invocation made during a visit to London, FES was set up by several women who also formed the original committee.[5]

As implied by its title, the society's main objective was to further educational work by providing grants and teachers for existing mission schools.[6] Missionaries were sent to train locals in preparation for a variety of tasks, including teaching in day and boarding schools, running orphanages, and organising Bible classes. Despite an emphasis on educational work, FES's primary motive was evangelism and the desire "for conveying the blessings of the Gospel to women of the eastern hemisphere".[7] Its creation represented a milestone in the missionary movement through formal recognition of the importance of women's contribution. FES was the first society in England, and probably the entire Christian world, set up "with the especial object of conveying, by women to women, the glad tidings of redemption".[8]

The notion of women securing salvation for other women, considered "captives",[9] developed into a theological theme within the society's self-understanding. Its role was seen in terms of bringing to an end the suffering experienced by women since the time of Eve in the Garden of Eden. Thus, the terms of the "Herald-Promise of Eden"[10] were regarded as throwing light on the reason for the society's special efforts. The terms of that promise were the placing of enmity between tempter and woman; between his seed and hers. "But", it was declared, "the fruit of his enmity has been bitter, to generation after generation of Eve's sad daughters".[11] Now, however, the gospel provided the power that "opens Harem doors, and proclaims liberty to zenana captives".[12] Moreover, women had participative authority because in Christ there was neither male nor female:

> This is the Magna Charta [sic] of our womanhood, sealed during His life on earth by the Lord from heaven in many significant actions, and signally confirmed, when, having risen from the dead, He committed the Gospel of the Resurrection, *first*, to the lips of women![13]

FES was revolutionary in its blatant proclamation of equality, legitimizing women's involvement in the missionary movement. However, this religiously motivated liberalism declared for western womanhood simply resulted in the transferral of sexism's inherent inequality into another domain. For it was assumed that white women, having discovered their own freedom, would act as saviours to their eastern sisters.

> The foe that entered Eden ... has forged fetters of ignorance, oppression, and degradation for the women; fetters which it might seem hopeless *for other women to attempt to strike off* [my emphasis], if One stronger than the strong man armed had not given us these marching orders.[14]

To be sure, English women were admirably encouraged to define "self" and free themselves from the "other" they were perceived as within the male norms of British society. Yet this very act of defiant emancipation relied upon inflicting the humility of "otherness" upon indigenous women. The inevitability of this shift is at the very heart of Foucault's theory of reverse discourses and Said's notion of "self" as defined in opposition to some invented "other".

FES's promotion of western women at the ideological expense of their eastern sisters reinforces my arguments concerning the ambiguous nature of Victorian religious feminism. Whilst advancing the cause of many British women and thus contributing to the historical development of the women's movement generally, it rarely resisted the dominant ideologies of orientalism and evangelicalism prevalent at home and throughout the empire. Accordingly, western Christendom was regarded as inherently superior in almost every respect compared to its Muslim/eastern counterpart. Thus English women, striving to release themselves from the perceived inferiority of their sex, remained steadfast within a race that continued to define itself as "naturally" superior.

Having begun its activities in China and India, FES soon expanded into other regions as the extent of work and financial support grew. Annual reports suggest Persia was one of, if not the, last and smallest sphere of work.[15] Certainly, Read was the only missionary ever sent there by the society. For the most part, FES was concerned with the selection and support of single women, though they also "assist[ed], in various ways, wives of missionaries belonging to other societies who [were] engaged in similar work".[16] This highly significant factor acknowledged the valuable efforts of missionary wives whose work, for the most part, went unnoticed and unrewarded by the mainstream missionary societies.[17] However, the support of FES towards married women also represented a certain contradiction. For the society maintained the inefficiency of wives as one of the reasons for its inception. Missionary wives, it was believed, were frequently "overpowered with the climate, unskilled in the languages, or untouched ... by the constraining love of Christ" and, therefore, failed to "gain access to the domestic prisons".[18]

This reflects something of the paradoxical role of wives within the modern missionary movement. On one hand, they were crucial to the efforts of mission stations especially as instigators of women's work in the formative years. Their early efforts paved the way for single women both practically and ideologically. For it proved there was work to be done and that female labourers were needed to carry it out. On the other hand, wives, as unpaid labourers, were seldom given formal recognition, training or financial reward.

Missionary wives were torn between two virtually impossible extremes and their extraordinary position was made explicit in the attitude of FES. The society acknowledged and approved their valuable presence by providing a forum for their views to be heard in its publications. Yet it also made clear that missionary wives were not only numerically insufficient but frequently incapable of genuine women's work for which single and independent ladies were necessary.

To carry out its evangelistic and educational aims, FES claimed it sought "careful probation and training, of well-qualified European ladies as Zenana Missionaries and School Teachers".[19] It remains unclear precisely what was meant, in particular, by the reference to training, of which there seems to have been very little. The appendices of *History of the Society for Promoting Female Education in the East* provide the only clues, by mention of a process included within the selection procedure, which appears to be the only preparation candidates received.[20]

As principal missionary organisations began accepting women it was, perhaps, inevitable that FES would become extinct. The society's financial situation had been unhealthy for some years and various appeals were made in the hope of raising more money. However, by 1898 it was clear that efforts were proving unsuccessful and hopes of continuing fast diminished. The opportunity for bringing FES to a suitable and dignified end came just one year later. In July 1899, the final issue of the society's in-house magazine announced the death of their long standing secretary, Miss Webb. The journal ended with a statement that this would be the final issue as the FES had decided to hand over its work to various larger organisations.[21] CMS accepted responsibility for twenty-four Anglican missionaries, however, Isabella Read (though still in Iran) had recently resigned and was not amongst them.[22]

Methodological problems associated with reconstructing a narrative of Read's life

Realistically, it is only possible to create a somewhat hazy history of Read's life and the person she was. Available sources provide patchy information which often leave one guessing at the outcome of events or filling in the gaps by imagining her thoughts and feelings through the thick veil of silence. Factual details by way of written evidence are virtually non-existent, as most FES papers were lost in a bombing raid during the Second World War. Nothing, for example, is known about Isabella's life before her arrival in Julfa other than that she came from Dublin in Ireland and was born circa 1851.[23] She is mentioned on several occasions in the CMS archives but very little appears of her own writing. Nevertheless, these passing references allow her career to be traced from the time of her arrival in Julfa, even though details sometimes remain unclear or incomplete.

In terms of first hand material from Read herself, there are two written sources available in the form of FES news letters. The *Female Missionary Intelligencer* (*FMI*) and *Missionary Pages for the Young* represent most of what remains of FES papers.[24] Read's contributions to the first of these journals in particular, provide valuable insights into her personality, although they rarely offer anything by way of biographical detail.

Apart from the dearth of accurate data, there are other factors making it difficult to study Isabella Read in a systematic manner. Two issues, in particular, cause certain confusion about exactly how she fitted into the mission schema, resulting in lack of clarity concerning her role. First, FES disbanded as an independent missionary society during Isabella's time in Persia. There had always been confusion about who exactly was responsible for her, yet the society's dissolution did little to clarify her position. Judging from the archives it would be easy to conclude that, fitting into neither camp, she was often forgotten or left unmentioned. For example, she never appears on the CMS list of active missionaries and, with one exception in 1894, her annual letters - if indeed she wrote any - are not included in the CMS collection. Secondly, Isabella Read was unique amongst her colleagues in that she married while in active service but did not have her work terminated. Her salary was reduced and her work later affected, but at the time of her marriage she was not forced to resign as a missionary in the way commonly expected of single women during that period.

In some respects Isabella's story is a sad one. Exceptional circumstances mark her as unusual and unique, yet she also appears somewhat lonely and out of place. Isabella toiled for many years as the only single woman missionary in the Persia mission. She represented a different society and continued working almost exclusively amongst the Armenian community even after the mission directed its main efforts towards the Muslim population. Her marriage to an Armenian was ultimately unsuccessful and, without the option of a divorce, Isabella was forced to live with the tragedy of his mental instability. Towards the latter part of her life, she found herself spurned by CMS, the society to whom she had devoted loyalty and commitment for many years.

It is easy to imagine Isabella as a lonely Irish woman, trapped in a foreign country and a disastrous marriage, dying unhappy and frustrated. However, this would serve little purpose in assessing her contribution to the Persia mission and, moreover, would probably be far from the truth. Her stay in Persia (1882-1919) spanned almost forty years - longer than any of her colleagues - and what remains of her writings suggests she was, for the most part, content and fulfilled. To be sure, the FES material represents only the earlier part of her working life, yet it indicates an open and defiant spirit, eager to encounter and learn from new experiences.

Separate from the mission in some senses, Isabella was very much part of it in other respects. Though the mission's emphasis moved away from Julfa, Isabella remained known, loved and respected by many. The Armenian community continued as her primary focus and it was there she made her home. However, at the time of her death, all three of her children were either working for CMS in Iran or soon would be. It is likely that Isabella died a great deal more sanguine than outward circumstances may suggest.

It remains impossible to paint a full colour portrait of Read. Yet even a sketched outline provides enough interest and detail to indicate her significance within the mission and church in Iran. In a way she was a shadowy figure, working on the boundaries of CMS's main involvement in Persia. Yet she cannot be overlooked as an early pioneer, particularly in the mission's educational efforts amongst the women of Iran.

Retrieving the past and weaving a forgotten history

Earlier in this book I discussed the distinction some scholars make between women's history as straightforward retrieval and feminist history as concerned with the past for the sake of the present. I argued that a sharp differentiation need not be made between the two, for both offer insights of import. However, I also emphasised the value of recovering and recreating the lives of historical women, to give them visibility and a voice of their own, as well as providing a basis for critical reflection. Accordingly, in this section I propose providing a chronology of Read's time in Iran, based on information gleaned from various available sources. The inevitable restrictions have already been outlined and should not undermine the project, but highlight the need for creatively re-imagining Isabella's role and her part in mission history.

Early responsibilities for educating girls in Julfa

Having been accepted as an FES missionary, Isabella travelled to Persia with Dr and Mrs Bruce who were returning after a visit to Britain. Illustrating the dominance of *English* power during the age of empire, the FES committee denied Isabella her Irish identity when formally acknowledging her work. For in noting her appointment to Persia, they mistakenly referred to her as "the first who has gone from *England* to that country".[25]

The party arrived in Julfa on 24 November 1882 and the thirty-one year old Read immediately took charge of the school previously set up by Bruce for Armenian girls. She had no formal missionary colleagues for nearly ten years until Laura Stubbs joined her in 1891.[26] Details of the inevitable struggles and hardships Isabella surely encountered are few. Yet the tremendous responsibilities, taken on so early in a strange and new environment, placed an extraordinary burden of expectation upon her. Bruce, clearly pleased with her work, informed both CMS and FES of his delight. To the latter he wrote to

> express our gratitude, not only to your Committee but to our Father in heaven, for the great satisfaction MISS READ gives to all who are interested in the work of our Girls' School. She is the right person in the right place. Her whole heart is in her work, and she is a true missionary, wholly devoted to her work. She not only gives her whole heart to the School, and to her pupils in it, but visits them in their houses, and wins the affections of all by making herself quite one with the people for whom she works.[27]

Evidence of Isabella's dedication and success is also clear from the growing number of pupils the school attracted. During 1884, the number of girls increased from seventy, at the end of the previous year, to one-hundred, and by Easter of the same year two-hundred pupils were in attendance.[28] The work was soon too much for one missionary alone and by 1888 Bruce was eagerly requesting more help. In view of CMS's policy against single women's employment, there was some confusion about which society should take responsibility for this matter. Bruce communicated the need to CMS, requesting that FES be contacted if necessary. However, neither organisation responded positively until in April 1889 an urgent telegram was sent to CMS, imploring one or other society to take action.[29]

Marriage and changing circumstances

The cause of Bruce's sudden anxiety was Miss Read's engagement to an Armenian teacher, Joseph Aidinyantz, employed by CMS and working at the Boys' School. For in accordance with regulations, Isabella was offering her resignation, thus leaving the future of the Girls' School uncertain. Bruce was eager that FES should send a replacement as soon as possible, though Read was willing to delay her resignation for as long as necessary. Moreover, whilst relieved to hear that FES had finally found a substitute missionary, Bruce remained unhappy at the prospect of relinquishing Read. His persistent reluctance in accepting her departure is exceptional and unique in the history of the Persia mission throughout the sixty-fifty year period until 1934. In September 1889 he wrote of his intention to appoint Read as matron of the Julfa orphanage, hoping CMS would grant her a salary of £25 per annum for this purpose.[30]

Chapter Six

Discussions about her future, recorded by almost everyone except herself, continued after Isabella's marriage somewhere between mid-September 1889 and early October the following year.[31] Bruce's determination to retain her services did not wane. He wrote to CMS, explaining the "peculiar position of Mrs Aidinyantz" (neé Read), describing her as "an invaluable worker" without whom "I do not know what we should have done in these times".[32]

The precise nature of Read's changing role remains unclear. There is some ambiguity about whether her hours were reduced or whether she took over as matron of the orphanage. What is certain, however, is that she continued as head of the Armenian Girls' School, retaining her status as a missionary in some form. Extraordinarily, Bruce also persuaded FES to pay her a half stipend of £50 per annum whilst she was needed at the school.[33] Thus, her links with FES continued, though they do appear to have been weakened. The society refused, for example, to send her an extra grant of £10 requested for medical assistance.[34] Furthermore, they shrugged off the responsibility of assigning another worker to Persia, causing bewilderment to Bruce who had been pleading for an additional lady missionary for some time.

During the next few years CMS expanded its work amongst the Muslims of Isfahan. Efforts in Julfa continued, however, and Isabella Aidinyantz remained an important and valuable part of the mission. She maintained her role as school principal, and in 1891 received formal assistance from CMS in the person of Laura Stubbs. By 1893 Robert Bruce had left Persia due to his wife's ill health, although he was still consulted in decisions affecting the mission. Rev. William St. Clair Tisdall followed Bruce as secretary of the Persia mission which was beginning to grow in numbers. A difference of opinion soon developed between the two men regarding Isabella's future role.

Problems arose when it became apparent that Laura Stubbs was dissatisfied with her work at the Girls' School. Tisdall believed she was ready for greater responsibility and, in accordance with his understanding of the agreement between Bruce and FES, advised that Aidinyantz' employment be terminated and Stubbs take over as principal. Bruce was appalled by this suggestion, considering it a misinterpretation of the arrangement made regarding Isabella after her marriage. Writing to Miss Webb, he resolutely pointed out the mistakes Tisdall had made in his assumptions about the case. His letter is of tremendous interest and worth quoting in some length, especially as no written account is available by Isabella herself.

> Your kind promises to continue to pay for Mrs Aidinyantz' services was not 'until some C.M.S. lady missionary should be ready to take her place' - but - 'as long as the missionary in charge says that her services are needed and as long as she does good work' ... Miss Stubbs was not sent out by C.M.S. to take Mrs Aidinyantz' place ... I do not believe that Miss Stubbs could do ... Mrs A's work - but she is very good and will do good in whatever department she may help in.[35]

Thus far Bruce's support for Isabella is somewhat defensive, based - one could argue - on a matter of pride or a difference of opinion and interpretation. However, he continues to present an extraordinary and unmistakable defence of her right, as a married woman, to work and be adequately paid for so doing.

> A male missionary when he marries gets an increase of salary. A lady missionary in her case - has her salary reduced to half. It is of great importance that she should be free from home cares and I should be very glad and thankful to hear that her salary was raised to £75 per annum instead of £50 as it now is.[36]

This support of Aidinyantz by Bruce was clearly sincere, coming from a genuine belief in her value as a missionary worker. For just a few months later he wrote to CMS complaining of too many women missionaries in Persia. Naming nine, of whom Isabella was the first, he concluded almost desperately, "But what will all these ladies Do [sic] in Julfa?"[37] It is unclear whether Isabella's salary was eventually increased or not, but Bruce won at least part of the battle for she did continue as head of the Girls' School for a while longer.

Isabella was the first of many single women to became engaged whilst in active service. Later there were never any incidents in which a suggestion was put forward for a married woman to remain as a missionary, or continue receiving her stipend. It seems that once the regulations were firmly in place, questioning them was futile. However, in Isabella's case, there was no precedence based on previous experience in the Persia mission. Bruce, whilst aware that the proportion of female to male missionaries was too high, was not prepared to lose a valuable worker simply because she happened to be married.

6a. Family photographs of the Aidinyantz' are extremely rare. This is one of very few to include either Isabella or her husband. Joseph Aidinyantz is on the right of the front row, Isabella is seated in the chair next to him and in front of her is their little boy. Their two girls are fifth from the right on the front row and on the right of the back row.

6b. The Aidinyantz children, 1902:
Nevarth, Apgar Read (who later married and lived in England), and the eldest Nouhie

The tightening of rules, strictly controlling female participation in the mission, often resulted in later women being more restricted than early pioneers. As numbers increased and the efficacy of women's work became apparent, it suddenly posed a threat to male supremacy. In response there was an attempt to restrain women's power by ensuring their activities were carried out within the acceptable boundaries of the dominant gendered ideology. In this way, full advantage could still be taken of their practical skills and involvement without endangering the balance of social equilibrium. Isabella Aidinyantz, meanwhile, remained an extraordinary exception to this principle.

Major change, when it came, was at Isabella's own instigation. In 1896, after nearly fourteen years of service, she requested and was granted a long over-due furlough by FES. While she and her husband set out for the journey to Ireland, Stubbs was given charge of the Girls' School. During their time abroad, Isabella became pregnant and was advised by doctors not to return to Persia until after the birth. Once the child was born, however, the couple changed their plans and decided to stay on "for family reasons" (for family photographs see figures 6a & b).[38]

Her resignation and the manner in which it was communicated left a number of people unhappy and resentful. Isabella wrote to CMS in September 1897 explaining that she was "very sorry indeed to be obliged to give up my work" and "resign my connection with my society... [I] think it right to let you know too, as the school is a C.M.S. school".[39] Either she failed to inform FES and the missionaries in Persia, or her communications never arrived. For in October CMS received correspondence from Stileman (now mission secretary), who had just heard the news, and was concerned about the problem it would cause the school. The institution, having "lived from hand to mouth" in Aidinyantz' absence, was eagerly expecting her return, for there was no-one suitably qualified or able to take over permanent responsibility.[40] He was unhappy that "Mrs A. has not communicated to us any of her plans or intentions for many months past", but hoped CMS or FES would soon send an appropriate substitute.[41] On contacting FES for clarification, CMS learnt that they had likewise not received any notice from her and would not, therefore, make any preparation for filling her place.[42] In the event, the Persia mission successfully maintained the Armenian Girls' School and Lily Buncher was sent by CMS to take over responsibility for it. FES never did provide a missionary to replace their sole representative in Persia and the society disbanded shortly afterwards in 1899.

The reality of being a wife on the mission field

There is no mention of Isabella Aidinyantz for the next four years, though she returned to live in Julfa in 1899.[43] Three years later in August 1902, on hearing that Stubbs was leaving the Armenian school, Isabella contacted Stileman. Explaining that when her own society was dissolved, "the ladies belonging to the Church of England were taken over by the C.M.S.", she continued, "I now desire to offer myself to the C.M.S.".[44] Stileman fully endorsed her application to PC, especially as Buncher was also due leave on furlough.

> Mrs A. is so well known to you by name ... that it is hardly necessary for me to say much about her. She is a very earnest Christian, spiritually minded, fully in sympathy with C.M.S. principles and methods, and has been specially trained for School work besides having had great experience in it. In addition to this she has lived amongst the people for years, and knows the Armenian language perfectly ...
> I hope that the P.C. will at once accept her offer.[45]

PC, however, did not immediately accept her offer and discussions continued over the ensuing months. Early in 1903 Stileman informed CMS of SC's proposal that Aidinyantz should take charge of the Armenian Girls' School during Buncher's absence and be paid not less than £100 per annum.[46] He stressed that this would not mean she was taken on as a missionary, in local or full connection, but merely that she was receiving payment for doing the job.[47]

The reason for Stileman's change of heart about Isabella's status as a missionary is, like so much else about her, somewhat unclear. The most probable explanation is gleaned from a reference in a letter written some years later. It suggests that PC's unwillingness to employ her was nothing to do with Isabella herself, but related to the fact that her husband was no longer a mission employee.[48] At any rate, sometime towards the beginning of 1904, Isabella once more began work in the school she had first taken charge of nearly twenty years previously. This time, however, she was no longer a missionary supported by an organisation but an independent worker paid through local mission funds, partly collected by her own relatives in Dublin.[49]

The mission was by now directing most of its attention towards work with Muslims. The Julfa schools remained as a reminder of early efforts but there was a general feeling within the mission that work amongst Armenians was second rate.[50] With the tide turning, strength of opinion began working against Mrs Aidinyantz. In June 1904 Stileman wrote to CMS expressing gratitude for the help received from Isabella during Buncher's absence.[51] However, the real motive behind his letter was a growing concern about how to dismiss Aidinyantz even though she was only engaged on a temporary basis: "I anticipate some difficulty ... in the matter, and fear that an effort will be made to keep on Mrs Aidinyantz in the school".[52] He regarded the problem as essentially financial, for though she was a valuable worker, "I do not think we should be justified in incurring the expense of keeping her on".[53] Unhappy at the thought of dismissing her himself, however, he asked CMS to intervene:

> It would greatly strengthen my hands in this matter if in one of your letters you mention that you have noted the temporary employment of Mrs Aidinyantz, and express the hope that this arrangement will not be continued after Miss Buncher's return.[54]

By the end of that year, Isabella's employment had been terminated. She continued working, however, for the Armenians themselves engaged her as a teacher in their own national school for girls.

Rejection at this stage was undoubtedly painful but worst was yet to come. The next suggestion that she should once more work in the mission's Armenian school came from CMS. The society had now expanded considerably and missionaries were active in other parts of the country also. This meant a continual shortage of staff in relation to the growing amount of work. The mission Conference, meeting on 12 February 1908, proposed that Mrs Aidinyantz be appointed in local connection to take over from Miss Buncher as head of the Armenian Girls' School so the latter could be sent to another station.[55]

Differences of opinion meant a decision could not be reached and the matter was referred to PC. Objections were raised under various guises. Bishop Stuart initially protested on the grounds that Aidinyantz should not leave her valuable work at the Armenian National School. He soon withdrew his opposition, however, on learning that she gave no Bible classes, had no part in the school's decision-making processes and only taught a few English classes.[56] Reluctance was also expressed by Rev. Mr Walker on the basis of Aidinyantz' age who, at fifty-seven, he believed was too old for such responsibility.[57] Stileman's objection came, primarily, from the now familiar understanding that the mission was distancing itself from work amongst Armenians. Writing from England on behalf of her ailing husband, Mrs Stileman explained the matter: "My husband feels strongly that it is most undesirable and he much hopes that the Committee will adhere to their previous decision on that subject".[58] This, however, was not the entire story and the letter mysteriously continued: "For other reasons also my husband thinks it would be a great mistake to bring her again into C.M.S. employment".[59]

Once more, the comment is likely to be a reference not to Isabella herself but her husband. Joseph Aidinyantz had suffered from poor mental health for some time and was currently in an asylum in Bombay, India. Several missionaries were concerned that if he were released, PC would decline Isabella's services, as they had done four years previously, on the basis that her husband was not a mission worker.[60] The extraordinary reality is that the main objection to Aidinyantz' employment was based, not on the fact that she was a married woman, or even a married woman living without her mentally unstable husband, but that *if he were released*, he would not be employed by CMS. At any rate, given the details of the situation, his return seemed highly unlikely, as explained by Rice:

> He [Isabella's husband] suffered delusions about money and his wife's duty of obedience to him and also about a servant of his whom he regarded as a divine character and he also nearly killed his wife by cutting her throat. One or two attempts were made to get him out of the asylum: on the last occasion Mrs Aidinyantz was in great trouble about it, and our Consul General here communicated with the asylum authorities and received an assurance that he should not be released without them first communicating with the Consul-General. Mr Aidinyantz is supposed to have had a relapse, and not to be so well as he was then thought to be.[61]

Notwithstanding these revelations, there were several missionaries in favour of Isabella's appointment. Rice, as mission secretary, supported her enthusiastically:

> Of Mrs Aidinyantz' zeal, experience and devotion I need say nothing ... I do not know her age, but she is very vigorous and capable, I should consider, of ten years of good work![62]

Buncher, also, was happy to relinquish her position at the school and move to another station.[63]

There is little from Isabella herself over this matter, though one can guess the frustration and anger she must have felt at such injustice. Though eager to return to the mission school, Isabella was not prepared to move at any cost. As negotiations began, her conditions were that she would not be employed for less than three years and that her salary should not be reduced from the £72 per annum she was currently receiving at the Armenian National School.[64] On hearing from Rice that PC was likely to reject the proposal, Aidinyantz - by now familiar with CMS methods - was not surprised. She replied, "Though I should be so glad to be back in what I always think of as my own dear school, your note was just what I expected".[65] Resigned to the eventual outcome, Isabella remained disgusted by the reasoning behind it.

> The Parent Committee might take into consideration that [my husband] was for years in C.M.S. employ until his mind became so affected that he was no longer fit to teach. If I had been engaged in the school work then, I do not think they would have dismissed me because he could not teach.[66]

Any confidence she may still have had in CMS was surely shattered, yet her faith in God and the mission of the church remained resolute. Thanking Rice for his personal support, she concluded her letter with a positive affirmation: "I know too that our gracious Lord will order all for the best".[67]

As far as official documents and archival sources are concerned, that is the end of any form of relationship between CMS and Isabella Aidinyantz. The reality was probably very different as she was bound to have regular contact with the European community that made up the mission. Her husband was eventually released from the asylum but stayed away from his family, living in Tehran until his death shortly before that of his wife. Isabella remained in Julfa where she had raised her three children, all of whom showed a desire to work for CMS. Surprising though this may seem, it suggests Isabella did not allow bitterness to distance her from the missionaries and what they stood for. However, she was also eager to secure a more certain and better defined relationship between CMS and her children than she had experienced herself.

In 1910, when her eldest daughter Armenouhie (Nouhie) was nineteen, Isabella made an application to CMS, requesting that they accept her as a missionary. Keen to ensure full connection, Isabella wrote,

> I should be sorry for her to be taken on in Local Connection, as I feel that her future usefulness and efficiency, under God, largely depend on her being trained before she begins her work. I am not in a position to bear the expenses, either of sending her to London, or of getting her trained. But if the C.M.S. are prepared to meet those expenses, they may remember, on the other hand, that she has practically lived all her life in the country ... and also ... she knows Armenian well, and can speak and read Persian.[68]

Once again, CMS were unwilling to oblige her wishes. It was not until 1917, after Nouhie had been helping in the mission on an unofficial basis for many years, that she was finally accepted and even then, only in local connection. Her sister Nevarth was welcomed by the society on similar terms, three years later in 1920, just months before their mother died. Meanwhile, her son - Apgar Read - having received medical training at Trinity College Dublin, was also preparing to return and work for CMS.[69] Isabella, however, did not live to see him again for she died from pneumonia on 6 December 1919 at the age of sixty-eight, shortly before Apgar's return.

Though she had no society of her own to pay her tribute as a long-standing missionary, colleagues in Persia mourned her and acknowledged her worth. Dr Donald Carr, having known her for many years wrote, "Mrs Aidinyantz will be a very great loss to all of us and indeed to the whole Armenian Community. She has been such a feature in Julfa for so long".[70] However, the only public recognition she received was a brief obituary in a CMS journal.[71] The short anonymous entry indicates nothing of her life's achievements other than the fact that she produced children also dedicated to the work of the society. No one was to know the great influence her two daughters would have in the future of the mission but regardless of this, Isabella Aidinyantz deserves to be remembered for more than *their* achievements. She was a significant figure who played a formative role in the CMS Persia mission and her part should not go unnoticed.

Isabella's attitude towards life in Persia and work as a missionary teacher

A study of Isabella Aidinyantz' personality and her approach to missionary work is necessarily limited to the earlier part of her time amongst the Armenians of Persia. With few exceptions, insights from her own writings are only available until 1896 when she resigned from FES. Nevertheless, these formative years are important in establishing her basic perspective towards life and work in Julfa.

Challenge within conformity: theology and the language of evangelicalism

The theology informing and motivating Isabella was of a type which satisfied both FES, in their selection procedure, and CMS with whom she had continued contact during her stay in Iran. She was from a low church Protestant tradition which formed the evangelical wing of the Church of England in the late nineteenth and early twentieth centuries. Various comments, some more explicit than others, indicate the leanings of her religious persuasion. There are, for example, passing references to the Eucharist and altar as the "Lord's Supper" and "Lord's Table" respectively.[72] Her writings also betray the value she placed on the centrality of the Bible. She often calculated the competence of staff according to their ability to teach Scripture.[73] Similarly, Aidinyantz laid great stress on the significance of single verses, encouraging students to find and discuss individual verses as a source of inspiration. Convinced of great advantage in memorising Scripture passages, on one occasion she was delighted to have "succeeded in getting all the classes to learn by heart some easy verses".[74] A third typically evangelical trait was the identification of faith as having arrived at a position of certainty regarding tenets of belief. This type of theology allowed little space for faith as a journey or process, including doubt as well as assurance, in its very essence. Accordingly, Isabella clearly distinguished between searching and the point of arrival: "I am very much interested about one of the school girls at present. I think she is really seeking, and perhaps she has even found".[75]

Finally, Isabella displayed unease with the notion of Armenian Orthodoxy. As a missionary working in their midst, perhaps this is to be expected. However, there were differences of opinion about what the mission's approach towards Armenians should be. Some felt they should be encouraged to convert, while others believed their faith simply required revitalisation after years of stagnation in an otherwise entirely Muslim environment. Still others held to the official Persia mission policy of non-interference, and advocated contact with Armenians only in the hope of eventually reaching Muslims through them.

Isabella's motives towards the Armenian people are never made explicit. Her husband was probably a convert to Anglicanism, yet her feelings were likely to be complex and convoluted. Living for so long in Julfa, Isabella in some senses became part of the Armenian community. She was always on the borders through her different religious and cultural traditions. However, familiarity, marriage and years of mutual contact made Julfa home in a very real way. Whether or not she believed conversion was necessary, Isabella was undoubtedly uncomfortable with Armenian religious practices such as "a superstitious veneration for the saints"; and her understanding of a "sincere Christian" was one who held to Protestant doctrines of faith.[76] Never wanting students to follow her views blindly, she enjoyed their challenging questions and listened to their opinions seriously, rejoicing if they were convinced of the need to change.

Despite such theological conformity, Isabella is in striking contrast to many other early women missionaries in Persia. Her official letters are somehow freer, dwelling more on details not directly relevant to her religious vocation. She seemed less concerned about satisfying readers' expectations by regaling them with the current rate of conversions or the latest potential converts. Instead, she delighted in describing her surroundings and relating interesting or informative aspects of daily life.

Two factors, in particular, may have allowed her the freedom to depart from expected norms. First, working amongst Armenians rather than Muslims meant the pressure to convert was less persistent. Whatever her or her readers' views on Orthodoxy, the people of Julfa were still baptised Christians: significantly nearer the "true faith" than their Muslim country-folk. Secondly, as the first single woman missionary in southern Iran, Isabella had no-one to emulate. Free to develop her own style, she took full advantage of her audience's ignorance of Persia. It was for them a mysterious enigma - an exotic construction of orientalist fantasy - which Isabella willingly fed with stories of life in Persia.

Influenced by these factors and/or simply due to her open personality and joy for the new experiences in life, Isabella Read's early letters in the *FMI* are resonant with intricate details of countless different themes. Her colleagues mentioned some of these in passing, but fear of self-indulgence meant they seldom dwelt on them without supplying a religious twist. Read, however, showed a refreshingly keen interest in her surroundings and expressed almost child-like pleasure in new experiences *for their own sake*, without constant need for theological qualification.

The impression one gets in reading Isabella's letters is of someone fascinated by life in Persia rather than a missionary with a specific purpose. She included detailed accounts of the people, the wild life, and the countryside, describing mundane routines of life as well as more unusual events, providing brief spells of amusement or variety.[77] On one occasion she recalled the visit of a photographer to Julfa, capturing something of the rarity of such an occasion. Recounting the episode, she described dressing up in the Armenian national costume and posing to have her picture taken. "I had great fun", although, "I have never felt anything so uncomfortable as the Armenian headdress".[78]

Isabella showed an unusual capacity for understanding and experiencing an incident from the "other's" point of view. Seldom tempted to exploit a situation by describing it as a prelude to a pertinent religious sentiment, she related events from perspectives other than that of a Christian missionary. The exclusivity of the orientalist language employed by so many of her colleagues when speaking of Iran and its people is largely absent from Isabella's writings.

Describing a recent visit from the *Imam Jum'eh* - a senior Muslim cleric - to the school, she revealed gratification without any religious animosity or the need to explicate evangelistic potential. "It was a great event ... for neither he nor his father had ever visited Julfa before".[79] Isabella understood the significance of this occasion on behalf of the people amongst whom she worked. The visit of a Muslim official to Julfa was a momentous occasion and a portent of improving relations between the two communities. She rejoiced with them, rather than place herself beyond them by emphasising her role as a missionary commentator.

Again, compared with many of her contemporaries, Read did not succumb to the pressure of articulating people's spiritual needs over and above their physical wants. Equally influenced by the philanthropic mood of Victorianism, her language resisted conforming to the evangelical ideology supporting it. Whilst colleagues were just as concerned to alleviate the corporeal needs of Iranians, many underplayed this in an anxious attempt to emphasise their duty as Christian missionaries. Isabella's theology was rooted in the tangible realities she witnessed and she did not define her understanding in explicitly religious terms for the sake of supporters at home. She was, for example, fully supportive of the Armenian decision to set up a school for children in nearby villages. In relating the events Isabella included no additional comments to provide religious justification for the project.[80]

Any challenge Read presented to the dominant expression of theological motifs was neither explicit nor especially strong. Her subtle approach was based more in what she did not say rather than what she did - a muted challenge, somewhat passively executed. For Read was theologically in line with colleagues and remained a missionary with religious motivation. Nevertheless, her ability to consider things from other perspectives and understand people on their own terms, softened her language and created a more sensitive tone. Remaining within the bounds of theological conformity, she exhibited a certain freedom in experiencing and exploring new possibilities without the need to justify herself or indulge readers at home. Hence the patronising tone, so prominent in religious writings at the turn of the century, is more tempered in the letters of Isabella Read.

Radical realism in commitment to educating girls

Read's initial venture in the Armenian Girls' School represented the earliest official female educational efforts in the work of the Persia mission. Robert and Emily Bruce had instigated the scheme, yet the work was only formalised with the arrival of Miss Read. Total commitment to the enterprise meant Isabella indulged her skills and efforts in ensuring its success.

There were no long-term plans and the entire undertaking, organised on a small scale, was reliant upon modest budgeting. Nevertheless, girls' education being virtually non-existent in Iran, almost anything Read offered was bound to be radically new. At the same time, parents had to be persuaded of the benefits involved in sending their daughters to school and the relevance of education for the future their children were likely to face. The curriculum, therefore, included a careful balance of religious, domestic and standard secular input. These responded to missionary concerns and the reality of Iranian women's lives, whilst also ensuring a higher standard of literacy for girls in a variety of subjects.

Isabella's letters incorporate detailed accounts of the school work to which she was evidently devoted. She revelled in her duties, not just for the religious opportunities they afforded but because of her love of teaching and the fondness she developed for the school and its young students. Information about school life is provided in a disjointed, sometimes rambling fashion, typical of the present-minded style of her writings generally. She was not submitting a systematic plan of her activities but wrote as thoughts came to her, developing themes and events that seemed important at that time. Included are such specifics as numbers of children attending school, details about organised outings, information on particular teachers and students, special events, and extra curricula activities.

Aidinyantz's administrative and teaching responsibilities were taken very seriously.[81] Above all, however, she delighted in seeing the children happy. Her school was primarily an educational establishment but she recognised the need for pupils to enjoy their environment. Understanding the particular restrictions upon girls and women in Iran, indeed experiencing some of the social strictures herself, she was eager for the students to benefit as much as possible. Isabella tried to foster free spirits in an environment where all too soon young girls were encumbered by the realities of adulthood. For the Christian community in Julfa was affected by many Muslim social requirements, as well as issuing its own code of female practice in which women were regarded first and foremost as wives and mothers.

Describing the regular outings enjoyed by pupils at the Boys' School, Isabella explained that these were much more difficult to organise for girls.[82] "The elder girls begged me to take them somewhere ... they hardly ever go anywhere except from home to school ... so I made arrangements to take them to a large enclosed place, where there is a garden, house, and trees".[83] A picnic breakfast was followed by a full day out in which she found the girls did not need much amusement, for "the freedom of strolling about amongst the trees, without *chuddars* [sic], and without anyone to say 'Don't,' seemed enough for them".[84]

Consideration for the well-being of the school and students, expressed in many of Isabella's *FMI* letters, was reflected equally towards her staff. Many personal references are included, naming teachers with whose work she was satisfied.[85] On one occasion she intervened on their behalf, pleading their case for a salary rise. In a most unconventional manner she by-passed the local mission protocol, presenting the teachers' request directly to CMS in London.[86] The final outcome is unclear and in a sense irrelevant. For the point is that Isabella formed close relationships with the Armenians, winning their trust and offering her own loyalty.

The educational window Isabella opened was two way. Regarding herself as teacher and principal, she gave of her skills and energy, expecting pupils to learn from her. Yet she also fostered an ability to be flexible, learning from her new environment and the people she encountered. For Isabella was emotionally and intellectually committed to the community into which she married. She was no longer merely an outsider with a package of superior educational and religious benefits to offer, or a religiously motivated woman who developed great love and compassion for the people of Iran. As a late nineteenth century missionary she was undoubtedly both of these, but Isabella was equally eager to be accepted by the people of Julfa and be welcomed as one of them.

A generous perspective on "otherness": Travel, holidays, and local customs

Unlike many early missionary letters from Iran, Isabella's vibrate with lengthy descriptions of events which fascinated and enchanted her. She highlights details and rejoices in the unfamiliar, not as subjects for criticism but as new opportunities and fresh experiences. Travelling in Persia was amongst the topics she dwelt upon. Indeed, her first contribution to the *FMI* is an elaborate account of the journey to Julfa in which she provides names of significant regions and the dates her party passed through them.[87] Descriptions of the changing geography, variable scenery and extent of journeying comforts, add up to fill the pages of her letters. Taking pleasure in the variety of experiences encountered, Isabella's descriptions were not padded with religious commentary but stood alone, self-justifyingly defiant.

I was much interested in watching the motley crowd on deck, Greek priests, Jews, Mohammedans, Tartars, Armenians, Cossacks; and the boat which came alongside, wherever the steamer stopped, with fruit and flowers.[88]

Having arrived in Persia, Read vividly depicts the changing scenery between Resht and Julfa: high mountains and extensive deserts, expanses scattered with frequent villages, contrasting miles of unpopulated regions. All these intrigued her and she indulged in them more like a travel writer than a missionary.

6c   6d

6c. Miss Parry, CMS missionary in Persia 1909-13, on mule back, c 1910.
6d. A Persian couple in palakis, placed over a mule.[89]

Excited by her new surroundings, Isabella was undeterred even by the most "wretched rooms in caravanserais" with their dusty floors, dirty walls, black roofs, and holes in the walls for windows, commenting instead: "it was wonderful how comfortable they looked when the servants had laid down a carpet".[90] Most of her contemporaries wrote sparingly about journeying details. In contrast, Isabella's lucid account has no religious overtones. The enthusiasm of a young woman in the face of new excitement left little room for thoughts of work, and she admits her pleasure openly: "I enjoyed the journey very much, there was so much novelty to me, who had never been outside the British Isles, and our party was very pleasant".[91]

Chapter Six

6e. Missionaries travelling in Kajavehs, c 1907

Unlike her penchant for travelling details, recalled modestly by most missionaries, Isabella's interest in Persian modes of transport does reflect a similar fascination expressed by many of her colleagues. Qajar Iran offered a variety of ways in which journeys could be undertaken, including on mule or horseback. However, the method captivating missionaries into vivid descriptions (probably due to its great discomfort) was the *kajaveh* (for various modes of transport in Qajar Iran see photographs 6c-g). In *Persian Sketches*, Bishop Linton fills almost two pages in a dedicated attempt to familiarise readers with this form of transportation. He describes the *kajaveh* as a pair of dog kennels covered with black tar cloth for protection from the weather, hanging over the back of a mule. To enter, each passenger stepped onto the back of a muleteer and was pushed head first into the enclosure.[92] Isabella also wrote about the *kajaveh*, describing her arrival in Iran with the Bruces and the journey from Resht to Julfa:

> Mrs Bruce travelled in a Kajavah, half-swung, half-balanced on a mule, and Miss Bruce and I took it in turns to sit in the opposite Kajavah, and to ride a pony. Kajavahs are the most uncomfortable thing imaginable. Miss Bruce and I both thought we should be sea-sick for the first hour or two we were in it; but, when we got accustomed to the motion, and to some plans for stowing our legs away, we got on much better; I even went to sleep for a while, one or two hot days.[93]

6f & g. According to Dr Carr these two photographs represent travelling "old style" & "new Style" for the missionaries in Persia

Holidays provided a further topic of interest for Isabella who enjoyed the novelty of change. The accounts present two distinctive differences compared with those written by other CMS women. First, Isabella delighted in vacations primarily because they represented a change of routine and break from regular duties. Responding positively if the women requested her attention, Isabella did not search for evangelistic opportunities: "I could only indulge in reading in the mornings when the women were busy ... in the afternoons they would not let me escape them. Sometimes I read for them or told them stories from the Gospels".[94] Though she was happy to entertain the women in their tedium, Read was realistic and largely unconcerned about the level of their interest in her religious offerings

> I had to try to be very brief. Nothing like sermonising would be tolerated for a moment, for the instant their attention flagged they would ask, 'why do you not where a silk dress? Why do you not where a silver belt? ...[95]

Secondly, and more unusually, Isabella took holidays without the company of other Europeans. Even while single, she did not travel with missionary colleagues but took as companions Armenian friends from Julfa. Indeed, on one occasion she was alone in a village for several days as her associates travelled ahead to another district. Far from exhibiting caution or concern, Isabella thrived on the opportunity to learn from this experience:

> It was pleasant to be alone amongst the people without anyone who understood one word of English, and in the few days that I lived quite amongst them I saw more of their customs than I had seen before.[96]

As she grew familiar with their ways, Isabella did not remain aloof or superior but attempted as much as possible to adapt her style to suit their habits. She understood the need for conforming to local ways if she was to be accepted by the people. Less inclined to convince them of the value of her standards, Read was not scornful of unfamiliar customs but eager to understand and appreciate them. When the villagers expressed dislike for Isabella's print cotton dress with its unusual frills, "to please them I wore a perfectly plain cotton dressing-gown, which was considered very nice".[97]

More than a change in fashion, however, holidays involved a considerable transformation in lifestyle. On one such occasion,

> during the whole month that I was away I never saw table or chair, and I lived in the most primitive fashion, taking my meals with the Armenians, eating their food and squatting on the floor by the door, talking to neighbours.[98]

Typically, Isabella thrived on the newness of her Persian experiences. In one letter she includes a light-hearted account of a long and tiresome holiday journey. Travelling for eighty to one-hundred miles on a donkey already laden with goods, they rode by night and slept during daylight hours. Isabella, however, had no complaints, writing simply, "the novelty made the journey to and fro very pleasant and amusing to me".[99]

Read's openness to the positive potential of new experiences, is also reflected in her attitude towards the people and customs of Iran. It was not uncommon for missionaries to outline indigenous traits in patronising terms. These frequently suggested, implicitly if not explicitly, that superior forms of belief and practice had not yet been discovered in Persia.

Isabella Aidinyantz was more inclined to show understanding when encountering differences of perspective or unfamiliar practices, often displaying humour to defuse a judgmental tone. She was fascinated by the distinctive clothing styles of Muslim and Armenian women and also by the disparity between the Armenian town and village women.[100] She delighted in describing the variety, not as proof of the various grades of women's degradation but as a point of interest for those eager to learn about life in Iran.

The peculiar strangeness did, of course, strike her at times and there was much she neither understood nor displayed sympathy towards. Concerned, for example, about spinal damage due to the excessive weight of village women's large headdresses, Isabella retained a critical approach to customs she considered harmful. "When we were in the villages, I tried to persuade them to change, and wear small things like the *Julfa* women, but they would not hear of it".[101] Her critique of Armenian traditions and their impact on women, however, did not obliterate Isabella's recognition of how strange she must appear to them. For she readily regarded herself "as a great curiosity, especially in the distant villages which had never before been visited by European women".[102] Here, once again, Read displays the capacity to see herself as "other", in contrast to the Armenian women's norm.

Customs regarded prohibitive for women were often dealt with by displays of humour. In remote Armenian villages, for example, a married woman was traditionally not permitted to speak to her mother-in-law until given permission to do so. Isabella explained that sometimes this situation lasted for years but wondered whether it proved useful in avoiding family arguments.[103] Her light-heartedness, however, did not negate serious criticism of a tradition in which women often counted for little. Feeling great empathy for her Armenian sisters, she was fiercely captious of the way she perceived the religious understanding of village women in particular:

> I found the poor women very ignorant indeed; the only thing they seemed to know was the story of Adam and Eve, and that Christ was crucified; their religion seems to consist in going to church and listening to a long sermon, not one word of which they understand.[104]

These disparaging remarks were not a superficial condemnation of Armenian women as inferior compared with their western counterparts. They were not a means by which Isabella scored religious points but grew, rather, from an interest in the condition of women generally.

For Isabella like many of her colleagues was motivated by a feminist concern for the well-being of women. Manifesting a woman-centred approach to life, her efforts were directed towards improving the plight of womankind in an environment where she believed they were belittled and undermined. Far from regarding their lack of religious knowledge as a weakness in the women themselves, Isabella blamed the male church. She accused the hierarchy of perpetuating an attitude of inferiority amongst Armenian women who were frequently regarded as insignificant and incompetent. This undermining of the female population expanded in some villages to include the notion that, being inadequate, girls and women were unworthy of education and incapable of learning:

> [The men] seem to think it utterly useless to teach *women*; one day I was talking to a number of women and girls, when a man passed by and laughingly said, 'Oh,

are you trying to teach the *women*? It is no use; they cannot understand anything.'[105]

Isabella's life in Iran was a testament to the inaccuracy of this belief. She dedicated herself to helping women improve their position through the benefits of education. Longing to understand them and become their friend, she also challenged them, for she wanted them to fulfil their potential in untraditional and unexpected ways. More willing than many to appreciate and enjoy the differences she perceived, nevertheless, Isabella was driven by an aspiration to advance the cause of Persian womanhood where she believed this to be necessary.

Intuitive empathy underlying empire's dominant ideologies

Compared with many early CMS women in Iran, much of the information in this chapter contrasts Isabella Read in a favourable light, especially in terms of sensitivity and sympathy towards Iranians and their customs. This, however, does not mean she should be sanctified as a pioneer ahead of her time. Read was not versed in liberalism, nor was she a radical reformer in the developing women's movement. Rather, she remained a product of the imperialist age whose dominant ideologies shaped her worldview. Convinced of the missionary incentive, Isabella was familiar and comfortable with the dualism dividing a superior West from an inferior East. As a young woman arriving in Persia, for example, she was struck by the telegraph poles running through the deserts, regarding them as symbols of a "link with the civilized world" she had left behind.[106]

Her motivation, certainly during the early documented years, was to encourage people towards accepting her vision of God and the church. She was a missionary with a purpose, seeking the right opportunities for sharing her religious faith with those she had come to serve. Nevertheless, Read's writings portray a more gentle and less confrontational style than many. Dealing less with faith as abstract truth or doctrine, she searched for the most appropriate ways to connect the faith and experience of those she sought to help. For the village women whose days were filled by hard labour in the fields, for example, she wanted theology and life to harmonise in a meaningful and pertinent combination. Noting how "the parable of the tares seemed most to arrest their attention, being just about the work in which they were engaged", she found that because of its relevance, "they readily took in its lessons".[107]

The impact of intercultural commitment

It is reasonable to assume that marrying an Armenian, raising children and living in Iran for almost forty years, influenced Isabella, at least partially, towards changing perspectives and a different understanding of herself and the world. It remains impossible to assess accurately the extent to which she retained a western outlook or was indigenized in her attitudes. Affected by Victorian evangelicalism, Isabella was motivated by a deep sense of benevolent responsibility, typical during the age of empire, and betrayed a thoroughly British tendency in her organised and methodical approach to life and work.[108] However, her extraordinary and long-term commitment to Iran fuelled a naturally flexible and adaptable personality, making her peculiarly open to change through new experiences.

There is enormous potential in the power of common language to bring diverse peoples together. For language, shaped by more than grammatical rules, is a rich product of any society's culture, self-understanding and worldview. Fluency in a shared language offers more than easy communication of factual information. It is a path to expressing and understanding cultural concerns at the deepest level. Armenian is a notoriously difficult language to learn and one with which Isabella struggled for a long time.[109] Nevertheless, it opened for her a new window of opportunity as she sought to become part of her adopted community in Julfa. Aidinyantz's commitment to learning the local language was not uncommon amongst missionaries. Indeed, it was a task expected of all. Yet the manner in which Isabella took holidays with locals and her marriage, which established her place within the Armenian community, suggest a level of commitment higher than most.

"Indefatigable in her efforts to overcome the difficulties of the Armenian language", Bruce reported that Isabella had soon "begun to study Persian, too".[110] Her children, therefore, grew up trilingually, with a sense of belonging to each of the cultures playing a part in their formation. It remains frustratingly difficult to find conclusive evidence about how Isabella or her children viewed themselves in the intersection of these various cultures. Proof about the extent to which western, Persian and Armenian society influenced them is virtually undocumented. Therefore, it is impossible to assess Isabella's critique of western dominance and superiority.

References by Aidinyantz concerning her children are rare, offering little of any interest. Clarifying that the children learnt all three languages, they confirm at the very least that her eldest daughter understood the Orient to the extent that she "knows Eastern modes of thought".[111] Mention of her husband is even scarcer, making it impossible to assess his influence upon Isabella's life. According to Dr Carr, Mr Aidinyantz "took to smoking Bhang" around 1906 "and went out of his mind".[112] It is difficult to imagine the impact this mental instability had upon the family at a time when such illnesses were considered scandalous and shameful.[113] Yet despite the breakdown of her marriage, Isabella chose to stay in Julfa rather than leave Persia, presumably eager that her children should experience and appreciate their Armenian heritage.

Archival evidence concerning the intercultural experiences of the Aidinyantz children is somewhat conflicting. If one senior missionary is to be believed, Mrs Aidinyantz' son was ashamed of his Armenian heritage whilst "his sisters on the other hand are ardent nationalists".[114] Nevertheless, the eldest daughter, Nouhie, considered English her native language and according to a colleague, "although her father [was] an Armenian, she would pass anywhere as a pure European having but her name to show that she is anything else".[115] Inadequate references make it difficult to form judgements concerning the cultural consciousness of Isabella and her children. Moreover, analysing the result of such diverse experiences is itself problematic. For the subtleties of cultural influencing can seldom be quantified or defined. The impact is powerful yet unpredictable, touching lives in unexpected ways. Those most closely associated with the experience may frequently deny or ignore the realities which can lie dormant for many years before suddenly materialising when least anticipated.

Regardless of precise details concerning Isabella's intercultural experiences and the extent of their influence, it is apparent that she developed deep love and affection for those amongst whom she made her home. Many CMS colleagues expressed similar feelings of warmth towards the people of Iran. However, Isabella was unusual in the respect she conveyed when detailing the lives of women whose experiences and priorities were far removed from her own. In one moving account Isabella reveals tremendous admiration underlying her friendship with poorer village women. Describing their daily endurance of heavy physical labour, she is candid with her readers, admitting that the hardships are more than she or many western women could tolerate:

> The women work very hard; they carry all the water from the springs; quite little girls have their tiny pitchers, and as they grow they are given larger ones. The women's pitchers were so large and heavy that I could only just carry them a little distance, and was much astonished to see the ease with which they put them on their shoulders and carried them considerable distances.[116]

Displaying less pity towards Iranian women, Isabella cultivated genuine sympathy through interest in them and their lives. Likewise, one detects a breadth of approach to the missionary task, liberating her from excessively narrow concern for the conversion of individuals. Her colleagues were often so preoccupied with the minutiae of local life that their own task became the extent to which their horizons could stretch. Isabella had a sense of detachment - a freedom from an overly parochial approach to life and faith. Her confidence was in a God whose visionary plan was broader than the work of individuals or that of the CMS mission in Persia. This assurance, together with the impact of her intercultural experiences, liberated Isabella from an intense preoccupation with her missionary calling and allowed her the autonomy to enjoy the people and learn from her new surroundings.

A distinctive style or impotent conviction?

Throughout this chapter Isabella Read has been described in terms which define her as somewhat unusual compared with many of her colleagues. Similarities have been stressed, yet Isabella stands out as essentially different from the CMS women in Iran. Her marriage to a local man alone was sufficient to distinguish her at a time when union between a westerner and easterner was rare and seldom encouraged. A question remains about whether the perceived distinction was a matter of straightforward style or founded on deeper ideological diversity which failed to find a more explicit voice in her writings.

In the case of stylistic modification it would be important not to overstate Read's role in Iran. Certainly, her expressed religious sentiment conformed to CMS expectations. Indeed, anything other than broad theological consonance would have made life and work intolerable. Nevertheless, Isabella's modes of expression and working methods appear very different, and the significance of this should not be undermined. Her inherent sense of western superiority was diminished and her self-identification based less on an "othering" of Iranian women in direct opposition to British norms. It has already been suggested that working amongst the Armenian population reduced the religious pressure to convert, yet this is not sufficient for elucidating her more moderate style. For her early *FMI* letters, compared with others from similar contexts, still emanate openness through their enthusiasm and respectful tone. In 1881, for example, Mrs

Emily Bruce wrote of her experiences in Julfa. Dismissing Armenian women's national dress as "very grotesque", she outlined her views of the people and explained her missionary ambitions:
> They are, as a rule, faithful wives and affectionate mothers; but they are brought up in the darkness of error and superstition much resembling those of Popery, and oh! how we long to be enabled to draw, not merely scores, but thousands of them within the sound of the pure Gospel, and still more into the knowledge of Him Who alone can cause the light to shine into their hearts.[117]

Similarly, an *FMI* article during 1895, by a woman missionary not based in Iran but with knowledge and experience of Armenians in Persia and other parts of the world, presented a fierce and uncompromising analysis. According to Miss Ferrier, Armenian people were
> for the most part sunk in the darkness of ignorance and superstition, their religion consisting in a weary round of fasts and ceremonies, having no effect upon the morals of the people, who believe that the most evil liver, if he have a priest at his dying bed, is sure of paradise.[118]

Nothing in Isabella's tone compares with the judgmental and negative comments expressed here and commonly articulated in missionary circles at the time. Her contrasting generosity grew from authentic commitment to the people and respect for their differences. On receiving tributes from supporters, amazed at her courage to work in Persia - a place devoid of human sympathy - Isabella's reply is polite but critical of such misplaced compassion: "I fear they give me credit for much more courage than I possess, and are too sympathetic with me in my loneliness here".[119] For, in fact, Read's sentiments were much more positive and she was "very happy, and very glad to be in *Persia*".[120]

A stylistic distinction between Isabella and her contemporaries would identify her as significant without essentially placing her beyond the ideological circle demarcated by CMS's theological and orientalist stance. It is far more interesting to regard her diversity as emanating from deeply held beliefs at variance with those of her colleagues. If, for a moment, we imagine this was the case, we are faced with the question of why her views were not made more explicit. If Isabella did have a more liberal approach towards other religions, a more positive notion concerning the relationship between East and West and a greater appreciation of diverse cultures, why was she not more outspoken? Two possibilities may be explored.

First, the consequence of Isabella illustrating more openly the ideas which are barely noticeable in her letters, would have been extremely difficult working relationships at best, and the loss of her job at worst. Neither CMS nor FES tolerated a liberal attitude to evangelism at the turn of the century.[121] If Isabella's ideas developed during her years in Persia and as a result of contact with locals, it is possible she chose caution rather than jeopardising her career. However, there is no evidence for a sudden (or gradual) change in Aidinyantz whose naturally open and flexible approach is apparent from the earliest days.

Secondly, and more likely, it is possible that Isabella's flirtation with more liberal concepts was *intuitive*, without possessing the theological framework necessary for construction in any self-conscious manner. Conditioned by the dominant contours of her day, Isabella's inner tendency towards religious and cultural generosity could not find freedom of expression or a linguistic peg upon which to attach itself within the conservative environment of the CMS Persia mission. The subconscious struggle between the liberal and traditional facets of her personality resulted in subtle nuances of difference that appear stylistic rather than being based on conviction to alternative ideologies. Had she been familiar with a diverse theological language or nurtured within a different framework, her intuitive sense of sympathy may have developed, eventually finding a distinct and clear voice of its own.

The precise nature of the factors distinguishing Isabella from many of her colleagues remains unclear. It is possible either that she simply employed a distinctive, more palatable style or that her deepest convictions were muted and impotent. For some it will be important to decide between these alternatives. Yet, I believe, this represents a futile exercise as the necessary evidence for a definitive judgement is not available. Instead, Isabella Aidinyantz should be regarded as a prime example of late nineteenth century womanhood, caught between the conflicting contours of tradition and modernity.

As a single woman she was involved in new ventures, thus expanding the possibilities for future generations. As a married woman she satisfactorily continued in paid employment, testifying to the unreasonable nature of regulations restricting most wives. Indeed, being the only woman in the Persia mission to combine both her roles, as a single and married woman, with being a missionary, she was a true pioneer. Her intuitive liberality appealed to such breaks with convention. Yet during her years in Iran and through contact with the CMS mission, she remained exposed to Victorian theological, orientalist and gender imperatives which shaped the entire British empire. The ideologies underlying evangelicalism which denounced other religions; acceptable sexual stereotypes that restrained women, as well as the negative "othering" of eastern peoples, continued influencing Read and moulding her missionary task. Theologically she expressed nothing out of the ordinary, and this assured her a secure place within the context of CMS. However, her natural resistance to orientalist assumptions gave her genuine sympathy for the people and an ability to overcome some linguistic restrictions in writing about Iranian women. Isabella Read remained within the boundaries of acceptability required of all Victorian women, yet her life is a reflection of the best efforts of her missionary colleagues in their attempts to extend friendship based on mutuality towards their Iranian sisters.

CHAPTER SEVEN

Emmeline Stuart:
Medical Missions and the History of Feminism

Women's medical work in mission history

The life of Emmeline Stuart is a multifarious narrative touching on several significant historical developments. Like many of her colleagues, she played an important part in the early progress of missionary endeavours in Iran. Similarly, she is of interest to women's religious history as a member of the ever increasing band of female activists during the Victorian era. However, as a qualified doctor, Emmeline Stuart also has her place in the more specific history of *medical* missions which are, in turn, an "epiphenomenon of the history of the medical profession".[1]

Her contribution in Iran is rooted both within the wider development of Victorian religious women's progress and the secular medical scene. Probably the most radical of her colleagues, Emmeline Stuart is notable for her part in the changing position of women within the CMS Persia mission. Her role, therefore, is especially pertinent to the progress of western feminism, though this chapter also includes a section concerning her attitude towards Muslims.

During the first half of the nineteenth century, the medical practitioner was an exceptional adjunct on the mission field and the notion of sending single women to work as missionaries was barely considered at all. However, by the end of the century the situation had changed dramatically and CMS, together with many other missionary organisations, realised that these two elements - female workers and qualified doctors - made up the most potent and effective workforce.[2] Thus, the missionary doctor - who could increasingly be a woman - and female workers generally, soon became indispensable assets within the missionary movement. Not surprisingly, those able to combine these components - ie female missionary doctors - were considered extremely influential within the programme to Christianise new lands.[3]

The development of medical missions in CMS

During its formative years in particular, CMS feared that emphasis on education and medicine would deter from the primary task of evangelism. As the centrality of the Bible gradually led towards the expansion of educational work, however, CMS official records remained silent about medical work, giving little by way of formal recognition to medical missionaries until the second half of the nineteenth century. Doctors and other medical workers were, of course, present from the start of CMS's activities abroad, carrying out "a form of pillbox ministry".[4] However, it was not until the 1860s that the medical mission was acknowledged as an essential arm of the missionary method.

In Iran the medical efforts of CMS men began with Dr Hoernle who served the Persia mission between 1879-90. After a hiatus of several years, work once again began under the superintendence of Dr Carr in 1894. Little attention was paid to the potential for women's medical expertise during the first twenty years after the arrival of Robert Bruce. Even the advent of Mary Bird in 1891 did not officially signify the start of medical work for women, as CMS was not intending any such developments in Iran. Nevertheless, Bird's unique and unconventional efforts laid the foundations, ensuring that women medical practitioners would soon be an inevitable part of the mission. She was followed in 1893 and 1894 by nurses, Henrietta Conner and Eleanor Davies-Colley. Eventually in 1897, with the arrival of Emmeline Stuart, a women's medical mission was formerly set up by CMS in Iran.

During the nineteenth century it is possible to identify a shift in the missionary approach of CMS generally. An emphasis on salvation - as a preparatory means for civilisation - in the first part of the century, gradually moved towards an increased commitment to the service alternative in the latter years. This subtle change brought into mission rhetoric a new vocabulary, embracing concern for the temporal as well as the spiritual needs of humanity. It moved eventually towards the mid twentieth century understanding of missionary work as a practical demonstration of the gospel of love and mercy. This shift is depicted by what I have referred to as the growing tension between pure evangelism as a mission philosophy, and the practical reality evidenced in the lives of missionaries striving to ameliorate physical needs.

Whilst the strain between theory and practice was apparent in the lives of Mary Bird and Isabella Read, it reaches its pinnacle in the work of medical practitioners as represented by Emmeline Stuart. For like all doctors, she was under immense pressure to improve the corporeal problems she encountered and, by virtue of her training, was better equipped for doing so than most ordinary missionaries. Whereas educational endeavours provided a relatively convenient bridge between evangelism and social improvement, the medical skills of doctors and nurses created a much greater tension. For preaching the gospel and offering secular education were not mutually exclusive, but could successfully be programmed alongside each other. By contrast, the demand for medical attention never ceased and time taken out for evangelism simply required stricter regulating of attention to physical needs. The religious requirements on one hand, and the professional incentive on the other, placed tremendous demands on the time and emotions of medical missionary women.

The reasons for this missiological shift from a salvific emphasis towards a model based more on service have been interpreted diversely. Some scholars stress socio-religious changes within British society whilst others emphasise the influence of early medical work on the mission field. Fitzgerald, for example, believes it was through the medical efforts of pioneering missionaries that an appreciation of Christian philanthropy developed, increasingly gaining greater legitimacy than the narrow muscular Christianity of previous years and encouraging organisations such as CMS to commit themselves to developing medical missions.[5] Conversely, Potter considers the rise of socialism and secularism to be the primary reason for developing interest in philanthropic work and the eventual acceptance of medical missions.[6] The changes, she believes, were rooted in growing awareness within Britain of deep social inequality between the classes, resulting in the evolution of socialist ideals and welfare work, both at home and on the mission field, through medical and other humanitarian efforts.

In either case, by the end of the century missionaries were recognising the benefits of medical work, especially in Muslim countries and other areas considered particularly unreceptive to the Christian message. In 1885 a CMS sub-committee recommended the specific use of medical missions where the Gospel could not easily be preached.[7] Mission ideology remained in place, through a firm assertion that all efforts should continue as subordinate to spiritual work. Yet the tension between missionary theory and practice was becoming explicit. For the impact of medical missions could no longer be undermined and they increasingly gained a reputation as the "golden key that opens the door of the heart of the most fanatical Moslem".[8]

As the twentieth century began, CMS was officially recognising its medical missions as a legitimate and valued aspect of outreach.[9] Walls divides the various strands of justificatory apologetics into four broad categories.[10] First, the imitative argument was based on obeying Christ's example and command to couple preaching with healing. Secondly, the humanitarian approach regarded philanthropy as a response to unnecessary suffering. Thirdly, the utilitarian defence maintained the need for medical provision to improve the efficiency and health of missionaries. Finally, the strategic objective advocated medical missions where none other could gain ground. Walls notes that though humanitarian concerns were especially strong at the turn of the century, the strategic motive was usually given prominence in missionary propaganda. Certainly, from the 1860s onwards medicine was regarded as an extremely useful vehicle for missionary advance in breaking down the "native wall of pride and prejudice, contempt and hatred" that commonly confronted "ordinary" methods.[11]

Female missionary doctors: Feminist progress or gendered servility?

Alongside the rise of the medical missionary, CMS and similar organisations experienced the advent of the single female missionary. This explosive combination of women's work and medical expertise produced a powerful dynamic, influencing the course of the missionary movement. However, the increased participation of women doctors in particular, not only changed the course of medical and mission history but also influenced the progress of feminism.

By late Victorianism, the two components commonly held to be the most vital within missionary methods were "women's work because it wins the home, and medical work because it wins the heart".[12] For whilst growing numbers of female evangelists and educationalists still found the doors of many zenanas firmly closed, medical women discovered they had the skills which gained them entrance into "the most inaccessible stronghold of heathenism, the home".[13] Unrivalled amongst their colleagues as agents of mission, therefore, women medical practitioners were praised as those most able to find "an entrance for the Gospel into the hearts and homes of ... patients".[14]

The appeal for medical women, soon ringing out across the missionary world, did not, however, represent a radical rethinking of the Victorian gender ideology and its acceptable male/female spheres of work. It was, rather, a calling directed specifically towards single women free of family responsibilities who, far from forsaking their true place in society, could extend their "natural" aptitude for maternal instincts and domesticity into the public realm. In other words, it was a vocation based upon, and justified by, an inherently feminine disposition towards service. This predilection for giving of oneself to others was exemplified most potently in physical motherhood, yet its "natural" predominance extended to womankind generally, providing an apology for the public role of single women. This meant ideologically and practically, women - particularly medical women whose lives were a symbol of self-giving - carried the greater part of the burden of the service ideal to which the missionary cause was increasingly committed.[15] Indeed, the success of this missionary strategy relied on a philosophy endorsing traditional sexual roles. For it recognised women as respondents to a feminised vocation entirely within bounds of ideological acceptability, not trespassing on the masculine domain but acting in complementarity alongside it.

According to radical feminism committed to equal rights for women, this understanding of female involvement within medical missions offers little by way of a positive history. However, for many religious feminists at the turn of the century, emphasis on feminine self-giving did not represent a contradiction. If considered contextually, therefore, the service model which motivated many women can be regarded as an important strand in the history of feminism. In 1913 Ruth Rouse, an apologist for the women's movement and the missionary cause, wrote a defence of both based on an interaction between their primary characteristics.[16] She regarded "the spiritual forces behind the women's movement" as "distinctly Christian in origin", identifying several similarities between the ethos and spirit of feminism and the missionary movement.[17]

Most notably, Rouse wrote of feminism's commitment to "striving for opportunity to *serve* the community" (my emphasis).[18] The women's movement, she argued, was marked by a desire for liberation, not just for its own sake, but for freedom to serve others. For "to the question 'To what end?' the women's movement answers clearly and universally 'To the end of service.'"[19] In other words, feminism's quest for emancipation was approved on the basis of a duality. The desire for liberation was validated but *only* as an incentive for freedom to dedicate one's life to the service of others. Rouse even included the more radical suffrage feminists within her reasoning, claiming they too "collectively ... demand the vote as an instrument for carrying out their schemes of service".[20]

Such views of feminism, as bound up with women's motivation to give of themselves in a distinctively feminine manner, represent a kind of female kenosis or self-emptying at the heart of the struggle for liberation. Clearly, Rouse's arguments - coming from within the separate spheres philosophy - were an attempt to consolidate feminism with the missionary incentive, thus approving the role of women within missions. Nevertheless, acknowledging the particular strand from within which she wrote does not undermine the significance of her views but clarifies the contrasts held in tension within the history of feminism.

However it is interpreted now, the service ideal offered female doctors myriad opportunities on the mission field at a time when the medical profession in Britain was hostile towards them. For most of the nineteenth century medical training for women remained the exception, and qualified female doctors found it almost impossible to practise their skills (for a chronology of developments in women's medical training see Appendix II). Unsurprisingly, a significant proportion of British women doctors were attracted to the mission field. For abroad they not only had the scope to exercise their medical vocation, but many found that "medicine acted as a special case, justifying roles which might otherwise have been regarded unwomanly and disruptive to society".[21] Thus, the feminine service ideal became a means of subversion through which women appeared to conform to accepted gender norms whilst, in fact, extending hitherto restricted boundaries.

Their unique position as women *and* doctors guaranteed female medical missionaries a distinguished place within the mission scheme. Involved in what were considered two of the most acute areas of activity, they could be confident about their role, knowing

> their reputation for exerting the most 'telling' effects on homes and hearts in heathen lands had placed them in the vanguard of the Protestant campaign to evangelise the world.[22]

Commissioned to apply the "double cure", women doctors were entrusted with the care of both bodily and spiritual sickness.[23] Engaged in combat with disease and sin they became an icon of the missionary movement, representing the noblest calling for Christian womanhood. On return to Persia after furlough, Emmeline Stuart was given instructions about her future work, referred to as "perhaps the most Christ-like of all forms of Missionary effort, - healing the sick and preaching the Gospel".[24] Women doctors came to symbolise the perfect fusion of mission theory and practice in their obedience both to spread the good news and alleviate suffering. Yet the potency of such imagery did nothing to impede the growing strain of unreasonable and extreme expectations.

Moreover, the unrivalled power women doctors were consigned in their ability to forward the cause of Christian mission proved unrealistically optimistic, at least if judged according to the number of converts. Missionaries had long been aware that Muslim countries represented the most difficult environment for harvesting rewards. Nevertheless, there were high hopes of success in Iran, for which CMS displayed confident anticipation during the entire sixty-five year period between 1869-1934. Indeed, in 1926 *The Call from the Moslem World* claimed no Anglican sphere in Islamic lands was so promising as Persia.[25] Much of the alleged success was credited to the work of medical missionaries and later accounts still frequently maintained that "the medical ministrations of Mary Bird, Emmeline Stuart, Donald Carr and others did much to attract Muslims" in Iran.[26] However, whilst medicine did succeed in enticing Persians, Iran was in reality very far from the responsive soil missionary apologists claimed it to be. Though the CMS hospitals and dispensaries were crowded with glad recipients of western medicine, gratitude rarely led to conversions and the number of converts remained few.

Nevertheless, assurance in their methods drove the missionaries towards ambitious plans for a land they believed could be transformed if only more doctors were forthcoming. Emmeline Stuart sent an impassioned appeal to the student missionary conference in London, urging them to "let a voice from Persia plead with the medical students today".[27] Her entreaty, voiced on behalf of the missionary cause, was based on the familiar service model. Yet it was also, albeit less explicitly, an invitation to women to extend the scope of their skills. For she was calling upon her Christian sisters to seize upon fresh possibilities - to leave behind the imposed restrictions at home and awaken to the dawn of new opportunity and freedom away from social strictures imposed by western gender norms.

> Can none of you come to help us? Are none of you nearly ready? In face of the great need out here will you decide to stay at home, where the professional ranks

are already over full? Here there is abundant room and scope for your energies. We are so few and so scattered, and the work is so immense. Where, I ask you to ask yourselves, will your lives most count for Christ? Where will you best serve your generation? Do you not hear the voice of the Master Himself saying, "Leave *all*, and follow me." He wants you in Persia. His work is at a standstill for lack of men [sic]. Who will say in answer to *His* call to-day, "Here am *I*, send *me*, send *me*?"[28]

This appeal by Stuart, issued to women and men in an effort to secure more workers for Iran, underlies much that justified the social and individual commitment of women in particular within the missionary programme. For female involvement, especially that of qualified medical practitioners, relied upon a duality which ensured their participation remained acceptable ideologically whilst at the same time representing a new venture. Women doctors conformed to tradition by personifying the missionary, and especially feminine, service ideal but also fashioned fresh possibilities for womankind by striving for new goals and achieving new objectives.

Professional commitment and the feminine threat

Stuart and other women doctors were secure in the knowledge that they were much needed by CMS. This gave them greater freedom to extend the boundaries of female involvement with less risk of exclusion from the mission schema. Nevertheless, problems and tensions still dogged their efforts. Always under pressure, both from themselves and the expectations placed upon them, to ensure the evangelistic side of their work did not suffer, the stress was often immense.

This is a theme frequently referred to by medical women and those writing about them. Philippa Braine-Hartnell informed CMS in 1899 that "Dr Emmeline finds it impossible when there is a stress of work, to prepare Dispensary addresses and ... it grieves her to see it neglected".[29] Stuart herself also expressed the conviction that medicine was subservient to evangelism, yet frequently regretted the tension inherent in this situation. In 1898, still struggling to learn Persian, she wrote,

> Even with the language at one's finger ends a medical missionary could never hope to undertake all the evangelistic work rendered possible by the existence of a Medical Mission, and without which it is hardly worthy of its name. The openings are so numerous that it would take several lay helpers to follow them up to any sufficient extent ... when the need for medical visits is over, who is to follow up the openings thus gained, and continue visiting and teaching the people?[30]

Acknowledging the theory of medical subordination to pure evangelism, Stuart was clear that in practice medical workers should not be compromised. Preaching the gospel was the most important aspect of the missionary programme, but should not deter those whose skills and qualifications enabled them to concentrate on physical cures and bodily needs. Instead, different missionaries should shoulder responsibility for the variety of requisite duties. Whilst medical workers must be free to fulfil their roles, "non-medical people are needed with more time for direct evangelistic work".[31] This concept represented an unashamed elevation of corporal deprivation as necessitating equal attention to spiritual requirements.

Opposition was voiced to this apparently "secular" view of mission and it was frequently expressed in response to the shifting emphasis of gender roles within the mission station. The arrival of women doctors represented a significant change in the hierarchical status of missionaries. Non-medical men, in particular, felt threatened by the relatively high position of authority granted to medically trained women. In an effort to defend their own role, several willingly elucidated the hazards of too much emphasis on medical work as damaging to the missionary aim. Blackett, a clergyman from Kerman, wrote in 1899, "valuable as medical work is, it is after all - from a missionary point of view - only a means to an end. We may secure the 'means' but miss the 'end'".[32]

Stuart's arrival in Persia was a turning point in the mission's history, for it symbolised the beginning of an ideological struggle between men's *perceived* notion of a woman's position in the station and the *reality* of a female doctor's presence. Stuart's professional status, combined with her confidence, strength and single-mindedness, was a potential risk to the gendered hierarchy of the mission and inevitably ushered in the start of a new era. This chapter will highlight the unsettling effect of her presence upon the mission as a whole and several individuals in particular.

Callaway has written about an earlier threat posed to male medicine generally through the establishment of the nursing profession.[33] This, however, was soon successfully controlled through the development of a gendered philosophy identifying nursing with feminine characteristics, thus clearly placing it in a subsidiary position. A division of labour was formalised within the familiar Victorian gender ideology of "hierarchical complementarity"[34] which kept nurses in subordination, carrying out complementary roles under the direction of male doctors. Accordingly, unqualified women in the Persia mission such as Mary Bird, as well as the two early nurses, Davies-Colley and Conner, were not a disruptive presence within the mission hierarchy. A female doctor, however, was more problematic, presenting a real threat to medical and non-medical colleagues through a potential subversion of the "natural" order of male superiority. In charge of every aspect of women's medical work, Stuart's responsibilities took her into spheres once the unchallenged preserve of men.

The opportunities her position accorded were often countered by efforts to contain her within acceptable ideological bounds. Therefore, her activities were mostly carried out within the context of Victorian gender norms, based on the feminised Christian ideal of service. However, from a historical perspective it is possible to regard her as a subversive presence, abiding by the rules where necessary, whilst all the time pushing at the boundaries, creating more space for the amelioration of missionary women's future.

The career of Dr Emmeline Stuart and her impact on the CMS Persia mission

A brief biography of Stuart's life and her arrival in Iran

Born in Edinburgh on 2 December 1866, Emmeline Stuart became one of the earliest women to train as a doctor at a British university, before beginning her career as a medical missionary with CMS. Her father was Robert Laidlaw Stuart and her uncle, Bishop Edward

Stuart, exercised episcopal oversight in Iran from 1894-1910. Two of her sisters, Marie and Gertrude, together with a cousin Annie, also served as missionaries with CMS in Persia.[35]

7a. Patients waiting outside the Julfa general hospital in 1895, two years prior to Stuart's arrival

7b. The Julfa Women's Hospital, 1904

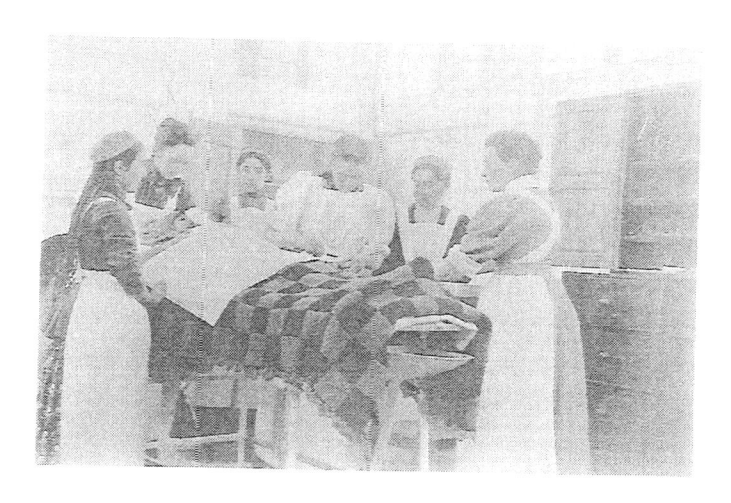

Chapter Seven 151

7c. Dr Stuart (centre) operating in the Julfa Women's Hospital, c 1899

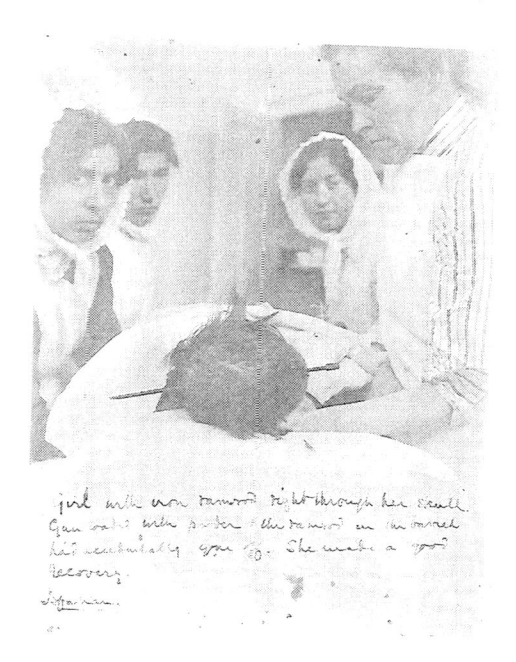

7d. Dr Stuart operating on a small girl, c 1907

Emmeline began her medical studies in 1891 at Queen Margaret College for women's higher education in Glasgow. The following year, QMC amalgamated with Glasgow University which, subsequent to the 1888 Scottish Universities Act and the 1892 Ordinances, was empowered to admit women students. Stuart continued her studies at the university, eventually graduating as a qualified doctor in 1895 before taking up a post as House Surgeon at the Clapham Maternity Hospital in London.[36] For some years a faithful member of the Student Volunteer Missionary Union (SVMU), Emmeline was one of their travelling secretaries prior to her time in Persia.[37]

Having been accepted as a CMS missionary two years earlier, the thirty year old Stuart finally departed for Julfa and the Persia mission on 25 March 1897. She spent the following thirty-seven years in Iran, first in Julfa and later in Isfahan and Shiraz, before retiring in 1934.[38] Leaving work and the country where she had spent most of her life was difficult for Emmeline. Energetic to the end, she resisted departure for as long as possible, but eventually acknowledged, "I am afraid it really is retirement for me - according to C.M.S. regulations for I have passed the retiring age and completed 37 years of service in Persia".[39] Yet still she craved the active life and refused to accept the finality which the change represented: "I have told Dr Cook that I am ready to stop-gap if required as my health is still very good".[40]

Linking early working techniques to the more modern approach which emerged under her leadership, Stuart's work represented a period of great transition within the mission environment. Responsible for setting up the women's medical mission in Iran, she oversaw the opening of women's hospitals in Julfa, Isfahan and Shiraz (see photographs 7a-d), and witnessed great change as the mission increased the number of its institutions and refined the methods of medical care in response to modern improvements. A commitment to better conditions for women drove her to work tirelessly for the bodily needs of patients. Concurrently, it resulted in her life-long struggle to improve the position of women missionaries within the Persia mission. Through professional contributions as a skilled doctor and her strength of personality as a woman, Emmeline Stuart became a distinct and valuable figure within the Persia mission. Both for those who remained after her and for Emmeline herself, the future without her was difficult to imagine. Yet her desire to return was never fulfilled. Having retired to England, she lived in Richmond, Surrey, until her death, aged eighty, in April 1946.

Sexual hierarchy: Resistance in embracing change

As early as 1890 Bruce tried to persuade CMS of the "great need for a medical missionary for the Persian women".[41] It was, however, the work of Mary Bird that awakened the mission to the real possibility of an improved position in Persia through the presence of a female doctor. Request for medical practitioners was invariably justified according to the strategic benefits they would accord to the overall missionary task. There are countless letters expressing the need for more medically trained workers as "*the* most hopeful means of gaining the esteem and affection of all classes of the people, and of bringing the Gospel to bear upon them".[42] General appeals for missionary doctors are interspersed by specific calls for female doctors, as "a medical mission lady, fully qualified, would be invaluable, and would enable us to reach women of all classes most widely".[43]

The missionaries, it seems, were unanimous in their desire for a female medically trained colleague. However, though they rationalised their needs in theory, once Stuart's arrival was imminent, the implications of inevitable changes had an unsettling effect upon them. Whilst all were desirous of her presence, some were concerned about the ramifications it would have upon the life and politics of the mission station. In particular, the presence of a potentially influential woman necessitated conspicuous boundaries of hierarchical structuring. Dr Carr was eager for Stuart's role to be clearly defined as either distinct from his, or part of the general medical mission under his superintendence.[44] PC had initially instructed Stuart to set up a separate women's hospital, and after careful consideration of the relationship between the two doctors by SC, it was confirmed that she should "take independent charge of a department of Mission work and that the said women's hospital should be under Dr Stuart's independent charge".[45]

Divergence of opinion remained, however, concerning the location of the new women's hospital. Many were anxious not only about Stuart's relationship with Dr Carr, but also the effect of her seniority upon the veteran missionary Mary Bird. Sympathies were divided between the safe and familiar, represented by an old and trusted colleague, and the potentiality of new possibilities concealed by the unknown young doctor. Excitement and anticipation for what might be, posed a threat to the security of established hierarchical structures.

Rather than facing the changing dynamics directly, an unsatisfactory solution was attempted through an effort to evade the dilemma. To render the problem irrelevant, a proposal was mooted to send Stuart to a location other than Julfa or Isfahan. It was hoped that the geographical distance between mission stations would minimise the unwanted impact of a new era without reducing the significance of progress and future opportunities. Accordingly, Stileman informed CMS that the missionaries unanimously supported a separate women's hospital, but not in the local vicinity:

> The work among Persian women here, has been, and can be fairly efficiently done by ladies not qualified in the professional sense working with the male doctors, but it would probably not be possible for unqualified ladies to establish medical missionary work in other centres where there are no male medical missionaries, but where qualified lady doctors would certainly be well received and be able to do invaluable missionary work amongst Persian women.[46]

For years the Persia missionaries had made requests for a woman doctor to improve the medical work already established. Now the petition was finally approved, their composure was shaken by the potential for transformation. Suddenly, past methods and achievements seemed comfortably adequate against an unknown future.

Stileman justified the suggestion to remove Emmeline from the mission's central location, assuring PC that Dr Stuart herself was present after Conference "to confer with us on the whole question" and that she was in agreement.[47] However, according to Bishop Stuart, his niece "was led to this conclusion by an impression that she was not really wanted here, and that her moving forward would be a solution to difficulties".[48] Removed from the immediate concerns of local missionary dynamics, CMS authorities in London disregarded the nervous propositions from

Persia. Able to see the larger picture and imagine the scope of fresh possibilities, Stuart was instructed to stay in Julfa and take independent charge of women's medical work.

The implications of this decision were played out during the ensuing years as Stuart and the Persia mission learned to live alongside each other. Sensitivity was maintained in rethinking the position of Mary Bird within the changing circumstances. As an experienced and respected member of the team, with a proven track record of ground-breaking capabilities, she was to begin work in a different station on her return from furlough. Meanwhile, missionaries in Julfa and Isfahan were compelled to accept and negotiate the new dynamics created by the presence of a female doctor in their midst.

A cautious challenge to the masculine values of empire

A cursory glance at the archival evidence indicates that Emmeline Stuart was a strong, confident, stubborn and capable character. Of the women represented in this book she is the one with whom contemporary feminists would find most in common. Enjoying considerable influence within the mission, Stuart was unafraid of voicing opinions and acting accordingly even if this placed her in a disparate position. She was a skilled physician whose competence combined with a persuasive and powerful personality, constituting a respected member of the mission team.

Whilst her unusual standing afforded Stuart greater freedoms, she remained a woman of her time whose words and actions were ultimately guided by the rules underlying the empire. In particular, like so many of her colleagues, Emmeline's language conformed to the standards of Victorian theological and orientalist expectations. Her role as a missionary feminist was more prominent, yet her unique style - often unconventional and unorthodox - was contained within the parameters of acceptability. In short, her part in the progress of the women's movement was set firmly within the religious strand of evangelical Christianity. Consequently, she seldom stepped outside the boundaries set by CMS regulations and the prevailing culture which understood her authority as operating within an extended version of the domestic sphere, ultimately subordinate to male leadership. Subversive though she was, had Emmeline been frequently too controversial, her position would have become untenable. Indeed, there is little evidence to suggest she was inclined to be disruptive in this way.

Notwithstanding or undermining wider cultural and religious restrictions, Stuart did have scope to deviate from strictly traditional forms of female behaviour. For the mission, believing she was the personification of their most potentially successful working method, needed her. She could lean on the boundaries constraining imperial women a little more heavily, secure in the knowledge that she was less expendable than many missionaries. Her role in the Persia mission, therefore, may be described as concessional, with all sides compromising in order to maintain the overall *status quo*. Whilst she conformed when necessary, her non-conformity was also tolerated, giving her more space than most for influencing change in women's status within the dominantly masculine mission hierarchy.

Not surprisingly, during the span of her career in Iran, Stuart experienced varying degrees of grudging acceptance, grateful co-operation and vehement opposition. Yet all the while, the confidence of her professional position meant that whilst normally operating within set ideological boundaries, she could occasionally stretch these to the limit. Seldom undermining male authority in action, she frequently bruised its supremacy through the strength of her verbal resistance. Her views are often expressed clearly and unashamedly, in a manner well beyond the customary feminine style of meek subservience and gentle humility. Several male colleagues found her unfamiliar approach threatening and troublesome, a factor which soon gained her the reputation of being awkward and difficult to work with.

Fiercely religious and of low church Protestant persuasion, Emmeline's theological stance was overwhelmingly in accordance with CMS approved standards and her motives were usually explicated in missionary rather than philanthropic terms. However, she displayed considerable freedom in expressing personal views *as a woman*, seldom shrouding preferences in providential rhetoric or qualifying them with apologies for daring to vocalise her thoughts. This is apparent from the earliest days even before arrival in Iran. CMS, who traditionally sent out, or "dismissed", missionaries prior to their departure from England was proposing to commission Stuart for work in Iran further in advance than was usual. Evidently dissatisfied with this decision Emmeline wrote to the society, plainly making her feelings known and avoiding any temptation to justify her view in terms of God's will. She writes simply and in an almost derogatory tone:

> Have I really to be dismissed so long before I go? I am afraid it will be a mere matter of form ... However, it matters the less as I should not feel I was really being 'dismissed' so many months beforehand. I should have forgotten all about it by January.[49]

Likewise, in direct relation to work on the field, Stuart never resorted to religious justification as a means of persuading CMS of a particular need. Nor did she hide behind the peculiar habit of undermining self in an effort to endorse an appeal. This form of feminised Christian subservience was a common feature of missionary women's writings in Iran between 1869-1934. Conformity to this model, as well as Emmeline's typical divergence from it, can be witnessed in the following two examples, both written in an effort to lighten the burden of Stuart's heavy work load. In 1899, Philippa Braine-Hartnell, tentatively presented CMS with a proposal that Annie Stirling should stay in Julfa (rather than move to a different station), where she was much needed for evangelistic work at the dispensary. Clearly concerned about mission protocol and female decorum, Braine-Hartnell's style is apologetic and embarrassed:

> ... you will pardon my pointing out that just this year there will be rather a block in Yezd ... and in the mean time Julfa is short of workers ... If I may just leave this suggestion in your hands, I hope you will forgive me if I am out of order in making any suggestion at all.[50]

Braine-Hartnell obviously detected a need and believed CMS had miscalculated their distribution of the missionary workforce. Though she takes a certain risk in voicing her opinion, thereby stepping outside expected etiquette for women, she is at great pains to avoid any forcefulness which may be interpreted as impudence. Conditioned to fulfil her expected role within the society, even the slightest deviation from docile subservience is accomplished with great difficulty.

On a similar occasion seven years later, Stuart's unabashed and outspoken approach is in direct contrast to usual female contributions. Presenting her case with no prevarication, she realises her views may be rejected but believes in the validity of her suggestion nevertheless. First, she speaks to Annie Stirling and secures her approval; next she presents her case unambiguously to CMS, confident that it is worthwhile and sensible.

> I ascertained from herself [Miss Stirling] that if the P.C. thought good on her return from furlough next Spring she would be quite willing to come to us. I do not know what the P.C. would say to such a suggestion, but I do not think it is unreasonable on my part.[51]

The model Stuart adopted in her work as a missionary woman demanded that she be taken seriously by colleagues. Her confidence and self-assurance, together with her status as a doctor, ensured that her position could not be ignored despite frequent attempts to undermine it.

Always remaining in an ideologically inferior position through the distinction of her sex, Stuart's rebellious style did not extend to any form of direct authority over male colleagues. Instead, experience of this hierarchical model was internalised and inverted by Stuart who, in turn, regarded her own position as a senior and influential missionary woman in analogous terms where possible. As head of the women's medical mission she saw her role comparatively, in terms of having authority over female colleagues. Paradoxically, her "self", which frequently resisted being defined as "other" by male supremacy, nevertheless relied for its full definition upon the ability to determine female colleagues as the inferior "other". Thus, Stuart played an ambiguous role in the mission hierarchy, acting as a kind of half-way post between masculine self-assurance and feminine self-deprecation.

The authority Emmeline commanded amongst the female missionaries was exhibited in a variety of ways, notably through mindfulness towards the personal needs of colleagues and attention to administrative responsibilities. Blessed with a strong constitution, Stuart enjoyed good physical health and, compared with many missionaries, rarely succumbed to illness. Nevertheless, she remained sensitive to the needs of those around her, constantly aware of what was best for the well-being of colleagues. She strongly urged CMS, for example, to permit the marriage of Dr Alicia Aldous to Rev. James Linton, arguing that Aldous' health was not up to the strains of full-time medical work in Persia and that a long engagement would be difficult for all concerned. Once married, however, Aldous would be healthier and happier and could continue helping in the dispensary where she already worked.[52]

Despite sympathy towards the personal needs of colleagues, Stuart displayed great irritation at the regulations which barred medical women who married outside the mission, from working in any capacity. "You will have heard that I am once more called upon to relinquish my nurse. This is the third nurse in succession who has managed to be married while with me".[53] Far from being a criticism of her colleagues' lack of commitment, this was a veiled attack on a genderized discriminating system. Not only were single women forced to choose between work and marriage, but in the process the mission's medical contribution also suffered. The paucity of missionaries was a continuing problem for CMS in Iran and the marriage of single women compounded this as valued workers were dismissed from the society, creating additional strains on the small group that remained.

Stuart showed great concern for her staff, caring for them and defending their rights with CMS. However, as superintendent of the women's medical team she also regarded her position in hierarchical terms. Presenting an entirely professional approach, she was eager to retain charge of the administrative and organisational side of the work. No such comparable position was possible for women in Britain at that time, for religiously motivated activities were always carried out under the strict authority of a clergyman. On the mission field, Stuart is representative of many whose roles took them well beyond what they could achieve at home. Even the realm of ordained ministers was encroached upon as senior women missionaries cared for their flock whilst guiding and supervising their activities.

Walls regards this as the increasingly acceptable prerogative of all mission doctors, male and female, resulting in the blurring of boundaries once so clearly defined, not only between men and women, but between lay and ordained missionaries.[54] Thus, Emmeline Stuart's role, which may be regarded as an inverted form of the masculine hierarchical model, was also subversive. For through her presence and authoritative style she undermined many traditional divisions between various ranks. Together with many other women missionary doctors, she played an important part in the overall democratisation of the church which experienced an increased lay and female participation during the late nineteenth and early twentieth centuries.

Stuart began her career in Persia by taking over the dispensary work started by Mary Bird. Soon, however, her attention was directed more towards developing a women's hospital in Julfa and its later transferral to Isfahan in 1906.[55] This formed part of a general move in shifting the mission's centre of gravity from the Armenian district to the Muslim area of town. With work expanding and spreading to other parts of the country, Stuart was soon joined by a steady stream of fifteen women doctors in the period up to 1934 (see Appendix VII). Nevertheless, there were several intervals, when colleagues were on furlough or sent to different stations, during which she was in sole charge of the entire medical mission. Supervising the men's hospital was not considered an ideal solution and was a task other women doctors were reluctant to take on.[56] Representing inappropriate female authority, the job was further hampered by practical difficulties. For Iran's strict segregational protocol made contact with patients of the opposite sex virtually impossible. Even Emmeline herself would resolve to empty the men's side of the hospital and refuse new intakes. Yet this usually proved impossible "as men were brought in from distant villages and were either too poor or too ill to go away and come back again for treatment. So I was obliged to take them in and do my best for them".[57]

In addition to hospital work, Stuart travelled to villages for several weeks at a time, itinerating and offering meliorative care. Motivated by tireless energy, religious loyalty, and professional integrity, Emmeline found work continued even during holidays, for people sought her out and it was impossible to refuse them. On one such occasion she and several colleagues were staying in a village near Yezd:

> We had a pleasant month together, but it was not exactly a complete holiday as patients appeared almost daily from all the country round, and the only way to secure any peace was to hold a dispensary for them on three mornings a week. We had a tent pitched under the trees, and after giving a little Gospel address I

prescribed for them one by one, and my sisters did the dispensing and dressings for me. Altogether, I treated 850 patients during my 'holiday' month, and performed sixty-six minor operations.[58]

During her years in Iran, Stuart was also invited by Bakhtiari tribes-people to spend time amongst them, providing medical care and attention (see photographs 7e).

7e. Dr Stuart with a hubble-bubble pipe, dressed in Bakhtiari tribal clothes, 1902

Offering western technological skills, for the most part unavailable in Persian medicine at the time, Emmeline became well known and highly respected for her work throughout the country. During the aftermath of the Anglo-Russian convention anti-foreign feeling was at its height and there was constant fear of violent aggression. Emmeline herself was attacked by a band of robbers who set upon her in Isfahan and, searching for money, threatened her with a knife. It was a sign of great honour, therefore, when in 1908 the Persian authorities offered Stuart a military escort on leaving Isfahan to begin her furlough. For the ten day journey across Iran, she rode by day on a gun-carriage and slept under its shelter by night.[59]

Emmeline's efforts in Iran typified those of many missionaries welcomed for the advantages they offered rather than the theological insights they tried to impart. Stuart's motivation was religious and she provided physical care in the hope that spiritual transformation would follow. Yet accepted and respected for her medical skills, the religious intent sustaining them remained virtually irrelevant to the majority of patients for whom conversion was never a serious option.

A theological rift and a geographical shift

Of the three women considered in this book, Emmeline Stuart experienced the widest amount of organisational change and diversity. Beginning work in the late 1890s, her career survived the changing emphasis of the mission's method and style as it moved from one century into the next and adapted itself to changing circumstances and new leadership. James Linton was consecrated Bishop in Iran on 18 October 1919, and remained in post until his retirement in 1935. Under his influence, missionary strategy and working patterns were transformed and a new, more modern era was ushered in. In particular, he promoted the notion that work should be carried out in greater co-operation with local Christians. True to Henry Venn's much earlier ideas about the role of CMS, his vision was one of an indigenous church, developing its own style and producing its own future leadership.[60] Linton was also keen to encourage movement "towards a slightly less rigid Protestantism" than had been typical of the mission hitherto.[61]

Whilst many agreed, in particular, with the need for greater Persian involvement, Linton's actions were regarded as too speedy by several senior missionaries and a clash of personalities hastened the inevitable rifts. The precise nature of the disagreements remains a mystery, for the archival evidence was either censored or is missing.[62] Matters came to a head, however, when Linton placed a cross on the communion table in the Isfahan church. Stuart was amongst those dissatisfied with the theological significance of such change which represented a move away from the low church conventions of CMS.[63] The tradition of those missionaries representing the earlier years of activity in Iran seemed threatened. The type of Christianity motivating their efforts and rendering their sacrifices worthwhile was being questioned, and in the process the value of their contribution also felt disputed.

Perhaps providentially, in 1922 the Indo-European Telegraph Department (IETD) requested that the mission provide their employees in Shiraz with medical supervision. Generous terms enabled the closed mission station to re-open, in the process, providing the reason for a number of missionaries to move away from Isfahan. Doctors Carr and Stuart, together with several others, many of whom had been in Iran for over twenty years, moved South and started work on the new hospital in Shiraz.

Stuart, arriving five weeks before Carr, began by opening a dispensary and visiting patients in their homes. She regarded the change in circumstances as a new opportunity and was keen "to leave the passed buried as far as difficulties in Isfahan are concerned".[64] Not given a formal farewell by colleagues, her departure from the place of her work for so many years was somewhat inauspicious and her escapist sentiments are hardly surprising. However, over the coming months and in view of a life-threatening illness experienced by Linton's wife, attempts were made to heal the divisions. Dr Carr continued to find the presence of the cross in St. Luke's church a hurtful reminder of the theological rift dividing the mission. Nevertheless, he was persuaded by Stuart to receive communion during a return trip to visit Alicia Linton, and found that it eased the tension between him and the bishop.[65] According to Carr the entire episode mellowed Stuart who by now had a reputation as a severe and confrontational character. He noted that having been in bed with neuritis for two weeks, she was led to take the Lord Jesus to overcome for her in the point where she has so often failed - I expect you know where that is - the quick tongue and sharp temper ... Dr Stuart has become so much more gentle, and her spiritual power will be greater than ever before.[66]

In 1924 Stuart finally received official recognition for her work in Isfahan and was able to lay past events to rest peaceably.[67] She spent her final ten years in Iran concentrating on expanding and developing medical work in Shiraz. Approaching retirement, she experienced deteriorating health and increasing government restrictions on her work. In the wake of growing nationalism, the Iranian authorities placed strict limitations upon the medical practice of foreign doctors, and several lawsuits were brought against Stuart and others for alleged medical negligence.[68] Nevertheless, by 1934 a thriving hospital was established and the indigenous church was growing in Shiraz. Stuart's part in the history of Iranian Anglicanism had reached its end, but foundations were laid for future work by the next generation of missionaries in greater co-operation with Persian Christians.[69]

7f. A group of missionary women in the CMS Persia mission, 1904
Emmeline Stuart is on the right

Growing confidence and feminist defiance

Resisting authority

Stuart exhibited a healthy disregard for authoritative commands she considered unreasonable and her time in Iran was interspersed with several public disagreements. She gained a reputation for being troublesome and difficult to work with. However, it remains impossible to know whether she was, in fact, unusually austere or whether the strength displayed by a woman in authority caused resentment in the mission. It is notable that all documented episodes in which she was at the forefront of internal disagreement, are written by male colleagues. Either the other women remained silent on the matter or, it seems, Emmeline did not cause the indignation of female co-workers.

Due to visit England for her first furlough in 1902, Stuart refused instructions to escort an ailing colleague who needed to return home for treatment. Her professional status superseded her position as a woman and meant she could not only strongly express her opinion but ultimately refuse to co-operate:

> I must absolutely decline the responsibility of taking [Florence Wilmott] home through Persia in the hot weather of May. From what I know of her condition such a journey in such weather would prove probably fatal to her, and I cannot consent to doing what I feel would be so fraught with danger to her. I strongly recommend her being left here till the end of September and then, if still thought necessary, I will take her home, but I cannot do so in May.[70]

Whereas the unwelcome views of most women could be ignored or discounted, medical expertise gave Stuart an authority that could not be disregarded. Indeed, having initially disagreed with her diagnosis, Carr eventually concurred and Wilmott remained in Persia until the heat of summer was over, before safely travelling back to England in the company of Emmeline Stuart.[71]

By the early twentieth century the steady rise of female participants was well established in the Persia mission (see photograph 7f). In 1905, for example, there were twenty-nine women (including wives) and only fourteen male missionaries present (see Appendix IV). Growing realisation that women played a vital role in the practical organisation of the mission meant male sensibilities were vulnerable. As mission secretary, Stileman wrote to CMS, bitterly complaining about several ladies bypassing his authority and making their own practical arrangements. The final straw was Dr Stuart's advice to Braine-Hartnell that she should take a holiday in Yezd and, on return, escort Marie Stuart back to Isfahan. A sense of panic is apparent in Stileman's letter as he tries desperately to regain the control he believes is his:

> Practically the whole of this long letter ... resolves itself into the simple question 'Are the ladies in this mission to be allowed to settle everything themselves, get Bishop Stuart to say "I agree" and go there own way?' It is simply *"Petticoat Government"* that I am fighting against, and I know that many will be thankful if it is made quite clear once for all that this thing is not to be! For the good of the whole mission, I trust this system may be knocked on the head.[72]

Stileman appears to be talking on behalf of other male colleagues also as he indicates a fear of female independence and its supposed impact upon the mission. Whilst offering little by way of rational argument, he nevertheless undermines the notion of change by the disparaging reference to "petticoat government", conjuring up a ridiculous scenario, unworthy of serious consideration. Damaging women's progress by belittling them was (and still is) a common feature of those who feel threatened by any shift in the balance of gender relationships. Such an approach is an attempt to maintain the *status quo* by eliminating all discussion.

Stuart's reluctance to accept irrational leadership also led to her resisting instructions from quarters higher than local mission authorities. During the First World War Persian sympathies tended towards the Germans who were fighting Russia, often considered a great threat to Iranian security. German agents infiltrated the country and hostility was aroused against the English as allies of Russia. In response, Britain took drastic action, including an evacuation order to all British residents.[73] CMS tried to resist this, in particular, pleading that medical practitioners be sanctioned to remain. Permission was not granted, however, and the missionaries all departed.

This incident indicates the extent of interaction between British missionaries and political authorities. The religious representatives were unhappy with the instruction to retreat and pleaded against it, for they were not under direct government orders. Nevertheless, they also felt the weight of loyalty and commitment towards their country's leadership and ultimately complied with the injunction to withdraw. Their justification was based on an interpretation of the circumstances as "not a religious question but purely a political one".[74] Accordingly, as explained to converts and fellow workers, they were not fleeing from danger but merely obeying orders.

Dr Stuart travelled to India with several colleagues, remaining there for approximately six months. In March 1916 she appears to have become frustrated and impatient with the situation. Taking events into her own hands, she decided to return to Persia against advice from British authorities in India. On hearing news that the British Consul was on his way back to Isfahan, she wrote: "I feel it is most important we, of the Medical Mission, should be among the first to get back to the towns from which we were expelled".[75] Mr Gough, British Secretary in the Punjab, vehemently disagreed with her, advising caution and discretion.[76] His primary concern was the inappropriate nature of women travelling and arriving on their own. Jessie Biggs, also eager to return, was proposing to do so along with Stuart. Gough, however, believed Biggs had been "overawed by Miss S." and remained anxious that

> the ladies would be alone in Persia without any male missionary at all. I cannot think that however capable and energetic Dr Emmeline Stuart may be, the [CMS] Committee would think it right that ladies should go there at once and be in Persia alone.[77]

In the event, Stuart did not wait for the necessary authorisation and, together with Biggs, began the journey to Isfahan. On the way, she wrote a lengthy letter to CMS in which she explained her reasons

> for acting as I did somewhat independently and, as I acknowledge, against C.M.S. rules for normal occasions. My only excuse is that this was an abnormal occasion.[78]

Having left Persia under abnormal circumstances and without direct orders from CMS, she argued that any sudden opportunity to return should be regarded as "part of the same abnormal chain of circumstances".[79] Therefore, she was unaware of "seriously transgressing C.M.S. rules", believing rather, that if she waited to arrange matters in the "correct and approved fashion", the opportunity for returning "to my station with the first party going back" would have been lost".[80]

> I know how difficult it would have been to explain to our people in Isfahan how their friends the missionaries instead of being the first to return to them when the way was opened, were the very last of all![81]

Whilst she was "exceedingly sorry to have upset Gough", she was convinced he knew "nothing about the ... state of things in Persia",[82] and she was therefore content with her decision.

> In all I have done I have had the approval of my own conscience though I acknowledge I have acted singularly ... I am truly sorry if I have incurred the displeasure of the P.C. as well as that of the Punjab secretary, but I can only say that, given the same abnormal circumstances and the same necessity for taking prompt action - I should do the same thing again.[83]

This extraordinary episode is a mark of Stuart's anachronistic position within CMS. Not only did she express strong opinions, but also acted accordingly without formal approval from those in authority over her. Such behaviour incurred serious risk of admonition and represents her willingness to step beyond the parameters of acceptability when the occasion demanded. In the event, CMS concurred with her spontaneous judgement, retrospectively endorsing her decision to return to Persia as she did.[84] However, Stuart could not have foreseen this when she resolved to leave India without the required permission.

The result was that the first missionaries to reach Isfahan after the evacuation were all women. Braine-Hartnell, having travelled via a different and approved route, arrived first on 15 May and was joined the following day by Stuart and Biggs. All three were pleased to receive a warm welcome from Persian friends.[85] Waiting for other colleagues before re-opening the hospital, Stuart occupied herself with dispensary work and home visits. The women were eventually joined by Drs Carr and Schaffter three weeks later, on 23 June 1916.

Women's share in the mission's administration

Whilst CMS grew increasingly dependent upon female co-operation in the Persia mission, it continually refused them any formal part in the society's organisational structure. Where women were given a voice, it was strictly in an advisory capacity for, both at home and on the mission field, they were barred from the right to vote and thus denied any real power to effect change.

From the 1890s, separate Women's Conferences became more common throughout CMS. Developing first as devotional meetings, these allowed women to organise their own meetings and reflected the gradual move towards increased co-operation between the sexes.[86] They remained, however, strictly within the bounds of "women's work" and were not regarded as a prelude towards equal partnership within the mission structures. Views emanating from Women's Conferences were given consideration at general Conference but not necessarily approved. Eventually in 1911 British missionary societies came together to consider the question of women's involvement. A report was published defining co-operation as more than mere complementarity and promoting the notion of working together at the same task and through a single organisation.[87] Slowly, individual stations began changing their policies and in 1917 women were given full voting rights on the CMS General Committee at home.

The relatively small size of the Persia mission meant the station could, up to a point, operate somewhat unusually. In the early days, especially while missionary numbers were low and organisational structures not yet securely in place, women enjoyed a more prominent voice within the mission. Those qualified according to the same rules governing male missionaries not only voted at the first Conference but Mary Bird was also selected onto SC.[88] Soon, however, stricter regulations were imposed and though women (single and married) were frequently present at Conference, often participating in discussions, they lost both their voting power and the right to be elected onto sub-committees.

The matter lay dormant until 1904 when a proposal was made to form a Women's Conference.[89] This was the beginning of a lengthy process which took a further twenty years before reaching a satisfactory conclusion in 1924 when women were eventually granted equal voting rights with male colleagues. Extraordinary delaying tactics were utilised by those fearing the smallest concession would result in a tidal wave of uncontrollable chaos. The archives seldom mention the actual names of female protagonists influencing this marathon pursuit for justice. However, there is no doubt that Emmeline Stuart was a prominent dissenter whose involvement is continually implicit, if not always explicit. Ironically, her efforts had contradictory results. Whilst acting as the focus for women's grievances, she also became the main obstacle to the achievement of their goal. For Stuart personified the reason why women should not be given the vote, as the additional power many felt she would gain became the justification for denying them this basic right.

Unlike their counterparts in many other CMS stations, the women in Persia eventually decided against the formation of their own Conference, believing that "no weight is ever given in Salisbury Square to the minutes of Women's conferences, and that to hold such conferences would be simply a waste of their time".[90] Writing some years later, Stileman maintained it was Emmeline Stuart and Philippa Braine-Hartnell who "emphatically refused" the idea of a Women's Conference, deciding instead "to agitate for *women's votes in the General Conference*".[91] Preferring to have two or three of their number given full voting rights, they persuaded Conference in 1905 to put this proposal to PC which in turn rejected the appeal. Nevertheless, the women and their supporters refused to relent and two years later, contrary to regulations, Emmeline was elected onto SC, the most powerful body in the mission. Predictably, the event was deprecated by Stileman who could "foresee great danger in giving her [Stuart] ... *one fourth of the voting power of the whole mission's local Governing Body*".[92] In view of the tremendous uproar, Stuart voluntarily resigned from SC, having succeeded in making an important point.

PC's resolute resistance to progress proved a great relief to those opposing change. Throughout the years between 1904-1907 various arguments were employed to ensure the *status quo* was maintained. These may be subdivided into four broad categories. First, the general view was that an inherent rectitude already existed within the structures and that women had little cause for complaining. They enjoyed considerable influence and were at liberty to give voice to their opinions in discussions preceding any Conference vote. In other words, change was not *necessary*, for the system was already fair. Secondly, there was a common belief that women could not be trusted with more power than they already possessed. Women were considered emotional to the point where their rational thought processes were severely hampered. It would, therefore, be *unwise* to assign them any further authority. Thirdly, the "slippery slope" argument was frequently presented as the reason why the vote should be withheld from women. Having given them rights in Conference, they would demand more power and there would "soon be an outcry that all subjects decided on the Standing Committee of Conference were settled by men alone".[93] In short, it was *dangerous* to give in to their petition for the right to vote on Conference.

Underlying these arguments - that it was unnecessary, unwise and dangerous to give women a greater share in the mission's administration - was a fourth, more basic factor. The power to vote represented a significant shift in the familiar ideological boundaries dividing men and women. By encroaching on hitherto exclusive male territory, the distinct parameters of the separate spheres philosophy would be blurred. Consequently, the basis of all social order and the unthreatening justification for women's public role (as an extended version of their private role) would be at risk of disintegration. Once women stepped outside the clear ideological confines that hemmed in their activities, ensuring they remained within the bounds of acceptability, the familiar hierarchy of men over women would be gone forever. Whilst women's increasing power was kept strictly separate (as for example in a Women's Conference), its subservience to male superiority was ensured. However, once they could exercise authority within the very same structures, the threshold to a new way of imagining reality was within sight. This fundamental fear lay at the heart of the opposition to women's right to vote on Conference.

Despite such serious resistance, none of the missionaries could appease the accelerating pace of modernity. Events took over and changing circumstances meant the voice of women demanding justice was soon echoed by other groups appealing for more influence within CMS structures in Iran. As the mission grew in size and spread to other regions, missionaries isolated through geographical distance began complaining about the unrepresentative nature of Conference.[94] At the same time, the newly founded St. Luke's church council in Isfahan, hitherto consisting of male missionaries and Persian converts, proposed the appointment of a senior lady missionary. The idea was that such a person would take over responsibility for the baptism of female candidates and the discipline of the growing number of women members.[95]

7g. St. Luke's Church, Isfahan which in the early days included a central curtain for the segregation of men and women

Though PC rejected the suggestion, the move towards more democratic structures in all areas of mission life had begun and the tide could not be turned. Early in 1913 once again the recommendation was made that women be elected onto Conference. Increasing numbers now felt

> the time has come when lady Missionaries should have a definite share in the administration of the Mission, and a recognized position in the Local Governing Body.[96]

However, divergence of opinion still divided the male missionaries and a decision could not be reached. Stileman wrote to CMS confidentially, explaining that those who voted against,

> did not do so because they were opposed to the *principle*, but because they feared that two members of the Stuart family would be elected, viz. Miss Stuart and Dr E.M. Stuart, and they did not think this would make for the harmony and welfare of the Mission.[97]

The struggle was no longer expressed in terms of a straightforward conflict between the sexes for, in a way, that battle had been lost. Now it was a personal issue, directed against individual women, especially Emmeline Stuart. Having already successfully moved beyond the strict limits of the feminine sphere by means of her profession and strength of character, there was nevertheless a sense that while the ideological basis for confining the scope of her power was still in place, she could ultimately be controlled within the mission's gender hierarchy.

Very slowly the screw was loosened and step by step women were permitted entrance into the "sanctuary" of an all male Conference. By mid 1913 they had won the right of election as full voting members, providing they remained numerically in a lower proportion to their male counterparts. In addition, it was agreed that of the three elected members on SC, one should be a woman.[98] Despite fears that Dr Stuart's power base would suddenly expand, in February 1914, it was not her but Miss Philippa Braine-Hartnell and Dr Catherine Ironside who became the first women officially elected as voting members of Conference.[99] Having achieved a major victory, in reality, the women were still severely restricted. For prevented from ever being in a majority, their voice was effectively subdued and their views could not carry full impact.

In 1917 the matter was again resurrected with a recommendation that women be entitled to an equal number of votes. As mission secretary, Walter Rice warmly endorsed this proposal:

> It has for many years been felt that Conference has been deprived of the votes of some of its oldest, and most experienced members through ladies not having votes, or, as is the case at present, through their being so insufficiently represented in the matter of voting.[100]

Meanwhile, the debate was protracted for several years, with obstacles continually presented. Old arguments mingled with new variants to ensure that strictures remained in place.[101] Increasingly unconvincing public opinion was voiced, disguising persistent alarm at the notion of Dr Stuart being given more power. One male missionary wrote:

> There is one outstanding personality among the women viz. Dr Stuart. She completely dominates all the other lady missionaries with possibly one exception. The submission of the ladies, body, soul and spirit, who live with her is complete. She is a singularly gifted woman, and has been greatly blessed in her work. She is however extremely head strong and difficult to work with unless she gets her own way. I should be sorry to see more administrative power put in her hands which is simply what it would amount to if more votes were given to the women missionaries.[102]

The recommendation that there should be equal numbers of male and female voters on Conference and one woman on SC, was finally ratified in December 1921.[103] It was not for a further three years, however, that the concluding scene of this extended drama was enacted. In 1924, the constitution of the Persia mission approved that all women, single and married, be granted the same voting rights as men, both on Conference and in elections for SC. Finally, a democratic decision was reached and voting in the Persia mission became the right of those with longer service, not the privilege of sex.[104]

Struggles surrounding the progress towards women's right to vote represent perhaps the most obvious way in which gender skirmishes were fought and new territorial maps drawn. Men and women operated successfully together while their separate spheres were clearly demarcated theoretically, if not in actuality. However, once a threat was perceived which questioned the very ideology, familiar structures no longer seemed safe and desperate attempts were made by some to maintain them. The mission's entire social foundation, based on Victorian gender hierarchy, was in danger of collapse. The fundamental understanding of a community based upon the complementarity of sexes operating within their separate spheres had to shift, however subtly, before women could be given equal rights to a share in the mission's administration.

Emmeline Stuart was at the heart of this struggle, encouraging others to move forward yet unaware she was holding them back, for to her male colleagues, she represented the greatest threat of all. Through her involvement, Stuart embodied transformation - in all its complexities - from an age of male superiority towards an era of greater co-operation. The conflict was personalised by those who regarded restrictions placed on Stuart as a wider safeguard against all threat of change. There was a sense that if only she could be stopped, then women's advancement in the mission could be prevented, or at least maintained within the bounds of controlled respectability.

The impression she made upon the life of the mission should be seen, primarily, within the context of the "equal but different" strand of feminist history. However, her salient role in the evolution of women's voting rights also presents Emmeline Stuart as a contributor to the more radical strand of the women's movement and its struggle for equal rights.

Social critique and missionary feminism

Emmeline Stuart was, like the majority of her colleagues in Iran, middle-class, well educated, financially secure and of a low church evangelical persuasion.[105] Imbued with many prevalent attitudes and assumptions of her day, she was further limited by the contemporary language of Victorian evangelicalism. Regarding East and West as profoundly different, she was seeped in an "orientalist" understanding of the "other" as essentially "inferior". In short, Stuart was - despite feminist tendencies - a product of the imperial age in which she lived.

Over the years, her views were aired through various publications for CMS journals. In one particular article, written in 1909, Stuart commented on the role of religion in relation to the social position of Persian women. It is a stinging attack on Islam as causing "the degradation of all we understand by the word 'womanhood'".[106] Basing her argument on two factors in particular, Stuart interpreted the problem as a product of religious rather than cultural heritage. First, she discusses the social condition of women resulting from polygamy, divorce and child-marriages, maintaining that these make "home, as we understand it ... an unknown quantity to the Moslems".[107] Secondly, the scandal of women's poor social status is blamed on Islam's refusal to permit them an education, inevitably leading to ignorance, "invariably accompanied by gross superstition".[108] The article concludes that Islam and civilisation are incompatible, and that ultimately "one must flee before the face of the other".[109]

By late twentieth century standards it would be easy to vilify Emmeline and dismiss her views as irrelevant to an investigation of feminist history. The extent of cultural and religious superiority, together with the strength of language she employs to denounce Islam, seem to undermine any valuable insights that may be present. However, according to the premise of this book, her observations must be analysed, not by our contemporary criteria, but within the Victorian/Qajar context. Accordingly, several factors need careful consideration.

Mindful of the dangers inherent in a distorted orientalism which refuses ever to be critical of Islam, it is important to look deeper and question whether her evaluation did not, in fact, have some arguable basis. Missionaries should not be regarded as entirely reliable for they were culturally biased, selective in the material they communicated, and motivated by an ardent desire to Christianise. Nevertheless, they enjoyed considerable contact with all types of Persian people and their familiarity with the lives of women, in particular, made them unique amongst most Victorian westerners abroad.

Emmeline Stuart was compelled to elucidate her views, not only as a missionary but also as a woman witnessing the suffering of other women. Whilst religious imperialism was certainly a factor in her writings, growing concern for the wholeness of womankind also provided an underlying motivation. Indeed, several of the issues she wrote about are today still part of the international debate regarding the oppression of women globally. Her oversight was succumbing to cultural naiveté through a complete association of the social scandal she witnessed with the religion of Islam. By setting Islam and Christianity in direct opposition, she presented her own theology, *a priori*, as the solution to the ills of Persian society. In the process she failed to understand that the problems of Iran, which may have been exacerbated by religion, also had other equally important explanations. The socio-economic and cultural reasons underlying the oppression of women made the problem a cross-religious phenomenon with diverse manifestations in different societies. Moreover, in each situation religious input could worsen women's circumstances by confining them within the parameters of particular theological codes of behaviour.

There is some irony in Stuart's inability to comprehend the complexities underlying the subject so important to her. Her aspiration that Iranian women should one day enjoy "the perfect freedom of English women"[110] does have a somewhat hollow ring. For at the very same time, Stuart and her colleagues were struggling for basic voting rights on Conference. Whilst women's inferiority was demonstrated differently in Victorian and Qajar society, nevertheless, they shared a common source. Both were confined to a secondary position by the cultural expression of their society's separate spheres philosophy. Therefore, though distinct in many respects, subservience to male superiority wove an invisible bond, making British and Persian women more similar than either realised.

Notwithstanding Stuart's incapacity for recognising any resemblance between her circumstances and those of Persian women, her critique of the Iranian situation need not be ignored entirely. Indeed, perhaps it gave her an added, and subconscious, dimension into their predicament. Moreover, in comparison to the choices she made to live as an independent single female, the plight of women in Iran was a great deal worse than her own. Her denunciation of a society that left women with virtually no control over their own lives is, therefore, worth considering cautiously.

Emmeline's indictment of women's treatment in Iran was not an angry accusation or an issuing of uncontrolled and random allegations. It was, rather, a considered opinion arising from her experiences. She showed insight and understanding, for example, in her condemnation of divorce as more problematic than polygamy, for the greater suffering it caused women and children whose fate was social isolation.[111]

Her advocacy for the improvement of women's plight can, for two reasons in particular, be regarded as an important phase in the historical development of feminism. First, arguing that a nation could make no real progress until it allowed women a rightful place, Stuart was encouraging Persian women, whom she regarded as *"full* of possibilities", to achieve their potential in the quest for a better life.[112] Having attained for herself considerable freedom from the confines of Victorianism, and struggling to procure even more, Emmeline was eager for all women to enjoy the rights that were theirs through virtue of being human. This need not be interpreted as a form of cultural imperialism or an attempt to impose western priorities on an eastern context. Rather, it was a desire for cross-cultural co-operation and mutuality - for women to unite in their efforts towards a better future. The precise nature of the western agenda did not have to be employed by Persian women who were capable of adapting or filtering the message of feminism to suit their own particular context.

Secondly, based on a theory suggested by Potter, Stuart's critique of Iranian women can be interpreted as a condemnation not just of Persian society but of the social condition of women in England. Potter admits that,

> for English women of religious background to be subscribing simultaneously to the problem of the degraded position of women at home, and conveying the advantages of British freedom to the women of the Orient seems a most remarkable instance of double think, and one wonders at the complacency ...[113]

She continues, however, arguing that missionary women developed a "zenana ideology", to explain the degradation of eastern women specifically and then applied it to raise consciousness about the plight of women generally.[114] In other words, they were launching a double-edged offensive against both eastern and western contexts.

Repudiation of the wrongs they witnessed abroad was far easier for missionary women than explicit criticism of their own situation. They bore no personal responsibility for it, nor did they suffer the extent of its consequences. Their apparently straightforward reproach, however, became a means by which "evils at home [were] being attacked in the guise of evils abroad".[115] According to Potter, this zenana ideology served even better than prostitution for lifting British feminism onto a more congenial moral plane. For whilst appearing complacent on the surface, its success as a cause for mobilising action suggests it contained an issue with which women in Britain wanted to contend. Therefore, largely by means of this ideology "feminism progressed further in the missions than it did in the church at home", ultimately, contributing to the overall advance of the women's movement.[116]

In this chapter I have argued that medical missions were a vital component in the history of feminist development. They accorded new possibilities to women at the turn of the century, encouraging them to fulfil their potential, whilst also helping prepare the ground for later innovations. By means of religious language which stressed vocation and a maternalism extending far beyond literal motherhood, women found increasing opportunities for moving into new and unknown territories. Initially their activities were contained within the limits of a safe ideology. However, the practical reality was consistently stretched until the very ideology itself was forced to recede. Emmeline Stuart, as a doctor and a woman, played a significant part within this wider picture. Hampered by the oppressive structures of Victorian language and discourses, she nevertheless participated in advancing the cause of the women's movement. In her own unique way, therefore, she authenticates the efforts of the CMS women in Iran as an influential strand within the historical development of feminism.

This brings to a close Part II of this book in which the conceptual themes of Part I were explored through the medium of biography. Mary Bird, Isabella Read and Emmeline Stuart, through the example of their lives and contributions, helped root the theories of chapters 1-4 within a cultural and historical reality. Accordingly, they provided contextual specificity for studying the influences of feminist, religious and orientalist assumptions underlying Victorian Britain during the age of empire.

CONCLUSION

As this book is being completed, Britain - along with much of the rest of the world - has just entered a new century and millennium. It is a period of intense change and uncertainty with people reflecting back to past achievements and failures whilst also looking to the future in hope, expectation and with some trepidation. Our values and priorities are reflected in how we view this time of transformation. For how we see ourselves and the world in which we live, has profound impact on how we regard the past and what we imagine for the future.

Whilst our context presents us with entirely different challenges and opportunities, the process of change is not dissimilar to that experienced by the CMS women in Iran at the turn of the last century. Their choices and actions were informed by the dominant contours of Victorianism that provided social, moral and cultural stability. In seeking a way forward, they aimed for a future which, whilst being a better place than the past, was nonetheless rooted within present reality. Indeed, they could only work for that future if it was manifestly realistic and practical in terms of their understanding and vision of the world.

The most complete understanding of the CMS women relies upon a sensitive appreciation of the complexities involved in historical research. The tension between past priorities and present concerns, the uneasy co-existence of generalised assumptions and particularised achievements, and the inherent paradoxes at the heart of the nineteenth century women's movement, all contribute to create a fuller, richer picture. Therefore, whilst using contemporary intellectual tools to analyse them, ultimately the CMS women should be judged by the standards of their own time, not the yardstick of our own priorities. Their achievements should be measured by an appreciation of the extent to which they conformed to or departed from the cultural norms and expectations of their day. It is this double-sided approach, incorporating past and present, which provides my work with its underlying comprehensiveness. The title of this book itself indicates the combined efforts of a conceptual consideration of religious feminism during the British empire *and* an analysis of the themes through the concrete specificity of a group of women rooted in a particular time and place.

Accordingly, Part I included a delineation of the ideological context of Victorian Britain (with its dominant influences of orientalism, evangelicalism and feminism), through a utilisation of late twentieth century interpretative concepts. This approach combined a desire to provide the relevant contextual setting with an intellectually credible method. Common nineteenth century assumptions regarding the three themes (empire, religion and gender) were outlined, the strength of their impact on British society acknowledged and internal developments within each discussed. Thus, the theoretical background for the work of CMS in Iran was examined both with relevance to the imperial programme itself and today's understanding of it.

Throughout Part I, I highlighted how orientalism regarded the East as essentially "other" and showed how its common linguistic motifs gave credence to western superiority in all areas of life. In addition the strength of evangelicalism within Victorian society was extremely influential both in providing religious justification for imperial views and in the interplay of women's growing involvement in public activities. Evangelical spirituality, at one and the same time, restricted and liberated women by confining them within acceptable gender boundaries whilst also motivating them to vocational responses which led to new and unprecedented opportunities. Churchwomen, therefore, played a significant part within the religious strand of Victorian feminism, by employing traditional ideologies (based on orientalist and evangelical assumptions) and expanding them to suit their practical requirements.

Nineteenth and early twentieth century women in Britain were negotiating the changing and conflicting contours of orientalist, evangelical and feminist perspectives. Meanwhile, those who worked abroad as missionaries had the additional task of confronting issues arising from encounters with other world religions. Part I ended with an acknowledgement of this aspect of missionary work through an expanded consideration of evangelical influence within early developments in the theology of religions. The CMS women in Iran were found to be both typical and untypical in their responses to the interfaith challenge.

Within the overall scene, as represented by the WMC's remarkably generous approach towards other faiths in 1910, those representing Persia now seem conservative and resistant to change. However, this was a feature of CMS culture at that time and also represented the response of other missionaries working in Muslim contexts. The CMS women in Iran were not unusual, therefore, in judging Islam negatively on the basis of unqualified generalisations and a willingness to associate the religion with the poor social condition of Iranian women. They further adhere to familiar patterns of their day through an ability to combine severe criticism of Islam in general terms, with genuine friendships and developing relationships. This orientalist tendency, allowing the general and particular to co-exist in this remarkable manner, was a Victorian peculiarity adopted by the CMS women and was a prominent feature of their work in Iran.

Part II provided an opportunity for further exploring the themes introduced in the previous chapters through a closer and more specific examination of CMS women's attitude towards the dominant ideologies of late Victorian society. Through the medium of biography the lives of three women were analysed with particular reference to their responses in each of the primary areas of theology, orientalism and feminism. The dynamics created by these three issues, in fact, underlay the entire section, for all three were of relevance to the individual women as well as their female colleagues. However, whilst their social, economic and religious contexts made them representative of most CMS women in Iran, individual interests and achievements also characterised each as unique and exceptional in her own way, thereby helping to highlight areas of specific interest within the fields of theology, orientalism and feminism.

Mary Bird's role gave rise, in particular, to greater appreciation of the CMS women's approach to theology and interreligious issues with reference to developing ideas within the theology of religions movement. Her attitude towards Islam and her relationship with Muslim women signified the general disposition of CMS women in this area. More successful than some in coming close to the people of Iran, her situation helps to highlight the dichotomy between missionary women's words and actions which enabled them to combine a general negativity towards Islam with a generous spirit towards Muslims. Isabella Read's somewhat unusual circumstances served to emphasise matters concerning orientalist assumptions of the day. Her resistance as well as her acquiescence in employing acceptable linguistic formulas evinced the tension inherent in the superior/inferior relationship which was a mark of empire during the late nineteenth and early twentieth centuries. By contrast, the life and work of Emmeline Stuart provided the most salient model for analysing the part played by missionary women within the overall history of feminism.

All three women, but most especially Stuart, embodied the failures and achievements of the CMS women in Iran by showing how their successes in some areas were dependent upon deficiency or limitation in others. Stuart's contributions clearly highlight significant advances in developing opportunities for women, justifying my contention that the CMS missionaries should be regarded as participants within the overall western women's movement. However, through complying with many orientalist and religious assumptions, her shortfalls characterise her as a Victorian woman moulded by the tenets of empire.

The CMS women did, of course, participate in the move towards gradual change in religious and orientalist outlook. Indeed their involvement, whilst highlighting several significant issues within the missionary context, also gives prominence to the more general situation concerning the relationship between East and West (Iran and England) during British imperial dominance. The extent of their contact with peoples of another faith and culture conformed to the typically narrow linguistic formulas of their day. Yet growing familiarity and acceptance of diversity also helped prepare the way for more open and honest dialogue in the future religious and cultural encounters between nations.

Notwithstanding their part within developing theological and orientalist ideas, the CMS women's most outstanding contribution was undoubtedly in the field of gender and the western women's movement. Their achievements, however, signified an inherent paradox within Victorian feminism which, whilst liberating for middle- and upper-class British women, relied upon an inferior "othering" of working-class women in England and so-called "heathen" women of the East. Furthermore, its success also necessitated religious authorisation from an essentially conservative Victorian evangelical theology. This ensured that women remained in an ideologically inferior position even whilst providing them with the motivation and justification for moving into the more public world of work.

Ultimately, all the efforts of CMS women in Iran between 1869-1934 were carried out within the overarching and powerful influence of evangelicalism upon all aspects of Victorian society. Mary Bird's instinct was for generosity towards Muslims, Isabella Read struggled for a post-orientalist approach in her writings, and Emmeline Stuart imagined a better world for all womankind. Yet each was severely hampered in her strivings by the strength of her evangelical convictions and the extent of its influence upon her. In short, none was able (or willing) to find a new theological framework necessary for justifying such major ideological shifts or a new language to accompany it. Ultimately, though experience changed their perceptions, the CMS women remained in essence culturally English and, as products of an imperialist and evangelical worldview, they were subject to its values and priorities.

This reliance upon western structures was, in fact, common to much that characterised the work of CMS and its women missionaries in Iran and elsewhere. For the mission's organisation, whilst responding to particular religious needs, nevertheless reflected much that was typical of imperial political structures generally. With the metropolis in London, as represented by CMS head-quarters and PC, the outlying stations became peripheral in terms of decision-making responsibilities. As part of the relentless imperial programme for globalisation, the networking of CMS activities in all its minutiae was directed from London as missionaries were responsible, finally, to authorities in Salisbury Square rather than to local mission leadership.

Moreover, the theory behind imperial benevolence - permeating the minds of most Victorian Britons abroad - was that the transfer of ideas would move from West to East. The perceived benefits of civilisation generally, education, medicine, the superior position of women, and for missionaries the Christian religion, were to be conveyed eastward with little provision allowed for the possibility that the movement may be two-way.

The CMS women were, of course, participants in this move towards globalisation. Whilst largely invisible in official structures, in reality, they were extremely influential, for the symbolic nature of their involvement was forcefully potent. In Iranian society at that time the co-operation of Muslim women in any such comparable programme was unthinkable. British society, for all its limitations, provided a milieu in which women, particularly single women, were beginning to realise new and hitherto unimaginable opportunities.

The socio-economic climate was favourable to women's involvement in paid employment. The religious tenor of evangelicalism also provided the upper echelons of Britain's female population with the incentive to broaden its horizons. The significance of monogamous marriage on one hand and Christian stress on celibacy on the other provided an ideological framework whereby women could extend their abilities from the private into the public arena. Married women, representing the very basis of sound society, were encouraged to extend their maternal influence further afield. Meanwhile, single women expanded such literal motifs, operating a form of social or benevolent motherhood and, by responding to the spiritual calling of vocation, became active participants in a movement for change.

Whilst the theory was in place for a one-sided transferral of imperial and religious benefits to be bestowed upon the unsuspecting East, the reality was often more fluid. It is evident from the example of the CMS women that though the theory retained its official status in their writings, in practice their relationships with locals frequently led to new insights and experiences. These subtly changed their perceptions without ever overthrowing or seriously undermining the deeply embedded theories of religious and cultural superiority.

One of my concerns throughout this book, and one which I outlined early on, has been to approach the protagonists with a complex historical methodology based on McLaughlin's dual perspective of "usability" and "responsibility".[1] Rather than attempting to judge the women missionaries from a straightforward late twentieth century standpoint as either right or wrong, I have tried to regard them and their actions as context specific, yet open to critical questioning. I have treated the CMS women with considerable respect, allowing them space to be heard on their own terms. Yet I have also examined them through the lens of a contemporary ideological and theoretical framework. I have, in short, attempted to be responsible towards their identity as Victorian women, whilst rendering them useful as subjects of current historical research.

The benefits of such an inclusive approach are to be found within the inherent tension it creates. The outcome, perhaps unsurprisingly, is not uncomplicated or straightforward but represents the composite nature of a bitter-sweet concoction. There are positive and negative factors to be acknowledged, both serving as useful guides to us as we play our part in the present and imagine the future it will lead to for following generations. It is obviously possible to learn from positive aspects of the CMS women's efforts. However, the inappropriate and unhelpful nature of their involvement serves to issue a warning to anyone entrenched in views which now seem acceptable but may look different in the light of historical hindsight.

From our perspective as inhabitants of a global village, much smaller and more compact than it was at the turn of the last century, we cannot avoid regarding the CMS women, in many respects, as misguided and erroneous. The benefits of modern technology have led to greater contact between East and West which has, in turn, created more understanding and appreciation. Bigotry and prejudice are still rife, yet western scholarship at least is much more wary of fanciful generalisations which demonise the "other" and categorise what is superior over that which is inferior. According to the breadth of experiences now available and the depth of understanding achieved, the CMS women display considerable limitation in their political, social and theological arguments. Swept along by the ideological tide of empire, they were often willing, uncritically, to uphold the values of Victorian England, endorsing the model as God-given, right and worthy of emulation. They displayed blindness towards the faults which marred their home society and the modifying influence of experience was soon distorted, stifling any forthcoming challenge into respectable silence.

Aware of their deficiencies and warned by the excesses of their wholehearted enthusiasm, it is nevertheless possible to extract positive lessons from the example of the CMS women in Iran. Within the dominance of narrow orientalist and religious views, and an era imposing heavy restrictions upon women, they achieved significant advances. Growing close to Persian people, they enjoyed notable contact with all types of Iranians, displacing many imaginary myths about the lives of easterners. Pioneers of greater contact between Orient and Occident, the greatest achievement of many was in the love and respect shown to them by Persians with whom they developed close and mutually respectful relationships. As Victorian women, the CMS missionaries showed extraordinary courage, dedication and autonomy in their decisions and the way they enacted these. Restricted by the weight of nineteenth century conventions, many displayed remarkable ingenuity and patience in struggling for better conditions. They exhibited considerable spiritual authority in responding to their vocation and participating in religious activities hitherto carried out by men alone. Accordingly, they may be regarded amongst the true pioneers of the women's movement within the Church of England, and their involvement should be seen as part of the long and troublesome path which led eventually to the ordination of women as priests in 1994.

Few commentators have acknowledged a relationship between the activities of missionary women and the progress of church feminism in Britain.[2] Yet there appears to be a natural and pertinent connection which could be explored on the basis of my research alone. The influence of Emmeline Stuart and other women missionary doctors upon the feminisation of British medicine has been alluded to in chapter 7. I believe that many similar links could be established between the significance of Victorian missionary women's work abroad and the development of feminism within Britain's churches in particular.

Indeed there are several ways in which the work I have carried out in this book could be developed by other research methods or expanded by further topics. The methodological slant which I have employed and the manner in which I have brought together mission studies and Iranian history, represents the opening of a tiny crack. For anyone interested in further research, there is ample scope for extensions and developments. Beyond the small crevice there is still a vast area of uncharted territory waiting to be explored.

The subject could usefully be considered from a perspective other than the missionary women themselves. The mission's impact upon Iran and the Iranian church, in particular, would provide a valuable approach to the material. Further linking the two fields of mission and Persian studies, this process would undoubtedly present different challenges to historians of the missionary movement and yield new insights for Iranian scholarship. Likewise, a closer examination of the role of CMS authorities in London upon the work of women missionaries would add an extra dimension to my research, enhancing our understanding of the extent to which the metropolis influenced the level of female involvement within the missionary movement.[3]

The period covered in this book, 1869-1934, represents the formative years of CMS's efforts in Iran as the missionaries faced challenges in their attempts to establish themselves within a new arena. Chronologically, if the topic were expanded through an examination of the post 1934 era, greater understanding of the encounter between western missionaries and the people of Iran would emerge. The involvement of later women missionaries differed according to their changing position in British society and their growing confidence within the mission structures. Furthermore, with the consolidation of the Pahlavi regime, the mission's entire relationship with the Iranian government and people began to change. Increasingly, they encountered hostility not just from religious circles, but from the growing tide of nationalism amongst the ordinary people. Anti-foreign feelings were often expressed more profoundly than anti-Christian sentiments. This, together with the impact of drastic centralisation programmes, led to the nationalisation or closure of missionary schools. The loss of educational establishments meant CMS, whilst forfeiting much of the direct influence it had hitherto enjoyed amongst the people, was forced to consider alternative working patterns.[4] Concurrently, the consolidation of the Persian church, through growing membership and increased Iranian leadership, necessitated a changing response from the missionaries. Inevitably, the extent and significance of women's participation shifted in the face of such enormous changes.

More broadly, this book has contributed to the wider area of women's involvement in the modern missionary movement and the British empire generally. I have deliberately augmented the confines within which mission studies usually operate and expanded the notion of empire beyond its common limitations. Both these are usually defined according to the geographical confines of formal British colonial rule. Iran, therefore, which was never colonised by the British, is normally neither considered a part of the British empire nor subjected to serious missiological study. By means of a more comprehensive interpretation of the term empire, I have tried to liberate mission studies from its usual boundaries and enhance the significance of imperial control. In reality, British imperial influence has had (and continues to have) far greater impact than the confines of literal colonialism may suggest. The part women played within this programme is varied and complex. A heavily contextualized bias, balanced by the creative tension of a "responsibly usable" approach, presents an engaging and challenging methodology. It advocates making past women visible and aims to give them epistemological dignity. At the same time it draws upon their experience as a means of better understanding contemporary feminism and improving future manifestations of the women's movement.

The CMS women in Iran have occupied my attention for over three years and life without them will seem strange. They have been companions with whom I have enjoyed many hours of silent dialogue. I have agonised over their historical significance, been challenged by their extraordinary achievements and have sympathised with their frequent failures. In many respects they and I are worlds apart, occupying different eras, maintaining divergent priorities and struggling with diverse challenges. Yet in other ways we are not that dissimilar. For I, like them, struggle within my own context to respond appropriately to the dominant discourses of my time. Indeed, more generally, Christians today are still searching for the right way to approach the priorities of a secular culture on one hand, and the realities of a multi-faith world on the other. In the words of David Bosch, "As we criticize our spiritual forebears, and do so relentlessly, let us remind ourselves that we would not have done any better than they did".[5] Though their efforts may now seem inadequate and unacceptable, the majority were motivated by good intentions and worthy causes. As pioneers in so many ways, they were mediating diversity and change within the developing fields of feminism, orientalism and religion. The CMS women in Iran, like most western Christians at the time, "in their emerging relationship with people of other cultures - did the only thing that made sense to them - they brought them the gospel as they understood it".[6]

Despite their shortcomings, these women are amongst our foremothers in faith. For it is through their efforts - good and bad - that we have arrived where we are today. We can reproach them for their many deficiencies, but the incentive towards a better future now rests with our own generation. I have enjoyed my journey with the CMS women, yet I look now to the growing number of young women in the small community that currently makes up the Anglican Church in Iran. They, like myself and many others, would not be here if it were not for the missionary women's efforts. Christian women in Iran today undoubtedly face new struggles, for their social and political environment presents them with different challenges. Yet to succeed, they must continue defying the ideological, theological and gender restrictions imposed upon them, whilst utilising any benefits available. Patience, ingenuity, courage, spiritual autonomy and humility are essential ingredients if Iranian Christian women, together with us all, are to create a better present and an improved future for following generations.

Notes

Introduction

1. Theories about the reasons and motivation for the development of the modern missionary movement are many and varied. Most commentators, however, agree that a combination of spiritual and socio-political factors were at play. For a variety of views see, for example, Stephen Neill (rev. 1986), *A History of Christian Missions*. Middlesex: Penguin; Brian Stanley (1990), *The Bible and the Flag: Protestant Missions and British Imperialism in the Nineteenth and Twentieth Centuries*. Leicester: Apollos; John Kent (1987), "Failure of a Mission: Christianity Outside Europe" in John Kent, *The Unacceptable Face: The Modern Church in the Eyes of the Historian*. London: SCM, pp 177-202; Max Warren (1970), "The Church Militant Abroad: Victorian Missionaries" in Anthony Symondson (ed.), *The Victorian Crisis of Faith*. London: SPCK, pp 57-70; Max Warren (1976), *I Believe in the Great Commission*. London: Hodder & Stoughton, pp 112-4; B. Worrall (1988), *The Making of the Modern Church: Christianity in England Since 1800*. London: SPCK, pp184-9.
2. On 12 April 1994 the organisation changed its name from Church Missionary Society to Church Mission Society. However, for the entire period covered by this book it was known by its former name which will be used unless the context specifically requires otherwise. For an account of how CMS started and details of its early years, see Eugene Stock (1899), *History of the Church Missionary Society, iii*. London: CMS, pp 68 f..
3. Within the last ten years scholars have begun publishing on the phenomenon of female involvement in the nineteenth century missionary movement and its significance upon the broader women's movement. See, for example, Fiona Bowie et al [eds.] (1993), *Women and Missions: Past and Present. Anthropological and Historical Perceptions*. Oxford: Berg; *Women's Studies International Forum*, 13:4 (1990) - several articles in this issue of the journal are dedicated to the subject of women and missions; Sean Gill (1994), *Women and the Church of England: From the Eighteenth Century to the Present*. London: SPCK, pp173-98; Frank Prochaska (1980), *Women and Philanthropy in 19th Century England*. Oxford: Clarendon Press, pp 19-72; and several chapters in Robert Bickers & Rosemary Seton [eds.] (1996), *Missionary Encounters: Sources and Issues*. Surrey: Curzon Press.
4. The word Persia is linguistically related to *Fars*, a region in the South-east of Iran, whose language - Persian - is dominant in the country. In the Persian language, the country has always been known as Iran - derived from the ancient Persian meaning "land of the Aryans" and signifying the early migrations of the Indo-Aryan people to the region. However, outside its boarders it was commonly known as Persia until, in 1935, Reza Shah ordered that the name Iran should be used by the rest of the world also. In the era covered by this book Persia was used to describe the country, however, the terms Iran and Persia, Iranian and Persian will be used interchangeably.
5. John Kent, op. cit., p 179, has commented that once colonialism ended and its realities became apparent, a new branch of church history emerged as missionary theorists began

analysing and transforming the old apologetic style of "not very critical biographies and ... complacent accounts of the work of missionary societies."

6   Missionary schools are often mentioned in passing in books on Iran but seldom does one find a reference to Iran or Persia in the index of a serious book on the history or theology of modern missionary movements. For two descriptive approaches to the subject see Hassan Dehqani-Tafti (1992), *Masih va Masihiyyat Nazd-e Iraniyan, I: Sayr-e Ejmali Dar Tarikh.* (Christ and Christianity Amongst the Iranians, i: A Short Historical Survey.) London: Sohrab Books, pp 59-76; and Robin Waterfield (1973), *Christians in Persia.* London: George, Allen & Unwin, pp 87f..

7   See Ursula King [ed.] (1994), *Feminist Theology from the Third World: A Reader.* London: SPCK, especially pp 4-5.

8   See, for example, Edward Said (1987), *Orientalism: Western Conceptions of the Orient.* London: Penguin (1995 reprint).

9   John Hick is one of the primary proponents of a pluralistic approach to religion that is severely critical of Christian attempts to evangelise people of other faiths in an effort to win converts. See, for example, John Hick & Paul Knitter [eds.] (1987), *The Myth of Christian Uniqueness.* London: SCM; and John Hick (1995), *The Rainbow of Faiths.* London: SCM.

10 For a discussion on scholars marginalizing religious impact see Susan Morgan (1997), *A Passion for Purity: Ellice Hopkins and the Politics of Gender in the Late-Victorian Church.* University of Bristol: PhD Thesis, pp 10-11. John Kent, op. cit., p 184, presents an example of post-imperialist anti-mission writing.

11 Elton Trueblood (1972), *The Validity of the Christian Mission.* NY: Harper & Row, p 29.

12 Frances Hiebert (1997), "Beyond a Post-modern Critique of Modern Missions: The Nineteenth Century Revisited" in *Missiology: An International Review*, 25: 3 (July), p 259.

13 Hiebert, op. cit., p 263.

14 See, for example, Lamin Sanneh (1993), *Encountering the West.* Maryknoll, NY: Orbis; Kwame Bediako (1995), *Christianity in Africa.* Maryknoll, NY: Orbis. With specific reference to a Persian Christian writing about his decision to convert to Christianity see Hassan Dehqani-Tafti's autobiography written some years ago: *Design of my World.* London: Lutterworth Press (1959).

15 Lamin Sanneh (1983), "The Horizontal and Vertical Mission: An African Perspective", *International Bulletin of Mission Research*, 7:4 (October), p 170. Though Sanneh is writing with specific reference to the situation in Africa, his insights are pertinent for the study of mission generally.

16 For a detailed development of this idea see William Jacob (1997), *The Making of the Anglican Church Worldwide.* London: SPCK.

17 ibid., p 298.

18 Maurice was a controversial and influential figure, who wrote prolifically during the nineteenth century. On the subject of Christianity's relationship with other faiths see, for example, Frederick Denison Maurice (1886), *The Religions of the World and their Relations to Christianity.* Cambridge: Macmillan & Co..

19 Note that more space has been allocated for delineating Iran's political, geographical and historical context, as it was there that the primary action took place.

Notes to Chapter One

Chp 1 - Imperialism and Feminism: In Search of an Integrated Methodology

1   The topic of this book lies somewhere within the broad category of "history", touching more specifically on areas of church history, mission studies, women's history, feminist history and Persian history. I mention the latter with care for I am aware of the problems associated with claiming to provide a history of a nation through its western missionary experience. In the 1960s and 70s it was not uncommon for scholars in the West to write histories of British missionary activity which were then passed off as histories of the indigenous people. Writing about the life and career of Peter Hinchliff, Adrian Hastings criticises his earlier work on mission activity in Africa for this very reason. "Well researched and useful as these works unquestionably are, they have always seemed to me markedly deficient in one, rather important, dimension - that of Africans themselves. Peter's 'African' history was a history of white people, Britishers in Africa. In that respect it was unfortunately too characteristic of the kind of 'colonial' history which passed everywhere for African history ...". See Adrian Hastings (1997), "From Africa to Oxford and Back: A Study of the Work of Professor Peter Hinchliff", *Theology*, 100:798 (Nov/Dec), p 403. Despite being Persian myself, I am duly cautioned by Hastings. Nevertheless, I do believe my book represents a part of the history of the church in Iran and that, as such, it may be considered an integral element of the history of a small minority of Persian people. This, in turn, makes it a component, however small, of Iran's past and a stage in the history of Iranian people. However, having approached the study not from the perspective of Persian people but from the missionaries' point of view, I am eager that it should be viewed essentially as a part of the history of nineteenth century Britain and the expanding Victorian church rather than the history of Iran.

2   Maxine Rodinson (1991), *Europe and the Mystique of Islam*. Seattle & London: University of Washington Press, p 84.

3   Mary Daly (1973), *Beyond God the Father: Toward a Philosophy of Women's Liberation*. Boston: Beacon, p 11.

4   Kim Knott (1995), "Women Researching, Women Researched: Gender as an Issue in the Empirical Study of Religion" in Ursula King (ed.), *Religion and Gender*. Oxford: Blackwell, p 214.

5   Sandra Harding [ed.] (1987), *Feminism and Methodology*. Milton Keynes: Open University Press, pp 2-3.

6   Daly, op. cit., p 11.

7   Daniel Maguire (1986), *The Moral Revolution*. San Francisco: Harper & Row, p 122.

8   James Bradley & Richard Muller (1995), *Church History: An Introduction to Research, Reference Works, and Methods*. Grand Rapids: Eerdmans, p 33.

9   Edward Said (1993), *Culture and Imperialism*. London: Vintage, pp 2-3.

10 Kathryn Pyne Addelson (1991), "The Man of Professional Wisdom" in Mary Fonow & Judith Cook (eds.), *Beyond Methodology: Feminist Scholarship as Lived Research*. Bloomington & Indianapolis: Indiana University Press, p 20.

11 Sheila Collins (1992), "Reflections on the Meaning of Herstory" in Carol Christ & Judith Plaskow (eds.), *WomanSpirit Rising: A Feminist Reader in Religion*. NY: HarperSanFrancisco, p 68.

12 Bradley & Muller, op. cit., p 36.
13 The Editorial Collective (1989), "Why Gender and History", *Gender and History*, 1:1, p 3.
14 Susan Morgan (1997), *A Passion for Purity: Ellice Hopkins and the Politics of Gender in the Late-Victorian Church*. University of Bristol: PhD Thesis, p 17.
15 Sean Gill (1994), *Women and the Church of England: From the Eighteenth Century to the Present*. London: SPCK, p 3.
16 Eleanor McLaughlin (1992), "The Christian Past: Does it Hold a Future for Women?" in Carol Christ & Judith Plaskow (eds.), *WomanSpirit Rising: A Feminist Reader in Religion*. NY: HarperSanFrancisco, pp 94-5.
17 Therefore, direct quotations from missionary letters will be used relatively extensively. Whilst these will be tempered by my own interpretations, it remains important that they are included as valid sources in their own right.
18 See, for example, Morgan, op. cit., pp 33-7.
19 There are now a growing number of such studies concentrating on all aspects of nineteenth century women's lives. See, for example, Gail Malmgreen [ed.] (1986), *Religion in the Lives of English Women 1760-1930*. London: Croom Helm; Pat Jalland (1986), *Women, Marriage and Politics, 1860-1914*. Oxford: Clarendon Press; Jane Lewis (1984), *Women in England 1870-1950: Sexual Divisions and Social Change*. London: Harvester Wheatsheaf; and Lilian Lewis Shiman (1992), *Women and Leadership in Nineteenth-Century England*. London: Macmillan.
20 Patricia Hilden (1982), "Women's History: The Second Wave", *The Historical Journal*, 25:2, p 501.
21 For fuller discussion surrounding the pitfalls involved in women's history see Harding [ed.], op. cit., pp 4-5; Hilden, op. cit., pp 507-8; Elizabeth Fox-Genovese (1982), "Placing Women's History in History", *New Left Review*, 133, p14; Judith Bennett (1989), "Feminism and History", *Gender and History*, 1:3, p 254; and Maria Mies (1991), "Women's Research or Feminist Research? The Debate Surrounding Feminist Science and Methodology" in Mary Fonow & Judith Cook (eds.), *Beyond Methodology: Feminist Scholarship as Lived Research*. Bloomington & Indianapolis: Indiana University Press, pp 60-84.
22 Gill, op. cit., p 3.
23 Gisela Bock (1989), "Women's History and Gender History: Aspects of an International Debate", *Gender and History*, 1:1, pp 8-9.
24 For more on the dangers inherent in some forms of feminist historiography see Bock, op. cit., p 8; Gill, op. cit., pp 3-4; Brian Harrison & James McMillan (1983), "Some Feminist Betrayals of Women's History", *The Historical Journal*, 26:2, pp 375-88; and Barbara Caine (1994), "Feminist Biography and Feminist History", *Women's History review*, 3:2, p 249.
25 Liz Stanley & Sue Wise (1991), "Feminist Research, Feminist Consciousness, And Experiences of Sexism" in Mary Fonow & Judith Cook (eds.), *Beyond Methodology: Feminist Scholarship as Lived Research*. Bloomington & Indianapolis: Indiana University Press, p 281.
26 Verta Taylor & Leila Rupp (1991), "Researching the Women's Movement: We Make Our Own History But Not Just As We Please" in Mary Fonow & Judith Cook (eds.), *Beyond*

Methodology: Feminist Scholarship as Lived Research. Bloomington & Indianapolis: Indiana University Press, p 127.

27 For a notable attempt to bring religion and gender into closer association, see Judith Plaskow (1993), "We Are Also Your Sisters: The Development of Women's Studies in Religion", *Women's Studies Quarterly*, 21:1-2, pp 9-21.

28 For negative approaches to the role of religion in the lives of British women see, for example, Shiman, op. cit., p 43; and Patricia Crawford (1993), *Women and Religion in England 1500-1720*. London: Routledge, p 4. For more positive interpretations see, for example, Gill, op. cit., especially pp 98-103; Morgan, op. cit., especially p 67; Barbara Caine (1992), *Victorian Feminists*. Oxford: University Press, p 12; and Frank Prochaska (1980), *Women and Philanthropy in 19th Century England*. Oxford: Clarendon Press, especially pp 222-30.

29 Elaine Graham (1995), *Making the Difference: Gender, Personhood and Theology*. London: Mowbray, p 26.

30 Caine (1992), op. cit., p 6.

31 Olive Banks (1993ed.), *Faces of Feminism: A Study of Feminism as a Social Movement*. Oxford: Blackwell, p 3; and Karen Offen (1988), "Defining Feminism: A Comparative Historical Approach", *Signs*, 14:1, p 132.

32 For an historical account of the word feminism see Offen, op. cit., pp 126-7.

33 The arguments used in this section to justify a broader use of the term feminism have largely been drawn from Offen, op. cit., p 134; Caine (1992), op. cit., p 6; and Olive Banks (1986), *Becoming a Feminist: The Social Origins of 'First Wave' Feminism*. Sussex: Wheatsheaf Books, p 159.

34 Brian Heeney (1982), "The Beginnings of Church Feminism: Women and the Councils of the Church of England 1897-1919", *The Journal of Ecclesiastical History*, 33:1 (January), p 91.

35 Philippa Levine (1987), *Victorian Feminism 1850-1900*. Tallahassee: Florida State University Press, p 18.

36 Offen, op. cit., p 128, has pointed out that like many other nineteenth century "ism" words (such as liberalism, conservatism and socialism), feminism was used by different groups to mean different things. Frequently, however, it referred to the "rights of women" rather than "rights equal to those of men".

37 Caine (1992), op. cit., p 52.

38 ibid., pp 16-7.

39 Brian Heeney in (1988), *The Women's Movement in the Church of England, 1850-1930*. Oxford: Clarendon Press, p 1, writes about the Church of England providing a great deal of anti-feminist doctrine and representing a major centre of resistance to the women's movement generally. As already mentioned, it should be noted that Heeney also refers to feminism as "a cause with many sides" although he appears to understand it more specifically as a fight for equality with men. See Heeney (1982), op. cit., pp 91 & 96.

40 From the 1880s in particular, feminism expanded rapidly to include new and varied ideas. For example, having been a predominantly middle-class phenomenon it increasingly involved working-class women whose participation diversified feminist theory and practice.

For details of changes within feminism during this period see, for example, Caine (1992), op. cit pp 241-50, and Levine, op. cit., pp 15-6.
41 Lavinia Byrne [ed.] (1993), *The Hidden Journey: Missionary Heroines in Many Lands*. London: SPCK, p 10.
42 A number of writers have acknowledged the opportunities which mission work raised for women in Britain through fund raising and support groups at home as well as active service abroad. Whilst this provided hundreds of women with a means of exercising their potential for work outside the home, their justification was based entirely on an extension of the domestic ideology. See, for example, Prochaska, op. cit., pp 23-93. As an example of scholarship which is critical of the missionary movement but still acknowledges the positive input of women, see John Kent (1987), "Failure of a Mission: Christianity Outside Europe" in John Kent, *The Unacceptable Face: The Modern Church in the Eyes of the Historian*. London: SCM, p 192.
43 Gill, op. cit., p 168.
44 Traditionally, in the days of uncritical histories of missionary societies earlier in the twentieth century, the link between British colonialism and imperialism was acknowledged as a natural product of its time. See, for example, Stephen Neill (1986 rev.), *A History of Christian Missions*. Middlesex: Penguin, pp 273-334. More recently, writers influenced by post-imperialist theories have been much more critical of missionary expansion as an exploitative arm of western imperialism. See, for example, Kent, op. cit.; and Greg Cuthbertson (1987), "The English-speaking Churches and Colonialism" in Charles Villa-Vicencio (ed.), *Theology and Violence: The South African Debate*. Johannesburg: Skotaville Publishers, pp 16-7. Others more committed to the missionary movement find themselves struggling with the subject. Stanley, for example, concludes that the missionary relationship to imperialism was complex and convoluted and while the missionaries were not indifferent to oppression and the desire for justice, their perceptions were too easily moulded by prevailing western ideologies. See Brian Stanley (1990), *The Bible and the Flag: Protestant Missions and British Imperialism in the Nineteenth and Twentieth Centuries*. Leicester: Apollos, p 184.
45 A number of secular studies have recently been published concerned with the role of women in the colonial services. For example, Helen Callaway (1987), *Gender, Culture and Empire*. Urbana: University of Illinois Press; Hilary Callan & Shirley Ardener [eds.] (1984), *The Incorporated Wife*. London: Croom Helm; Clare Midgley (1995), "Ethnicity, 'Race' and Empire" in June Purvis (ed.), *Women's History: Britain 1850-1945. An Introduction*. London: UCL, pp 247-76. For the relationship between missionary women and empire see Judith Rowbotham (1996), *"This is no Romantic Story": Reporting the Work of British Female Missionaries, c. 1850-1910*. NAMP Position Paper Number 4. Cambridge: University of Cambridge, North Atlantic Missiology Project; Margaret Strobel (1987), "Gender and Race in the Nineteenth- and Twentieth-Century British Empire" in R. Bridenthal et al (eds.), *Becoming Visible*. Boston: Houghton Mifflin, pp 374-96; Nupur Chaudhuri & Margaret Strobel (1990), "Western Women and Imperialism", *Women's Studies International Forum*, 13:4, pp 289-94. This issue of *WSIF* was dedicated to studies

Notes to Chapter One 185

of women and empire with a number of contributors writing about missionary women in particular.
46 For details of its early history see C. Eldridge (1978), *Victorian Imperialism*. London: Hodder & Stoughton, p 1.
47 Rosebury quoted in A. Thornton (1959), *The Imperial Idea and its Enemies*. London: Macmillan, p x.
48 Edward Said (1978), *Orientalism: Western Conceptions of the Orient*. London: Penguin (1995 reprint), p 7; and Said (1993), op. cit., p 132.
49 Said (1993), op. cit., p 8.
50 Eldridge, op. cit., p 3.
51 Michael Doyle (1986), *Empires*. Ithaca: Cornell University Press, p 45.
52 Said (1993), op. cit., pp 131-2.
53 Judith Bennett (1993), "Women's History: A Study in Continuity and Change", *Women's History Review*, 2:2, p 174.
54 Ronald Hyam (1992), *Empire and Sexuality: The British Experience*. Manchester: University Press, p 179. This view has, however, recently been challenged by Andrew Porter who believes that missionaries were, in fact, amongst the weakest agents of cultural imperialism.
55 Said (1978), op. cit., p 100. It is commonly maintained that missionary societies followed in the path forged by British imperialist expansion. A number of commentators argue from a somewhat different angle, emphasising instead the notion that a great deal of imperial ethos arose as a direct result of evangelicalism and its cultural influence upon British society. See, for example, Hyam, op. cit., pp 56-7; and Kathryn Tidrick (1990), *Empire and the English Character*. London: Tauris, p 3.
56 For more detail, see Callaway, op. cit., p 30.
57 Rowbotham, op. cit., p 30.
58 Midgley, op. cit., p 263.
59 ibid..
60 Antionette Burton (1990), "The White Woman's Burden: British Feminists and the Indian Woman, 1865-1915", *Women's Studies International Forum*, 13:4, pp 295-308.
61 B. Worrall (1988), *The Making of the Modern Church: Christianity in England Since 1800*. London: SPCK, p 8.
62 Nancy Paxton (1990), "Feminism Under the Raj: Complicity and Resistance in the Writings of Flora Annie Steel and Annie Besant", *Women's Studies International Forum*, 13:4, p 333.
63 Michel Foucault (1978), *The History of Sexuality, i: An Introduction*. New York: Pantheon, p 26.
64 Foucault, op. cit., p 101; and Jane Haggis (1991), *Professional Ladies and Working Wives: Female Missionaries in the London Missionary Society and its South Travancore District, South India in the 19th Century*. University of Manchester: PhD Thesis, p 33.
65 Strobel (1987), op. cit., p 375.
66 Said (1978), op. cit., pp 1-2.

67 For more on the connection between Foucault and Said's theories of "otherness" see Mehrzad Boroujerdi (1996), *Iranian Intellectuals and the West: The Tormented Triumph of Nativism*. N.Y.: Syracuse University Press, pp 1-7.
68 Haggis, op. cit., p 336.
69 Boroujerdi has written about this eastern desire to emulate the West, referring to it as "orientalism in reverse", a phrase coined earlier in the twentieth century by the Syrian philosopher Sadik Jajal al-Azm. Orientalism in reverse is the process by which "oriental" intellectuals aim to appropriate their true identity on the basis of many of the biases imposed by orientalism. It cannot satisfactorily be called occidentalism for its point of departure is essentially introverted. Primarily concerned with understanding its "own" Orient, it is only secondarily interested in the "other's" Occident. Whilst it shares the assumption about a fundamental ontological difference between East and West, orientalism in reverse begins from the point of infatuation with the dominating West. See Boroujerdi, op. cit., pp 10-4 & 12.
70 According to Neill, op. cit., p 220, regardless of missionary strategy, converts were frequently imitative, requiring everything to be done in its traditional western way. For a discussion of the mixed benefits of empire see, for example, Said (1993), op. cit., pp 18-9. For the views of several writers concerning the positive influence of women missionaries see, for example, Hyam, op. cit., p 49; and and Andrew Porter (1996), *"Cultural Imperialism" and Missionary Enterprise*. NAMP Position Paper Number 7. Cambridge: Univeristy of Cambridge, North Atlantic Missiology Project, pp 19-22. Kent, a vehement critic of the missionary endeavour has already been quoted acknowledging female missionaries as among the positive influences of the age of empire.
71 Isichei has underlined this in her study of African missionary work, concluding that female converts, far from resenting the imposition of Christianity, generally experienced it as beneficial and empowering. See Elizabeth Isichei (1993), "Does Christianity Empower Women? The Case of Anaguta of Central Nigeria" in Fiona Bowie et al (eds.), *Women and Missions: Past and Present. Anthropological and Historical Perceptions*. Oxford: Berg, p 209.
72 ibid., especially p 6.
73 Said (1993), op. cit., p xxi.
74 Porter, op. cit., p 25.
75 Gill, op. cit., p 191.
76 Stanley, op. cit., p 160.
77 Said (1978), op. cit., p 205, argues that during the nineteenth century there was a distillation of essential ideas about the Orient: its sensuality, for example, and its tendency towards despotism; its aberrant mentality, habits of inaccuracy, backwardness etc ... This meant that when the term "oriental" or "Orient" was used, it provided sufficient reference to be identified as a specific body of information which was, moreover, considered morally neutral and objectively valid.
78 Hyam, op. cit., pp 16-8.
79 Rodinson, op. cit., pp 78, 106, 127.
80 Strobel (1987), op. cit., p 383.

Notes to Chapter One

81 Hyam, op. cit., p 202.
82 Mies, op. cit., pp 69-70.
83 For a helpful discussion of these problems see Morgan, op. cit., pp 32-3.
84 Copies were also kept of outgoing "Letters" from CMS head-quarters in London to individual missionaries. These, however, have not been used as an information source for this book which concentrates on events and their interpretation from the view point of the missionaries themselves.
85 The censorship of correspondence retained in the files is a rare feature. However, there are occasional letters dealing with controversial issues which include sections that have been entirely inked out.
86 Towards the end of the period, excerpts used for publication became shorter and shorter. More problematic, however, is the fact that after publication, the original copies were discarded, severely limiting an already restricted collection.
87 For more information on the gender based classification of missionary letters generally see Haggis, op. cit., pp 90-8.
88 Bennett (1993), op. cit., p 175.
89 Said (1978), op. cit., pp 42-3.
90 ibid., p 156.
91 ibid., p 157.
92 I use the term missiology with great circumspection throughout this book, strictly as shorthand for mission studies or mission history. It is a controversial word, sometimes accused of being nothing more than an excuse for missionary apologetics (see Kent, op. cit., p 184). In reality, there is no common agreed definition and different writers use the term to mean different things. For some it is meaningless unless it moves from theory to the practice of missionary participation and is, therefore, a forum for discussing and improving practical methods. For others, it is an intellectual discipline concerned with the contextual study of the church's missionary activity. For a fuller discussion about the nature of the term missiology, see James Scherer (1987), "Missiology as a Discipline and What it Includes", *Missiology*, 15:4 (October), pp 507-22.
93 For a fuller discussion concerning the use of photographs and visual evidence in historical studies, see Paul Jenkins (1996), "Four nineteenth-century pictorial images from Africa in the Basel Mission Archive and Library Collections" in Robert Bickers & Rosemary Seton [eds], *Missionary Encounters: Sources and Issues*. Surrey: Curzon Press, pp 95-113.
94 Said (1978), op. cit., p 8.
95 Caine (1994), op. cit., pp 252-3.
96 The terms "victim" and "agent" are applied to historical women by Judith Bennett (1989), op. cit., p 262, who argues they were disposed to both. Though they were not *passive* victims, they still colluded with patriarchal standards, and whilst not *free* agents, they nevertheless encountered ideological, institutional and practical barriers which they had to overcome.
97 Toby Epstein Jayaratne & Abigail Stewart (1991), "Quantitative and Qualitative Methods in the Social Sciences: Current Feminist Issues and Practical Strategies" in Mary Fonow &

Judith Cook (eds.), *Beyond Methodology: Feminist Scholarship as Lived Research*. Bloomington & Indianapolis: Indiana University Press, p 98.

98 Addelson, op. cit., p 31.

99 It is largely this factor that has guided the emphasis of my research. Not free to visit Iran, I have had to rely, for the most part, on British sources rather than considering the subject in a more balanced way from the perspective of the Persian church as well as CMS. It should be noted, however, that even if trips to Iran had been possible there is virtually nothing available by way of textual material as most of the diocesan papers were destroyed or looted in the aftermath of the revolution. For details of the manner in which the revolution affected both my family and the Persian Anglican Church, see Hassan Dehqani-Tafti (1981), *The Hard Awakening*. London: Triangle, SPCK.

100 Said (1978), op. cit., p 20.

101 Patricia Hill Collins (1991), "Learning from the Outside Within: The Sociological Significance of Black Feminist Thought" in Mary Fonow & Judith Cook (eds.), *Beyond Methodology: Feminist Scholarship as Lived Research*. Bloomington & Indianapolis: Indiana University Press, pp 35-54.

102 Mary Fonow & Judith Cook (1991), *Beyond Methodology: Feminist Scholarship as Lived Research*. Bloomington & Indianapolis: Indiana University Press, p 9.

103 Johnson (1975) quoted in Stanley & Wise (1991), op. cit., p 267.

104 Callan & Ardener [eds], op. cit., p 11.

105 Kenneth Cragg (1985 rev.), *The Call of the Minaret*. London: Collins, p 181.

106 Hilary Rose (1982), "Making Science Feminist" in Elizabeth Whitelegg et al (eds.), *The Changing Experience of Women*. Oxford: Martin Robinson, p 368.

107 See Ursula King [ed.] (1995), *Religion and Gender*. Oxford: Blackwell, p 222.

Chp 2 - A Meeting of West and East: The Victorian/Qajar Period Contextualized

1. For further details concerning both the Qajar tribe and dynasty, see Ann Lambton (1987), *Qajar Persia*. London: Tauris. The following is a list of the shahs from the Qajar dynasty between 1787-1925:

Agha Muhammad	1787-97
Fath Ali	1798-1834
Muhammad	1834-48
Naser-e-din	1848-96
Muzaffar-e-din	1896-1907
Muhammad Ali	1907-9
Sultan Ahmad	1909-25

2. Writing as late as 1970, Max Warren, in "The Church Militant Abroad: Victorian Missionaries" in Anthony Symondson (ed.), *The Victorian Crisis of Faith*. London: SPCK, p 58, commented on the long-term survival of Victorian influences, and questioned "whether we are not still in many respects Victorians"? A comment should also be made about my occasional use of the words "England" or "English" as interchangeable for "Britain" or "British". Although there were included among the missionaries a number of Welsh, Scottish and Irish women and men, the policies of CMS and many of the ideas proliferating its work were English in origin. Also, in Persian, the word *Engelestaan* - literally, England, was commonly used to mean Britain or the United Kingdom and, moreover, as Wright points out, "in those far off days" people from Great Britain "were all known as 'the English'". See Denis Wright (1977), *The English Amongst the Persians*. London: William Heinemann Ltd, p xv.

3. Arnold Wilson (1932), *Persia*. London: Ernest Benn Limited, p 26. Many visitors to Iran have provided lengthy descriptions of the country's geography, climate and other physical characteristics. See, for example, Donald Wilber (1955), *Iran: Past and Present*. Princeton: University Press, pp 3-13; and Ella Sykes (1910), *Persia and its People*. London: Methuen & Co. Ltd, pp 1-12.

4. These figures were taken from Ervand Abrahamian (1982), *Iran Between Two Revolutions*. Princeton, New Jersey: Princeton University Press, p 12; and Rouhi Shafii (1997), *Scent of Saffron: Three Generations of an Iranian Family*. London: Scarlet Press, p 1. See also B. Gilbar (1976/77), "Deomographic Developments in Late Qajar Persia, 1870-1906", *Asian and African Studies*, 2, pp 125-56; and Gavin Hambly (1991b), "The Traditional Iranian City in the Qajar Period" in Peter Avery (ed.), *The Cambridge History of Iran*, vii: *From Nadir Shah to the Islamic Republic*. Cambridge: University Press, pp 542-3. Despite such details provided by scholars, the reality is that non-existent census data means the Qajar years remain a "dark age for Iranian statistics" (Abrahamian, op. cit., p 12), and most figures are estimated by projecting back from twentieth century census information. Indeed, the period is poorly served by documentation of any kind and, as Hambly points out, "the researcher remains dangerously dependent upon the subjective accounts of European diplomats, travellers and missionaries" (Hambly, op. cit., p 542).

5. Roger Stevens (1962), *The Land of the Great Sophy*. London: Methuen & Co. Ltd, p 7.

6 Persian is the dominant language spoken by approximately half the population. For a summary of other racial groups and languages see, for example, Nikki Keddie (1981), *Roots of Revolution: An Interpretative History of Modern Iran.* (Includes a section by Yann Richard.) New Haven: Yale University Press, p 26.

7 Upton writes: "Until the mid-[nineteen]twenties movement and transportation overland were almost exclusively on foot, on donkey, camel, or horse-back, or in some type of horse-drawn conveyance - a carriage for persons, a heavy, springless wagon for merchandise". Joseph Upton (1960), *The History of Modern Iran: An Interpretation.* Cambridge, Massachusetts: Harvard University Press, p 21.

8 See Abrahamian, op. cit., pp 18-25.

9 Malcolm Yapp (1977), "1900-1921: The Last Years of the Qajar Dynasty" in Hossein Amirsadeghi (ed.), *Twentieth Century Iran.* London: Heinemann, p 2.

10 Ann Lambton (1954), *Islamic Society in Persia.* London: London University, p 16-7.

11 A number of royal women were also among the appointed governors of provinces though their role was solely for the purpose of receiving revenue. Keddie, op. cit., pp 26-7.

12 Abrahamian, op. cit., p 41.

13 Yapp, op. cit., p 2.

14 Stephen Neill (1986 rev.), *A History of Christian Missions.* Middlesex: Penguin, p 81.

15 These minority groups included Assyrian and Armenian Christians, Jews, Zoroastrians and Baha'is. For details see Abrahamian, op. cit., p 12.

16 For details of the historical and doctrinal differences between Shi'ism and Sunnism see, for example, Yann Richard (1995), *Shi'ite Islam.* Trl. by Antonia Nevill. Oxford: Blackwell; and Ilya Petrushevsky (1985), *Islam in Iran.* Trl. by Hubert Evans. London: Athlone Press.

17 Bernard Lewis (1995), *The Middle East: 2000 Years of History from the Rise of Christianity to the Present Day.* London: Weidenfeld & Nicolson, p 331.

18 This was a particularly common notion in the nineteenth century. For examples of scholars promoting this view see Petrushevsky, op. cit., p 32. For details of why the theory was prominent see Lewis, op. cit., pp 75-6.

19 Stevens, op. cit., p 41.

20 Richard, op. cit., p 78.

21 ibid., p 91.

22 ibid., p 101. For details and descriptions of the most important Shi'ite religious rites in Iran also see ibid., pp 97-101.

23 Roy Mottahedeh (1985), *The Mantle of the Prophet: Religion and Politics in Iran.* New York: Pantheon Books, p 313.

24 Stevens, op. cit., p 32.

25 Mottahedeh, op. cit., p 164.

26 Stevens, op. cit., p 36. Prior to the 1979 revolution there was much criticism of this Persian tendency towards pre-Islamic self-understanding by a number of prominent writers. Ali Shariati (1933-77), now widely regarded as the main ideological brain behind the revolution, believed that Islamic civilisation had completely cut Iran off from its pre-Islamic past and that "a return to our roots means not a rediscovery of pre-Islamic Iran, but a return to our Islamic, especially Shiah roots" (quoted in Mottahedeh, op. cit., pp 330-1). His

Notes to Chapter Two

writings were amongst those that convinced many middle-class Iranian intellectuals of the need for a complete break with the Shah's regime through an Islamic Revolution. Certainly, total identification with Islam at the expense of pre-Islamic Persian culture was a feature of the revolutionary temperament. However, the paradoxical nature of the Islamic/pre-Islamic Persian character is evident again today, perhaps more strongly than ever, especially among the middle-classes who found that identification with Islam alone did not provide the historical rootedness for which they searched. Shafii (op. cit., p 5), for example, writes passionately about the Arabs who "ruined the long-lasting Persian civilization".

27 With the exception of China which has attracted a great deal of missiological scholarship.

28 During most of the period in which CMS was active in Iran, the balance of influential power swung between Russia and Britain, although there were other nations, including Germany and the USA, also involved in Iranian politics. The USA became an effective body in the region from the mid twentieth century, just as Britain was withdrawing due to the ending of its oil interests. For a summary of earlier US involvement in Iran see W. Morgan Shuster (1912), *The Strangling of Persia: A Record of European Diplomacy and Oriental Intrigue*. London: T. Fisher Unwin. It should be noted, however, that my book is concerned solely with the position of the British in Iran. For a concise and helpful chapter on the intricacies of foreign investments in Iran see Yapp, op. cit.. For Iranian relations with Great Britain in particular, see Rose Greaves (1991), "Iranian Relations with Great Britain and British India, 1798-1921" in Peter Avery (ed.), *The Cambridge History of Iran, vii: From Nadir Shah to the Islamic Republic*. Cambridge: University Press, pp 374-425.

29 Wright, op. cit., p 2.

30 George Curzon (1892), *Persia and the Persian Question*, ii. London: Longmans, Green & Co, p 602. Lord Curzon travelled to Iran between 1889-90, was very influential in British foreign policy and became Foreign Secretary in 1919. For a detailed outline of British policy in Persia during this period see Curzon, op. cit., pp 585-634; Wright, op. cit.; and Gordan Waterfield (1973), *Professional Diplomat: Sir Percy Loraine*. London: John Murray, pp 59-138.

31 Stevens, op. cit., p 31. Gallagher and Robinson developed their thesis of British imperialism during the 1950s, arguing that it aimed towards the integration of new regions into an expanding economy through combining commercial penetration and political influence. They believed, however, that it limited the use of military power and encouraged stable governments in order to provide conditions which would best suit British interests. See C. Eldridge (1978), *Victorian Imperialism*. London: Hodder & Stoughton, pp 74-6.

32 Indirect imperialism which operates regardless of colonial status has been identified as a kind of informal imperialism by Stanley. See Brian Stanley (1990), *The Bible and the Flag: Protestant Missions and British Imperialism in the Nineteenth and Twentieth Centuries*. Leicester: Apollos, p 35.

33 See Max Warren (1976), *I Believe in the Great Commission*. London: Hodder & Stoughton, p 113; and David Bosch (1991), *Transforming Mission: Paradigm Shifts in Theology of Mission*. Maryknoll, New York: Orbis, p 307.

34 Wright, op. cit., p xiv; and Sattareh Farman Farmaian (1992), *Daughter of Persia: A Woman's Journey from her Father's Harem Through the Islamic Revolution*. London: Bantam Press, p 83.
35 Wright, op. cit., p xiv. Many writers have commented upon this unusual situation. Cottam, for example, articulated it in terms of a peculiar paradox. "Nowhere in the world", he wrote, "is British cleverness so wildly exaggerated as in Iran, and nowhere are the British more hated for it". R. Cottam (1964), *Nationalism in Iran*. Pittsburgh, p 217.
36 For details see Mottahedeh, op. cit., pp 295f..
37 Al-e Ahmad quoted in ibid., p 296. For more on Jalal Al-e Ahmad see also Mehrzad Boroujerdi (1997), *Iranian Intellectuals and the West: The Tormented Triumph of Nativism*. N.Y.: Syracuse University Press, pp 53, 65-76.
38 Abrahamian, op. cit., pp 3-6, 419.
39 ibid., pp 426, 435.
40 ibid., pp 448-9.
41 Gordon Hewitt (1971), *The Problem of Success: A History of the Church Missionary Society, 1910-1942, i*. London: CMS Press Ltd, p 377.
42 It should also be noted that there were periods during which relations between the mission and Persian people were more relaxed. For example, during times of difficulty such as the famines of 1870-1 and 1918-19, the work of missionaries was appreciated and animosity towards them lessened.
43 The enthusiasm with which Britain grasped this opportunity can be seen by the increased number of officials and government representatives stationed in Iran. From having no consulates in 1841, the number had risen to twenty-three in 1921. See Wright, op. cit., p 75.
44 In addition to a seventy year railway concession running from the north of the country to the south, Reuter was handed exclusive rights, for seventy years throughout Persia, for tramways, mining, irrigation, water works and exploitation of the state forests. He was also given a twenty-year monopoly over the Persian customs and the first option on any further concessions for public utilities, roads, postal services, manufacturing plants and banks. In return, twenty percent of the railway profits and fifteen percent of all other profits were to go to the Shah. The result of this extraordinary situation, according to the French Statesman Thiers, was that nothing of Persia was left to the people except the atmosphere. See Wright, op. cit., p 103.
45 Curzon, op. cit., p 480.
46 The consul in Tabriz even feared a massacre of Christians. See Wright, op. cit., p 107. For further details of the Tobacco Concession see Lambton (1987), op. cit., pp 223-76. It is usually agreed that the *ulama* stirred up feeling against the British, encouraging popular revolt. For a presentation of this view see, for example, Nikki Keddie (1966), *Religion and Rebellion in Iran: The Iranian Tobacco Protest of 1891-1892*. London: Frank Cass. However, more recently, Fereydun Adamiyat has argued that the strength and spontaneity of popular feeling alarmed the *ulama* who did all they could to calm and channel the reaction. They joined the demonstrators in order not to lose their influence and in the hope of reaching a compromise with the monarchy. (Fereydun Adamiyat, *Shuresh bar emtiyaz-nama-ye Rehzi*, Tehran: Payam, 1360/1981, summarised in Richard, op. cit., p 92.

Notes to Chapter Two

47 Wright, op. cit., p 107; and Edward Browne (1910), *The Persian Revolution of 1905-1909*. 1966 Impression, London: Frank Cass & Co., p 57.
48 Firuz Kazemzadeh (1968), *Russia and Britain in Persia, 1864-1914*. Yale: University Press, p 502.
49 Lambton (1987), op. cit., p 277; and Abrahamian, op. cit., p 90. For full details of the struggle surrounding the Constitutional Revolution, the civil war and the fifteen years following these events, see for example, Browne, op. cit.; Lambton (1987), op. cit., pp 319-30; Abrahamian, op. cit., pp 69-101; and Vanessa Martin (1989), *Islam and Modernism: The Iranian Revolution of 1906*. London: Tauris. The period is also well covered by the more narrative, autobiographical style of Farman Farmaian, op. cit., pp 26-41.
50 Wright, op. cit., pp 172 & 174.
51 For details of the extraordinary machinations surrounding the 1919 Agreement see, for example, Wright, op. cit., pp 178-80; Yapp, op. cit., pp 20-2; and Waterfield, op. cit., pp 59-66.
52 For more on Reza Shah, and British involvement during the period between 1921 and his downfall in 1941 see, for example, Wilfred Knapp (1977), "1921-1941: The Period of Riza Shah" in Hossein Amirsadeghi (ed.), *Twentieth Century Iran*. London: Heinemann, pp 23-52; and Abrahamian, op. cit., pp 118-68.
53 Hambly, op. cit., p 588.
54 ibid., p 586.
55 Sykes, op. cit., p 208; and Shuster, op. cit., p 183.
56 For example, spinning, weaving, cooking, agriculture and animal husbandry. See Keddie (1981), op. cit., p 26.
57 Farman Farmaian, op. cit., p 7.
58 For greater details in the variety of Persian women's lives see, for example, Keddie (1981), op. cit., p 14; and Sima Bahar (1983), "A Historical Background to the Women's Movement in Iran" in Farah Azari (ed.), *Women of Iran: Conflict with Fundamentalist Islam*. London: Ithaca Press, pp 170-1.
59 Questions include details such as the age of puberty and marriage, the span of child-bearing years, the size and mortality rates of families, the roles of mothers and others in child-rearing, women in the work force, the position of single women in society, the practical implications of women's social and legal status.
60 Hambly, op. cit., p 586.
61 For more on Muslim family law see Keddie (1981), op. cit., pp 97-8; and Petrushevsky, op. cit., pp 143-51. For more information on temporary marriages see Shahla Haeri (1989), *Law of Desire*. London: Tauris, especially pp 76, 82, 192.
62 This subject is explored in a novel by Grace Visher Payne (1950), *The Unveiling*. Philadelphia: The Westminster Press. See, for example, pp 57-9.
63 Farman Farmaian, op. cit., p 77.
64 The Shah's wives and women in other harems were especially influential as they joined the battle against the Tobacco Concession by breaking their pipes and boycotting the smoking of tobacco. For details of a few exceptional women who were willing to speak out on socio-political affairs see Bahar, op. cit., pp 171-2.

65 For details of this and various other incidents see Bahar, op. cit., pp 173-4; and Mangol Bayat-Philipp (1978), "Women and Revolution in Iran, 1905-1911" in Lois Beck & Nikki Keddie (eds.), *Women in the Muslim World.* Cambridge, Massachusetts: Harvard University Press, pp 302-4.

66 For more information surrounding this event see Abrahamian, op. cit., pp 108-10; Keddie (1981), op. cit., p 77; Shafii, op. cit., pp 17-8; and Shuster, op. cit., pp 157-208. Shuster himself was the American financial adviser to which the Russians objected.

67 Bayat-Philipp, op. cit., p 306.

68 The first women's magazine, *Danesh* (Knowledge) was published in Tehran in 1911.

69 Wiebke Walther (1993), *Women in Islam: From Medieval to Modern Times.* Princeton & New York: Markus Wiener Publishing, p 225.

70 For more on the history and development of the *madresseh* see Mottahedeh, op. cit., pp 89-147; and Petrushevsky, op. cit., pp 75-6. For details of *maktab* education in Iran see Mottahedeh, op. cit., pp 67-8, 90.

71 Missionary schools occasionally receive a mention, particularly in autobiographies of Persian women who often credit them with having provided a positive influence. See, for example, Farman Farmaian, op. cit., pp 56-60, 73-5; and Shafii, op. cit., pp 8 & 32.

72 Keddie (1981), op. cit., p 108.

73 ibid., p 108; and Gavin Hambly (1991a), "The Pahlavi Autocracy: Riza Shah, 1921-1941" in Peter Avery (ed.), *The Cambridge History of Iran, vii: From Nadir Shah to the Islamic Republic.* Cambridge: University Press, p 235.

74 A number of positive reforms did come into effect under Reza Shah such as the raising of the legal age for marriage (see Keddie (1981), op. cit., p 98). Also, women students were admitted to the University of Tehran from its foundation in 1935 and, by the late 1930s, had access to many professions including government posts. However, they were still exploited in many areas such as the textile and carpet industries in which they had long been the primary workers, employed on low wages and under poor conditions.

75 Shafii, op. cit., p 22. See also, Farman Farmaian, op. cit., pp 95-6; and the novel, *The Unveiling,* by Payne, op. cit., which provides an insight into the difficulties that this law caused for many Iranian families.

76 Farman Farmaian, op. cit., p 91.

77 Unless otherwise stated or clarified by the context, throughout this book I use the term "church" to mean the Anglican communion abroad and/or the Church of England.

78 Several helpful books have been published on religion and society in nineteenth and twentieth century Britain. See, for example, John Moorman (1973ed.), *A History of the Church in England.* London: A & C Black; Elisabeth Jay (1986), *Faith and Doubt in Victorian Britain,* Context and Commentary Series. Basingstoke: Macmillan; B. Worrall (1988), *The Making of the Modern Church: Christianity in England Since 1800.* London: SPCK.

79 Moorman, op. cit., p 417.

80 Biblical criticism originated in Germany during the eighteenth century, yet by 1900 most serious scholars in Britain had accepted its main conclusions.

81 The publication of *Essays and Reviews* in 1860 was indicative of contemporary liberalism, its toleration of a breadth of Christian opinion and the desire to express theological truths in a manner relevant to the times.

82 For more details on the trial of Edward King and disagreements over the revision of the Prayer Book, see David Bebbington (1989), *Evangelicalism in Modern Britain: A History from the 1730s to the 1980s*. London: Routledge, pp 147 & 205, 220-1.

83 Worrall, op. cit., p 41.

84 An appreciation of the nature of evangelicalism and its relationship with British society during the late nineteenth and early twentieth centuries is vital as it formed the theological backdrop against which the missionary activities took place. For an excellent account of it history, essential doctrines and how it changed, see Bebbington, op. cit..

85 Worrall, op.cit. p 9.

86 Bebbington, op. cit., pp 115-7.

87 Evangelical divisions were most apparent in 1922 when CMS, "the barometer of the Evangelical party" (Cockayne quoted in Bebbington, op. cit., p 217), experienced a schism, leading to the formation of the more conservatively Scripture-based BCMS.

88 These four characteristics are applied by Bebbington as stable elements within an otherwise changing phenomenon. For a full account of their significance, see Bebbington, op. cit., pp 2-17. The evangelical and western missionary movements had always been closely linked. The religious revivals of early evangelicalism provided the catalyst for organised missionary activity, while the setting up of societies such as CMS in 1799 was largely responsible for the subsequent influence of evangelicalism upon the mainstream church.

89 Holroyd quoted in Bebbington, op. cit., p 150.

90 See, for example, Sean Gill (1994), *Women and the Church of England: From the Eighteenth Century to the Present*. London: SPCK, p 83.

91 Hugh McLeod (1981), *Religion and the People of Western Europe, 1789-1970*. Oxford: University Press, p 29; for a discussion of why this may have been the case, see pp 29-34.

92 Lilian Lewis Shiman (1992), *Women and Leadership in Nineteenth-Century England*. London: Macmillan, p 6. During much of the nineteenth century women's employment opportunities were very limited. Most professions were hostile to the idea of including women, whose only realistic hope of a career lay in governessing or teaching. As the women's movement progressed there was a growing belief that education was the key to success and from the 1850s, in particular, there were many efforts to improve female education. With the advent of state education from 1870, the church's monopoly disappeared and by the end of the century the situation had much improved. The church had long provided elementary education for girls especially through the provision of Sunday schools. However, few received the thorough tutelage which boys enjoyed through regular attendance at day schools. Secondary and higher education, mainly a middle-class prerogative, was much more contentious for it threatened the notion that women's primary sphere was in the home. The church included advocates on both sides of the argument (see Gill, op. cit., pp 115-23), though following the acceptance of women missionaries, most societies shared the view that their female workers should be well educated. By 1900 there were many institutions offering higher education to women, with the notable exception of

Oxford and Cambridge Universities which barred full female membership until 1919 and 1948 respectively. For more detailed information on women's education during the period see Gill, op. cit., pp 112-30; Shiman, op. cit., pp 82-5; and Philippa Levine (1987), *Victorian Feminism 1850-1900*. Tallahassee: Florida State University Press, pp 26-56, which includes a useful chronology of the major landmarks.

93 The reasons for the increased social problems included population growth, urbanisation, rising unemployment and other such effects of industrialisation. For fuller details of these and other interconnected issues see, for example, Worrall. op. cit., pp 37-9.

94 Frank Prochaska (1980), *Women and Philanthropy in 19th Century England*. Oxford: Clarendon Press, p 223.

95 Bebbington, op.cit. p 212.

96 Gill, op. cit., p 14.

97 For details see McLeod, op. cit., p 30; and Prochaska, op.cit. p 2.

98 This theory was traced by evangelicals to specific scriptural references, especially, Genesis 2-3, 1 Corinthians 11, and 1 Timothy 2.

99 Gill, op. cit., p 78.

100 For more on the importance of motherhood at the turn of the century see Gill, op. cit., pp 103f.; Jane Lewis (1984), *Women in England 1870-1950: Sexual Divisions and Social Change*. London: Harvester Wheatsheaf, pp 92-7; and Susan Morgan (1997), *A Passion for Purity: Ellice Hopkins and the Politics of Gender in the Late-Victorian Church*. University of Bristol: PhD Thesis, pp 95, 239-45.

101 Lewis (1984), op. cit., p 95. The official census of 1851 verified that there were approximately 400,000 more women than men in Britain. A growing urgency developed over the problem of what should be done with these so-called redundant or "surplus" women. Clearly, they could not all marry, however, allowing them better education and employment opportunities meant admitting a basic flaw in the separate spheres ideology which required women to remain in their "natural" realm at home.

102 Sarah Lewis (1839) quoted in Morgan, op. cit., p 240.

103 Saleeby quoted in Anna Davin (1978), "Imperialism and Motherhood", *History Workshop*, 5 (Spring), p 51.

104 Brian Heeney (1988), *The Women's Movement in the Church of England, 1850-1930*. Oxford: Clarendon Press, p 14.

105 Lewis (1984), op. cit., p 93.

106 Barbara Ramusack (1990), "Cultural Missionaries, Maternal Imperialists, Feminist Allies: British Women Activists in India, 1865-1945", *Women's Studies International Forum*, 13:4, pp 310-19.

107 Jay, op. cit., p 19.

108 For more on Victorian women's concepts of suffering see Morgan, op. cit., p 246f.. Gill (op. cit., pp 85-7), has pointed out the ambiguities involved in the efforts to negotiate women's involvement in the church during this period on the basis of feminising Christology. Many were unhappy with stressing the sacrificial characteristics of Christ in terms of feminine attributes such as sympathy and compassion. These were regarded as undermining such distinctly masculine qualities as his leadership and assertiveness. Consequently, a

Notes to Chapter Two

mysterious unity of Christ's manly and womanly characteristics was advocated in the concept of chivalry - "that interplay of masculine strength and feminine weakness" in which the contradictory gender expressions in Christ were reconciled.

[109] Gill, op. cit., p 4.

[110] Heeney has outlined the slow progression of women in the democratisation process of the church from the late nineteenth century onwards. See Brian Heeney, op. cit.; and Brian Heeney (1982), "The Beginnings of Church Feminism: Women and the Councils of the Church of England 1897-1919", *The Journal of Ecclesiastical History*, 33:1 (January), pp 89-109. The movement to provide the Church of England with the machinery for self-government and increased lay involvement began c. 1880. However, women were excluded from both the Parochial Church Councils (PCCs) formed in 1897, and the Representative Church Council in 1903 for which they were not even permitted to vote. Modest concessions were eventually granted in 1914 when women were authorised to stand for election onto PCCs. It was not until the Enabling Act of 1919, however, that full equality on the various Church Councils was finally conceded to women. Despite the tireless work of the Church League for Women's Suffrage from its foundation in 1909, realistically, the impetus for change came not because of the church's conversion to feminism but due to the 1918 Parliamentary Reform Act, granting some women the vote and allowing them to become Members of Parliament. Women's liturgical participation in any capacity remained controversial throughout this period. In 1916 a heated debate broke out for one month from 10 February through letters to the *Guardian*, over whether women should be permitted to read lessons in church. In the same year the Archbishop's planned revival in the National Mission of Repentance and Hope extended the controversy into the area of preaching. The success of the anti lobbyists resulted in initial permission being withdrawn. Some women - most notably Maude Royden - began to break the regulations and accept invitations to preach. However, by 1930 virtually no progress had been made towards the authorisation of women preachers. On the rare exceptions when permission was given for a woman to preach or pray in a consecrated building, the congregation was made up of women and children only.

Chp 3 - The CMS Persia Mission and its Women Missionaries

1   These are mythical stories, not historical facts. For further details about such myths and legends, and references to original sources, see Hassan Dehqani-Tafti (1993), *Masih va Masihiyyat Nazd-e Iraniyan, II: Dar She'r-e Farsi, Douran-e Sabk-e Kohan (Klasik).* (Christ and Christianity Amongst the Iranians, ii: In the Classical Period of Persian Poetry.) London: Sohrab Books, pp 183-4; and Robin Waterfield (1973), *Christians in Persia.* London: George Allen & Unwin, p 16.
2   For more on these details and the growth of Christianity in Iran until the seventh century, see Hassan Dehqani-Tafti (1992), *Masih va Masihiyyat Nazd-e Iraniyan, I: Sayr-e Ejmali Dar Tarikh.* (Christ and Christianity Amongst the Iranians, i: A Short Historical Survey.) London: Sohrab Books, pp 15 & 24-5; Norman Thomas [ed.] (1995), *Readings in Mission.* London: SPCK, pp 11-12; John Foster (1939), *The Church of the T'ang Dynasty.* London: SPCK; Max Warren (1976), *I Believe in the Great Commission.* London: Hodder & Stoughton, p 95; David Bosch (1991), *Transforming Mission: Paradigm Shifts in Theology of Mission.* Maryknoll, New York: Orbis, p 204; and Waterfield, op. cit., pp 16-28.
3   For details see Dehqani-Tafti (1992), op cit. pp 23-58; and Waterfield, op cit. pp 33-7.
4   Bernard Lewis (1995), *The Middle East: 2000 Years of History from the Rise of Christianity to the Present Day.* London: Weidenfeld & Nicolson, p 210. Lewis uses this term to describe the *dhimmis* because not all religious minorities were recognised but only those considered by Islam to be people of the book, ie Christians, Jews and Zoroastrians.
5   Greatly influenced by Nestorius during the fifth century, these Christians do not use the term Nestorian to define themselves. Within other branches of Christianity, Nestorianism is often considered a heresy, however, members of the Church of the East do not regard themselves as a splinter group, but part of the orthodox historical church. The Church of the East enjoyed a particularly strong position in Iran at the time of the Arab invasion.
6   Technically this Armenian district was known as New Julfa, however, the commonly used abbreviated name will be used throughout this book.
7   For fuller details on the ancient churches in Iran see Dehqani-Tafti (1992), op. cit., pp 87-97; and Waterfield, op. cit., pp 47-64.
8   See Dehqani-Tafti (1992), op. cit., pp 91-7.
9   See Denis Wright (1977), *The English Amongst the Persians.* London: William Heinemann Ltd, p 113.
10 Kenneth Cragg (1992), *Troubled by Truth: Life Studies in Inter-faith Concern.* Edinburgh: Pentland Press, p 27. By all accounts Martyn was an extraordinary person who has continued to attract much missiological attention. For information on his life and work see, for example, Constance Padwick (1922), *Henry Martyn: Confessor of the Faith.* London: CMS Press.
11 For details see Wright, op. cit., pp 114-7; and Dehqani-Tafti (1992), op. cit., pp 66-7; and Waterfield, op. cit., p 124.
12 For details on the Archbishop of Canterbury's mission see Wright, op. cit., pp 121-2; and Waterfield, op. cit., pp 124-7.

Notes to Chapter Three

13 CMJ and CMS formed close ties towards the end of the century with missionaries co-operating from both societies, first in Isfahan and later Tehran. See Waterfield, op. cit., pp 112-23; and Gordon Hewitt (1971), *The Problem of Success: A History of the Church Missionary Society, 1910-1942, i*. London: CMS Press Ltd, p 380-1.

14 For more details on the work of the American Presbyterian mission see Dehqani-Tafti (1992), op. cit., pp 77-82; Hewitt, op. cit., pp 380-1; Waterfield, op. cit., pp 133-45; and John Elder (1960), *History of the American Presbyterian Mission in Iran*. Literature Committee of the Church Council of Iran.

15 Quoted in Thomas (ed.), op. cit., pp 44-5.

16 Quoted in Cragg, op. cit., p 24.

17 The official language of the Court in India was Persian and it was considered useful for missionaries to be familiar with it so they could converse with influential people in the country. Iran was an ideal place for Bruce (as it had been for Martyn before him) to improve his Persian.

18 For more on Robert Bruce and his early years in Persia see, for example, Eugene Stock (1899), *History of the Church Missionary Society, iii*. London: CMS, pp 123-4.

19 It should be noted that the ordinand and the majority, though not all, of the confirmees were converts from the Armenian Church. At this stage there were very few Muslim converts in the Persia mission. It was not CMS policy to work towards dissent in the Armenian congregation, and their unofficial policy of non-interference was eventually ratified in 1921 (see G2/PE/P3 1921: 43). Nevertheless, the missionaries did not dissuade any who showed interest in conversion and, especially in the early years, were pleased to welcome them.

20 Denis Wright (op. cit., p 121) comments on the formation of the diocese of Iran, saying that Charles Stileman was consecrated "the first Bishop of Isfahan - an appointment which must have seemed an extraordinary act of presumption to those Persians who were aware of it". Wright, however, does the missionaries an injustice. Aware of the problems inherent in such an act, it was decided that the episcopal title would be Bishop *in* Iran, not Bishop *of* Iran, or indeed Isfahan as Wright mistakenly records. The subtle differentiation is of clear significance.

21 On one occasion it took Bishop Stuart nearly four months to complete a return visit from Julfa to Baghdad (see G2/PE/O 1897: 91).

22 Julian Pettifer & Richard Bradley [eds.] (1990), *Missionaries*. London: BBC Books.

23 Quoted in Hewitt, op. cit., p 296.

24 Hewitt, op. cit., p 388.

25 Personal interview on 22 February (1995) in Basingstoke, Hampshire.

26 Jeffrey Cox (1992), "Independent English Women in Delhi and Lahore, 1860-1947" in R.W. Davis & R.J. Helmstadter (eds.), *Religion and Irreligion in Victorian Society: Essays in Honour of R. K. Webb*. London: Routledge, p 181. Cox refers to this institutionalising tendency as one aspect of a complicated strain of imperialism which was the heritage of late-Victorian Christianity.

27 Jocelyn Murray (1985), *Proclaim the Good News: A Short History of the Church Missionary Society*. London: Hodder & Stoughton, p 290.

28 This is not to say that the Anglican Church in Iran was entirely successful in its efforts to become an indigenous church. Some have argued that real indigenisation is impossible for Anglicanism which remains a peculiarly English invention and one that does not successfully transfer to other cultures. For more on this see F.W. Dillistone (1980), *Into All the World: A Biography of Max Warren*. London: Hodder & Stoughton, p 128.
29 Personal interview on 22 February (1995) in Basingstoke, Hampshire.
30 None of this is to suggest that the search for an integrated identity is straightforward for the Persian Christian - far from it. The struggle for defining self in relation to a "foreign" religion and in response to the reactions of compatriots cannot be escaped. Feelings of "not belonging" often mean an existence on the boundaries. Yet in a sense this characteristic is true of Christianity generally which, according to Andrew Walls' "pilgrim principle", means every Christian has "dual nationality". For "all Christians of whatever nationality, are landed by adoption with several millennia of someone else's history, with a whole set of ideas, concepts, and assumptions which do not necessarily square with the rest of their inheritance". See Andrew Walls (1996), *The Missionary Movement in Christian History: Studies in the Transmission of Faith*. Edinburgh: T & T Clark, pp 8-9.
31 Isabella Read went to Iran under the auspices of FES before CMS accepted single women as missionaries. However, she worked for the CMS mission in Julfa and was under its direction. Read was later on the CMS pay-roll for a brief period and has been included as a subject in this book. The first CMS single women arrived in Julfa in 1891.
32 There is, for example, an archival reference to a conference of the Persia and Baghdad missions in G2/PE/O 1886: 52.
33 As a point of reference this list has been duplicated in Appendix III.
34 See, for example, Brian Stanley (1990), *The Bible and the Flag: Protestant Missions and British Imperialism in the Nineteenth and Twentieth Centuries*. Leicester: Apollos, pp 11-13.
35 Personal interview on 22 February (1995) in Basingstoke, Hampshire.
36 In his interview (1995), Dehqani-Tafti mentions, in particular, Vera Eardley, CMS missionary in Iran between 1925-1960, and Nevarth Aidin, eldest daughter of Isabella Read and a missionary for CMS in Persia from 1920-58.
37 None of the statistics I provide include Isabella Read of the FES, for I have collected the information from CMS record books in which she was never included.
38 Rosemary Seton (1996), "'Open Doors for Female Labourers': Women Candidates of the London Missionary Society, 1875-1914" in Robert Bickers and Rosemary Seton (eds.), *Missionary Encounters: Sources and Issues*. Surrey: Curzon Press, p 58. See also, John Isherwood (1979), *An Analysis of the Role of Single Women in the Work of the Church Missionary Society, 1804-1904, in West Africa, India and China*. University of Manchester: MA Thesis, p 5.
39 For an account of CMS in Ireland see Jack Hodgins (1994), *Sister Island: A History of the Church Missionary Society in Ireland 1814-1994*. Dunmurry: Transmission Publication.
40 For more on the history of women's training in CMS during this period see, for example, Isherwood, op. cit., p 6; and Eugene Stock (1899 & 1916), *History of the Church Missionary Society*, iii, pp 703-4, 672 & iv, pp 467, 470. London: CMS.

Notes to Chapter Three 201

41 See H. Weitbrecht (1913), "The Training of Women Missionaries", *Church Missionary Review*, 44 (May), pp 298-302.
42 Allan Becher Webb (1993), *Sisterhood Life and Woman's Work in the Mission-Field of the Church*. London: Skeffington & Son, p 3.
43 See Eleanor Jackson (1997), *"A True Mother in Israel": The Role of the Christian Mother as Evangelist in Nineteenth-Century India*. NAMP Position Paper Number 30. Cambridge: University of Cambridge, North Atlantic Missiology Project, p 11.
44 See, for example, Deborah Kirkwood (1993), "Protestant Missionary Women: Wives and Spinsters" in Fiona Bowie et al (eds.), *Women and Missions: Past and Present. Anthropological and Historical Perceptions*. Oxford: Berg, p 28.
45 Writing about the South Travancore District in southern India, Haggis notes that by the time single women arrived in the 1880s and 1890s, a sphere of work had already been developed with thousands of pupils attending the missionary schools and other educational establishments. See Jane Haggis (1991), *Professional Ladies and Working Wives: Female Missionaries in the London Missionary Society and its South Travancore District, South India in the 19th Century*. University of Manchester: PhD Thesis, p 236.
46 Emily Bruce worked virtually single-handed for almost ten years before Isabella Read joined the station in Julfa. (The Bruces' daughters also lived in Iran and participated in the early years of CMS's work. One of them married Dr Hoernle, the earliest medical missionary, in 1885 but died in childbirth the following year.) Teaching in the Armenian Girls' School and participating in district visiting, her isolated efforts were hardly sufficient for establishing "women's work" in Iran. Recognising this herself, Emily wrote several articles entreating women to join the missionary enterprise in Persia. The FES which sponsored, primarily, single women missionaries also represented a number of wives by including information about them in its journals and providing them with opportunities to write about their work. Several articles by Emily Bruce, describing her work and the position of the mission in Julfa, supply the only written sources about her. See *FMI* (1879), xxi, pp 161-2; *FMI* (1881), i, pp 170-3; and *FMI* (1882), ii, pp 1-2.
47 For an excellent discussion concerning the distinction between single and married women missionaries see Haggis, op. cit., pp 234-8.
48 Personal recollection.
49 Those who married within the first two or three years, were also required to recompense CMS for the cost of their training and travel.
50 Seton, op. cit., p 66.
51 G2/PE/P4 1930: 64.
52 This included travelling costs and the "married man's allowance" which husbands received as a small addition to their usual missionary salary.
53 G2/PE/O 1899: 56.
54 G2/PE/O 1893: 36.
55 Edward Said (1987), *Orientalism: Western Conceptions of the Orient*. London: Penguin (1995 reprint), pp 95-103.
56 ibid., p 101.

Chp 4 - Attitudes Towards Islam and Theological Self-Perceptions

1. Kenneth Cracknell (1995), *Justice, Courtesy and Love: Theologians and Missionaries Encountering World Religions, 1846-1914*. London: Epworth Press.
2. ibid., p 191.
3. ibid., pp 261-81.
4. ibid., pp 1-180.
5. For detailed discussion of these categories by Cracknell see ibid., pp 4-34.
6. ibid., p 34.
7. ibid., pp 197-226.
8. ibid., pp 227-31.
9. See, for example, ibid., pp 206 and 219.
10. ibid., p 219.
11. ibid., p 231.
12. The statistics have been calculated by me on the basis of material received from the librarian at the Henry Martyn Mission Studies Library in Cambridge where copies of the questionnaires are held.
13. Cracknell, op. cit., pp 231-6.
14. ibid., p 236.
15. His writings include, *The Sources of Islam: A Persian Treatise*, translated and abridged by William Muir. Edinburgh: T & T Clark (1901); *The Religion of the Crescent*, London: SPCK, 3rd edition revised (1910); *Christianity and Other Faiths*, London: SPCK (1912).
16. *World Missionary Conference, 1910; Report of Commission IV: The Missionary Message in Relation to Non-Christian Religions*. London: Oliphant, Anderson & Ferrier (?1910), pp 122-55.
17. William St. Clair Tisdall quoted in Cracknell, op. cit., p 236.
18. The following information is from personal email correspondence received from Kenneth Cracknell on 18/11/96 and 19/11/96.
19. Personal email correspondence from Kenneth Cracknell, 18/11/96.
20. Personal email correspondence from Kenneth Cracknell, 19/11/96.
21. Realistically, it is not possible to undertake a gendered analysis of the CMS women in Iran by comparing them with other female respondents of the Commission IV questionnaire. For the number of women represented by the questionnaire was too low (5 from a total 149) for such a calculation. It remains difficult to know exactly how and why the respondents were selected. According to Cracknell, "We have no minutes of the Commissions' preparatory meetings (if [they] were [to be found] in the CMS archives it would be like finding the Dead Sea Scrolls)... I think that the respondents were by and large known personally ... to one or other of the Commissioners ... I have never seen an open invitation to respond to Commission four in the missionary journals or magazines..." (Personal email correspondence, 19/11/96).
22. Cracknell (1995), op. cit., pp 202, 219, 285.
23. ibid., p 202.
24. ibid., p 219.

Notes to Chapter Four

25 G2/PE/O 1892: 53.
26 Bird - G2/PE/O 1898: 28.
27 Bird - G2/PE/O 1893: 87.
28 Ethel Stuart - G2/PE/O 1903: 36.
29 Included in a joint letter from "the missionaries of the C.M.S. labouring in Persia" to the Home Committee in London registering a complaint at the decision not to "occupy Isfahan" but continue "concentrating their forces in Julfa". Laura Stubbs and Mary Bird are among the five to sign. G2/PE/O 1893: 105.
30 Mary Bird *Annual Letters* (1895), p 12.
31 Wilkes - G2/PE/O 1895: 57.
32 G2/PE/0 1891: 85.
33 G2/PE/O 1892: 53.
34 There were many similarities between the situation of CMS women in Iran and their counterparts in Iraq. Indeed, occasional references have been made to the work and writings of the latter in this chapter. However, there is also need for caution as it would be wrong to assume too many generalised similarities. This issue about the cause of indigenous women's ignorance is an example of the diversity about which one should be aware.
35 "The Social Conditions of Women in Muslim Lands", *Church Missionary Review*, August 1909, p 462.
36 G2/PE/O 1890: 136.
37 G2/PE/O 1891: 90.
38 G2/PE/O 1901: 143.
39 G2/PE/O 1895: 77.
40 For a useful discussion of missionaries as social commentators with specific relevance to the Indian situation see Geoffrey Oddie (1996), "Missionaries as Social Commentators: The Indian Case" in Robert Bickers and Rosemary Seton (eds.), *Missionary Encounters: Sources and Issues.* Surrey: Curzon Press, pp 197-210.
41 Mary Bird *Annual Letters* (1895), p 11.
42 G2/PE/O 1919: 67.
43 This is particularly true of the printed annual letter extracts and articles written for CMS journals rather than the ordinary letters.
44 See, for example, Emmeline Stuart *Annual Letters* (1899), pp 77-8; and (1900), pp 262-3; Mary Bird *Annual Letters* (1895), pp 10-12; and (1896), pp 20-24.
45 See Edward Said (1987), *Orientalism: Western Conceptions of the Orient.* London: Penguin (1995 reprint), p 101.
46 See Frances Hiebert(1997), "Beyond a Post-modern Critique of Modern Missions: The Nineteenth Century Revisited", *Missiology: An International Review,* 25:3 (July), pp 259-77.
47 G2/PE/O 1916: 72.
48 Westlake - G2/PE/O 1903: 140.
49 Cracknell (1995), op. cit., p 285.

50 It is ultimately impossible to know whether the views of the CMS women were in accord with their own instincts or a result of indoctrination through training which brought them in line with the conservative CMS ethos.
51 Cracknell (1995), op. cit., p 260.
52 Martha Adamson - G2/PE/O 1906: 123.
53 Biggs - G2/PE/O 1903: 120; writing in connection with the recent persecution of Babis, in which one man had been killed by Muslim fanatics.
54 G2/PE/O 1901: 143.
55 "In Persian Villages", *Mercy and Truth* (1898), ii, pp 7-10.
56 Emmeline Stuart, "New Hospital for Women in Julfa", *Mercy and Truth* (1899), iii, p 150.
57 In *Mercy and Truth* (1899), iii, p 263.
58 Helen Barrett Montgomery (1910), *Western Women in Eastern Lands: An Outline Study of Fifty Years of Woman's Work in Foreign Missions*. NY: Macmillan, p52.
59 Emmeline Stuart *Annual Letters* (1900), p 263.
60 G2/PE/O 1909: 73.
61 Nancy Paxton (1990), "Feminism Under the Raj: Complicity and Resistance in the Writings of Flora Annie Steel and Annie Besant", *Women's Studies International Forum*, 13:4, p 338.
62 Adrienne Rich quoted in Paxton, op. cit., p 338.
63 G2/PE/O 1907: 109.
64 G2/PE/O 1914: 48.
65 G2/PE/O 1900: 154.
66 "First Impressions", *Mercy and Truth* (1903), vii, p 266.
67 G2/PE/O 1904: 41.
68 G2/PE/O 1916: 32.
69 G2/PE/O 1923: 57.
70 G2/PE/O 1928: 1 and 1933: 17.
71 G2/PE/O 1929: 96.
72 G2/PE/O 1920: 76.
73 G2/PE/O 1930: 51.
74 G2/PE/O 1897: 170.
75 G2/PE/O 1907: 188.
76 "First Impressions", *Mercy and Truth* (1903), vii, pp 267-8. See also G2/PE/O 1905: 84.
77 "Work Among Women in Yezd", *Mercy and Truth* (1901), v, p 135.
78 Denis Wright (1977), *The English Amongst the Persians*. London: William Heinemann Ltd, pp 119, 155.
79 I am here not concerned with how the Muslim world has chosen to react to this change but with the duty of Christianity in looking forward. For as pointed out by Kenneth Cragg, "there is a Christian obligation to Islam that neither begins nor ends in how Muslims respond". See his, *The Call of the Minaret* (1985). London: Collins, p 304.
80 Seyyed Hossein Nasr (1989), "God" in Seyyed Hossein Nasr (ed.), *Islamic Spirituality I: Foundations*. London: SCM, p 312.
81 G2/PE/O 1896: 120.
82 G2/PE/O 1903: 105.

Notes to Chapter Four

83 G2/PE/O 1902: 92.
84 G2/PE/O 1925: 82.
85 G2/PE/O 1912: 61.
86 "Joyful, Joyful Shall the Meeting Be", *Mercy and Truth*, (1900), iv, pp 285-6.
87 G2/PE/O 1900: 148.
88 Braine-Hartnell - G2/PE/O 1898: 113.
89 G2/PE/O 1895: 57.
90 G2/PE/O 1902: 102.
91 G2/PE/O 1908: 154.
92 Cracknell (1995), op. cit., p 245.
93 G2/PE/O 1901: 104.
94 G2/PE/O 1905: 126.
95 G2/PE/O 1921: 91.
96 G2/PE/O 1905: 33.
97 G2/PE/O 1904: 62.
98 G2/PE/O 1906: 123.
99 G2/PE/O 1907: 173.
100 G2/PE/O 1923: 76.
101 G2/PE/O 1915: 48.
102 G2/PE/O 1914: 54
103 ibid..
104 See, for example, Clara Colliver Rice (1923), *Persian Women and Their Ways*. London: Seeley, Service & Co., p 90.
105 Phillips - G2/PE/O 1895: 58.
106 G2/PE/O 1893: 87
107 G2/PE/O 1894: 7.
108 G2/PE/O 1894: 182; the declaration was signed by all those in the CMS Persia mission which included three men, two wives and four single women.
109 G2/PE/O 1896: 135.
110 Cragg, op. cit., p 198.
111 Stileman - G2/PE/O 1891: 14.
112 G2/PE/O 1891: 90.
113 G2/PE/O 1907: 148.
114 Biggs - G2/PE/O 1902: 97.
115 G2/PE/O 1900: 82.

Chp 5 - Mary Bird: A Passion for Evangelism and a Heart for the Women of Iran

1   See, for example, F.W. Dillistone (1980), *Into All the World: A Biography of Max Warren*. London: Hodder & Stoughton, p 71.
2   For a discussion about the religious motives of missionaries in the modern era see Anne Wind (1995), "The Protestant Missionary Movement from 1789-1963" in Frans Verstraelen et al (eds.), *Missiology: An Ecumenical Introduction*. Michigan: Eerdmans, pp 240-1. With specific reference to the motives of women see Lydia Huffman Hoyle (1996), "Nineteenth-Century Single Women and Motivation for Mission", *International Bulletin of Missionary Research*, 20:2 (April), pp 58-64.
3   Two of the general books on the nineteenth century missionary movement that mention Mary Bird are very different in style. Lavinia Byrne [ed.] (1993), *The Hidden Journey: Missionary Heroines in Many Lands*. London: SPCK, pp 37-8, 163, is an uncritical publication which reproduces extracts from the writings of women missionaries in an effort to give voice to them. Sean Gill's (1994), *Women and the Church of England: From the Eighteenth Century to the Present*. London: SPCK, p 195, provides a more detailed analysis and includes a chapter on the modern missionary movement. He mentions Bird, however, only in passing. During the first half of the twentieth century two biographical books, and a chapter in a third, were written about Mary Bird. Whilst these offer no analysis of her life, they do present details of her character and early life. See Clara Colliver Rice (1916), *Mary Bird in Persia*. London: CMS; Jessie Powell (1949), *Riding to Danger: The Story of Mary Bird of Persia (Iran)*. London: The Highway Press; and Jennie Chappell (1920?), "Mary Bird" in *Three Brave Women: Stories of Heroism in Heathen Lands*. London: Partridge & Co., pp 121-60. Other books on the history of CMS in Persia also offer details of Bird's time in Iran. See Eugene Stock (1899), *History of the Church Missionary Society, iii*, London: CMS, p 530; Gavin Hewitt (1971), *The Problems of Success: A History of the Church Missionary Society, i*, London: CMS, pp 383-4; Robin Waterfield (1973), *Christians in Persia*. London: George, Allen & Unwin, pp 154-7; Hassan Dehqani-Tafti (1992), *Masih va Masihiyyat Nazd-e Iraniyan, I: Sayr-e Ejmali Dar Tarikh*. (Christ and Christianity Amongst the Iranians, vol I: A Short Historical Survey.) London: Sohrab Books, p 69.
4   Mary Bird (1899), *Persian Women and Their Creed*. London: CMS. For three other books written by CMS women missionaries in Iran see Clara Colliver Rice (1923), *Persian Women and Their Ways*. London: Seeley, Service & Co.; Gwen Gaster (1959), *Our Blind Family*. London: CMS; and Molly Williams (1994), *The Rich Tapestry of my Persian Years: Memoirs of Maud Hannah (Molly) Williams, a Missionary Nurse, 1937-1974*. Victoria, Australia: Keith Cole.
5   Chappell, op. cit., p 123.
6   Rice (1916), op. cit., p 91.
7   ibid., p 4.
8   For a portrayal of the Victorian attitude to missionaries, see the novel by Tim Jeal (1996), *The Missionary's Wife*. London: Warner Books, especially pp 17-8.
9   Rice (1916), op. cit., p 5. Clara Colliver Rice was the wife of Walter Rice, a missionary in Iran between 1901-21. She worked with Mary Bird for many years and knew her well. The

Notes to Chapter Five

book she wrote on Bird's life is a valuable source, including many quotations from Mary Bird's own writings and personal letters.
10 Powell, op. cit., p 13.
11 ibid..
12 In Mary Bird (1899), op. cit., p 2; and Rice (1916), op. cit., p 174.
13 Bird (1899), op. cit., p 103.
14 Quoted in Rice (1916), op. cit., p 165.
15 Chappell, op. cit., p 123.
16 Bird (1899), op. cit., p 25.
17 Photographs taken from Rice (1916), op. cit., p 8.
18 Lavinia Byrne (1993), op. cit., p 37.
19 Bird (1899), op. cit., pp 26-7.
20 Resolution passed by the Persia mission in 1894, quoted in Hewitt, i, (1971), op. cit., p 383.
21 Quoted in Rice (1916), op. cit., p 64.
22 ibid., p 65.
23 ibid..
24 ibid., pp 65-6.
25 ibid., p 66.
26 Bird (1899), op. cit., pp 63 & 31.
27 Mary Bird *Annual Letters* (1891-2), p 417.
28 ibid..
29 Bird (1899), op. cit., p 78.
30 Quoted in Rice (1916), op. cit., p 68.
31 Chappell, op. cit., p 124.
32 Quoted in Rice (1916), op. cit., p 86.
33 In "A woman's work among the women of Julfa", *Mercy and Truth* (1898), ii, p 33.
34 Bird (1899), op. cit., p 39.
35 For details of some treatments offered by locals see, for example, Bird (1899), op. cit., pp 43-4; and Powell, op. cit., pp 45-52.
36 Powell, op. cit., p 42.
37 See, for example, G2/PE/O 1892: 63 and 1893: 68.
38 G2/PE/O 1893: 98.
39 Quoted in Rice (1916), op. cit., p 121; and Bird (1899), op. cit., p 37.
40 There are many references indicating that later medical missionaries valued Bird's skill and commitment whilst remaining convinced she would not attempt dangerous work for which she was not adequately qualified. See, for example, Rice (1916), op. cit., pp 113-4.
41 Mary Bird *Annual Letters* (1892-3), p 122.
42 Bird (1899), op. cit., p 39.
43 Rice (1916), op. cit., p 6.
44 ibid..
45 Quoted in ibid., pp 173-4.
46 ibid., p 7.
47 Bird (1899), op. cit., p 42.

48 ibid., p 35.
49 Kenneth Cragg (1985 rev.), *The Call of the Minaret*. London: Collins, p 198.
50 Tisdall as mission secretary wrote on several occasions and Mary Bird herself confirmed his pleas for help, providing details of the number of patients and those requiring house visits after their treatment was completed. She wrote, for example, that between 25 July and 30 November 1893, the dispensary in Julfa - open for just two mornings each week - registered 2244 attendances. For details see G2/PE/O 1893: 72, 77, 87; and Mary Bird *Annual Letters* (1893-4), pp 8-9.
51 In 1891 Isabella Bishop wrote about her brief journey through Isfahan and the anti-foreign sentiment of the people, describing the experience as a "bad half-hour". See Isabella Bishop (1891), *Journeys in Persia and Kurdistan*, i. London: John Murray, p 244.
52 Mary Bird *Annual Letters* (1894-5), p 8.
53 See Hewitt (1971), op. cit., p 384.
54 Quoted in Rice (1916), op. cit., p 70.
55 Mary Bird *Annual Letters* (1894-5), pp 8-9; and Mary Bird (1899), op. cit., p 41.
56 Tisdall - G2/PE/O 1895: 53.
57 There was, for example, an attempt to poison her by the wife of a local *mullah*. For details, see Powell, op. cit., pp 62-3.
58 Chappell op. cit., p 142. For more details on the story of Sakineh see, for example, Bird (1899), op. cit., pp 80-7; and Powell, op. cit., pp 78-88.
59 Rice (1916), op. cit., p 113.
60 Stileman - G2/PE/O 1897: 34.
61 Records do not indicate exactly how long this was for, though it appears to have been almost two months. Dr Stuart left Britain for Persia on 25 March, taking approximately one month to arrive, and Mary Bird had departed from Julfa by 12 June.
62 G2/PE/O 1897: 131.
63 Bird (1899), op. cit., p 49.
64 Stileman - G2/PE/O 1898: 50.
65 During her furlough, Bird worked tirelessly to promote the cause of Persia in Britain. She spoke at meetings, raised awareness of financial needs and was always eager to recruit potential missionaries.
66 Stileman - G2/PE/O 1898: 135.
67 G2/PE/O 1898: 137.
68 Stileman writes that he is uncertain what to do about Dr Latham's appointment as "Dr White is very anxious to have her at Yezd as soon as possible, and Mr Blackett seems equally anxious not to have her at Kerman" (G2/PE/O 1898: 140).
69 Stileman - G2/PE/O 1898: 135.
70 See Stileman - G2/PE/O 1898: 135.
71 Minutes of the tenth Persia Missionary Conference - G2/PE/O 1899: 6.
72 G2/PE/O 1900: 15.
73 G2/PE/O 1901: 100.
74 ibid..
75 Mary Bird *Annual Letters* (1902), p 217.

Notes to Chapter Five

76 It is generally true that there is less information on work in other stations compared with that in Isfahan. There does seem to have been a bias towards Isfahan, the centre of the mission and residence of the bishop, and this did on occasions cause controversy. Missionaries from outer stations complained, for example, that their views were not being given due consideration.
77 Rice (1916), op. cit., pp 129-30.
78 ibid., p 122.
79 G2/PE/O 1903: 75.
80 G2/PE/O 1904: 60.
81 ibid.. In a touch of irony, the testimonial was presented to the British Consul, Major Sykes, who had intervened on behalf of Blackett to prevent Bird's appointment to Kerman.
82 In Rice (1916), op. cit., pp 162-3.
83 G2/PE/P3 1911: 33.
84 G2/PE/P3 1911: 54. See also G2/PE/P3 1911: 33. Limitations were imposed to ensure that Bird's untrained skills were suitably restricted within the more formal structures of the developing medical mission.
85 Rice - G2/PE/O 1913: 68.
86 "Village work amongst women in Persia", *Mercy and Truth* (1914), xviii, p 140.
87 ibid..
88 Rice (1916), op. cit., p 103.
89 Bird, *Mercy and Truth* (1914), op. cit., p 141.
90 Allinson - G2/PE/O 1914: 87.
91 Dodson - G2/PE/O 1914: 85.
92 Allinson - G2/PE/O 1914: 87.
93 Dodson - G2/PE/O 1914: 85.
94 ibid..
95 ibid..
96 Rice (1916), op. cit., p 181.
97 Bird (1899), op. cit., pp 20-1.
98 Chappell, op. cit., p 160.
99 ibid., pp 159-60.
100 In Rice (1916), op. cit., p 161.
101 ibid., pp 65-6.
102 ibid., p 5.
103 According to Gill this notion of feminine submission grew increasingly requisite as, during the course of the nineteenth century, the male ideal of compassionate Christian care and service was lost through the professionalisation of the clergy. See Sean Gill, op. cit., p 191.
104 Andrew Walls (1996), *The Missionary Movement in Christian History: Studies in the Transmission of Faith*. Edinburgh: T & T Clark, p 260.
105 In Chappell, op. cit., p 137.
106 Bird (1899), op. cit., pp 94 & 100.
107 ibid., p 35.
108 Gill, op. cit., p 195.

[109] She, for example, devotes a chapter in her book to disproving and undermining the five pillars of Islam. For details see Bird (1899), op. cit., pp 5-15.
[110] ibid., p 5.
[111] Rice (1916), op. cit., p 6.
[112] G2/PE/P3 1914: 80.
[113] On one occasion she recalled debating Christianity for three hours with a village governor near Kerman. At its conclusion she was eager for them to arrive at a point of mutuality and "proposed that we should pray that He who is the Truth should guide us into all truth". Put this way, "he at once agreed, and told all the servants present to bow for prayer". See Mary Bird *Annual Letters* (1903), p 141.
[114] Rice (1916), op. cit., p 136.
[115] Bird *Annual Letters* (1903), p 141.
[116] Quoted in Rice (1916), op. cit., p 142.
[117] Jane Robinson (1990), *Wayward Women: A Guide to Women Travellers*. Oxford: University Press; p 154.
[118] On rare occasions Mary Bird would hear of the effects of her work. After the death of one particular female patient, a message was brought to Bird, asking her to visit the deceased woman's daughter and read to her from the Bible. Apparently hearing the Christian gospel had comforted the patient, and her dying wish was that her daughter also should hear the message of hope. Bird (1899), op. cit., pp 78-9.
[119] Kenneth Cragg, op. cit., p 324.
[120] In Rice (1916), op. cit., p 193.

Notes to Chapter Six 211

Chp 6 - Isabella Read: Mission as an Open Window on Education

1   See, for example, Molly Williams (1994), *The Rich Tapestry of my Persian Years: Memoirs of Maud Hannah (Molly) Williams, a Missionary Nurse, 1937-1974*. Victoria, Australia: Keith Cole, pp 126f..

2   American Presbyterian missionaries were active in the northern part of Persia as early as 1835 and included among their number several single women.

3   This is an acronym for Female Education Society, a name by which the Society for Promoting Female Education in the East was also known.

4   Some sources use the alternative spelling, Abeel.

5   For a copy of Abel's speech entitled, "An appeal to Christian ladies in behalf of female education in China and the adjacent countries by Rev. David Abeel", see *History of the Society for Promoting Female Education in the East*. London: Edward Suter (1847), Appendix A, pp 261-5.

6   For a copy of the society's general regulations and bylaws, including its objectives and aims, see ibid., pp 275-81.

7   *Society for Promoting Female Education: Reports Nos. 60-64*, (1895-99). This information was provided at the beginning of each report.

8   "Light through Eastern Lattices: A Plea for Zenana Captives" in *Tracts Relating to Missions 1882-85*, no. 3, p 1. This was written in 1884 as the FES was celebrating its fiftieth jubilee.

9   ibid., p 2.

10   ibid., p 1.

11   ibid..

12   ibid..

13   ibid., pp 1-2.

14   ibid., p 6.

15   *Society for Promoting Female Education: Reports Nos. 60-64*, (1895-99). Each annual report begins with a list of countries represented by the society, in which Persia always appears last. References to work in Iran are usually very short compared to other areas. Furthermore, a file held by the CMS archivist in London with information on FES papers makes no mention of Persia as a sphere of work. The list also provides dates when work began in each country and all these, with the exception of Shefa Amr in Palestine, are before Read's arrival in Julfa. It is unclear why Persia has been omitted from the list.

16   *Society for Promoting Female Education: Reports Nos. 60-64*, (1895-99). Once more, this information is provided before each report.

17   Mrs Emily Bruce of Persia, for example, wrote articles for the *Female Missionary Intelligencer*.

18   "Light through Eastern Lattices: A Plea for Zenana Captives" in *Tracts Relating to Missions 1882-85*, no. 3, p 5.

19   *Society for Promoting Female Education: Reports Nos. 60-64*, (1895-99). This objective was printed at the beginning of each report.

20   Each applicant to FES was required to answer, in writing, questions approved by the committee. These included such details as their understanding of several leading Christian

doctrines, difficulties they might encounter as a missionary, their motives, preparations they had made, their method of studying Scripture, and their level of education and ability to teach. (For a copy of the full "Questions for Candidates" see *History of the Society for Promoting Female Education in the East*, op. cit., pp 281-3.) Applicants provided two referees who also answered questions pertaining to the candidate's piety and ability to teach. (For a copy of "Questions for Referees" see ibid., pp 283-4.) If these proved satisfactory, potential missionaries were admitted for a probationary period of one month, during which three committee members conversed with them privately. There is no indication of how long these discussions lasted or how frequently they occurred. The committee then made its final recommendation based on the written report of its three members.

21 *FMI* (1899), ixx, pp 81-2 & 108.
22 Despite the dissolution of FES, supporters were encouraged to continue raising funds, and working parties existed until, at least, 1915.
23 I have approximated the year of Read's birth, her age on arrival in Persia and at the time of her death, on the basis of an archival reference in 1908 in which Isabella is said to be fifty-seven years old (see G2/PE/O 1908: 95).
24 The FES papers now available are housed at the British Library. These include, *Missionary Pages for the Young*, a monthly news letter for young people about the work of the FES between 1879-87; *Female Missionary Intelligencer* (*FMI*), a monthly journal, between 1858-99, with information by and about active missionaries; *Society for Promoting Female Education: Reports 60-64*, the society's annual reports between 1895-99; and *History of the Society for Promoting Female Education in the East*. London: Edward Suter (1847).
25 "Home Proceedings", *FMI*, (1882) ii, p 175.
26 Though they were never formally accepted as missionaries, Mrs Bruce and her two daughters undoubtedly helped at the school. For occasional references to their involvement, see for example, *FMI* (1884), iv, p 179; *FMI* (1886), vi, p 101; and *FMI* (1887), vii, p 47.
27 "Letters from Julfa", *FMI* (1884), iv, p 177.
28 *FMI* (1884), iv, pp 142 & 178.
29 G2/PE/P1 1889: 20. See also, G2/PE/P1 1888: 12 & 24. For Bruce's letter, outlining the details for urgent support, see G2/PE/P1 1889: 28.
30 G2/PE/P1 1889: 80.
31 The last reference to Isabella as Miss Read appears in G2/PE/P1 1889: 80 and the first as Mrs Aidinyantz is in G2/PE/P1 1890: 115. From here onwards, Isabella's maiden and married names will be used interchangeably.
32 G2/PE/O 1890: 115.
33 Bruce - G2/PE/P1 1890: 115.
34 Miss Webb - G2/PE/P1 1890: 120.
35 G2/PE/O 1893: 136.
36 ibid..
37 G2/PE/O 1894: 131.
38 Aidinyantz - G2/PE/O 1897: 155. None of the existing material is clear about when her three children were born. It seems that the eldest daughter (Nouhie) was born c. 1891, her

Notes to Chapter Six 213

second daughter (Nevarth) a couple of years later and that this occasion is a reference to the birth of her son (Apgar).
39 ibid..
40 G2/PE/O 1897: 163.
41 ibid..
42 Miss Webb - G2/PE/P2 1897: 169. It is perhaps noteworthy that Isabella's decision to prolong her furlough was mentioned in various FES papers, ("1897: 62nd Report" in *Society for Promoting Female Education: Reports Nos. 60-64*, 1895-99, p 20; and "Home Proceedings" in *FMI* (1896), xvi, p 174), whilst her resignation does not appear in any of the surviving material. This may reflect the development of a rift between her and the FES, but is more likely due to poor documentation.
43 The date of her return is referred to in Aidinyantz - G2/PE/O 1902: 133.
44 ibid..
45 G2/PE/O 1902: 132.
46 G2/PE/O 1903: 44.
47 ibid..
48 Rice - G2/PE/O 1908: 65.
49 Stileman - G2/PE/O 1904: 166.
50 As early as 1893 Bruce alluded to this and voiced his concern: "I am sorry to say there is a temptation among our lady missionaries to look down on work for Armenians ... [but] the girls' school in Julfa being the only effort at female education in the whole of our mission field ... is of the utmost importance for the evangelization of Persia". G2/PE/O 1893: 136.
51 G2/PE/O 1904: 109.
52 ibid..
53 ibid..
54 ibid..
55 G2/PE/P3 1908: 65.
56 In Rice - G2/PE/O 1908: 65.
57 G2/PE/O 1908: 95.
58 G2/PE/O 1908: 87.
59 ibid..
60 G2/PE/O 1908: 65.
61 ibid..
62 ibid..
63 G2/PE/O 1908: 67.
64 As pointed out by Rice (G2/PE/O 1908: 65), this was still considerably less than CMS would expect to pay a woman missionary of their own.
65 G2/PE/O 1908: 68.
66 ibid..
67 ibid..
68 G2/PE/O 1910: 68.
69 Unlike her daughters, Isabella's son's time with CMS was short lived, for his theological views were not in accord with those of the society. In 1922, after working for CMS for

barely two years, SC requested his contract not be renewed. There had been several complaints about him lacking in the "spiritual" sphere, not working well with others, and being "a very bad mannered boy" (Linton - G2/PE/O 1922: 93). At around the same time, his sisters were preparing to travel to England for training at The Willows, before returning as missionaries in full connection. CMS had again refused to pay their expenses but the mission was supportive of them: "They are good workers, and unless they have meanwhile imbibed their brother's views we should probably be very glad to have them back" (ibid.).

70 G2/PE/O 1902: 6.
71 "Obituary", *CM Gleaner* (April 1920), p 85.
72 See, for example, *FMI* (1883), iii, p 21; *FMI* (1889), ix, p 15; and *Missionary Pages for the Young: New Series*, no. 3, July 1885, p 2.
73 *FMI* (1884), iv, pp 142 & 179; *FMI* (1886), vi, p 102.
74 *FMI* (1884), iv, p 179. For other similar references see, for example, *FMI* (1893), xiii, p 124; and *Missionary Pages for the Young*, xxi, January 1884, p 4.
75 *FMI* (1896), xvi, p 34.
76 *FMI* (1887), vii, p 98; and *FMI* (1894), xiv, p 139.
77 See, for example, *FMI* (1884), iv, pp 181-3.
78 ibid., p 181.
79 ibid., p 183.
80 See *FMI*, vol VI, July 1886, pp 101-2.
81 See, for example, *FMI* (1893), xiii, p 124; *FMI* (1884), iv, p 180; and *FMI* (1886), vi, p 103.
82 This point is elucidated by Isabella as being primarily because of the paradoxical nature of Islamic law which stated that girls and boys could not go out together but neither could a group of girls and women walk unchaperoned by men. See *FMI* (1887), vii, p 47.
83 *FMI* (1884), iv, p 180.
84 ibid., p 180-1.
85 See, for example, ibid., p 179; *FMI* (1886), vi, p 102; and *FMI* (1894), xiv, pp 140-1.
86 For details see G2/PE/O 1904: 127 & 170.
87 *FMI* (1883), iii, pp 17-22.
88 ibid., p 17.
89 Photograph taken from Clara Colliver Rice (1923), *Persian Women and Their Ways*. London: Seeley, Service & Co., p 168.
90 *FMI* (1883), iii, p 20.
91 ibid., p 21.
92 For details see James Linton (1923), *Persian Sketches*. London: CMS, pp 9-10.
93 *FMI* (1883), iii, p 19.
94 *FMI* (1889), ix, p 14.
95 ibid..
96 ibid., p 14.
97 *FMI* (1887), vii, p 100.
98 ibid., p 98.
99 ibid..

Notes to Chapter Six 215

100 For descriptions of women's national dress see, for example, *FMI* (1884), iv, pp 181-2; and *FMI* (1887), vii, p 100.
101 *FMI* (1896), xvi, p 34.
102 *FMI* (1887), vii, p 100.
103 *FMI* (1884), iv, p 184.
104 *FMI* (1887), vii, p 98.
105 ibid., p 99.
106 *FMI* (1883), iii, p 21.
107 *FMI* (1887), vii, p 99.
108 This is apparent, among other things, in the way she encouraged students to set up and run a YWCA. See, for example, *FMI* (1887), vii, p 46; and *FMI* (1888), viii, pp 2-4.
109 There are many references to the difficulties she encountered with Armenian, the frustration it caused and the amusing situations it led to. See, for example, *FMI* (1884), iv, pp 144, 180; *FMI* (1886), vi, p 103; *FMI* (1887), vii, p 99; *Missionary Pages for the Young*, xxi, January 1884, p 3; and *Missionary Pages for the Young: New Series*, no. 3 (July 1885), p 2.
110 *FMI* (1884), iv, p 177.
111 The two references are as follows. First, in *FMI* (1894), xiv, p 141, Isabella writes, "My time is fully occupied between school and household duties, and looking after our two little girls. The elder of them, *Armenvuhee* [sic], who is three and a half years old, speaks English, Armenian and a little Persian." Secondly, the letter of application to be accepted as a missionary, written by Isabella on behalf of Nouhie, includes the reference to her daughter's understanding of eastern culture (G2/PE/O 1910: 68). It should be noted that Isabella's two daughters claim many references later in the CMS archives as they became active and valuable members of the mission. These, however, date from a period after Isabella's death and primarily concern their work in the mission schools.
112 G2/PE/O 1916: 131. Virtually the only occasion Isabella herself mentioned her husband was approximately two years after their marriage, when she wrote: "My husband is doing most interesting work in classes of Mohammedan men and boys". See *FMI* (1893), xiii, p 125.
113 During the course of my research I had a telephone conversation with Isabella Aidinyantz's grandson who lives in England. (Whilst her daughters remained single, Isabella's son married and had children.) In talking about his grandparents, Michael Aidin was aware of the breakdown of their marriage but knew nothing of his grandfather's mental illness. He told me that the Aidinyantz marriage had remained an unspoken enigma within the family for there was a sense of shame at its failure.
114 Linton - G2/PE/O 1922: 93.
115 Dr Emmeline Stuart - G2/PE/O 1917: 17; see also Rice - G2/PE/O 1910: 68.
116 *FMI* (1887), vii, p 101.
117 *FMI* (1881), i, pp 171-2.
118 *FMI* (1895), xv, p 111.
119 See *FMI* (1889), ix, p 15.
120 *FMI* (1883), iii, p 22.
121 This is evidenced, for example, by the dismissal of Aidinyantz' son whose theological views were not in accord with CMS.

Chp 7 - Emmeline Stuart: Medical Missions and the History of Feminism

1   Andrew Walls (1996), *The Missionary Movement in Christian History: Studies in the Transmission of Faith*. Edinburgh: T & T Clark, p 211.
2   For more on the development of single women's missionary contribution throughout the nineteenth century see Sean Gill (1994), *Women and the Church of England: From the Eighteenth Century to the Present*. London: SPCK, pp 173-205; and John Isherwood (1979), *An Analysis of the Role of Single Women in the Work of the Church Missionary Society, 1804-1904, in West Africa, India and China*. University of Manchester: MA Thesis.
3   During an end-of-century review of mission developments in 1897, the importance of both women's contribution and medical expertise was formally noted by the Medical Missionary Association. For a detailed quotation see Rosemary Fitzgerald (1996), "A 'Peculiar and Exceptional Measure': The Call for Women Medical Missionaries for India in the Later Nineteenth Century" in Robert Bickers and Rosemary Seton (eds.), *Missionary Encounters: Sources and Issues*. Surrey: Curzon Press, p 175.
4   Walls, op.cit., p 211.
5   Fitzgerald, op. cit., p 194.
6   Sarah Potter (1974), *The Social Origins and Recruitment of English Protestant Missionaries in the Nineteenth Century*. University of London: PhD Thesis, pp 218-33.
7   See Isherwood, op. cit., p 165.
8   M.E. Hume-Griffith (1909), *Behind the Veil in Persia and Turkish Arabia*. London: Seeley & Co., p 140.
9   The first paid female member of staff at CMS House in London, Georgina Gollock, included medical work, alongside educational efforts and evangelism, as the three primary methods of the society's programme for work abroad. See Georgina Gollock (1909), *The Story of the C.M.S.*. London: CMS, pp 32-3.
10 Walls, op. cit., pp 212-3.
11 *Authorised Report of the Second Missionary Conference held at Oxford, May 2-3, 1877*, quoted in Rosemary Fitzgerald, op. cit., p 186.
12 Martyn Clarke (1905), quoted in Fitzgerald, op. cit., p 174. Throughout this section I have drawn extensively from the findings of Rosemary Fitzgerald whose chapter, though it is written with specific relevance to the situation in India, is highly relevant within the context of this book also.
13 *Report of the Ecumenical Conference on Foreign Missions*, 1900, quoted in Fitzgerald, op. cit., p 176.
14 J. Lowe (1886), quoted in Fitzgerald, op. cit., p 175. The increased value CMS placed on medical skills for women is also apparent in the changing patterns of missionary training provided for female recruits. By the turn of the century, all women missionaries were receiving basic medical skills and a centre was provided specifically designed for medically qualified women to receive missionary training. For details see Eugene Stock (1916), *History of the Church Missionary Society*, iv. London: CMS, p 470; and Georgina Gollock (1898), "The Training of Women Missionaries", *Church Missionary Intelligencer*, NS 23 (January), pp 39-43.
15 See also Potter, op. cit., p 220.
16 Ruth Rouse (1913), "The Ideal of Womanhood as a Factor in Missionary Work", *International Review of Missions*, 2:5 (January), pp 148-64.

Notes to Chapter Seven

17 ibid., p 151.
18 ibid., p 153.
19 ibid..
20 ibid., p 154.
21 Sara Tucker (1990), "Opportunities for Women: The Development of Professional Women's Medicine in Canton, China, 1879-1901", *Women's Studies International Forum*, 13:4, p 357. For more detailed figures on women doctors joining missionary organisations see Fitzgerald, op. cit., p 195.
22 Fitzgerald, op. cit., p 175.
23 ibid., p 185.
24 G2/PE/0 1909: 174.
25 See Gordon Hewitt (1971), *The Problem of Success: A History of the Church Missionary Society, 1910-1942*, i. London: CMS, p 388.
26 Lyle Vander Werff (1977), *Christian Mission to Muslims: The Record*. California: William Carey Library, p 165.
27 *Students and the Missionary Problem. Addresses Delivered at the International Student Missionary Conference, London* (1900). London: SVMU, p 512.
28 ibid., p 513.
29 G2/PE/O 1899: 107.
30 Emmeline Stuart, *Annual Letters* (1898), p 21.
31 ibid..
32 G2/PE/O 1899: 3.
33 Helen Callaway (1987), *Gender, Culture and Empire*. Urbana: University of Illinois Press, p 98.
34 ibid..
35 Edward Craig Stuart worked as a missionary in India from 1850 before being consecrated Bishop of Waiapu in New Zealand twenty-seven years later. As a middle-aged widower, the desire to return to the East led him to resign his see and volunteer for work in Persia. He travelled to Iran with his daughter Annie who remained a close colleague and companion, serving the Persia mission throughout his time and beyond. Together with his three nieces, Emmeline, Marie and Gertrude (who married the CMS missionary Rev. A.K. Boyland in 1903), Bishop Stuart and the four female members of his family gave a total of 144 years of missionary service in Iran (see Appendices III & VI for a breakdown of the years).
36 I am grateful to Lesley Richmond, Deputy Archivist at the University of Glasgow, for providing me with most of this information.
37 Stock, op. cit., iv, p 516.
38 Officially she should have retired in 1926 at the age of sixty and after thirty years of missionary service; however, requests were made to PC for an extension which was granted. See Linton - G2/PE/O 1926: 79.
39 G2/PE/O 1934: 33.
40 ibid..
41 G2/PE/O 1890: 134.
42 A joint letter written by the CMS missionaries in Persia - G2/PE/O 1893: 105.
43 Tisdall - G2/PE/O 1893: 75.

44 G2/PE/P2 1897: 74.
45 Minutes of SC - G2/PE/O 1897: 129.
46 G2/PE/O 1897: 130.
47 ibid..
48 G2/PE/O 1897: 131.
49 G2/PE/O 1896: 129.
50 G2/PE/O 1899: 107.
51 G2/PE/O 1906: 77.
52 G2/PE/O 1910: 75.
53 G2/PE/O 1910: 39.
54 Walls, op. cit., p 219.
55 She writes enthusiastically about the opening of both these hospitals in *Annual Letters* (1899), pp 77-8; and "The Women's Hospital Isfahan", *Mercy and Truth* (1906), x, pp 368-70.
56 In Rice - G2/PE/O 1910: 96, the undesirability of leaving Stuart in charge of the entire medical work is expressed; and in G2/PE/O 1929:60 Linton writes of Dr Katherine Hodgkinson's refusal to take on the men's side of the medical work in Kerman.
57 Emmeline Stuart, *Annual Letters* (1898), p 21.
58 Emmeline Stuart, *Annual Letters* (1905), p 11.
59 Eugene Stock, op. cit., iv, p 135.
60 For more details about Henry Venn's theories at the beginning of the nineteenth century see, for example, David Bosch (1991), *Transforming Mission: Paradigm Shifts in Theology of Mission*. Maryknoll, New York: Orbis, pp 331-2.
61 Robin Waterfield (1973), *Christians in Persia*. London: George, Allen & Unwin, p 165.
62 G2/PE/O 1922: 75 are the minutes of SC during which a resolution was passed imposing severe conditions upon the work of Dr Carr. However, the actual resolution has been inked out and the details have been lost to history. Later papers indicate there was a great deal of opposition from members of the mission to the passing of this resolution which was eventually revoked. See also, G2/PE/O 1922: 84 and 1923: 39 & 76.
63 For further details see Waterfield, op. cit., pp 165-6. These ruptures may be seen within the context of the disquiet caused by the disruptions within CMS as a whole, which eventually led to a split in the society and the creation of BCMS in 1922.
64 G2/PE/O 1923: 39.
65 Carr - G2/PE/O 1923: 77.
66 ibid..
67 Formal thanks were offered to Stuart in the Minutes of Conference - G2/PE/O 1924: 2.
68 For details see Linton - G2/PE/O 1928: 37; Linton - G2/PE/P4 1934: 10; and Hewitt, op. cit., pp 392-3.
69 For an account of continuing medical work in Shiraz see the autobiography by Molly Williams (1994), *The Rich Tapestry of my Persian Years: Memoirs of Maud Hannah (Molly) Williams, a Missionary Nurse, 1937-1974*. Victoria, Australia: Keith Cole, especially pp 59-70 & 83f..
70 Stuart - G2/PE/O 1902: 71.

Notes to Chapter Seven 219

71 Stileman - G2/PE/O 1902: 71.
72 Stileman - G2/PE/O 1905: 63.
73 The missionaries were informed of this in September 1915; see G2/PE/P3 1915: 68. For more on Anglo-Iranian relations during the war see, for example, Denis Wright (1977), *The English Amongst the Persians*, pp 171-84.
74 Carr - G2/PE/O 1915: 76.
75 G2/PE/O 1916: 43.
76 G2/PE/O 1916: 35.
77 G2/PE/O 1916: 62 & 44.
78 G2/PE/O 1916: 51.
79 ibid..
80 ibid..
81 ibid..
82 ibid..
83 ibid..
84 See Stuart - G2/PE/O 1916: 71, in which Emmeline refers to a letter from Wigram dated 27 April 1916.
85 ibid..
86 See Isherwood, op. cit., pp 250-1.
87 See Minna Gollock (1912), "The Share of Women in the Administration of Missions", *International Review of Mission*, 1:4, pp 674-87.
88 The rules for male missionaries stated that the right to vote was given after the second language exam had been passed. The first missionary Conference in Persia was held on 26 July 1894; see Minutes - G2/PE/O 1894: 155.
89 See Minutes of the fifteenth meeting of the Persia Conference - G2/PE/O 1904: 33. The recommendation was proposed by Annie Stirling and seconded by Jessie Biggs, though none of the women could actually vote for the outcome.
90 Stileman - G2/PE/O 1906: 36. Salisbury Square was the location of CMS head-quarters in London.
91 G2/PE/O 1907: 178.
92 G2/PE/O 1907: 124. For details of the events between 1904-1907 see, for example, G2/PE/O 1905: 3; G2/PE/P3 1905: 3; G2/PE/P3 1907: 117; and Rice - G2/PE/P3 1907: 118.
93 G2/PE/O 1905: 5.
94 See, for example, Dodson - G2/PE/P3 1910:52 and Minutes - G2/PE/P3 1910: 53a.
95 Stileman - G2/PE/P3: 120.
96 Minutes of Conference - G2/PE/O 1913: 16.
97 G2/PE/O 1913: 17.
98 Minutes - G2/PE/P3 1913: 96 and Minutes - G2/PE/O 1913: 40. Several missionaries remained unconvinced, purporting that the decision was unscriptural. However, the vote was eventually carried by a majority of one.
99 Minutes of the thirty-fourth Conference of the Persia mission - G2/PE/O 1914: 18.
100 G2/PE/O 1917: 87.
101 For details, see Linton - G2/PE/O 1918: 5 and Marrable - G2/PE/O 1918: 6.

102 Marrable - G2/PE/O 1918: 6.

103 Minutes - G2/PE/P3 1922: 5.

104 The following is a copy of the voting regulations approved by the constitution of the Persia mission in 1924. For more details see G2/PE/P3 1924: 2 and G2/PE/P3 1924: 23. For a copy of the constitution of the LGB of the Persia mission see G2/PE/P3 1924: 26.

(1) All missionaries, wives and those in local connexion may be present at conference and station sub-conferences, and all missionaries - men and women - of three years standing who are off probation, and wives of missionaries of five years standing or of three years standing who have passed 2nd exam and are working under instruction of LGB may vote. Others may only vote if given authority by PC.

(2) SC - to consist of head of mission and four others of those entitled to vote who are resident in Isf, to be elected by ballot of all voting members of the mission.

105 Although Stuart was paid a salary by CMS, there are several references to her paying her own travelling expenses, helping other missionaries pay their expenses, and offering to reduce her income if it meant CMS could send additional workers. See, for example, G2/PE/O 1914: 26, G2/PE/O 1933: 83, G2/PE/P2 1897: 125, G2/PE/P3 1911: 66, G2/PE/P4 1930: 83.

106 "The Social Condition of Women in Muslim Lands", *Church Missionary Review* (1909), August, p 458.

107 ibid., p 459.

108 ibid., p 462.

109 ibid., p 463.

110 ibid..

111 ibid., p 460.

112 ibid., pp 463-4.

113 Sarah Potter, op. cit., p 226.

114 ibid..

115 ibid..

116 ibid..

Conclusion

1. Eleanor McLaughlin (1992), "The Christian Past: Does it Hold a Future for Women?" in Carol Christ & Judith Plaskow (eds.), *WomanSpirit Rising: A Feminist Reader in Religion.* NY: HarperSanFrancisco, pp 94-5.
2. Some writers concerned with the issue of women's ordination have included information about missionary work by highlighting it as a part of professional female participation in the church's life. See, for example, Kathleen Bliss (1952), *The Service and Status of Women in the Churches.* London: SCM, especially pp 104-10. However, few make any direct or even implicit link between the two issues. For other books on the ordination of women priests within the Church of England see, for example, Margaret Webster (1994), *A New Strength, A New Song: The Journey to Women's Priesthood.* London: Mowbray; Jonathan Petre (1994), *By Sex Divided: The Church of England and Women Priests.* London: Fount. And for more general information on women and priesthood see, for example, Karen Jo Torjesen (1993), *When Women Were Priests: Women's Leadership in the Early Church and the Scandal of their Subordination in the Rise of Christianity.* NY: HarperSanFrancisco; and Monica Furlong (1998), *Act of Synod - Act of Folly?* London: SCM.
3. This would involve, in particular, close examination of the archive "Letters" which represent literature sent by CMS head-quarters to missionaries working abroad.
4. From the early 1930s through to the 1940s the future of missionary schools lay in the balance. The CMS archives reflect a growing obsession with attempts to keep control of such establishments. Isabella Read's daughters - Nouhie and Nevarth Aidin - both headteachers of missionary schools, were at the forefront of these struggles and played major roles as the mission adjusted to its new circumstances.
5. David Bosch (1991), *Transforming Mission: Paradigm Shifts in Theology of Mission.* Maryknoll, New York: Orbis, p 237.
6. ibid., p 344.

Appendix I

Map of Iran

Copied from Hossein Amirsadeghi [ed.] (1977), *Twentieth Century Iran*. London: Heinemann, p xv.

Appendix II

A chronology of the development of medical opportunities for women doctors in Britain during the nineteenth-century

1849   A British woman by the name of Elizabeth Blackwell qualified as a doctor, graduating from the University of Geneva in New York, America.

1858   The Medical Registration Act prepared the way for a Medical Register in Britain.

1859   Elizabeth Blackwell was included on the first Medical Register.

1874   The London School of Medicine for Women was founded, giving women the opportunity to receive medical training.

1876   The Russell Gurney Enabling Act allowed medical corporations to examine women, allowing them to be included on the Medical Register.

1879   London University recognized the London School of Medicine for Women and began granting them degrees.

1891   Bristol University became the first university to accept women for medical training.

Other universities followed:-

1892   Glasgow University

1893   Newcastle University

1894   Edinburgh University
              University College of South Wales & Monmouthshire

1895   Aberdeen University

1898   St. Andrews University

1899   Manchester University

1900   Birmingham University

This information was supplied by archivists at the British Medical Association (BMA), the Wellcome Institute for the History of Medicine, and Glasgow University.

Appendix III

A list of senior and influential men in the Persia mission between 1869-1934

Name and most significant position held	Presence in Iran
Robert Bruce - founder of the Persia mission	(1969-1894)
Charles Stileman - mission secretary, bishop from 1912	(1892-1916)
William St. Clair Tisdall - mission secretary	(1893-1907)
Edward Stuart - bishop	(1894-1910)
Donald Carr - medical doctor	(1894-1930)
Walter Rice - mission secretary	(1901-1921)
James Linton - educationalist, bishop from 1919	(1908-1935)
William Thompson - educationalist, bishop from 1935	(1914-1961)

Appendix IV

Statistics of CMS Missionaries in Iran, 1875-1980, based on figures in CMS Annual Record Books (Isabella Read of FES not included)

Key: * See right hand column for more information // My own calculation, not made explicit in CMS records

	Year	Wives	[Drs.]	Singles	[Drs]	Women	Clergy	Laymen	Drs	Men	Total	*Comments
1	1875	1*				1	1			1	2	Wives don't appear by name but only as little "m"
2	1876	1*				1	1			1	2	Wives don't appear by name but only as little "m"
3	1877	1*				1	1			1	2	Wives don't appear by name but only as little "m"
4	1878	1*				1	1			1	2	Wives don't appear by name but only as little "m"
5	1879	1*				1	2		1	2	3	Wives don't appear by name but only as little "m"
6	1880	1*				1	2			2	3	Wives don't appear by name but only as little "m"
7	1881	1*				1	2		1	2	3	Wives don't appear by name but only as little "m"
8	1882	1*				1	2			2	3	Wives don't appear by name but only as little "m"
9	1883	1*				1	2		1	2	3	Wives don't appear by name but only as little "m"
10	1884	1*				1	2		1	2	3	Wives don't appear by name but only as little "m"
11	1885	2				2	2		1	2	4	
12	1886	1*				1	2		1	2	3	Wives don't appear by name but only as little "m"
13	1887	1*				1	2		1	2	3	Wives don't appear by name but only as little "m"
14	1888	1*				1	2		1	2	3	Wives don't appear by name but only as little "m"
15	1889	1*				1	2		1	2	3	Wives don't appear by name but only as little "m"
16	1890	1*				1	2			2	3	Wives don't appear by name but only as little "m"
17	1891	1		2		3	2			2	5	Wives are named from this year with a few exceptions - eg war yrs
18	1892	2		2		4	3			3	7	
19	1893	3		2		5	3		1	4	9	
20	1894	5		4		9	4	1	1	6	15	
21	1895	4		5		9	5	1	1	7	16	
22	1896	4		5	1	9	6	1		7	16	
23	1897	4		7		11	6	2		8	19	
24	1898	5		6	1	11	5	2		7	18	
25	1899	5		9	2	14	6	2		8	22	
26	1900	7		10	2	17	7	3	3	10	27	
27	1901	8	/1/	12	1	20	8	4	3	12	32	
28	1902	10	/1/	12	2	22	8	5	4	13	35	
29	1903	11	1	16	3	27	8	5	4	13	40	
30	1904	11		18	4	29	8	5	4	13	42	
31	1905	11	1	18	4	29	8	6	3	14	43	
32	1906	11	1	20	4	31	9	7	4	16	47	
33	1907	12	1	20	4	32	9	7	4	16	47	

Appendix IV continued ...

	Year	Wives	Drs.	Singles	Drs	Women	Clergy	Laymen	Drs	Men	Total	*Comments
34	1908	11		17	4	29	6	7	4	13	42	
35	1909	12		16	4	28	7	7	4	14	42	
36	1910	12		19	5	31	6	7	4	13	44	
37	1911	13	1	19	4	32	8	5	4	13	45	
38	1912	13	1	20	4	33	8	6	5	14	47	
39	1913	13	/1/	21	4	34	8	6	5	14	48	
40	1914	11	/1/	22	5	33	7	6	5	13	46	
41	1915	11	/1/	21	5	30	6	7	5	13	43	More detailed statistics available at front of Annual Record Book
42	1916	11	/1/	19	4	30	6	7	5	13	43	
43	1917	10	/1/	19	4	29	6	6	5	12	41	
44	1918	11	/1/	18	4	29	7	6	5	13	42	
45	1919	9	/1/	18	4	27	5	6	5	11	38	More detailed statistics available at front of Annual Record Book
46	1920	9	/1/	22	4	31	6	6	6	12	43	
47	1921	9	/1/	25	4	34	6	5	4	11	45	More detailed statistics available at front of Annual Record Book
48	1922	9	/1/	27	5*	36	7	7	5	14	50	Only 4 indicated in list unless they're counting Mrs Linton (unlikely)
49	1923	7	/1/	25	5*	32	7	7	5	14	46	Only 4 indicated in list unless they're counting Mrs Linton (unlikely)
50	1924	9	/1/	26	5	35	6	7	5	13	48	
51	1925	9	/1/	27	5	36	7	6	4	13	49	
52	1926	8	/1/	27	5	35	6	6	3	12	47	
53	1927	8	/1/	31	7	39	5	6	4	11	50	
54	1928	8	/1/	33	7	41	7	6	4	13	54	
55	1929	7	/1/	37	9	44	7	5	4	12	56	
56	1930	8	/2/	34	7*	42	8	6	5	14	56	Only 6 appear in lists, perhaps 7th is one of wives
57	1931	8	/3/	33	4*	41	8	6	5	14	55	Lists show 5 single and 3 married Drs
58	1932	10	/3/	35	5*	45	7	9	5	16	61	Lists show 6 single and 3 married Drs
59	1933	11	/3/	33	6	44	7	9	5	16	60	
60	1934	10	/3/	32	6*	42	8	8	4	16	58	Lists show 5 single and 2 married Drs
61	1935	9	/2/	30	5	39	7	9	5	16	55	
62	1936	10	/3/	27	5*	37	8	10	5	18	55	Lists show 4 single and 3 married Drs
63	1937	9	/3/	24	4*	33	8	7	4	15	48	Lists show 3 single and 3 married Drs
64	1938	10	/3/	24	3*	34	6	8	4	14	48	Lists show 4 single and 3 married Drs
65	1939	10	/3/	22	4	32	6	8	4	14	46	
66	1940	10	/3/	21	3	31	6	6	4	12	43	
67	1941	10	/3/	23	3*	33	6	5	3	11	44	Lists show 4 single and 3 married Drs
68	1942	10	/3/	21	4	31	7	4	3	11	42	
69	1943	10	/3/	21	4	31	8	4	3	12	43	
70	1944	9	/2/	20	4	29	7	4	3	11	40	
71	1945	8	/2/	18	3	26	7	3	2	10	36	

Appendix IV continued ...

	Year	Wives	[Drs]	Singles	[Drs]	Women	Clergy	Laymen	Drs	Men	Total	*Comments
72	1946	7	/1/	18	4*	25	5	4	3	9	34	Lists show only 3 single and 1 married Dr.
73	1947	6	/2/	19	4*	27	5	3	2	8	35	Lists show only 2 single and 2 married Drs
74	1948	5	/2/	17	2*	22	5	2	1	7	29	Lists show only 1 single and 2 married Drs
75	1949	5	/2/	17	3*	22	5	2		7	29	
76	1950	8	/2/	17	3*	25	5	3	2	8	33	Lists show only one of the single Drs
77	1951	8	/2/	18	3*	26	5	3	3	8	34	Lists show only one of the single Drs
78	1952	7	/2/	13	1*	20	4	3	3	7	27	Lists show only 2 of the single Drs
79	1953	4	/2/	11	3*	15	3	1	2	4	19	Lists show 2 single Drs
80	1954	3	/1/	12	2	15	2	2	2	4	18	Lists show only 2 single Drs
81	1955	4	/1/	13	3*	17	2	2	2	3	21	Lists show only 2 single Drs
82	1956	6	/1/	13	1*	19	3	3	1	6	25	Lists show 2 single Drs
83	1957	6	/1/	16	2	22	3	4	2	6	29	Statistics now give 1 figure for all lay people & don't separate Drs
84	1958	9	/1/	18*	/2/	23	5	4	/2/	9	36	Includes 4 single women marked in italics
85	1959	10*	/1/	16*	/1/	26	5	5*	/2/	10	36	Figures include 1 wife, 4 singles & 1 layman marked in italics
86	1960	9*	/1/	16*	/1/	25	4	5*	2	9	34	Figures include 1 wife, 4 singles & 1 layman marked in italics
87	1961	7*	/1/	15*	/1/	22	3	5*	2	8	30	Figures include 1 wife, 2 singles & 1 layman marked in italics
88	1962	7*	/1/	12	/1/	19	2	6*	3	8	27	Figures include 3 wives and 2 laymen marked in lists in italics
89	1963	8*		15	/1/	23	2	7*	/4/	9	32	Figures include 3 wives & 2 laymen marked in lists in italics
90	1964	8	/2/	17	/1/	25	2	7	2	9	34	
91	1965	8	/1/	11		19	3	3	/3/	10	29	
92	1966	7	/1/	9		16	3	6	3	9	25	
93	1967	9	/1/	10		18	4	6	/2/	8	29	
94	1968	10	/1/	10		20	4	6	/2/	10	30	
95	1969	11	/1/	11		22	4	7	/2/	11	33	
96	1970	12	/1/	13		25	4	8	/3/	12	37	
97	1971	10	/1/	14		24	3	8	3	11	35	
98	1972	8	/1/	11		19	2	7	/4/	9	28	
99	1973	6	/1/	10		16	1	6	3	7	23	
100	1974	6	/1/	10		16	1	5	/3/	6	22	
101	1975	6	/1/	10		16	1	5	3	6	22	
102	1976	4	/1/	8		12	1	3	2	4	16	
103	1977	7	/1/	12		19	1	6	3	7	26	
104	1978	7	/1/	11		18	1	6	3	7	25	
105	1979	4	/1/	6		10	1	3	2	4	14	
106	1980	1		4		5	1			1	6	

Appendix V

Chronological list of CMS single women missionaries in Iran, 1891-1934, based on figures in CMS Record Books Isabella Read of FES not included. For alphabetical list see Appendix VI and for separate list of women doctors see Appendix VII

	Name	Years	Breakdown	Total	Comments
1	BIRD, Mary	1891-1904; 1911-14	13 + 3	16	
2	STUBBS, Laura	1891-1902		11	
3	DAVIES-COLLEY, Eleanor (1897 f. Mrs White)	1893-97; 1897-1913	4 + 16	20	
4	STIRLING, Annie	1893-1932		39	
5	CONNER, Henrietta	1894-1901		7	
6	BRAINE-HARTNELL, Philippa	1896-1927		31	
7	STUART, Dr Emmeline	1897-1934		37	
8	BUNCHER, Lily	1898-1908		10	
9	LATHAM, Dr Urania (1901 f. Dr Malcolm)	1898-1901; 1901-07	3 + 6	9	
10	STUART, Gertrude (1903 f. Mrs Boyland)	1898-1903; 1903-29	5 + 26	31	
11	BRIGHTY, Mary Ellen	1899-1936		37	
12	McCLURE, Margaret	1901-7		6	
13	McKim, Henrietta	1901-11		10	
14	WILLMOT, Florence	1901-2		1	
15	TAYLOR, Dr Elsie	1901-4		3	
16	BIGGS, Jessie	1902-30		28	
17	STUART, Anne	indep. 1894-1902; CMS 1902-26	8 + 24	32	
18	WESTLAKE, Dr Winifred	1902-32		30	
19	PROCTER, Ethel	1903-8		5	
20	WARD, Mabel	1903-20		17	
21	SKIRROW, Emily	1902-11		9	
22	MOLONY, Dr Lucy	1903-30		27	
23	MACKLIN, Alice (1916 f. Mrs White)	1903-16; 1916-22	13 + 6	19	
24	MOTHERSOLE, Kate	1904-7		3	
25	IRONSIDE, Dr Catherine	1905-21		16	
26	THOMAS, Edith	1905-39		34	
27	PHILLIPS, Ethel	1905-9		4	
28	ADAMSON, Martha (1908 f. Mrs Scorer)	1906-8; 1908-12	2 + 4	6	
29	MOORE, Jane	1908-38		30	

Appendix V continued ...

	Name	Years	Breakdown	Total	Comments
30	ALDOUS, Dr Alicia (1910 f. Dr Linton)	1909-10; 1910-34	1 + 24	25	
31	CARRICK, Margaret	1910-14		4	
32	PARRY, Zoë	1909-13		4	
33	PETLEY, Emma	1909-44		35	
34	GAUNTLETT, Annie	1911-22		11	
35	STUART, Marie	indep. 1903-5; CMS 1911-38	2 + 27	29	
36	BROWNRIGG, Bertha (1920 f. Mrs Schaffter)	1912-20; 1920-46	8 + 26	34	
37	SALISBURY, Ruth	1912-24		12	
38	CONSTABLE, Dr Evelyn	1914-16; 1921-2	2 + 1	3	
39	VERINDER, Alice	1914-17; 1923-49	3 + 26	29	
40	KINGDON, Winifred	1914-35		21	
41	AIDIN, Armenouhie	1917-41; 1942-57	24 + 15	39	Retired in 1957, stayed in Iran and died there
42	LLOYD, Mary	1920-47		27	
43	McKITTERICK, Frances	1920-30		10	
44	SEAGRAVE, Elsie	1920-25		5	
45	STRATTON, Eva	1920-51		31	
46	TWEEDIE, Winifred	1920-35		15	
47	AIDIN, Nevarth	1920-58		38	
48	BIRCH, Frances	1921-2		1	
49	JUNKINSON, Mrs Lottie	1920-22		2	
50	WOODROFFE, Janet	1921-49		28	
51	HODGSHON, Elizabeth	1921-36		15	
52	BAILLIE, Dr Emily	1922-30; 1933-39	8 + 6	14	
53	PRICE, Dr Mary	1924-28		4	
54	EARDLEY, Vera	1925-52; 1955-58; 1959-60*	27 + 3 + 1	31	Retired in 1958 but returned for one year
55	RICHARDSON, Hester	1925-26		1	
56	MacDONOGH, Ethel	1925-32		7	
57	PIGOTT, Dr Lucy	1927-39		9	
58	JAMES, Florence	1926-43		17	
59	GERRARD, Ella	1926-45		19	
60	GRIMSHAW, Elizabeth	1926-29		3	
61	NIGHTINGALE, Hilda	1927-42		15	
62	HODGKINSON, Dr Katherine (1929 f. Dr Richards)	1926-29; 1929-45	3 + 16	19	
63	EARDLEY, Irene	1927-36		9	
64	BIRT, Lilian	1928-51		23	
65	HENN, Lylie	1927-58		31	
66	ANDERSON, Eadith	1928-34		6	
67	EVANS, Kathleen (1937 f. Mrs Carpenter)	1928-31; 1936-37; 1937-42	3 + 1 + 5	9	

Appendix V continued ...

	Name	Years	Breakdown	Total	Comments
68	BURNETT, Dr Olive	1929-30		1	
69	HENRIQUES, Dr Stella	1929-47		18	
70	PIGOTT, Dr Wilfreda (1935 f. Dr Iliff)	1929-35; 1935-43	6 + 8	14	
71	EVANS, Jessica	1929-34		5	
72	COLBORNE, Leonora	1930-32		2	
73	SMART, Catherine	1930-51; 1954-61	11 + 7	18	
74	MORRIS, Mrs Marjorie	1930-35		5	
75	ROBINSON, Marie	1932-44		12	
76	MESS, Dr Elizabeth	1932-44		12	
77	HEATHER, Rhoda	1933-34		1	
78	DEAN, Jessie	1933-36		3	

Appendix VI

Alphabetical list of CMS single women missionaries in Iran, 1891-1934, based on figures in CMS Record Books. Isabella Read of FES not included. For chronological list see Appendix V and for separate list of women doctors see Appendix VII

	Name	Years	Breakdown	Total
1	ADAMSON, Martha (1908 f. Mrs Scorer)	1906-8; 1908-12	2 + 4	6
2	AIDIN, Armenouhie	1917-41; 1942-57	24 + 15	39
3	AIDIN, Nevarth	1920-58		38
4	ALDOUS, Dr Alicia (1910 f. Dr Linton)	1909-10; 1910-34	1 + 24	25
5	ANDERSON, Eadith	1928-34		6
6	BAILLIE, Dr Emily	1922-30; 1933-39	8 + 6	14
7	BIGGS, Jessie	1902-30		28
8	BIRCH, Frances	1921-2		1
9	BIRD, Mary	1891-1904; 1911-14	13 + 3	16
10	BIRT, Lilian	1928-51		23
11	BRAINE-HARTNELL, Philippa	1896-1927		31
12	BRIGHTY, Mary Ellen	1899-1936		37
13	BROWNRIGG, Bertha (1920 f. Mrs Schaffter)	1912-20; 1920-46	8 + 26	34
14	BUNCHER, Lily	1898-1908		10
15	BURNETT, Dr Olive	1929-30		1
16	CARRICK, Margaret	1910-14		4
17	COLBORNE, Leonora	1930-32		2
18	CONNER, Henrietta	1894-1901		7
19	CONSTABLE, Dr Evelyn	1914-16; 1921-2	2 + 1	3
20	DAVIES-COLLEY, Eleanor (1897 f. Mrs White)	1893-97; 1897-1913	4+16	20
21	DEAN, Jessie	1933-36		3
22	EARDLEY, Irene	1927-36		9
23	EARDLEY, Vera	1925-52; 1955-58; 1959-60	27 + 3 + 1	31
24	EVANS, Jessica	1929-34		5

Appendix VI continued ...

	Name	Years	Breakdown	Total
25	EVANS, Kathleen (1937 f. Mrs Carpenter)	1928-31; 1936-37; 1937-42	3 + 1 + 5	9
26	GAUNTLETT, Annie	1911-22		11
27	GERRARD, Ella	1926-45		19
28	GRIMSHAW, Elizabeth	1926-29		3
29	HEATHER, Rhoda	1933-34		1
30	HENN, Lylie	1927-58		31
31	HENRIQUES, Dr Stella	1929-47		18
32	HODGKINSON, Dr Katherine (1929 f. Dr Richards)	1926-29; 1929-45	3 + 16	19
33	HODGSHON, Elizabeth	1921-36		15
34	IRONSIDE, Dr Catherine	1905-21		16
35	JAMES, Florence	1926-43		17
36	JUNKINSON, Mrs Lottie	1920-22		2
37	KINGDON, Winifred	1914-35		21
38	LATHAM, Dr Urania (1901 f. Dr Malcolm)	1898-1901; 1901-07	3 + 6	9
39	LLOYD, Mary	1920-47		27
40	MacDONOGH, Ethel	1925-32		7
41	MACKLIN, Alice (1916 f. Mrs White)	1903-16; 1916-22	13 + 6	19
42	McCLURE, Margaret	1901-7		6
43	McKim, Henrietta	1901-11		10
44	McKITTERICK, Frances	1920-30		10
45	MESS, Dr Elizabeth	1932-44		12
46	MOLONY, Dr Lucy	1903-30		27
47	MOORE, Jane	1908-38		30
48	MORRIS, Mrs Marjorie	1930-35		5
49	MOTHERSOLE, Kate	1904-7		3
50	NIGHTINGALE, Hilda	1927-42		15
51	PARRY, Zoë	1909-13		4
52	PETLEY, Emma	1909-44		35

Appendix VI continued ...

	Name	Years	Breakdown	Total
53	PHILLIPS, Ethel	1905-9		4
54	PIGOTT, Dr Lucy	1927-39		9
55	PIGOTT, Dr Wilfreda (1935 f. Dr Iliff)	1929-35; 1935-43	6 + 8	14
56	PRICE, Dr Mary	1924-28		4
57	PROCTER, Ethel	1903-8		5
58	RICHARDSON, Hester	1925-26		1
59	ROBINSON, Marie	1932-44		12
60	SALISBURY, Ruth	1912-24		12
61	SEAGRAVE, Elsie	1920-25		5
62	SKIRROW, Emily	1902-11		9
63	SMART, Catherine	1930-51; 1954-61	11 + 7	18
64	STIRLING, Annie	1893-1932		39
65	STRATTON, Eva	1920-51		31
66	STUART, Anne	indep. 1894-1902; CMS 1902-26	8 + 24	32
67	STUART, Dr Emmeline	1897-1934		37
68	STUART, Gertrude (1903 f. Mrs Boyland)	1898-1903; 1903-29	5 + 26	31
69	STUART, Marie	indep. 1903-5, CMS 1911-38	2 + 27	29
70	STUBBS, Laura	1891-1902		11
71	TAYLOR, Dr Elsie	1901-4		3
72	THOMAS, Edith	1905-39		34
73	TWEEDIE, Winifred	1920-35		15
74	VERINDER, Alice	1914-17; 1923-49	3 + 26	29
75	WARD, Mabel	1903-20		17
76	WESTLAKE, Dr Winifred	1902-32		30
77	WILLMOT, Florence	1901-2		1
78	WOODROFFE, Janet	1921-49		28

Appendix VII

Chronological list of CMS women missionary doctors in Iran, 1891-1934
For lists of all single women missionaries in Iran during this period see Appendices V & VI

	Name	Years in Iran	Total
1	STUART, Dr Emmeline	1897-1933	36
2	LATHAM, Dr Urania (1901 m. & became Dr Malcolm)	1898-1901; 1901-07	9
3	TAYLOR, Dr Elsie	1901-4	3
4	WESTLAKE, Dr Winifred	1902-32	30
5	MOLONY, Dr Lucy	1903-30	27
6	IRONSIDE, Dr Catherine	1905-21	16
7	ALDOUS, Dr Alicia (1910 m. & became Dr Linton)	1909-10; 1910-34	25
8	CONSTABLE, Dr Evelyn	1914-16; 1921-2	3
9	BAILLIE, Dr Emily	1922-30; 1933-39	14
10	PRICE, Dr Mary	1924-28	4
11	HODGKINSON, Dr Katherine (1929 m. & became Dr Richards)	1926-29; 1929-45	19
12	PIGOTT, Dr Lucy	1927-39	9
13	BURNETT, Dr Olive	1929-30	1
14	PIGOTT, Dr Wilfreda (1935 m. & became Dr Iliff)	1929-35; 1935-43	14
15	HENRIQUES, Dr Stella	1929-47	18
16	MESS, Dr Elizabeth	1932-44	12

BIBLIOGRAPHY

Primary Sources
I   Unpublished archival material
II CMS & FES journals, and missionary reports
III Other primary sources including interview, and Persian material

Secondary Sources
I   Books and articles
II Theses and dissertations

Primary Sources

I UNPUBLISHED ARCHIVAL MATERIAL

- G2/PE/O - Original Papers and letters sent to CMS headquarters. Reference followed by the year and record number. (Held in the Heslop Room, Birmingham University Library.)

- G2/PE/P1-4 - Precis of the Original Papers, typed at headquarters, provide information from some of the letters for which the original has been lost. Reference followed by the year and record number. (Held in the Heslop Room, Birmingham University Library.)

II CMS & FES JOURNALS, AND MISSIONARY REPORTS

(Note: The following journals and reports have been extensively consulted. References to individually quoted articles are provided in the End Notes to each chapter.)

- *Annual Letters*. London: Church Missionary House. (Held in the Mission Studies Library at Partnership House, London.)

- *Church Missionary Intelligencer,* vols 1-57, 1849-1906. (Held in the Mission Studies Library at Partnership House, London.)

- *Church Missionary Review,* vols 58-78, 1907-27. (This journal succeeded the *Church Missionary Intelligencer.* Copies are held in the Mission Studies Library at Partnership House, London.)

- *Church Missionary Gleaner,* vols 1-19, 1841-1869; and New Series vols 1-48, 1874-1921. (Held in the Mission Studies Library at Partnership House, London.)

- *Female Missionary Intelligencer,* New Series vols 1-22, 1858-80; and New Series vols 1-19, 1881-99. (Held in the British Library, shelf mark PP 950 b)

- *Mercy and Truth: A Record of CMS Medical Missions.* CMS: London. (Held in the Heslop Room, Birmingham University Library.)

- *Methods of Mission Work Among Moslems;* Being those Papers read at the First Missionary Conference on behalf of the Mohammedan World held at Cairo April 4th-9th, 1906. N.Y. & London: Revell. (For Private Circulation Only.)

- *Missionary Pages for the Young,* no.s 1-24, January 1879 - October 1884; and *Missionary Pages for the Young: New Series,* no.s 1-12, January 1885 - October 1887. (Held in the British Library, shelf mark PP 913 ba)

- *Society for Promoting Female Education: Reports Nos. 60-64.* 1895-99. (Held in the British Library, shelf mark 4767 cc 29)

- *Students and the Missionary Problem;* Addresses Delivered at the International Student Missionary Conference, London, 1900. London: SVMU.

- *World Missionary Conference, 1910; Report of Commission IV: The Missionary Message in Relation to Non-Christian Religions.* London: Oliphant, Anderson & Ferrier. ?1910.

- *World Missionary Conference, 1910; Report of Commission V: The Training of Teachers.* London: Oliphant, Anderson & Ferrier. ?1910

III OTHER PRIMARY SOURCES INCLUDING INTERVIEW, & PERSIAN MATERIAL

- Bird, Mary (1899), *Persian Women and Their Creed.* London: CMS.

- Chappell, Jennie (1920?), *Three Brave Women: Stories of Heroism in Heathen Lands.* London: Partridge & Co..

- Dehqani-Tafti, Hassan (1992), *Masih va Masihiyyat Nazd-e Iraniyan, I: Sayr-e Ejmali Dar Tarikh.* (Christ and Christianity Amongst the Iranians, vol I: A Short Historical Survey.) London: Sohrab Books.

- _____ (1993), *Masih va Masihiyyat Nazd-e Iraniyan, II: Dar She'r-e Farsi, Douran-e Sabk-e Kohan (Klasik).* (Christ and Christianity Amongst the Iranians, vol II: In the Classical Period of Persian Poetry.) London: Sohrab Books.

- _____ (1995), Personal Interview (22 February), Basingstoke, Hampshire.

- *History of the Society for Promoting Female Education in the East.* London: Edward Suter, 1847. (Held in the British Library, shelf mark 4766 b. 16)

- Powell, Jessie (1949), *Riding to Danger: The Story of Mary Bird of Persia (Iran).* London: The Highway Press.

- *Register of Missionaries and Native Clergy 1804-1904.* (Printed by CMS for private circulation.)

- Rice, Clara Colliver (1916), *Mary Bird in Persia.* London: CMS.

- _____ (1923), *Persian Women and Their Ways.* London: Seeley, Service & Co..

- *Society for Promoting Female Education in China, India and the East.* London: Edward Suter, ?1840. (Held in the British Library, shelf mark 4193 cc 22)
- *Tracts Relating to Missions 1882-85.* (Held in the British Library, shelf mark 4766 BB 38[3])

Secondary Sources

I BOOKS AND ARTICLES

Abrahamian, Ervand (1982), *Iran Between Two Revolutions.* Princeton, New Jersey: Princeton University Press.

Addelson, Kathryn Pyne (1991), "The Man of Professional Wisdom" in Mary Fonow & Judith Cook (eds.), *Beyond Methodology: Feminist Scholarship as Lived Research.* Bloomington & Indianapolis: Indiana University Press, pp 16-34.

Amirsadeghi, Hossein [ed.] (1977?), *Twentieth Century Iran.* London: Heinemann.

Arnold, David & Bickers, Robert (1996), "Introduction" in Robert Bickers and Rosemary Seton (eds.), *Missionary Encounters: Sources and Issues.* Surrey: Curzon Press, pp 1-10.

Arnstein, Walter (1986), "Queen Victoria and Religion" in Gail Malmgreen (ed.), *Religion in the Lives of English Women 1760-1930.* London: Croom Helm, pp 88-128.

Azari, Farah (1983), *Women of Iran: Conflict with Fundamentalist Islam.* London: Ithaca Press, pp 190-225.

Bahar, Sima (1983), "A Historical Background to the Women's Movement in Iran" in Farah Azari (ed.), *Women of Iran: Conflict with Fundamentalist Islam.* London: Ithaca Press, pp 170-89.

Banks, Olive (1986), *Becoming a Feminist: The Social Origins of 'First Wave' Feminism.* Sussex: Wheatsheaf Books.

———— (1993 ed.), *Faces of Feminism: A Study of Feminism as a Social Movement.* Oxford: Blackwell.

Bayat-Philipp, Mangol (1978), "Women and Revolution in Iran, 1905-1911" in Lois Beck & Nikki Keddie (eds.), *Women in the Muslim World.* Cambridge, Massachusetts: Harvard University Press, pp 295-308.

Bebbington, David (1989), *Evangelicalism in Modern Britain: A History from the 1730s to the 1980s.* London: Routledge.

Bediako, Kwame (1995), *Christianity in Africa.* Maryknoll, New York: Orbis.

Bendroth, Margaret Lamberts (1993), *Fundamentalism and Gender: 1875 to the Present.* New Haven and London: Yale University Press.

Bennett, Judith (1989), "Feminism and History", *Gender and History*, 1:3, pp 250-72.

———— (1993), "Women's History: A Study in Continuity and Change", *Women's History Review*, 2:2, pp 173-84.

Bickers, Robert (1996), "'To Serve and Not to Rule': British Protestant Missionaries and Chinese Nationalism, 1928-1931" in Robert Bickers and Rosemary Seton (eds.), *Missionary Encounters: Sources and Issues*. Surrey: Curzon Press, pp 211-39.

Bishop, Isabella (1891), *Journeys in Persia and Kurdistan, vols. I & II*. London: John Murray.

Blake, Susan (1990), "A Woman's Trek: What Difference Does Gender Make?", *Women's Studies International Forum*, 13:4, pp 347-56.

Kathleen Bliss (1952), *The Service and Status of Women in the Churches*. Londond: SCM.

Bock, Gisela (1989), "Women's History and Gender History: Aspects of an International Debate", *Gender and History*, 1:1, pp 7-31.

Boroujerdi, Mehrzad (1996), *Iranian Intellectuals and the West: The Tormented Triumph of Nativism*. N.Y.: Syracuse University Press.

Børresen, Kari Elisabeth (1995), "Women's Studies of the Christian Tradition: New perspectives" in Ursula King (ed.), *Religion and Gender*. Oxford: Blackwell, pp 245-55.

Bosch, David (1991), *Transforming Mission: Paradigm Shifts in Theology of Mission*. Maryknoll, New York: Orbis.

Bowie, Fiona et al [eds.] (1993), *Women and Missions: Past and Present. Anthropological and Historical Perceptions*. Oxford: Berg.

Bradley, James & Muller, Richard (1995), *Church History: An Introduction to Research, Reference Works, and Methods*. Grand Rapids: Eerdmans.

Browne, Edward (1910), *The Persian Revolution of 1905-1909*. 1966 Impression, London: Frank Cass & Co..

Brown, Maria (1965), "Teaching in Isfahan" in Barry Till (ed.), *Changing Frontiers in the Mission of the Church*. London: SPCK, pp 101-10.

Brownfoot, Janice (1984), "Memsahibs in Colonial Malaya: A Study of European Wives in a British Colony and Protectorate, 1900-1940" in Hilary Callan & Shirley Ardener (eds.), *The Incorporated Wife*. London: Croom Helm, pp 186-210.

Burton, Antoinette (1990), "The White Woman's Burden: British Feminists and the Indian Woman, 1865-1915", *Women's Studies International Forum*, 13:4, pp 295-308.

Bynum, Caroline Walker (1992), *Fragmentation and Redemption: Essays on Gender and the Human Body in Medieval Religion*. New York: Zone Books.

Byrne, Lavinia [ed.] (1993), *The Hidden Journey: Missionary Heroines in Many Lands*. London: SPCK.

Bibliography

Caine, Barbara (1992), *Victorian Feminists*. Oxford: University Press.

_____ (1994), "Feminist Biography and Feminist History", *Women's History Review*, 3:2, pp 247-61.

Callan, Hilary (1984), "Introduction" in Hilary Callan & Shirley Ardener (eds.), *The Incorporated Wife*. London: Croom Helm, pp 1-26.

Callan, Hilary & Ardener, Shirley [ed.] (1984), *The Incorporated Wife*. London: Croom Helm.

Callaway, Helen (1987), *Gender, Culture and Empire*. Urbana: University of Illinois Press.

Cannon, Lynn Weber et al (1991), "Race and Class Bias in Qualitative Research on Women" in Mary Fonow & Judith Cook (eds.), *Beyond Methodology: Feminist Scholarship as Lived Research*. Bloomington & Indianapolis: Indiana University Press, pp 107-18.

Chaudhuri, Nupur & Strobel, Margaret (1990), "Western Women and Imperialism", *Women's Studies International Forum*, 13:4, pp 289-94.

Collins, Patricia Hill (1991), "Learning from the Outside Within: The Sociological Significance of Black Feminist Thought" in Mary Fonow & Judith Cook (eds.), *Beyond Methodology: Feminist Scholarship as Lived Research*. Bloomington & Indianapolis: Indiana University Press, pp 35-59.

Collins, Sheila (1992), "Reflections on the Meaning of Herstory" in Carol Christ & Judith Plaskow (eds.), *WomanSpirit Rising: A Feminist Reader in Religion*. New York: HarperSanFrancisco, pp 68-73.

Cottam, R.W. (1964), *Nationalism in Iran*. Pittsburgh.

Cox, Jeffrey (1992), "Independent English Women in Delhi and Lahore, 1860-1947" in R.W. Davis & R.J. Helmstadter (eds.), *Religion and Irreligion in Victorian Society: Essays in Honour of R. K. Webb*. London: Routledge.

Cracknell, Kenneth (1995), *Justice, Courtesy and Love: Theologians and Missionaries Encountering World Religions, 1846-1914*. London: Epworth Press.

Cragg, Kenneth (rev. 1985), *The Call of the Minaret*. London: Collins.

_____ (1992), *Troubled by Truth: Life Studies in Inter-faith Concern*. Edinburgh: Pentland Press.

Crawford, Patricia (1993), *Women and Religion in England 1500-1720*. London: Routledge.

Curzon, George (1892), *Persia and the Persian Question*, ii vols. London: Longmans, Green & Co..

Cuthbertson, Greg (1987), "The English-speaking Churches and Colonialism" in Charles Villa-Vicencio (ed.), *Theology and Violence: The South African Debate*. Johannesburg: Skotaville Publishers.

Daly, Mary (1973), *Beyond God the Father: Toward a Philosophy of Women's Liberation.* Boston: Beacon.

Davin, Anna (1978), "Imperialism and Motherhood", *History Workshop,* 5 (Spring), pp 9-65.

Davis, Natalie Zemon (1995), *Women on the Margins: Three Seventeenth-Century Lives.* Cambridge, Massachusetts: Harvard University Press.

Dawson, E.C. (1925), *Missionary Heroines of the Cross.* London: Seeley, Service & Co..

De Groot, Adrianus (1995), "One Bible and Many Interpretive Contexts: Hermeneutics in Missiology" in Frans Verstraelen et al (eds.), *Missiology: An Ecumenical Introduction.* Michigan: Eerdmans, pp 144-56.

Dehqani-Tafti, Hassan (1959), *Design of my World.* London: Lutterworth Press.

_____ (1981), *The Hard Awakening.* London: Triangle, SPCK.

Dillistone, F.W. (1980), *Into All the World: A Biography of Max Warren.* London: Hodder & Stoughton.

Donaldson, Margaret (1990), "'The Cultivation of the Heart and the Moulding of the Will': The Missionary Contribution of the Society for Promoting Female Education in China, India and the East" in W. Sheils and D. Wood (eds.), *Women in the Church; Studies in Church History,* 27. Oxford: Blackwell, pp 429-42.

Doyle, Michael (1986), *Empires.* Ithaca: Cornell University Press.

Drury, Clare (1994), "Christianity" in Jean Holm (ed.), *Women in Religion.* London: Pinter, pp 30-58.

Edkins, Joseph (1893), *The Early Spread of Religious Ideas: Especially in the Far East.* London: Religious Tract Society.

Elder, John (1960), *History of the American Presbyterian Mission in Iran.* Literature Committee of the Church Council of Iran.

Eldridge, C. (1978), *Victorian Imperialism.* London: Hodder & Stoughton.

Evans, Richard (1977), *The Feminists: Women's Emancipation Movements in Europe, America and Australasia, 1840-1920.* London: Croom Helm.

Farman Farmaian, Sattareh (1992), *Daughter of Persia: A Woman's Journey from her Father's Harem Through the Islamic Revolution.* London: Bantam Press.

Fitzgerald, Rosemary (1996), "A 'Peculiar and Exceptional Measure': The Call for Women Medical Missionaries for India in the Later Nineteenth Century" in Robert Bickers and Rosemary Seton (eds.), *Missionary Encounters: Sources and Issues.* Surrey: Curzon Press, pp 174-96.

Fonow, Mary & Cook, Judith (1991), *Beyond Methodology: Feminist Scholarship as Lived Research.* Bloomington & Indianapolis: Indiana University Press.

Forman, Charles (1987), "Responses to James Scherer's Paper from Different Disciplinary Perspectives: Church History", *Missiology*, 15:4 (October), p 523.

Foster, John (1939), *The Church of the T'ang Dynasty*. London: SPCK.

Foucault, Michel (1978), *The History of Sexuality, vol I: An Introduction*. New York: Pantheon.

Fox-Genovese, Elizabeth (1982), "Placing Women's History in History", *New Left Review*, 133, pp 5-29.

France, Richard (1995), "The Ramsden Sermon: A Shift in the Centre of Gravity of Christian Mission?", *Theology*, 98:785 (Sep/Oct), pp 338-44.

Francis-Dehqani, Gulnar (2000), "CMS Women in Persia: Perceptions on Muslim Women and Islam, 1884-1934" in Kevin Ward & Brian Stanley (eds.), CMS and World Christianity 1799-1999, Curzon Press: London (forthcoming).

Furlong, Monica (1998), *Act of Synod - Act of Folly?* London: SCM.

Gail, Marzieh (1951), *Persia and the Victorians*. London: George Allen & Unwin.

Gaitskell, Deborah (1996), "Women and Education in South Africa: How Helpful are the Mission Archives?" in Robert Bickers and Rosemary Seton (eds.), *Missionary Encounters: Sources and Issues*. Surrey: Curzon Press, pp 114-28.

Gartrell, Beverley (1984), "Colonial Wives: Villains or Victims?" in Hilary Callan & Shirley Ardener (eds.), *The Incorporated Wife*. London: Croom Helm, pp 165-85.

Gaster, Gwen (1959), *Our Blind Family*. London: CMS.

Gibb, H.A.R. (1947), *Modern Trends in Islam*. Chicago: University Press.

Gilbar, B. (1976/77), "Demographic Developments in Late Qajar Persia, 1870-1906", *Asian and African Studies*, 2, pp 125-56.

Gill, Sean (1994), *Women and the Church of England: From the Eighteenth Century to the Present*. London: SPCK.

Gollock, Georgina (1909), *The Story of the C.M.S.*. London: CMS.

Gollock, Minna (1912), "The Share of Women in the Administration of Missions", *International Review of Mission*, 1:4, pp 674-87.

Gordan, Linda (1978), "What Should Women Historians Do?", *Marxist Perspectives*, 3, 128-36.

Gort, Jerald (1995), "Human Distress, Salvation and Mediation of Salvation" in Frans Verstraelen et al (eds.), *Missiology: An Ecumenical Introduction*. Michigan: Eerdmans, pp 194-210.

Graham, Elaine (1995), *Making the Difference: Gender, Personhood and Theology*. London: Mowbray.

Greaves, Rose (1991), "Iranian Relations with Great Britain and British India, 1798-1921" in Peter Avery (ed.), *The Cambridge History of Iran, vol. 7: From Nadir Shah to the Islamic Republic*. Cambridge: University Press, pp374-425.

Griffiths, Valerie (1987), "Women in Mission" in Kathy Keay (ed.), *Men, Women and God: Evangelicals on Feminism*. Basingstoke: Marshall Pickering, pp 62-77.

Haeri, Shahla (1989), *Law of Desire: Temporary Marriage in Iran*. London: Tauris.

Hambly, Gavin (1991a), "The Pahlavi Autocracy: Riza Shah, 1921-1941" in Peter Avery (ed.), *The Cambridge History of Iran, vol. 7: From Nadir Shah to the Islamic Republic*. Cambridge: University Press, pp 213-43.

_____ (1991b), "The Traditional Iranian City in the Qajar Period" in Peter Avery (ed.), *The Cambridge History of Iran, vol. 7: From Nadir Shah to the Islamic Republic*. Cambridge: University Press, pp 542-89.

Harding, Sandra [ed.] (1987), *Feminism and Methodology*. Milton Keynes: Open University Press.

Harrison, Brian (1978), *Separate Spheres: The Opposition to Women's Suffrage in Britain*. London: Croom Helm.

Harrison, Brian & McMillan, James (1983), "Some Feminist Betrayals of Women's History", *The Historical Journal*, 26:2, pp 375-89.

Hastings, Adrian (1997), "From Africa to Oxford and Back: A Study of the Work of Professor Peter Hinchliff", *Theology*, 100:798 (Nov/Dec), pp 402-10.

Hayward, Charles (?1950), *Women Missionaries*. London: Collins.

Heeney, Brian (1982), "The Beginnings of Church Feminism: Women and the Councils of the Church of England 1897-1919", *The Journal of Ecclesiastical History*, 33:1 (January), pp 89-109.

_____ (1988), *The Women's Movement in the Church of England, 1850-1930*. Oxford: Clarendon Press.

Hendricks, Barbara (1997), "The Legacy of Mary Josephine Rogers", *International Bulletin of Missionary Research*, 21:2 (April), pp 72-80.

Hewitt, Gordon (1971 & 77), *The Problem of Success: A History of the Church Missionary Society, 1910-1942, vols. I & II*. London: CMS Press Ltd.

Hick, John (1995), *The Rainbow of Faiths*. London: SCM.

Hick, John & Knitter, Paul [eds.] (1987), *The Myth of Christian Uniqueness*. London: SCM.

Hiebert, Frances (1997), "Beyond a Post-modern Critique of Modern Missions: The Nineteenth Century Revisited", *Missiology: An International Review*, 25:3 (July), pp 259-77.

Hilden, Patricia (1982), "Women's History: The Second Wave", *The Historical Journal*, 25:2, pp 501-12.

Hodgins, Jack (1994), *Sister Island: A History of the Church Missionary Society in Ireland 1814-1994*. Dunmurry: Transmission Publication.

Honig, Anton (1995), "Asia: The Search for Identity as a Source of Renewal" in Frans Verstraelen et al (eds.), *Missiology: An Ecumenical Introduction*. Michigan: Eerdmans, pp 306-32.

Hoyle, Lydia Huffman (1996), "Nineteenth-Century Single Women and Motivation for Mission", *International Bulletin of Missionary Research*, 20:2 (April), pp 58-64.

Hume-Griffith, M. E.(1909), *Behind the Veil in Persia and Turkish Arabia*. London: Seeley & Co..

Hyam, Ronald (1992), *Empire and Sexuality: The British Experience*. Manchester: University Press.

Isichei, Elizabeth (1993), "Does Christianity Empower Women? The Case of Anaguta of Central Nigeria" in Fiona Bowie et al (eds.), *Women and Missions: Past and Present. Anthropological and Historical Perceptions*. Oxford: Berg, pp 209-28.

Jacob, William (1997), *The Making of the Anglican Church Worldwide*. London: SPCK.

Jackson, Eleanor (1997), *"A True Mother in Israel": The Role of the Christian Mother as Evangelist in Nineteenth-Century India*. NAMP Position Paper Number 30. Cambridge: Univerisity of Cambridge, North Atlantic Missiology Project.

Jalland, Pat (1986), *Women, Marriage and Politics, 1860-1914*. Oxford: Clarendon Press.

Jay, Elisabeth (1986), *Faith and Doubt in Victorian Britain*, Context and Commentary Series. Basingstoke: Macmillan.

Jayaratne, Toby Epstein & Stewart, Abigail (1991), "Quantitative and Qualitative Methods in the Social Sciences: Current Feminist Issues and Practical Strategies" in Mary Fonow & Judith Cook (eds.), *Beyond Methodology: Feminist Scholarship as Lived Research*. Bloomington & Indianapolis: Indiana University Press, pp 85-106.

Jayaweera, Swarna (1990), "European Women Educators Under the British Colonial Administration in Sri Lanka', *Women's Studies International Forum*, 13:4, pp 323-32.

Jeal, Tim (1996), *The Missionary's Wife*. London: Warner Books.

Jenkins, Paul (1996), "Four Nineteenth-Century Pictorial Images from Africa in the Basel Mission Archive and Library Collections" in Robert Bickers and Rosemary Seton (eds.), *Missionary Encounters: Sources and Issues*. Surrey: Curzon Press, pp 95-113.

Jenkinson, William & O'Sullivan, Helene [eds.] (1993), *Trends in Mission: Toward the Third Millenium*. Maryknoll, New York: Orbis.

Jongeneel, Jan & van Engelen, Jan (1995), "Contemporary Currents In Missiology" in Frans Verstraelen et al (eds.), *Missiology: An Ecumenical Introduction*. Michigan: Eerdmans, pp 438-57.

Kazemzadeh, Firuz (1968), *Russia and Britain in Persia, 1864-1914*. Yale: University Press.

Keddie, Nikki (1966), *Religion and Rebellion in Iran: The Iranian Tobacco Protest of 1891-1892*. London: Frank Cass.

_____ (1981), *Roots of Revolution: An Interpretative History of Modern Iran*. (Includes a section by Yann Richard.) New Haven: Yale University Press.

Kelly-Gadol, Joan (1987), "The Social Relation of the Sexes: Methodological Implications of Women's History" in Sandra Harding (ed.), *Feminism and Methodology*. Milton Keynes: Open University Press, pp 15-27.

Kent, John (1987), "Failure of a Mission: Christianity Outside Europe" in John Kent, *The Unacceptable Face: The Modern Church in the Eyes of the Historian*. London: SCM, pp 177-202.

King, Ursula [ed.] (1994), *Feminist Theology from the Third World: A Reader*. London: SPCK.

_____ [ed.] (1995), *Religion and Gender*. Oxford: Blackwell.

Kirkwood, Deborah (1984), "The Suitable Wife: Preparation for Marriage in London and Rhodesia/Zimbabwe" in Hillary Callan & Shirley Ardener (eds.), *The Incorporated Wife*. London: Croom Helm, pp 106-19.

_____ (1993), "Protestant Missionary Women: Wives and Spinsters" in Fiona Bowie et al (eds.), *Women and Missions: Past and Present. Anthropological and Historical Perceptions*. Oxford: Berg, pp 23-42.

Knapp, Wilfred (1977), "1921-1941: The Period of Riza Shah" in Hossein Amirsadeghi (ed.), *Twentieth Century Iran*. London: Heinemann, pp 23-52.

Knott, Kim (1995), "Women Researching, Women Researched: Gender as an Issue in the Empirical Study of Religion" in Ursula King (ed.), *Religion and Gender*. Oxford: Blackwell, pp 199-218.

Kordi, Gohar (1991), *An Iranian Odyssey*. London: Serpent's Tail.

_____ (1995), *Mahi's Story*. London: The Women's Press.

Lambton, Ann (1954), *Islamic Society in Persia*. London: University of London.

_____ (1987), *Qajar Persia*. London: Tauris.

Levine, Philippa (1987), *Victorian Feminism 1850-1900*. Tallahassee: Florida State University Press.

Lewis, Bernard (1995), *The Middle East: 2000 Years of History from the Rise of Christianity to the Present Day*. London: Weidenfeld & Nicolson.

Lewis, Jane (1984), *Women in England 1870-1950: Sexual Divisions and Social Change.* London: Harvester Wheatsheaf.

Linton, James (1923), *Persian Sketches.* London: CMS.

McLeod, Hugh (1981), *Religion and the People of Western Europe, 1789-1970.* Oxford: University Press.

Magee, Penelope Margaret (1995), "Disputing the Sacred: Some Theological Approaches to Gender and Religion" in Ursula King (ed.), *Religion and Gender.* Oxford: Blackwell, pp 101-20.

Maguire, Daniel (1986), *The Moral Revolution.* San Francisco: Harper & Row.

Malmgreen, Gail [ed.] (1986), *Religion in the Lives of English Women 1760-1930.* London: Croom Helm.

Martin, Vanessa (1989), *Islam and Modernism: The Iranian Revolution of 1906.* London: Tauris.

Maughan, Steven (1996), "'Mighty England Do Good': The Major English Denominations and Organisation for the Support of Foreign Missions in the Nineteenth Century" in Robert Bickers and Rosemary Seton (eds.), *Missionary Encounters: Sources and Issues.* Surrey: Curzon Press, pp 11-37.

Maurice, F.D. (1886), *The Religions of the World and their Relations to Christianity,* London: Macmillan.

McLaughlin, Eleanor (1992), "The Christian Past: Does it Hold a Future for Women?" in Carol Christ & Judith Plaskow (eds.), *WomanSpirit Rising: A Feminist Reader in Religion.* New York: HarperSanFrancisco, pp 93-106.

Midgley, Clare (1995), "Ethnicity, 'Race' and Empire" in June Purvis (ed.), *Women's History: Britain 1850-1945. An Introduction.* London: UCL, pp 247-76.

Mies, Maria (1991), "Women's Research or Feminist Research? The Debate Surrounding Feminist Science and Methodology" in Mary Fonow & Judith Cook (eds.), *Beyond Methodology: Feminist Scholarship as Lived Research.* Bloomington & Indianapolis: Indiana University Press, pp 60-84.

Millman, Marcia & Kanter, Rosabeth Moss (1987), "Introduction to Another Voice: Feminist Perspectives on Social Life and Social Science" in Sandra Harding (ed.), *Feminism and Methodology.* Milton Keynes: Open University Press, pp 29-36.

Montgomery, Helen Barrett (1910), *Western Women in Eastern Lands.* New York: Macmillan.

Moorman, John (1973 ed.), *A History of the Church in England.* London: A & C Black.

Mottahedeh, Roy (1985), *The Mantle of the Prophet: Religion and Politics in Iran.* New York: Pantheon Books.

Müller, Karl et al [eds.] (1997), *Dictionary of Mission: Theology, History, Perspectives*. Maryknoll, New York: Orbis.

Murray, Jocelyn (1985), *Proclaim the Good News: A Short History of the Church Missionary Society*. London: Hodder & Stoughton.

Nasr, Seyyed Hossein (1989), "God" in Seyyed Hossein Nasr (ed.), *Islamic Spirituality I: Foundations*. London: SCM, pp 311-23.

Neill, Stephen (rev. 1986), *A History of Christian Missions*. Middlesex: Penguin.

Newbigin, Lesslie (rev. 1995), *The Open Secret: An Introduction to the Theology of Mission*. London: SPCK.

Nightingale, Florence (1979 ed.), *Cassandra*, With an Introduction by Myra Stark. New Haven, Connecticut: The Feminist Press, 1860 reprint.

Oddie, Geoffrey (1996), "Missionaries as Social Commentators: The Indian Case" in Robert Bickers and Rosemary Seton (eds.), *Missionary Encounters: Sources and Issues*. Surrey: Curzon Press, pp 197-210.

O'Connor, June (1995), "The Epistomological Significance of Feminist Research in Religion" in Ursula King (ed.), *Religion and Gender*. Oxford: Blackwell, pp 45-63.

Offen, Karen (1988), "Defining Feminism: A Comparative Historical Approach", *Signs*, 14:1, pp 119-57.

Padwick, Constance (1922), *Henry Martyn: Confessor of the Faith*. London: CMS Press.

Paton, David (1953), *Christian Missions and the Judgement of God*. London: SCM.

Paxton, Nancy (1990), "Feminism Under the Raj: Complicity and Resistance in the Writings of Flora Annie Steel and Annie Besant", *Women's Studies International Forum*, 13:4, pp 333-46.

Payne, Grace Visher (1950), *The Unveiling*. Philadelphia: The Westminster Press.

Peel, J. (1996), "Problems and Opportunities in an Anthropologist's Use of a Missionary Archive" in Robert Bickers and Rosemary Seton (eds.), *Missionary Encounters: Sources and Issues*. Surrey: Curzon Press, pp 70-94.

Petre, Jonathan (1994), *By Sex Divided: The Church of England and Women Priests*. London: Fount.

Petrushevsky, Ilya (1985), *Islam in Iran*. Trl. by Hubert Evans. London: Athlone Press.

Pettifer, Julian & Bradley, Richard [eds.] (1990), *Missionaries*. London: BBC Books.

Plaskow, Judith (1993), "We Are Also Your Sisters: The Development of Women's Studies in Religion", *Women's Studies Quarterly*, 21:1-2, pp 9-21.

Porter, Andrew (1996), *"Cultural Imperialism" and Missionary Enterprise.* NAMP Position Paper Number 7. Cambridge: Univerisity of Cambridge, North Atlantic Missiology Project.

Prior, Michael (1997), *The Bible and Colonialism: A Moral Critique.* Sheffield: Academic Press.

Prochaska, Frank (1980), *Women and Philanthropy in 19th Century England.* Oxford: Clarendon Press.

Quinn, V. & Prest, J. [eds.] (1987), *Dear Miss Nightingale: A Selection of Benjamin Jowett's Letters to Florence Nightingale 1860-1893.* Oxford: Clarendon Press.

Ramusack, Barbara (1990), "Cultural Missionaries, Maternal Imperialists, Feminist Allies: British Women Activists in India, 1865-1945", *Women's Studies International Forum,* 13:4, pp 309-22.

Renier, G. (1950), *History: Its Purpose and Method.* New York: Harper & Row.

Richard, Yann (1995), *Shi'ite Islam.* Trl. by Antonia Nevill. Oxford: Blackwell.

Robinson, Jane (1990), *Wayward Women: A Guide to Women Travellers.* Oxford: University Press.

Rodinson, Maxime (1991), *Europe and the Mystique of Islam.* Seattle & London: University of Washington Press.

Rose, Hilary (1982), "Making Science Feminist" in Elizabeth Whitelegg et al (eds.), *The Changing Experience of Women.* Oxford: Martin Robinson, pp 352-72.

Rouse, Ruth (1913), "The Ideal of Womanhood as a Factor in Missionary Work", *International Review of Missions,* 2:5 (January), pp 148-64.

Rowbotham, Judith (1996), *"This is no Romantic Story": Reporting the Work of British Female Missionaries, c. 1850-1910.* NAMP Position Paper Number 4. Cambridge: University of Cambridge, North Atlantic Missiology Project.

Said, Edward (1978), *Orientalism: Western Conceptions of the Orient.* London: Penguin (1995 reprint).

_____ (1993), *Culture and Imperialism.* London: Vintage.

Sanneh, Lamin (1983), "The Horizontal and Vertical Mission: An African Perspective", *International Bulletin of Mission Research,* 7:4 (October), pp 165-171.

_____ (1993), *Encountering the West.* Maryknoll, New York: Orbis.

Scherer, James (1987), "Missiology as a Discipline and What it Includes", *Missiology,* 15:4 (October), pp 507-22.

Semple, Rhonda (1997), *Women, Gender and Changing Roles in the Missionary Project: The London Missionary Society and the China Inland Mission, 1885-1910.* NAMP Position

Paper Number 39. Cambridge: Univerisity of Cambridge, North Atlantic Missiology Project.

Seton, Rosemary (1996), "'Open Doors for Female Labourers': Women Candidates of the London Missionary Society, 1875-1914" in Robert Bickers and Rosemary Seton (eds.), *Missionary Encounters: Sources and Issues.* Surrey: Curzon Press, pp 50-69.

Shafii, Rouhi (1997), *Scent of Saffron: Three Generations of an Iranian Family.* London: Scarlet Press.

Shiman, Lilian Lewis (1992), *Women and Leadership in Nineteenth-Century England.* London: Macmillan.

Shorter, Aylward (1988), *Toward a Theology of Inculturation.* London: Geoffrey Chapman.

Shuster, W. Morgan (1912), *The Strangling of Persia: A Record of European Diplomacy and Oriental Intrigue.* London: T. Fisher Unwin.

Smith, George (1892), *Henry Martyn: Saint and Scholar.* London.

Stanley, Brian (1990), *The Bible and the Flag: Protestant Missions and British Imperialism in the Nineteenth and Twentieth Centuries.* Leicester: Apollos.

_____ (1996), "Some Problems in Writing a Missionary Society History Today: The Example of the Baptist Missionary Society" in Robert Bickers and Rosemary Seton (eds.), *Missionary Encounters: Sources and Issues.* Surrey: Curzon Press, pp 38-49.

Stanley, Liz & Wise, Sue (1991), "Feminist Research, Feminist Consciousness, And Experiences of Sexism" in Mary Fonow & Judith Cook (eds.), *Beyond Methodology: Feminist Scholarship as Lived Research.* Bloomington & Indianapolis: Indiana University Press, pp 265-83.

Stevens, Roger (1962), *The Land of the Great Sophy.* London: Methuen & Co. Ltd.

Stock, Eugene (1899, 1916), *History of the Church Missionary Society,* vols. *I-III & IV.* London: CMS.

Strobel, Margaret (1987), "Gender and Race in the Nineteenth- and Twentieth-Century British Empire" in R. Bridenthal et al (eds.), *Becoming Visible.* Boston: Houghton Mifflin, pp 374-96.

Sykes, Ella (1910), *Persia and its People.* London: Methuen & Co. Ltd.

Symonds, Richard (1993), *Far Above Rubies: The Women Uncommemorated by the Church of England.* Leominster: Gracewing.

Taylor, Verta & Rupp, Leila (1991), "Researching the Women's Movement: We Make Our Own History But Not Just As We Please" in Mary Fonow & Judith Cook (eds.), *Beyond Methodology: Feminist Scholarship as Lived Research.* Bloomington & Indianapolis: Indiana University Press, pp 119-32.

The Editorial Collective (1989), "Why Gender and History", *Gender and History*, 1:1, pp 1-6.

The Editors (1995), "Introduction: What Do We Mean by Missiology" in Frans Verstraelen et al (eds.), *Missiology: An Ecumenical Introduction*. Michigan: Eerdmans, pp 1-7.

Thomas, Norman [ed.] (1995), *Readings in Mission*. London: SPCK.

_____ (1996), "World Mission Conferences: What Impact Do They Have?", *International Bulletin of Missionary Research*, 20:4 (October), pp 146-53.

Thornton, A. (1959), *The Imperial Idea and its Enemies*. London: Macmillan.

Thorogood, Bernard (1988), *The Flag and the Cross: National Limits and Church Universal*. London: SCM.

Tidrick, Kathryn (1990), *Empire and the English Character*. London: Tauris.

Tisdall, W. St. Clair (1901), *The Sources of Islam: A Persian Treatise*. Trl. & abridged by William Muir. Edinburgh: T & T Clark.

_____ (rev. 1910), *The Religion of the Crescent*. London: SPCK.

_____ (1912), *Christianity and Other Faiths*. London: SPCK.

Torjesen, Karen Jo (1993), *When Women Were Priests: Women's Leadership in the Early Church and the Scandal of their Subordination in the Rise of Christianity*. New York: HarperSanFrancisco.

Trimingham, J. Spencer (1948), *The Christian Approach to Islam in the Sudan*. Oxford: University Press.

Trueblood, Elton (1972), *The Validity of the Christian Mission*. New York: Harper & Row.

Tucker, Marjorie (1990a), "American Women's Open Door to Chinese Women: Which Way Does it Open?", *Women's Studies International Forum*, 13:4, pp 369-80.

Tucker, Sara (1990b), "Opportunities for Women: The Development of Professional Women's Medicine in Canton, China, 1879-1901", *Women's Studies International Forum*, 13:4, pp 357-68.

Upton, Joseph (1960), *The History of Modern Iran: An Interpretation*. Cambridge, Massachusetts: Harvard University Press.

Walls, Andrew (1996), *The Missionary Movement in Christian History: Studies in the Transmission of Faith*. Edinburgh: T & T Clark.

Walther, Wiebke (1993), *Women in Islam: From Medieval to Modern Times*. Princeton & New York: Markus Wiener Publishing.

Warren, Max (1970), "The Church Militant Abroad: Victorian Missionaries" in Anthony Symondson (ed.), *The Victorian Crisis of Faith*. London: SPCK, pp 57-70.

_____ (1976), *I Believe in the Great Commission*. London: Hodder & Stoughton.

Waterfield, Gordon (1973), *Professional Diplomat: Sir Percy Loraine*. London: John Murray.

Waterfield, Robin (1973), *Christians in Persia*. London: George, Allen & Unwin.

Watt, William Montgomery (1991), *Muslim-Christian Encounters: Perceptions and Misperceptions*. London: Routledge.

Webb, Allan Becher (1883), *Sisterhood Life and Woman's Work in the Mission-Field of the Church*. London: Skeffington & Son.

Webster, Margaret (1994), *A New Strength, A New Song: The Journey to Women's Priesthood*. London: Mowbray.

Werff, Lyle Vander (1977), *Christian Mission to Mulsims: The Record*. California: William Carey Library.

Wessels, Anton (1995), "The Middle East: Cradle and Crucible" in Frans Verstraelen et al (eds.), *Missiology: An Ecumenical Introduction*. Michigan: Eerdmans, pp 11-30.

Wilber, Donald (1955), *Iran: Past and Present*. Princeton: University Press.

Williams, Molly (1994), *The Rich Tapestry of my Persian Years: Memoirs of Maud Hannah (Molly) Williams, a Missionary Nurse, 1937-1974*. Victoria, Australia: Keith Cole.

Williams, Peter (1993), "'The Missing Link': The recruitment of Women Missionaries in Some English Evangelical Missionary Societies in the Nineteenth Century" in Fiona Bowie et al (eds.), *Women and Missions: Past and Present. Anthropological and Historical Perceptions*. Oxford: Berg, pp 43-67.

_____ (1997), *The CMS and the Indigenous Church in the Second Half of the Nineteenth Century*. NAMP Position Paper Number 31. Cambridge: Univerisity of Cambridge, North Atlantic Missiology Project.

Willis, Justin (1996), "The Nature of a Mission Community: The Universities' Mission to Central Africa in Bonde" in Robert Bickers and Rosemary Seton (eds.), *Missionary Encounters: Sources and Issues*. Surrey: Curzon Press, pp 128-52.

Wilson, Arnold (1932), *Persia*. London: Ernest Benn Limited.

Wind, Anne (1995), "The Protestant Missionary Movement from 1789-1963" in Frans Verstraelen et al (eds.), *Missiology: An Ecumenical Introduction*. Michigan: Eerdmans, pp 237-52.

Worrall, B. (1988), *The Making of the Modern Church: Christianity in England Since 1800*. London: SPCK.

Wright, Denis (1977), *The English Amongst the Persians*. London: William Heinemann Ltd.

_____ (1985), *The Persians Amongst the English*. London: Tauris.

Yapp, Malcolm (1977), "1900-1921: The Last Years of the Qajar Dynasty" in Hossein Amirsadeghi (ed.), *Twentieth Century Iran*. London: Heinemann, pp 1-22.

Yates, Timothy (1994), *Christian Mission in the Twentieth Century*. Cambridge: University Press.

Yeo, Eileen (1992), "Social Motherhood and Sexual Communion of Labour in British Social Science, 1850-1950", *Women's History Review*, 1:1, pp 63-87.

Young, Pamela Dickey (1990), *Feminist Theology/Christian Theology: In Search of Method*. Minneapolis: Fortress Press.

II THESES AND DISSERTATIONS

Francis-Dehqani, Gulnar (1999), *Religious Feminism in and Age of Empire: CMS Women Missionaries in Iran, 1869-1934*. Bristol University: PhD Thesis.

Haggis, Jane (1991), *Professional Ladies and Working Wives: Female Missionaries in the London Missionary Society and its South Travancore District, South India in the 19th Century*. University of Manchester: PhD Thesis.

Isherwood, John (1979), *An Analysis of the Role of Single Women in the Work of the Church Missionary Society, 1804-1904, in West Africa, India and China*. University of Manchester: MA Thesis.

Morgan, Susan (1997), *A Passion for Purity: Ellice Hopkins and the Politics of Gender in the Late-Victorian Church*. University of Bristol: PhD Thesis.

Potter, Sarah (1974), *The Social Origins and Recruitment of English Protestant Missionaries in the Nineteenth Century*. University of London: PhD Thesis.

Powell, Avril (1983), *Contact and Controversy Between Islam and Christianity in Northern India, 1833-1857: The Relations Between Muslims and Protestant Missionaries in the North-Western Provinces and Oudh*. SOAS, University of London: PhD Thesis.